America on Film
and Tape

America on Film and Tape

A Topical Catalog of
Audiovisual Resources
for the Study of
United States History,
Society, and Culture

HOWARD B. HITCHENS, *General Editor*

Vidge Hitchens, *Associate Editor*

Bibliographies and Indexes in American History, Number 3

Greenwood Press
Westport, Connecticut • London, England

11970619

Library of Congress Cataloging in Publication Data

Main entry under title:

America on film and tape.

(Bibliographies and indexes in American history,
ISSN 0742-6828 ; no. 3)
Includes index.
1. United States—Civilization—Audiovisual aids—
Catalogs. I. Hitchens, Howard B. II. Hitchens, Vidge.
III. Title. IV. Series.
E169.1.A471873 1985   016.973   85-8011
ISBN 0-313-24778-1 (lib. bdg. : alk. paper)

Library of Congress Catalog Card Number: 85-8011
ISBN: 0-313-24778-1
ISSN: 0742-6828

First published in 1985

Greenwood Press
A division of Congressional Information Service, Inc.
88 Post Road West, Westport, Connecticut 06881

Printed in the United States of America

The paper used in this book complies with the
Permanent Paper Standard issued by the National
Information Standards Organization (Z39.48-1984).

10 9 8 7 6 5 4 3 2 1

Contents

Contributors

Dr. George Basalla
Professor of History
University of Delaware

Dr. William D. Coplin
Professor, The Maxwell School
Syracuse University

Nancy deLaurier
Curator, Slides and Photographs
Department of Art and Art History
University of Missouri/ Kansas City

Dr. John B. Garver, Jr.
Chief Cartographer
National Geographic Society
Washington, DC

Vidge Hitchens
VANITCH
Frankford, DE

Dr. John W. Larner
American Historical Association
Washington, DC

Dr. Lawrence E. Mintz
Professor, American Studies
University of Maryland

Dr. Patrick O'Meara
Director, African Studies Program
Indiana University

Dr. Miles Orvell
Professor, Department of English
Temple University

Dr. Nancy W. Stein
Professor of Sociology
Normandale Community College
Bloomington, MN

Dr. Richard Sylla
Professor, Economics and Business
North Carolina State University

Dr. John Vlach
Professor, American Studies
George Washington University

Preface

This selection of audiovisual materials has been developed to serve scholars, teachers, and anyone with an interest in experiencing or studying United States history, society and culture in a way that goes beyond reading about it. The study of our society and culture is a formal interdisciplinary program in several hundred American colleges and universities as well as many educational institutions in other countries. Traditionally, American Studies programs have depended for instructional purposes on the vast and ever-growing body of published literature about the United States in the academic disciplines that have come to be combined into American Studies, beginning with History and Literature. Increasingly, films, slides, audio and video cassettes, and recordings of different kinds are being used to supplement and enhance the printed materials in these disciplines and, consequently, in American Studies. Since there is no clear common agreement among scholars as to which disciplines should and should not be included in American Studies, this catalog has been developed by taking an eclectic approach, with information ordered in the following fourteen categories: Anthropology, Architecture, Arts, Economic History, Folklore, Geography, History, International Relations, Language-Literature-Journalism, Performing Arts, Political Science, Popular Culture, Science and Technology, and Sociology.

The amount and variety of audiovisual materials that reflect America has grown substantially in the last fifty years, particularly in the past decade because of the widespread availability of low-cost audiovisual equipment and materials. The major difficulties in compiling the catalog have been in selecting appropriate materials of the best quality and insuring a reasonable balance in quality and number of items among the fourteen categories. It has to be a selection of what is available, for a complete listing would include materials that are duplicative and of uneven quality; and the book would be many times larger.

The selection process used here depended largely on the consultation of highly selective filmographies from such professional associations as the Educational Film Library Association (EFLA), the Consortium of University Film Centers (CUFC), and the American Sociological Association. Major distribution agencies, such as the National AudioVisual Center, Modern Talking Picture Service, and the Educators Progress Service, were also very helpful. Persons consulted by the General Editor included association staff members, faculty in American Studies programs, and producers of audiovisual materials. The director of the American Studies Association, John Stephens, was especially helpful in locating professional consultants and section editors.

Much of the groundwork for this catalog was first done as a project for the United States Information Agency, and a debt is owed Dr. Leslie High of USIA, who initiated it and provided support. The present contents have been expanded to include some free loan materials as well as those for purchase or rental. As a result, the catalog, though selective, is the most comprehensive compilation of audiovisual materials for American Studies now available.

The process of developing this catalog involved the professional judgment of experts who served as Section Editors for each of the fourteen categories used. The work and dedication involved in making these selections on the part of each of the Section Editors is gratefully acknowledged. The product could never have been developed without the cooperation, hard work, and good will of all the professionals involved in this project.

I would also like to acknowledge the assistance of Rachel Theus and
Kerry Cadden, who helped in the word processing and editing of the catalog.
Finally, the indomitable spirit and hard work of my Associate Editor, Vidge
Hitchens, who prepared the Performing Arts section and did a great deal of the
editorial work on the whole document, were instrumental to its completion.

Howard B. Hitchens

Introduction

Most people would expect that the vast audiovisual industry in the United States provides a thorough reflection of all elements of the society and culture in its products. Such is not the case. On reflection, one realizes that certain aspects of human activity lend themselves more readily to audiovisual exploitation than others. Obviously, a live theatrical performance tends to lose something when it is captured on film or video recording -- a phenomenon that has been demonstrated time and again. Therefore, this catalog of audiovisual resources is rich beyond imagination in some aspects of American culture, such as Civil War history, while it can be poor in other areas. On the whole, though, the user will find something to suit his or her need or taste in each of the fourteen categories here used to define American Studies.

The criteria used in selecting these materials took into account the fact that the materials are intended for use with secondary and post-secondary level students, and the adult population generally. Other criteria are:

> The formats of audiovisual materials to be included are 16mm films, 35mm slide sets, audio cassettes, video recordings, and filmstrips (filmstrips and slide sets often are accompanied by recorded sound).

> Materials to be included are judged to be essential for the study of each area - not just nice to know. In most areas there are many more items available than are listed here.

> Feature films are included only if they are readily available for educational use.

> Materials are the most current possible on each topic.

> Most materials listed have been judged to be of high quality as indicated by their having won various awards, having been included in carefully selected specialized lists of academic resources, or having been used successfully for instructional purposes.

Although there have been other efforts to address the general American Studies curriculum in bits and pieces, no other guide provides a selective list of audiovisual resources for the entire spectrum, which here comprises fourteen disciplines. In addition to the materials cited here, many others are available from various sources for further exploration and study. The following suppliers of audiovisual resources for the individual disciplinary areas deserve mention.

o Landslides
  Box 475
  Cambridge, MA 02139

Collection of aerial 35mm slides of various regions of the USA.

o Sandak, Inc.
  180 Harvard Avenue
  Stamford, CT 06902

Arts of the United States
Collection of 2500 slides based on the survey of that title.

o Center for Southern Folklore
  1216 Peabody Avenue
  PO Box 40105
  Memphis, TN 38104

American Folklore Films and
Videotapes
Large collection of unique items.

o Instructional Resources Corp.
  6824 Nashville Road
  Lanham, MD 20706

The American History Slide
Collection - An assembly of 2100
35mm slides indexed, captioned,
boxed and organized by experts
in American history.

o Social Studies School Service
  PO Box 802
  10000 Culver Blvd.
  Culver City, CA 90203

Global education bibliography.

o American Sociological Association
  1722 N Street, N.W.
  Washington, D.C. 20036

Using Films in Sociology Courses:
Guidelines and Reviews

o Educators Progress Service, Inc.
  Randolph, Wisconsin 53956

Guides to free audiovisual materials.

Additional sources of audiovisual materials are contained in the editors' introductions to some of the sections of this catalog. Particular attention should be paid to suggestions in the introductions to the sections on Arts; Language, Literature and Journalism; Political Science; and Science and Technology.

How to Use This Catalog

There are three ways to approach the use of this catalog: directly to the subcategory in which one is interested (e.g. Arts, Sculpture); or through a study of the outline of subject categories (at the end of this section) to help determine one's area of interest; or by finding a known title in the Index of Titles.

The Subject Category Outline is provided to help the user narrow his search more quickly. After the search is narrowed to a specific subcategory of, for example, the Arts, one can find that section in the Arts section quickly. Since the topics of some subcategories overlap, all sections which might conceivably pertain to the area of interest should be consulted.

If the title of the work is known, direct consultation of the Title Index should be made. Often a key word such as a surname can lead directly to a desired title (e.g. Andrew Wyeth or Ansel Adams in the Arts section). An appropriate resource should be found for any desired area of study through a search of the Subject Category Outline and the specific sections of the catalog.

Each entry in the catalog has the following information:

Title

Intended Audience Level   S = Secondary School (Many of the materials with this code can probably be used with students at ages 13-15 years, as well as those in technical schools.)
C = College or University
A = Adult or General audience

Audiovisual Format (videotape, film,etc.)

The format codes are:
16mm = 16mm motion picture
FS, Cassette = filmstrip, with audio cassette
35mm = Set of 35mm slides
35mm, Cassette = set of slides with sound
Audio Cassette = audio cassette
U = 3/4" U-matic video recording
V = VHS video recording
B = Beta video recording
Phonodiscs

Sound or Silent – Sd, or Sl

Length – Given in minutes, slides or frames (frs). Unavailable if not listed

Year of Release Unavailable if not listed

Distributor (Where an abbreviation is used, it can be found in the alphabetical directory provided as an appendix)

Description of the Content

Here is a sample entry:

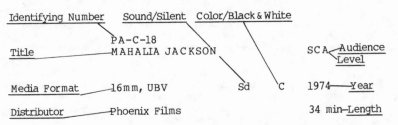

A portrait of gospel singer Mahalia Jackson and footage of her performing eleven songs.

Content Description

        To acquire an audiovisual product not already available in a library or media center contact the distributor listed with the entry. An alphabetical Directory of Distributors whose materials are contained in this catalog is provided as an appendix. Prices of materials and rental or loan conditions can be ascertained from the distributors.

        The editor and contributors have attempted to provide a strong selection of the best available materials, and an accurate rendering of data basic to making a selection and contacting the source. Nevertheless, there remain many possibilities for error, and obviously additions will be needed to enter valuable new materials that are being produced constantly. Therefore, suggestions for corrections, deletions, and additions are welcome. Please address them to the editor in care of the publisher.

Subject Category Outline

POPULAR CULTURE (PopC)

SCIENCE AND TECHNOLOGY (ST)

SOCIOLOGY (Sy)

America on Film
and Tape

Anthropology

John Vlach

Anthropology, defined as the study of mankind, is social science that searches for universal laws of human behavior. Such an endeavor is not, then, confined to any particular geographical, historical, or social entity. Anthropologists could, in theory, study human beings of any time or place belonging to any class or race. In practice, however, they have concentrated their research, until fairly recently, on the members of so-called primitive, peasant, or simple societies. In the United States, this has meant that the mainstay of anthropological investigation has been the study of the Indian. The following list, in containing more films on Native Americans than any other group, reflects this particular disciplinary emphasis.

During the last few decades, however, there has been more awareness of the circumstances affecting other minority groups besides Indians. Hispanic and Asian-Americans, for example, have exerted political and economic influences on the larger society and as a consequence they have also attracted scholarly attention. As these non-Indian groups have become legitimized as proper subjects for study, other immigrant populations have also been visited by anthropological researchers. A cursory review of this listing will indicate that the expressed goal of studying all of mankind is finally being pursued by anthropologists as they turn their lenses on groups close to home rather than exclusively on exotic people far away. Ethnographic investigation of retirement communities, stock car drivers, and college sororities would have been unthinkable, or at least considered trivial, by the previous generations of anthropologists. This filmography indicates not only the changes in the field of anthropology but the development of a new confidence as anthropologists begin to study people more like themselves.

ANTHROPOLOGY (An)

An-A	The Discipline
An-B	Native Americans
An-C	Ethnicity – General
An-D	Hispanic Americans
An-E	Asian Americans
An-F	Euro-Americans
An-G	Regional America
An-H	Special Groups

4   America on Film and Tape

Anthropology - The Discipline

An-A-1
FRANZ BOAS (1858-1942)   A
        UBV   Sd   C
        Documentary Educl Resources   59 min
A portrait of Boas, the "father of American anthropology," using archival
photographs, including work by Edward Curtis, and film footage of the Pacific
Northwest where Boas did repeated field work. Excerpts from his writings,
anecdotes and stories from people who knew him, including the Kwakiutl,
complete the portrait.

An-A-2
DIALECTS   A
        16mm   Sd   B   1958
        INUAVC   30 min
Explains and demonstrates dialect differences in standard English. Five guests
from different geographical areas of the United States illustrate pronounced
differences. Shows how language variations are divided into geographical areas.

An-A-3
OTHER PEOPLE'S GARBAGE   A
        16mm, UVB   Sd   C   1980
        PBS Video   58 min
A look at efforts to understand day-to-day life in the recent past, including
archeology, oral history and public records. Archeologists are seen working in
three areas: a 19th-century California coal mining town, slave quarters on a
Georgia cotton plantation and Boston sites uncovered during subway
construction.

Anthropology - Native Americans

An-B-1
AGHVEGHNIIMI - AT THE TIME OF WHALING   A
        16mm   Sd   C   1974
        Documentary Educational Resources   38 min
Filmed in Gambell, Alaska, during the whaling season. The people of the
community determined the content of the film to produce a record of the
community from the perspective of its own people. Shows a contemporary Eskimo
whaling community and its continuity as a culture through changing times.

An-B-2
AMERICAN INDIANS SERIES   A
        FS, Cassette   Sd   C   1972
        Coronet   42-54 frs
Each of the four color filmstrip programs in this series explores the culture and
history of the natives of a specific region of North America. Students will learn
of the American Indian tribes of the North Pacific Coast -- including parts of
Canada and Alaska, the Plains region of the United States, the Northeast U.S.
and southern Canada, and the Southeastern states. The narratives examine the
tribes' religious ceremonies and mythologies, their lives today, and their arts and
crafts. Other topics considered include the effects of the white man's
encroachment and conquest, and the Indians' difficulty in preserving their

heritage in the modern world. Each program consists of 6 filmstrips, 6 cassettes, and a guide. American Indians of the North Pacific Coast. American Indians of the Plains. American Indians of the Northeast. American Indians of the Southeast.

An-B-3
ANNIE MAE, BRAVE HEARTED WOMAN   A
          16mm   Sd   C   1980
          Brown Bird Productions, Inc.   84 min
Events of recent native American history are traced through the personal perspective of Annie Mae Pictou Aquash, a young native American woman whose commitment to social change ressulted in her death.

An-B-4
COMPLETING OUR CIRCLE   A
          16mm   Sd   C   1978
          MGHT   27 min
Traditions and arts of the Plains and West Coast Indians, the Inuit, and early European settlers are shown by using techniques to animate artifacts not photographed before.

An-B-5
DISPOSSESSED, THE   A
          16mm   Sd   C   1971
          University of California EMC   33 min
The struggle of California's Pit River Native Americans to regain their lands through reoccupation. Their meetings, reoccupation moves and arrests are seen, while individuals talk about land, poverty, legal rights and how their problems relate to the larger U.S. scene.

An-B-6
HERITAGE IN CEDAR   A
          16mm, U   Sd   C   1979
          Univ. of Washington Press   29 min
A survey of northwest coast Native American cedar woodworking. Included are a decaying Haida settlement; objects in the new University of British Columbia anthropology museum; Makah objects at the Ozette site in Washington; the 'Ksan village in British Columbia, where new carvings are done in the old way; and Hoh Village in Washington, where some traditional arts were never lost.

An-B-7
NAVAJO WAY, THE   A
          16mm   Sd   C   1975
          Films, Inc.   52 min
Interwoven in the story of Mary Grey Mountain, her son Robert Lee, and an aged medicine man, Long Salt, is the story of their people, the Navajo. Focuses on the dignity of being a Navajo. Suggests that the largest of American Indian tribes has been able to survive within the white man's culture because of their strong commitment to their traditions.

An-B-8
NEW INDIANS, THE   A
          16mm, U   Sd   C   1977
          Coronet   59 min
North American Indians face problems but take pride in their ancient traditions.

An-B-9
NORTH AMERICAN INDIANS TODAY   SCA
      16mm, U   Sd   C   1977
      NGS   25 min
Meet today's Indians, proud of their identity and searching for their cultural
heritage.

An-B-10
POW-WOW!   SCA
      16mm   Sd   C   1980
      Coronet   15 min
A dazzling display of North American Indian dances at a gathering of more than
20 tribes: the sacred Fire Dance; the Gourd Dance; the Intertribal Dance, and
the War Dance.

An-B-11
SHINNECOCK   A
      16mm   Sd   C   1976
      Phoenix Films   21 min
In North America, the Indians of the East Coast were the first to come in
contact with the white man. Explains how the Shinnicocks, their culture, and
heritage have been lost in the quicksand of time.

Anthropology - Ethnicity - General

An-C-1
AMERICA'S ETHNIC HERITAGE-GROWTH AND EXPANSION   S
      FS, Cassette   C   1976
      BFA   50 frs
Chronicles America's growth from 1800 to 1890 through the contributions of the
Scandinavians, Irish, Chinese and Japanese.

An-C-2
IMMIGRANT EXPERIENCE, THE:
  THE LONG, LONG JOURNEY   A
      16mm   Sd   C   1973
      LCA   31 min
First-person narration consists of the recollections of an old Polish-American
who looks back on a lifetime of hard work and recalls his initial experiences as a
youthful emigrant to the United States. The emphasis is on the difficulties
encountered by the minority child who is different from his school mates,
whether he be "Greenback," "Wop," or "Kike," on the economic hardships, and on
the conflict between retaining a traditional ethnic culture and the pressure to
become, as soon as possible, a "real American." Frequent use of Polish dialogue
with subtitles lends an air of authenticity.

An-C-3
ISLAND CALLED ELLIS, THE   A
      16mm   Sd   C   1966
      MGHT   53 min
Using Ellis Island's 30-acre locale, this film documents immigration in the decade
prior to World War I. Rare archive films of the "new" European immigrant show
the impact of Ellis Island on the newly-arrived people.

An-C-4
MINORITIES USA: THE AMERICAN DILEMMA   S
      FS, Cassette   C
      Coronet   15 min
Examines stereotype, prejudice, discrimination and scapegoating of minorities in
USA.

An-C-5
NATION OF IMMIGRANTS   A
      16mm   Sd   B   1969
      Films, Inc.   53 min
In-depth review of immigration to the United States beginning with European
discovery of the new world and arrival of earliest settlers. Contrasts dreams and
hopes of later immigrants with the hate-mongering and bigotry which faced them.
Based on book of same title by the late President Kennedy; narrated by Richard
Basehart; introduction by the late Senator Robert F. Kennedy.

Anthropology - Hispanic Americans

An-D-1
EL BARRIO - THE PUERTO RICAN   S
      FS, Cassette   C   1972
      Multi-Media Productions
Views Puerto Ricans as an ethnic group and discusses their contributions to
America's culture, economy and society.

An-D-2
WE'RE MOVING UP   A
      UBV   Sd   C   1980
      Films, Inc.   80 min
Hispanics are the fastest-growing minority in the U.S., with the current U.S.
total of twelve million increasing daily.

An-D-3
RESURRECTION   A
      16mm   Sd   C   1973
      Yale University Media Design Studio   27 min
A Mexican-American family celebrating Easter in Los Angeles.

An-D-4
YO SOY CHICANO   A
      16mm   Sd   C   1972
      INUAVC   59 min
The Chicano experience, from its roots in pre-Columbian history to the present.

Anthropology - Asian Americans

An-E-1
CHINESE AMERICAN, THE   A
      16mm   Sd   C   1973
      Handel Film Corporation   20 min
Illustrates how San Francisco's Chinatown developed following the earthquake of
1906 into the famous tourist attraction it is today.

An-E-2
JADE SNOW WONG   A
    16mm   Sd   C   1976
    Films, Inc.   27 min
Jade Snow, born into a traditional Chinese American family in the early 20's,
works as a maid and with this money and scholarships, graduates from college
with honors.

An-E-3
JAPANESE AMERICAN, THE   A
    16mm   Sd   C   1974
    Handel Film Corporation   30 min
Traces the emigration of the Japanese to the West Coast of the U.S. Illustrates
the deteriorating relations between the two countries climaxed at Pearl Harbor.

An-E-4
JENNY   S
    16mm, BVU   Sd   C   1977
    Carousel Films   19 min
A profile of a Japanese American family who teach their eight-year old daughter
the traditions and arts of their ancestors.

Anthropology - Euro-Americans

An-F-1
CITIZEN CARNEY   A
    16mm   Sd   C   1980
    Walter Thomas   47 min
Investigates the lifestyle of a band of American Gypsies who work and travel
from the Northwest Pacific to the Sunbelt.

An-F-2
DEMETRI ALEXANDROS' DIVE   S
    16mm, UVB   Sd   C   1977
    EBEC   9 min
The story of a young Greek boy who wants to dive for the cross in a community
church ceremony, but is denied permission because he is too young.

An-F-3
RAANANAH: A WORLD OF OUR OWN   SCA
    16mm   Sd   C   1980
    Marlene Booth   29 min
The story of Raananah, a Jewish communal settlement in New York state.

An-F-4
STORY OF ROMANIAN AMERICANS IN PICTURES, THE   A
    FS, Cassette   B   1977
    PUAVC
The history of Romanian Americans from their emigration to America in the
1900's to the American Bicentennial in 1976.

An-F-5
UNIQUE HERITAGE - POLISH AMERICANS   A
        FS, Cassette   C   1975
        Multi-Media Productions
Examines relationship between the cultural heritage of the Polish - Americans
and the lifestyle of American society.

An-F-6
VILLAGE IN BALTIMORE, A   A
        16mm   Sd   C   1981
        Doreen Moses   58 min
Set in the ethnic neighborhood of "Greek Town" in Baltimore, Maryland, deals
with the assimilation levels of four young Greek-American women -- their
personal and professional goals, and the importance of their families.

                        Anthropology - Regional America

An-G-1
LAFOURCHE: THE FORK OF THE MISSISSIPPI   A
        16mm   Sd
        Nicholls State University   30 min
Deals with the lifestyles and cultural heritages of the people who live on the
banks and delta lands around Bayou Lafourche.

An-G-2
LIFE IN RURAL AMERICA   S
        FS, Cassette   C   1973
        NGS   12-14 min
Presents the problems and rewards of living on the land. Five sound filmstrips:
The Family Farm; Cowboys; Coal Miners of Appalachia; Harvesters of the Golden
Plains; Settlers on Alaska's Frontier.

An-G-3
LIVING IN THE U.S. SERIES: A
        16mm, U   Sd   C   1974
        Coronet

LIVING IN THE MIDDLE ATLANTIC STATES   15 min
New York, Pennsylvania, New Jersey, Delaware, Maryland and West Virginia
contain more than a quarter of the nation's population.. A department store
worker, factory foreman, truck farmer, toll collector and railroad yardmaster
talk about living and working in megalopolis.

LIVING IN THE MIDWESTERN STATES   13 min
The midwestern states of Ohio, Michigan, Indiana, Illinois and Wisconsin
integrate transportation, manufacturing, marketing and farming. A farmer,
secretary, commodities trader and automobile assembler talk about how their jobs
relate to the Midwest and the rest of the nation.

LIVING IN THE NEW ENGLAND STATES   13 min
Depicts the people of Maine, Massachusetts, Vermont, New Hampshire,
Connecticut and Rhode Island. People in lobstering, innkeeping, shoemaking and
electronic research reflect on changes from the Colonial New England.

LIVING IN THE PACIFIC STATES   14 min
Washington, Oregon and California. Five people in various occupations -- logging,
aerospace, fishing, recreation and farming -- talk about their work and reasons
for living in the Pacific states.

LIVING IN THE ROCKY MOUNTAIN STATES   15 min
Montana, Idaho, Wyoming, Colorado, Utah and Nevada. A park ranger, mining
foreman, meat inspector, engineer and geology student talk about living and
working there.

LIVING IN THE SOUTHERN STATES   14 min
Virginia, Kentucky, Tennessee, North Carolina, South Carolina, Georgia, Florida,
Arkansas, Alabama, Mississippi and Louisiana. Talks with a tug-boat captain, a
geneticist and workers at a poultry farm, peanut butter factory and textile mill.

LIVING IN THE SOUTHWESTERN STATES   15 min
Arizona, New Mexico, Oklahoma and Texas. A cowhand, a Native American, a
prospector, an oil worker and a tour guide talk about living in the region.

LIVING IN THE UNITED STATES   13 min
Introductory film for this series.

An-G-4
LOUISIANA STORY   A
         16mm   Sd   B   1948
         MGHT   77 min
A 12-year old Cajun boy's world of nature in the Louisiana bayou country is
disturbed by the arrival of oil derricks. A classic ethnographic film by Robert
Flaherty.

An-G-5
MOUNTAINS OF GREEN, STREETS OF GOLD   A
         16mm, U   Sd   C   1978
         Films, Inc.   27 min
A story about Appalachians who left good jobs in Cleveland to return to the
mountains of West Virginia.

An-G-6
HAD YOU LIVED THEN --
   LIFE IN A MIDWESTERN SMALL TOWN   A
         16mm, U,V,B   Sd   C   1976
         Paramount Pictures, Inc.   18min
The invention of the automobile and electric lights changed the lives of many in
the early 20th century.

An-G-7
THROUGH ALL TIME:
   THE AMERICAN SEARCH FOR COMMUNITY   A
         16mm, U   Sd   C   1977
         University of California EMC   28 min
These two films explore the American search for community by examining the
dilemmas facing small towns.

TRADITIONAL SMALL TOWNS combines views of numerous towns throughout
America.

PLEASURE DOMES AND MONEY MILLS visits resort and recreation towns.

Anthropology - Special Groups

An-H-1
AIN'T NOBODY'S BUSINESS   A
          16mm   Sd   C   1970
          Mountain Moving Picture Co.   52 min
Women of various ages, races and backgrounds talk about their work --
prostitution. There are interviews with Margo St. James, a male vice squad
member, and footage of the First World Meeting of Prostitutes.

An-H-2
BODYBUILDERS   A
          U   Sd   1976
          University Community Video   28 min
Top contenders at the 1976 Mr. Minnesota competition and their dedication to
body building are seen in and out of competition.

An-H-3
HARD CHARGERS, THE   A
          16mm, U   Sd   C   1971
          Time-Life Multimedia   52 min
The story of stock car racing in the South and its relationship to southern values
and culture.

An-H-4
HARE KRISHNA PEOPLE, THE   A
          16mm   Sd   C   1973
          Greenwood Press   30 min
An intimate insight into the lives and beliefs of the Hare Krishna people.

An-H-5
JESUS PEOPLE   A
          16mm   Sd   C   1972
          Pyramid Films   43 min
A cinema-verite look at the "Jesus People."

An-H-6
SOUTH BEACH   A
          16mm   Sd   C   1978
          Cinema 5   30 min
The everyday life of retirees in South Miami Beach, Florida and how they begin
to organize for political action.

An-H-7
VINA   A
          16mm   Sd   C   1973
          Yale University Media Design Studio   28 min
Follows two Trappist monks -- one old, one young -- during their daily rout-
ines and their intimate spiritual moments.

Architecture

John Vlach

Architecture consists of man-made structures; the built environment as opposed to the natural environment. As such, architecture is a very inclusive topic. Architecture as practiced and studied, however, consists of the structures designed by professional architects. Since these structures, which are usually monumental in nature and intention, constitute only five percent of the built environment, very little architecture has ever been seriously studied. When we look at the list of visual resources on American architecture, we find it dominated by surveys of high-style, professionally designed buildings.

A good deal of what follows here is devoted to the works of famous, often eccentric, architects; men who were cult figures. Even the national and regional surveys are generally serial statements placing major architects in a chronological order. Cities are on occasion treated more centrally than architects. But these works tend to consider only the outstanding monumental structures designed by the likes of Wright, Sullivan, or Richardson. The same canon is confirmed repeatedly from different directions.

What of the rest of American Building? How is it presented? If it is presented, it stands as anonymous architecture; as the work of colonial ancestors. It is regarded as significant but without detailed historical explanation. Current scholarship in architectural history, particularly in vernacular architectural history, is rapidly filling in the wide gaps in the American building record. We now have the beginnings of a history for the ignored ninety-five percent of the built environment. Perhaps future visual resources will portray this new knowledge.

ARCHITECTURE (Arc)

Arc-A	General
Arc-B	Domestic
Arc-C	Architects
Arc-D	Buildings
Arc-E	Regional
Arc-F	Urban

Architecture - General

Arc-A-1
ARCHITECTURE AS A LANGUAGE,1840-1876   A
     35mm, Cassette   C   1974
     Sunburst Communications   80 Slides
Shows how architecture of the 19th century reflected the progress and enthusiasm
of the time.

Arc-A-2
ARCHITECTURE IN AMERICA, 17th-20th CENTURY   A
     35mm   1967
     SANDAK   60 Slides
Views the variety and ingenuity of American architecture from early colonial
times through 1950's.

Arc-A-3
COMMUNES OF THE SOUTHWEST U.S.A.   A
     35mm   C   1972
     Environmental Communications   50 Slides
Offers an historical look at shelters built to house alternative communities,
ranging from adobe huts to domes built of space-age materials.

Arc-A-4
CONCRETE ARCHITECTURE IN NORTH AMERICA   C,A
     35mm   C   1972
     KaiDib Films International   494 Slides
Examines a large number of structures in the U.S. and Canada which employ
reinforced concrete in their construction.

Arc-A-5
200 YEARS OF AMERICAN ARCHITECTURE   A
     35mm   C   1973
     EDDIM   20 Slides
American architecture in the past 200 years.

Arc-A-6
TOWERS AND PALACES, THE SEARCH FOR AN AMERICAN   TRADITION IN
ARCHITECTURE   A
     FS,Cassette   C   1971
     Rand McNally   90 frs
Discusses pursuit of an American tradition in the years after the Civil War.
Includes the development of the skyscraper.

Arc-A-7
200 YEARS OF AMERICAN TASTE IN ARCHITECTURE   A
     35mm   C   1974
     EDDIM   20 Slides
Shows America's taste from colonial through eclectic, to the present.

Architecture - Domestic

Arc-B-1
AMERICAN HOUSING STYLES   A
        35mm   C   1974
        Weston Walch   22 Slides
American housing styles by William Kenneth Reid.

Arc-B-2
CHICAGO   A
        35mm   C
        Johnson Architectural Images   220 Slides
Chicago is the birthplace of modern American architecture. Architects like
Jenney, Burnham & Root, Adler & Sullivan, Wright, Turnock, Holabird & Roche,
Shaw, Schmidt and Nimmons provided the creative focus evidenced in the buildings
of the early Chicago School. This set of 220 color slides examines many of the
landmarks of the Chicago School; in addition, the Prairie School and several
noteworthy structures in historical styles are presented.

Architecture - Architects

Arc-C-1
ARCHITECT OF THE NEW AMERICAN SUBURB, H. H.
RICHARDSON   A
        16mm   Sd   C   1978
        Fogg Fine Arts Films   26 min
Traces the life and work of Henry Hobson Richardson. Shows 17 suburban buildings
he designed in and around Boston between 1867 and 1886.

Arc-C-2
ARCHITECTURE: MIDDLE ATLANTIC STATES, 1860-1915   A
        35mm
        Educational Art Transparencies
Features work of Henry Hobson Richardson in Albany and Pittsburgh, Second
Empire architecture in Washington, D.C. and Philadelphia and the work of Louis
Sullivan in Buffalo.

Arc-C-3
FRANK LLOYD WRIGHT - ORGANIC ARCHITECT   A
        FS, Cassette   C   1977
        Aids of Cape Cod   71 frs
Biographical study of architect Wright, who revolutionized American architecture.

Arc-C-4
LOUIS I. KAHN: ARCHITECT   A
        16mm   Sd   C
        Visual Resources, Inc.   27 min
Depicts the imposing architectural achievements of Kahn, the teacher who is
shaping the concepts of a generation of young architects.

Arc-C-5
PALLADIO THE ARCHITECT AND HIS INFLUENCE
IN AMERICA   C,A
    16mm   Sd   C   1979
    Fogg Fine Arts Films   48 min
Palladio is the most imitated architect in the world. Shows villas and palaces of
Vicenza, Venice churches, country villas and Palladio's influence on Jefferson and
other American architects. Made for a general public interested in the arts and
Italian civilization, and for practitioners or students of architecture.

Architecture - Buildings

Arc-D-1
AMERICAN PICTURE PALACES   A
    16mm   Sd   C   1982
    Smithsonian Institution   23 min
The heyday, decline and rebirth of an American treasure: the Picture Palace.
Explores the achievement of visionary architects and showmen. Its live footage
and stills of palaces across the country demonstrate how these extravagances of
the Jazz Age have become practical solutions to the performaing arts' needs of
today and how they help revitalize our cities.

Arc-D-2
MOVIE PALACE MODERN   A
    35mm   1975
    Environmental Communications   45 Slides
Surveys movie theaters decorated by A.B. Heinsbergen from the era of silent
moves to the 1970's.

Arc-D-3
PLACE TO BE, A: THE CONSTRUCTION OF THE EAST BUILDING
OF NATIONAL GALLERY OF ART   A
    16mm   Sd
    CPB   60 min
Traces the creation and the construction of the East Building of the National
Gallery of Art, from the pencil of architect I.M. Pei to the craftsmen who
constructed the building to artists whose works are displayed there.

Arc-D-4
THOMAS JEFFERSON-NEO-CLASSICIST   A
    35mm
    Johnson Architectural Images   20 Slides
Jefferson's design of the State Capitol in Richmond, Virginia, is the first public
building based on the complete Roman temple form. Monticello, his own estate
outside Charlottesville,is based on a Palladian scheme. The Rotunda of the
University of Virginia was inspired by the Roman Pantheon. All are superb
examples of American Neo-classical architecture at its finest.

Architecture - Regional

Arc-E-1
ARCHITECTURE: MIDDLE ATLANTIC STATES, 1820-1860   A
    35mm   C   1975
    Educational Art Transparencies   39 Slides
Presents examples and histories of architecture in Middle Atlantic states from
1820-1860.

Arc-E-2
ARCHITECTURE OF THE AMERICAN MIDDLE WEST,
1915 TO PRESENT   S,C,A
    35mm   C   1975
    Educational Art Transparencies   56 Slides
Features Frank Lloyd Wright's Usonian houses and work for the Johnson Wax
Company; E. Saarinen's work at Cranbrook Academy; Minoru Yamasaki's buildings
in Detroit and Glencoe, Illinois; Columbus, Indiana and Chicago today.

Arc-E-3
ARCHITECTURE: MIDDLE ATLANTIC STATES,
1915-PRESENT   A
    35mm   C   1975
    Educational Art Transparencies   64 Slides
Depicts architecture in Middle Atlantic states from 1915-present.

Arc-E-4
ARCHITECTURE OF THE MIDDLE ATLANTIC REGION: COLONIAL
    AND GEORGIAN STYLES   A
    35mm   C   1975
    Educational Art Transparencies   39 Slides
Features Philadelphia structures and residences of Fairmont Park.

Arc-E-5
ARCHITECTURE OF THE MIDDLE ATLANTIC REGION:
    FEDERAL PERIOD   A
    35mm   C   1975
    Educational Art Transparencies   47 Slides
Features projects of Latrobe, Godefroy and William Thornton.

Arc-E-6
ARCHITECTURE OF THE SOUTHEASTERN STATES
    1860 TO THE PRESENT   A
    35mm   C   1975
    Educational Art Transparencies   78 Slides
Examples of architecture structures from 1860 to 20th century.

Arc-E-7
ARCHITECTURE OF THE SOUTHEASTERN STATES:
    FEDERAL PRERIOD TO THE CIVIL WAR   A
    35mm   C   1975
    Educational Art Transparencies   61 Slides
Architectural landmarks in Richmond, Virginia; Charleston, South Carolina and
Savannah, Georgia.

Arc-E-8
FEDERAL ARCHITECTURE IN NEW ENGLAND   A
    35mm   C   1975
    Educational Art Transparencies   71 Slides
Presents a survey of federal architecture in New England. Features the work of
Charles Bulfinch of Boston.

Arc-E-9
NEW ENGLAND ARCHITECTURE, 1890-PRESENT   A
    35mm   C   1975
    Educational Art Transparencies   51 Slides
Architecture in New England from 1890 to present. Features Boston Public
Library, Newport houses, and recent developments in Boston, Cambridge and
Hartford.

Arc-E-10
THREE PREHISTORIC INDIAN DWELLINGS   A
    35mm   C   1976
    Environmental Communications   25 Slides
The dwellings in this slide series clearly illustrate the natural union of man with
his environment. The geological dictates of the site resulted in the use of
available materials. Ruins of major prehistoric settlements in the American
southwest can be seen at Canyon de Chelly, Arizona; Mesa Verde, Colorado; and
Chaco Canyon, New Mexico.

Architecture - Urban

Arc-F-1
THE AMERICAN CITY IN THE 20TH CENTURY   A
    35mm   C   1973
    SANDAK   8 Slides
Views 20th century urban life under the various aspects of government, education
and the arts, commercial enterprises, housing and living needs and transportation.

Arc-F-2
CITY   A
    16mm   Sd   B   1939
    Museum of Modern Art   55 min
A screen classic which makes a strong appeal for the planning of cities to take
care of human needs. Commentary by Lewis Mumford. Music by Aaron Copeland.

Arc-F-3
CITY AND THE SELF   A
    16mm   Sd   C   1973
    Time-Life Films   55 min
Dramatically explores and scientifically demonstrates the basic facts of city life:
anonymity, distrust of others and the city dweller's lack of moral involvement.

Arc-F-4
HOW TO LOOK AT A CITY   A
    16mm   Sd   B   1964
    INUAVC   30 min
Basic issues of city planning, density, variety and human scale are examined as
they apply to New York City. Information is interwoven with somewhat

sentimental vignettes of the responses of adventurers, lovers and the starstruck to the city. Narrated by architect and author Eugene Raskin.

Arc-F-5
WASHINGTON, D.C., OUR NATION'S CAPITAL   A
            35mm   C   1976
            GPITVL   40 Slides
Presents sites in Washington, D.C., such as the Capitol, White House and Supreme Court. Relates historic background and pertinent information to each scene.

Arts

Nancy deLaurier

The following selections of audiovisual materials on American art reflect the availability of topics as much as they reflect the artistic significance of the topics and the quality of the audiovisual material. The topics include the "fine arts" of painting, drawing, printmaking and sculpture as well as the crafts and "useful arts", and folk arts. The time periods represent our ancient prehistoric cultures through to the 1980's; the geographical spread of topics ranges from coast to coast and from our southern states to the Eskimos of Alaska. The artists and topics are either important in themselves, or represent a significant type of American art form, including folk arts, which evoke the life of the people from colonial to contemporary times.

There is a wide range of quality in any collection of photographic materials, especially in color. For this listing only slides known to be of good quality were included. To preserve the color and good photographic image, film materials should be stored in closed metal containers and kept cool and dry. Film is easily scratched and fingerprinted, and attracts dirt - so precautions must be taken in handling film to avoid these detractors.

Other major suppliers of slides in American art are:

Rosenthal Art Slides, 5456 Ridgewood Court, Chicago, IL 60615

The Dunlap Society, Lake Champlain Road, Essex, NY 12936

Barney Burstein, 2745 E. Atlantic Blvd., #305, Pompano Beach, FL 33062

Miniature Gallery, 60 Rushett Close, Long Ditton, Surrey, England, KT7 OUT (one major set on American painting)

The -Slide Buyers Guide-, published by the Visual Resources Association, lists sources of art and architecture slides, their subject areas, and quality ratings. The 1980 (latest) edition is available from:

Nancy deLaurier
204 Fine Arts
Univ. of Missouri/ Kansas City
Kansas City, MO 64110

ARTS

Arts - Surveys (General Topics)

Arts-A-1
ARTS OF THE UNITED STATES   A
    35mm   C
    SANDAK   2000 slides
Comprehensive series of more than 2000 slides.

Arts-A-2
CREATIVE AMERICANS 1800-1900   C
    U   C   1972
    Time-Life Multimedia   27min
Looks at major American artistic achievements of the 19th century.

Arts-A-3
DICTIONARY AND GUIDE TO
  MOVEMENTS IN MODERN ART   A
    35mm   C   1972
    SANDAK   160 slides
Examples of major art movements and styles in American art in the 19th and 20th
centuries.

Arts-A-4
ICONS OF POPULAR CULTURE   CA
    35mm   C   1971
    SANDAK   25 slides
Examines icons as reflected in art in U.S. contemporary culture and their possible
warnings to the outside world.

Arts-A-5
THE STRUCTURE OF COLOR   CA
    35mm   C   1971
    SANDAK   56 slides
Documents 1971 exhibition of 39 paintings of the proceeding 20 years which are
structured primarily by color.

Arts - Times, Places, Styles

Arts-B-1
AFTER JACKSON POLLOCK   SCA
    FS, Cassette   C   1970
    McIntyre Visual Publications   33 frs
Shows the distinctive styles and techniques of various well-known American
painters who dominated the contemporary scene in the 1950s and 1960s.

Arts-B-2
AMERICAN ART, 1865-1913   S
    16mm   Sd   C   1968
    EDDIM   15min
More than 300 examples of American art for the period which anticipated
America's entry into the mainstream of world art.

Arts-B-3
AMERICAN ART SINCE 1945   A
     35mm   C   1975
     SANDAK   102 slides
Shows art by Gorky, Still, Motherwell, Warhol and others, representing trends in
American art since 1945.

Arts-B-4
AMERICAN GENIUS: 1960s-1970s   SC
     FS, Cassette   C   1972
     EDDIM   84 frs
Shows how the emerging social consciousness of the 1960s erupted in physical
violence and found expression in anti-hero movies, pop art, the living theatre and
rock music.

Arts-B-5
ART BY TALENTED TEENAGERS   SCA
     FS   C   1979
     Scholastic Magazines, Inc.   200 frs
Features entries from -Scholastic Magazine-'s 52nd Annual National High School
Art Exhibition.

Arts-B-6
ART IN AMERICA   SCA
     16mm   Sd   C   1976
     Handel Film Corp.   25min
Depicts prominent artists of the 18th and 19th centuries in New England.
Discusses portraiture, historical paintings of the American Revolution, maritime
paintings and scrimshaw. Includes indigenous art of the Eskimos, Hawaiians and
Indians.

Arts-B-7
BARRIO MURALS OF SANTA FE   SCA
     35mm   C   1976
     Environmental Communications   10 slides
This slide series documents the vigorous and boldly-colored creations of Los Artes
Guadalupanos de Aztian, a collective in New Mexico, and various other public
works executed through Fall, 1972. Included with the slides is a supplementary
booklet, with slide-by-slide descriptions, and a map showing the locations of the
works illustrated.

Arts-B-8
BILLBOARD ENVIRONMENT, THE   SCA
     35mm   C   1976
     Environmental Communications   68 slides
This series of outstanding examples of outdoor advertising is the result of a
four-year documentation process (1970-1973), augmented by the inclusion of
several archival works from the mid-1960s. Billboards have been banned or
severely regulated in several locations. The series includes a considerable variety
of applications of forms of outdoor advertising: the most subtle and sophisticated
messages promoting recording artists along the Sunset Strip; exciting designs
which break free of the conventional rectangle; printed and painted examples;
billboard artists at work; photographs of billboards taken in their street context
and while "in progress" at the advertising studios.

Arts-B-9
CALIFORNIA CUSTOM CARE   SCA
          35mm   1976
          Environmental Communications   34 slides
In the decentralized, exploded scale of California, the automobile culture has
defined and established itself as an indigenous reality. A Californian's car is not
only a necessity, it is his home away from home. From this cultural milieu
developed the fantastic art form of automobile customization. This slide series
documents a variety of mind-bending, eye-popping customized automobiles of 1932
vintage to the present. Examples were selected from several custom car shows
and from vehicles encountered on California highways, and include the work of
George Barris—the Picasso of this art form.

Arts-B-10
CHICAGO MURALS   SCA
          35mm   1976
          Environmental Communications   60 slides
These murals represent a unique contribution to the mural renaissance of the
sixties and seventies. They present a documentation of the Public Art Workshop
and the Chicago Mural Group.

Arts-B-11
CITY WALLS, NEW YORK   A
          35mm   1976
          Environmental Communications   36 slides
This recently updated slide series provides a survey of wall paintings by City
Walls, Inc., an organization which has been responsible for the execution of
several dynamic wall paintings in New York City. Included are many major works
by various artists, from the time of its inception in 1969 to the present, together
with a few early works that pre-date the formal founding of City Walls, Inc. City
Walls, Inc. projects are primarily abstract paintings concerned with form and color
and their relationship to the total urban environment.

Arts-B-12
COLONIAL PERIOD IN THE MIDDLE ATLANTIC STATES   A
          35mm   C   1968
          SANDAK   25 slides
Depicts the period through the homes of people, architecture of the Pennsylvania
Dutch, public buildings, furniture, and everyday objects.

Arts-B-13
CONTEMPORARY AMERICAN ART—1973 Whitney   A
          35mm   C   1973
          Whitney Museum   46 slides
Gives examples of the painting and sculpture shows at the 1973 Whitney Museum
exhibition of contemporary American art.

Arts-B-14
CONTEMPORARY ART IN AMERICA, 1950-67   SCA
          35mm   C   1967
          SANDAK   1980 Sls
Focuses on major movements from 1960 to the present. Includes the new American
paintings, abstract sculpture in the 1960s, the art of assemblage, Op Art, Pop Art
and primary structures.

Arts-B-15
CURATOR'S CHOICE   A
        U   Sd   C
        ABC Video Enterprises   25min
Provides an idea of how art is collected and valued by museum curators. Six art
curators explain their purchase choices and the responsibilities they have as fine
art assayers.

Arts-B-16
FINE ART IN FEDERAL BUILDINGS   A
        16mm   Sd   C   1974
        NAVC   5 min
Describes Program for Fine Art in Federal buildings and shows a stabile by
Alexander Calder.

Arts-B-17
THE HAND AND THE SPIRIT   CA
        35mm   C   1973
        SANDAK   50 slides
Shows relationships of U.S. religious art during 18th and 19th centuries to
changing religious trends in America.

Arts-B-18
HUDSON RIVER SCHOOL   SCA
        35mm   C   1967
        SANDAK   20 slides
American landscape painters.

Arts-B-19
L.A. CHICANO GRAFFITI   SCA
        35mm   C   1976
        Environmental Communications   73 Slides
Chicano graffiti in the Los Angeles area assume a distinctive calligraphic
character, emphasizing style and design as much as vigorous verbal messages.
These inscriptions, called placas or plaqueasos by those who write them, follow
clearly established lettering patterns tha have been perpetuated for several
decades.   The places are analyzed in a visual essay through their stylized
alphabets, verbal codes, and aggresive designs. The slides represent the different
types of placas, their principal alphabet styles, various designs, and their effect
over the years on certain walls.

Arts-B-20
L.A. CHICANO STREET MURALS   SCA
        35mm   C   1976
        Environmental Communications   70 slides
This series documents the strong and vibrant murals and supergraphics that have
appeared throughout the Chicano community, and explores the role of the Chicano
artists as community energizers and spokesmen.

Arts-B-21
MAJOR MOVEMENTS OF THE 60'S   SCA
        35mm   C   1970
        SANDAK   30 slides
Presents examples of the visual arts movements of the 1960's. Explains op art,
magic realism, kinetic art, luminal art, pop art, grotesque, post-abstract
expressionism, minimal art and technological innovations in methods and materials

for creating two and three dimensional shapes and objects.

Arts-B-22
MARIO SANCHEZ--PAINTER OF
 MEMORIES
                                                     SCA
     16mm   Sd   C   1978
     Bowling Green Films   17min
Study of the life and work of Cuban-American wood painter Mario Sanchez.

Arts-B-23
MASTERPIECES FROM THE WORCESTER ART   A
     35mm   C   1976
     SANDAK   43 slides
Shows examples of European and American art, ranging from 14th century Italy to
20th century America.

Arts-B-24
THE MECHANICAL PARADISE   A
     16mm, UVB   Sd   C   1980
     Time-Life Video   52min
The series explores the social history of the twentieth century through artists'
eyes.

Arts-B-25
MURALS, CENTRAL U.S.A.
                                                 SCA
     35mm   C   1976
     Environmental Communications   25 slides
This slide series offers examinations of murals and supergraphics from such cities
as: Cincinnati, Ann Arbor, Minneapolis, Dayton, Fort Worth, Little Rock, Dallas,
Yellow Springs, St. Louis and Atlanta.

Arts-B-26
MUSEUM: BEHIND THE SCENES AT
 THE ART INSTITUTE OF CHICAGO   A
     16mm   Sd   C
     The American Federation of Arts   28min
A behind-the-scenes look at a major American museum; and the work of curators
in organizing the exhibitions, the installers who handle the works of art, and the
conservators who are involved in the care and preservation of the paintings and
prints.

Arts-B-27
A NATION OF PAINTERS   A
     16mm   Sd   C   1978
     EBEC   7min
Shows various painters and their works.

Arts-B-28
NEW ART OF THE AMERICAN WEST   SCA
     16mm   Sd   C
     MTPS   23min
Shows how several artists of the southwest use the inspiration of the land, its
vagaries and vastness, to create highly original works that reflect their vision of
the American West. Each demonstrates how the west has influenced his/her views
and artform.

Arts-B-29
NEW YORK PAINTING AND SCULPTURE 1940–1970   SCA
        35mm   C   1970
        SANDAK   50 slides
Shows painting and sculpture by the artists who have worked in New York during
its most creative period.

Arts-B-30
1975 BIENNIAL EXHIBITION--CONTEMPORARY
    AMERICAN ART FROM THE WHITNEY   SCA
        35mm   C   1975
        SANDAK   60 slides
Shows the work of contemporary American artists from the biennial exhibition at
the Whitney Museum of American Art in New York.

Arts-B-31
19TH CENTURY AMERICA   SCA
        35mm   C   1970
        Metropolitan Museum of Art   100 slides
Shows painting, sculpture, furniture, decorative arts and period rooms from the
19th century.

Arts-B-32
SAN FRANCISCO BAY AREA MURALS   SCA
        35mm   C   1976
        Environmental Communications   45 slides
The Bay Area mural movement is indicative of a conscious reaction to the sterile,
formal, functionless, neo-dada and minimalistic art of the past few decades. It is
truer to the beliefs that you've got to have art, art in the environment, reflecting
and affecting the daily lives of people, and with an affirmative vision of our
future.

Arts-B-33
SAN FRANCISCO BAY AREA WOMEN ARTISTS   SCA
        35mm   1976
        Environmental Communications   40 slides
A dramatic visual variety of sensibilities, styles, concepts and involvements are
illustrated in this definitive series of San Francisco Bay area women artists.
Represented are the works of 27 painters who live and work in and around San
Francisco.

Arts-B-34
A SENSE OF DISCOVERY, THE NATIONAL MUSEUM
    OF AMERICAN ART   A
        16mm   Sd   C
        Smithsonian, Office of Telecomm.   28min
Explores both the art and unique educational and research programs that
distinguish this museum. Also depicts its efforts to show not only prominent, but
also the less well-known but important artists, and movements that have
profoundly influenced the progress of art, both in the United States and abroad.

Arts-B-35
STREET PAINTINGS OF L.A.   SCA
        35mm   C   1976
        Environmental Communications   56 slides
This slide series provides an overview of the street painting movement over a

period of six years and includes the major works of such groups and individual artists as the L.A. Fine Arts Squad, The Fool, Wayne Holwick and Arthur Mortimer.

Arts-B-36
SUPERGRAPHICS   SCA
        35mm   C   1976
        Environmental Communications   29 slides
With the new total environment orientation of architects, artists, and graphic designers, our cities are getting an immense face lift. Paint has provided the answer for a quick, inexpensive means of revitalizing drab urban areas. The spatial experimentation of supergraphics can be superficial, or it can become an architecture in itself. Whimsy and humor often become design elements to surprise and delight the city dweller. Arrows, letters, symbols, and color explode normal static rectilinear architectural forms into lively visual happenings.

Arts-B-37
SURVEY OF WALL PAINTINGS   SCA
        35mm   1976
        Environmental Communications   29 slides
The works of various community muralists, individual and other groups are represented in this series, paralleled with the less self-conscious work of advertising wall paintings. The paintings are widely divergent in conception, style and effect, and are executed by groups with equally different social and political motives. This slide series is a useful sampling of the public art that is flourishing in metropolitan areas throughout the East - New York, Boston, Cincinnati, Montreal, etc.

                    Arts - Painting, Prints, Photography

Arts-C-1
AARON SISKIND   SCA
        35mm   B   1981
        Light Impressions 1.   30 slides
The work represented in this set surveys the work of Siskind from the late 1930s until the late 1950s. Included in this set: Sea Weed (1940s), Martha's Vineyard (1950s), Terrors and Pleasures of Levitation, and more.

Arts-C-2
AARON SISKIND   SCA
        35mm   B   1981
        Light Impressions 2.   30 slides
The work of this set covers the period from 1965 to 1979. Among the work included: Homage to Franz Kline, the work from Rome, the Badlands, and Utah, Corfu olive trees, recent New York City work, Cusco and more.

Arts-C-3
AARON SISKIND   SCA
        35mm   B   1981
        Light Impressions 3.   25 slides
During the 1930s and 1940s, Siskind was involved in the photo as a document. He was a member of the Photo League. Among the work in this set: Harlem Document, The Most Crowded Block in the World, and the Portrait of a Tenement.

Arts–C–4
ABSTRACT EXPRESSIONISM, NEW YORK SCHOOL   CA
        35mm, Cassette   1974
        SANDAK   25 slides
Examines the characteristics of abstract expressionism as an art movement.

Arts–C–5
ABSTRACT PAINTINGS: THE GESTURAL TRADITION   A
        35mm   C
        Art Now, Inc.   22 slides
Presents works of artists in the gestural tradition of abstract expressions in such
as Jasper Johns, Karel Appel and Willem de Kooning.

Arts–C–6
THE AMERICA OF CURRIER AND IVES:
  FROM SAIL TO STEAM   SA
        35mm   C   1974
        Coronet   59 slides
Shows relationship of Currier and Ives prints of sailing ships, steamboats and
railroads to the development of America and the westward movement.

Arts–C–7
THE AMERICA OF CURRIER AND IVES:
  URBAN AMERICA IN THE MAKING   SCA
        FS, Cassette   C   1974
        Coronet   61 slides
Shows how Currier and Ives pictured city life in the mid–1800s.

Arts–C–8
AMERICAN PAINTING––17TH AND 18TH CENTURIES   SCA
        35mm   C   1968
        SANDAK   20 slides
Visual description of the early American styles in painting, including such artists
as Copley, Feke and West.

Arts–C–9
AMERICAN PAINTING 1850–1900   A
        FS, Cassette   C
        LIFE   66 frs
Shows the traditional painting of the period and the development of new styles
influenced by the 20th century. Shows works of Sargent, Cassatt, Hassam and
Whistler.

Arts–C–10
AMON CARTER MUSEUM OF WESTERN
  ART   SCA
        35mm
        Amon Carter Museum   12 slides
An essay on the Amon Carter Museum, its founding and its collection.

Arts–C–11
ANDREW WYETH   SC
        35mm   C
        EDDIM   20 slides
Examines Wyeth's work as it relates to his favorite locales and sitters, to help
the viewer understand his technique and aesthetic direction.

Arts-C-12
ANSEL ADAMS, PHOTOGRAPHER   A
          16mm   Sd   B   1958
          IFB   20min
Shows the life and work of Ansel Adams: his equipment, home, interests, and his
attitude toward art, photography and life.

Arts-C-13
ART OF THE REAL: U.S.A. 1948-1968   SCA
          35mm   C
          SANDAK   34 slides
Examples from the Museum of Modern Art's acquisitions reflecting major trends of
the 1960s in painting and sculpture.

Arts-C-14
HARRY CALLAHAN,Photographer   SCA
          35mm   1981
          Light Impressions   30 slides
The works included in this slide set are: a suite of "Eleanor" images, a series of
"Weed" or line images, a series of multiple exposures, urban pedestrians, and the
"Beach" series.

Arts-C-15
HARRY CALLAHAN, Photographer   SCA
          35mm   1981
          Light Impressions   30 slides
A further exploration into the work of Callahan. This set includes: a series of
urban facades, the recent images from Cuzco, Peru, more multiples including the
series of nudes in urban store windows, the work with the television screen as
icon and his "cutout" collages.

Arts-C-16
HARRY CALLAHAN, Photographer   SCA
          35mm   C   1981
          Light Impressions   25 slides
Noted primarily as a master of black and white photography, this set reveals
Callahan's work with color from the 1940s to the present.

Arts-C-17
CHARLES BURCHFIELD   SCA
          16mm   Sd   C
          IFB   14min
Illuminates Burchfield's sketches and watercolors of American life, revealing the
development and growth of the artist's inner vision. His work reflects the
fantasies of an imaginative eye and a predilection toward realism.

Arts-C-18
CHARLES M. RUSSELL   SCA
          35mm   C
          Amon Carter Museum   12 slides
An essay on Russell, his life and times, with an assessment of his role as the
"cowboy" artist.

Arts-C-19
CONTEMPORARY AMERICAN PRINTS 1955-1966   SCA
          35mm   C   1966
          SANDAK   40 slides
The forty slides of graphics contained in this listing document American graphics
during the years 1955-1966. The full range of print-making media is illustrated by
the inclusion of intaglio, lithography, wood block and relief, serigraphy, and mixed
techniques.

Arts-C-20
CONTEMPORARY PHOTOGRAPHERS   SCA
          35mm   1981
          Light Impressions   50 slides
Since its inception in 1971, Light Gallery has been primarily interested in 20th
Century photography and the contemporary working photographer. Those included
in this volume are, in Light's judgment, among the most innovative and exciting
picture-makers today.

Arts-C-21
DESIGN FOR PEOPLE   SCA
          16mm   Sd   C   1974
          National Endowment for the Arts   13min
Presents survey of opinions and reactions to Federal graphics used in such places
as customs, immigration, education and on postage stamps.

Arts-C-22
DRAWINGS: A PLURALIST DECADE   A
          16mm   Sd   C
          USIA   19min
Examines the drawings of 66 American artists that compose the American Exhibit
at the 1980 Venice Biennale, the theme of which is "Drawings of the 1970s: The
Pluralist Decade."

Arts-C-23
EDWARD STEICHEN, Photographer   SCA
          35mm   1981
          Light Impressions   35 slides
1. Covers the period from the late 1890s to the late 1920s. Included in this set:
Diagram of Doom, Laughing Boxes, Milk Bottles, a series of photos of Therese and
Isadora Duncan, Triumph of the Egg, Time-Space Continuum, portraits of Rodin,
Steiglitz, Eleanora Duse, and a self-portrait. Also included are some advertising
and silk design images.

2. Covers the period from the late 1920s to the late 1940s. Included in this set:
The Maypole, What Price Glory?, On the Clinic Stairs, various fashion
photographs, portraits of Amelia Earhart, Gary Cooper, Greta Garbo, Gloria
Swanson, Marlene Dietrich, Charles Laughton, and Paul Robeson. Also in this set
are images made by Steichen of naval events during World War II.

Arts-C-24
THE EIGHT AND THE ASHCAN SCHOOL   SC
          35mm   C
          EDDIM   20 slides
Shows paintings by the eight artists of the Ash Can School who present their
diversified, individual styles and interests.

Arts-C-25
ELECTROWORKS   SCA
          35mm   1981
          Light Impressions   80 slides
The International Museum of Photography has organized "Electroworks," a major
exhibition of the work produced with office copy machines. An entire generation
of artists now refer to the office copiers as the media with which they work. This
slide set examines a selection of works from this exhibit, including the range of
objects.

Arts-C-26
FAMOUS AMERICANS AND HISTORICAL
     EVENTS IN PAINTING   SCA
          35mm   C   1968
          SANDAK   25 slides
Presents a series of events and historical personages from colonial times to the
period prior to the civil war as reflected in paintings.

Arts-C-27
FARM SECURITY ADMINISTRATION   SCA
          35mm   1981
          Light Impressions   80 slides
The use of photography to record social facts dates back to the beginning of the
medium, but between 1935 and 1943 a small group of photographers working for
the Farm Security Administration of the Federal government raised the
documentary method to an influential aesthetic style.

Arts-C-28
FREDERIC REMINGTON   SCA
          35mm
          Amon Carter Museum   12 slides
An essay on Remington, his life and influence as a painter of the western scene.

Arts-C-29
FREDERIC REMINGTON   SCA
          STERLED   27min
A portrait of the pre-eminent artist of the American West.

Arts-C-30
FOCUS: FOUR AMERICAN PHOTOGRAPHERS   A
          16mm   Sd   C
          USIA   29min
Profiles four American photographers, showing them at work as they explain how
and why they do photography.

Arts-C-31
FRANZ KLINE REMEMBERED   A
          16mm   Sd   C   1982
          Direct Cinema   28min
A film portrait of the late Abstract Expressionist painter Franz Kline. Through
the use of photographs, period footage, and interviews with fellow artists and
friends, Franz Kline, the man, the painter and his time come vividly to life.

Arts-C-32
GEMINI G.E.L.   A
    35mm   1976
    Environmental Communications   70 slides
Since 1966, Gemini G.E.L. has collaborated with some of America's best known
modern artists in the creation of multiple works of art. Located in Los Angeles,
Gemini is an experimental lithography workshop. This slide series presents a
selection of some of the most outstanding and well-known works that have
emerged as a result of a decade of collaborative efforts.

Arts-C-33
JAMES ROSENQUIST   A
    35mm   1976
    Environmental Communications   40 slides
Mylar, plastic sheets, bits of wood, wire, twine, plexiglass, neon and electric
light, and paint are the materials employed by James Rosenquist in his art works.
This series of slides shows the works of James Rosenquist from 1958 to 1975.

Arts-C-34
LEWIS HINE   A
    35mm   B   1981
    Light Impressions   30 slides
In 1903 Lewis Hine, who was a teacher at the Ethical Culture School, first picked
up a camera. After five years of gradually increasing involvement with the
medium, photographing slums in Washington and the immigrants on Ellis Island,
Hine declared himself a professional photographer. Hine's work can be divided into
two major periods. The first, prior to World War I, was devoted to reformist
causes, to the abolition of sweat shops and child labor, to cleaning up the slums
and providing decent living. The second period, following his return from the war
as a captain in the Red Cross, was devoted to a portrayal of the American
working man, whether building the Empire State Building or creating a huge
dynamo.

Arts-C-35
LADDIE JOHN DILL   A
    35mm   1976
    Environmental Communications   25 slides
This slide series illustrates the evolution of Dill's work from his early neon-light
sculptures to his latest cement and glass paintings.

Arts-C-36
LEE KRASNER: THE LONG VIEW   SCA
    16mm   Sd   C   1978
    The American Federation of Arts   30 min
Documentary film explores development and life as a woman artist, marriage to,
and death of, Jackson Pollock, and life alone. Shows much of her work and stills
of her with Pollock.

Arts-C-37
THE MAKING OF A MURAL   A
    16 mm   C   1976
    Helios Film Productions   15min
Bill Walker, pioneer black mural artist, is shown creating -The Worker-, a mural
which depicts the history of the Amalgamated Meatcutters Union. Poetry,
historical quotes, and labor songs are united with a visual montage of labor
struggles.

Arts-C-38
A MAN AND A RIVER   A
        16mm   Sd   C   1973
        Environmental Protection Agency   15min
Students of art and environmentalists alike will appreciate this look at the
inspiration for and the works of the late Thomas Hart Benton, American painter,
conservationist, raconteur. Here we canoe with Tom Benton down his favorite
river--the Buffalo--as he reminisces about his early enjoyment of free flowing
rivers in natural surroundings, and the importance of preserving them for future
generations. Interspersed along the water route we view some of Benton's
paintings and drawings--from his "cottonloading" sternwheeler of 1928 to the lyric
paintings of his favorite river spots like -Bat House Cave-. Sensitively narrated by
Richard Chamberlain, Benton's contentment when communing with nature provides
an eloquent plea for conscious public conservation of the Nation's natural
treasures.

Arts-C-39
MARY CASSATT, IMPRESSIONIST FROM PHILADELPHIA   SCA
        16mm   Sd   C   1978
        Films, Inc.   28min
Devoted to Mary Cassatt, one of the five greatest American artists of the 19th
century, along with Homer, Sargent, Whistler, and Eakin.

Arts-C-40
A NATION OF PAINTERS   SCA
        16mm   Sd   C   1977
        EBEC   7min
The dreams and hopes of a young nation are recorded by American painters in the
time between the Revolution and the Civil War. Often painting for a night's
lodging or a meal, these enthusiastic, untrained artists express an exuberance and
optimism that reflect the national confidence in the future greatness of the
United States.

Arts-C-41
NEW AMERICAN PAINTING--ABSTRACT EXPRESSIONISM   CA
        35mm   1959
        SANDAK   61 slides
Shows examples of modern American abstract expressionist painting from an
exhibit organized by the Museum of Modern Art, New York, in 1958.

Arts-C-42
NICHOLAS MURAY   A
        35mm   B   1981
        Light Impressions   25 slides
Born in Hungary, Muray was trained in Budapest. At the beginning of WWI, Muray
emigrated to the U.S. and immediately obtained a job as a color technician and
engraver. By the 1920s, living in New York City, his reputation as an
accomplished portraitist had spread. From the highly nostalgic images of a 1933
Dodge and of Joan Crawford posing for a Rogers Brothers Silverplate, to the
clear and sophisticated articulations for plastics and food advertisements, his
pictures represent a brief survey of photogrpahic advertising during this period.

Arts-C-43
PAINTERS PAINTING   A
          16mm   Sd   C   1972
          New Yorker Films   117 min
Covers painting from 1940 to 1970, the period when an American art was finally
produced. Includes de Kooning, Rauschenberg, Warhol, Frankenthaler and others.
Improvised and casual in studios and galleries.

Arts-C-44
PAINTINGS ABOUT AMERICA   SCA
          35mm   C   1971
          Center for Humanities, Inc.   160 slides
Deals with paintings about America by American artists to show the social,
intellectual, literary, and economic transitions that accompanied the growth of
the United States.

Arts-C-45
THE PHOTOGRAPHER'S HAND   SCA
          35mm   1981
          Light Impressions   35 slides
This slide set reproduces an exhibition of hand-altered and hand-made photographs
which was first shown at the International Museum of Photography at George
Eastman House during the summer of 1979.

Arts-C-46
POSTERS OF PROTEST   A
          35mm   1976
          Environmental Communications   102 slides
The Posters of Protest released with naked force the satirical purpose often
implicit or veiled in Pop Art. Directly deriving images and symbols from
commercial and popular culture, mocking that culture and the established political
society with it, the weapons of consumerism are turned against consumerism
itself.

Arts-C-47
REACHING OUT--KEN TYLER, MASTER PRINTER   CA
          16mm   Sd   C   1978
          Univ. of California EMC   28min
Shows lithographic Ken Tyler working with such other artists as Roy Lichtenstein,
David Hockney and author Michael Crichton. Presents Tyler commenting on the
possibilities of his medium, how he got started in his career, and some of his
major work.

Arts-C-48
ROBERT RAUSCHENBERG   SCA
          16mm   Sd   C   1979
          Blackwood Productions   45min
Robert Rauschenberg's art embodies the life-embracing and participatory spirit
that characterizes much of American art since 1950. The film traces his life and
work from the days at Black Mountain College to the climactic retrospective,
held in 1977 at The Museum of Modern Art in New York. The film was made with
the participation of John Cage and Merce Cunningham.

Arts-C-49
FLIP SCHULKE   A
    35mm   1981
    Light Impressions   25 slides
Photo essayist who travels throughout the U.S.A. and abroad on photographic
assignments and projects. This portfolio of work shows that it is possible to
combine art, creativity, sensitivity and introspection as well as communicate ideas
of realistic and imagined subjects.

Arts-C-50
SUPER REALISM: PAINTING AND SCULPTURE   SC
    35mm   C
    EDDIM   20 slides
Shows examples of paintings and sculpture by the leading super real artists.
Discusses stylistic similarities and differences.

Arts-C-51
U.S. EYE   SCA
    35mm   1981
    Light Impressions   136 slides
Sixty five artists from all sections of the United States were chosen for inclusion
in "U.S. EYE," a fine art photography exhibition planned as part of the National
Fine Arts Committee's program to showcase American Art at the 1980 Olympic
Games in Lake Placid, N.Y.

Arts-C-52
VISUAL COMMUNICATIONS   SCA
    35mm   C
    SANDAK   180 slides
Surveys the wide variety of American graphic designs from the 18th century to
the present day. Includes examples of advertising, cartoons, catalogs, record
covers and posters.

Arts-C-53
WEEGEE THE PHOTOGRAPHER   SCA
    35mm   B   1981
    Light Impressions   30 slides
Born Arthur Fellig, Weegee (1899-1968) was an immigrant from Austria who built
his reputation as a free-lance news photographer with a bulky 4x5 Speed Graphic
press camera in the days before the miniature camera. He began his career
chasing ambulances and responding to the police radio; as his vision developed, his
subject matter expanded to cover gangsters and celebrities, movie stars and slum
dwellers, high society and the Bowery, all portrayed with compassion but without
sentimentality.

Arts-C-54
WEEGEE'S WOMEN   SCA
    35mm   1981
    Light Impressions   30 slides
Whether doing street reportage of studio cheesecake, Weegee looked at women
with the same voyeuristic and irreverent eye that he turned on the rest of New
York City's amazing human drama. He captured a certain real quality about
women that transcends both myth and stereotype: the women of his photographs
are more like memories than images.

Arts–C–55
BRETT WESTON   SCA
        35mm   B   1981
        Light Impressions   25 slides
This set of slides covers a range of this gifted photographer's work from the early
1930s to the present day, from California to New York and Europe and Japan.

Arts–C–56
WINSLOW HOMER   SCA
        35mm   C   1975
        EDDIM   20 slides
Surveys the development of the 19th century artist.

Arts–C–57
THE WORKS OF EDWARD RUSCHA   SCA
        35mm   1976
        Environmental Communications   25 slides
An historical survey of the work of contemporary Los Angeles artist Edward
Ruscha from 1962 until the present. This series of 25 slides documents most of his
well known paintings and prints.

Arts–C–58
THE WORLD OF ANDREW WYETH   A
        16mm   Sd   C
        IFB   26min
Notes significant facts in the life of one of the great realistic painters, especially
the influence of his father, N.C. Wyeth. Explores 49 paintings, giving both an
overall impression of each canvas and a close look at specific details. Technical
assistance was provided by Wyeth's son, Nicolas; the introduction is by Henry
Fonda, a personal friend.

Arts–C–59
WYNN BULLOCK   SCA
        35mm   B   1981
        Light Impressions   30 slides
The slide set covers representative imagery from Bullock's lifetime in creative
photography, especially his nudes and the lush, romantic land– and sea–scapes he
created in his adopted home of Monterey.

Arts–C–60
YANKEE PAINTER: THE WORK OF WINSLOW HOMER   SCA
        16mm   Sd   C
        World Vision Enterprises   26.5min
More than 37 sketches, oils, and watercolors are reviewed. With Homer as its
champion, watercolor became an American specialty.

                        Arts – Sculpture

Arts–D–1
AMERICAN SCULPTURE––17TH–19TH CENTURIES   SCA
        35mm   C   1968
        SANDAK   40 slides
Folk, Spanish Colonial, and Professional sculpture developments are represented in
these slides.

Arts-D-2
ART IN AMERICA. PART 8. SCULPTURES
    16mm   Sd   C
    Handel Film Corp.
Title describes content.

SCA
1980
28min

Arts-D-3
CERAMIC SCULPTURE: SIX ARTISTS
    35mm
    American Crafts Council
Selections from the exhibition co-sponsored by the Whitney Museum of American Art and the San Francisco Museum of Modern Art; includes work by Voulkos, Mason, Arneson, Price, Gilhooly and Shaw.

SCA
1982
30 slides

Arts-D-4
THE DINNER PARTY
    35mm
    SANDAK
The Dinner Party is a complex work of art celebrating the accomplishments of women throughout history. It consists of thirty-nine place settings set on an open triangular table 46.5 feet on each side. The table rests on a porcelain floor upon which is written the names of 999 women of achievement in western civilization.

SCA
1981
80 slides

Arts-D-5
DUDLEY CARTER
    16mm   Sd   C
    Sher Films
A ninety-year-old woodsman turned axe sculptor carves three monumental cedars for a vast modern shopping center. Interweaving of life story with the present he tells of history, and a life well led.

SCA
1983
29min

Arts-D-6
FORMS IN METAL
    35mm
    American Crafts Council
Metalsmithing in America from the 1700s to the present.

A
1975
59 slides

Arts-D-7
GEORGE SEGAL
    16mm   Sd   C
    Blackwood Productions, Inc.
Portrait of George Segal, one of America's most eloquent and engaging artists; shows Segal at work on two important public commissions, a memorial for Franklin Roosevelt which will eventually be installed near the Tidal Basin in Washington and the other, a sculpture to commemorate the tragic events at Kent State University in 1971.

CA
1971
58min

Arts-D-8
JIM PALLAS: ELECTRONIC
SCULPTOR
    16mm   Sd   C
    The Little Red Filmhouse
Jim Pallas assembles whimsical sculptures which spin, rise, fall, light up, inflate and deflate as they respond to body heat, motion, and sounds. Pallas prepares a dance company for the unveiling of his latest environmental sculpture designed to display intricate light patterns triggered by movements of a passerby.

SCA
12min

Arts-D-9
L.A. NEON   A
        35mm   1976
        Environmental Communications   44 slides
These photographic images provide a nostalgic glimpse of the disappearing art of
bent glass tubes filled with various gases which was perfected in the 1920s and
given its full expression in the 1930s and 1940s.

Arts-D-10
MARK DI SUVERO   SCA
        35mm   1976
        Environmental Communications   40 slides
The slides in this series document sculptor Mark di Suvero and his assistants at
work installing the pieces in the environments of New York's city parks and public
places, and show the finished pieces in their sites. They provide an impressive
record of a unique and ambitious exhibit, the scope of which is unlikely to occur
again for a long time, and an exciting chronicle of the assemblage process itself.

Arts-D-11
MICHAEL HALL: SCULPTOR   SCA
        16mm   Sd   C   1980
        Marx/Handley Productions   10min
Large sheets of steel and I-beams, welded and braced and bolted, take on images,
provoke questions and become more understandable as Michael Hall speaks of his
kind of constructivism, derived from his American and Midwestern roots. Trestles,
billboards, fences, objects in the landscape, become sculptural ideas and pieces as
images explore Hall's interpretation of urban/rural environments.

Arts-D-12
PUBLIC OUTDOOR SCULPTURE OF NEW YORK   SCA
        35mm   C   1976
        Environmental Communications   20 slides
Since 1967, New York City has been the scene of a dramatic increase in public
outdoor sculpture. A variety of art works have appeared in various public
sites--plazas, traffic islands, parks, playgrounds--altering and enhancing the
cityscape in interesting and unexpected ways. Corporations, government agencies,
and individual donors have responded by bringing the art works of internationally
recognized sculptors to New York City's public spaces. Some of the artists in this
survey are: Alexander Calder, Jean Dubuffet, Henry Moore, Louise Nevelson,
Isamu Noguchi, Pablo Picasso.

Arts-D-13
RICHARD HUNT: SCULPTOR   SCA
        16mm   C   1970
        EBEC   14min
Eyesores of the junkyards--discarded metal, abandoned cars, scraps -- change into
fantastic sculptures under the creative hands of this great American black artist.
The camera follows Hunt as he collects junk, welds, sketches, and works on a
sculpture of John Jones, the first black man to be elected to public office in
Illinois. A rich study of an artist who utilizes the urban environment.

Arts-D-14
RICHARD SERRA   A
        35mm   C,B   1976
        Environmental Communications   50 slides
These slides communicate the diversity and excitement of Serra's work--from

theatre pieces to improvisational environments to the process works and the latest monumental raw-steel structures. Some of the works included: Elevations, Log Measure - Sawing Five Fir Trees, Cutting Device: Base-Plate-Measure, Duplicate, Sight Point.

Arts-D-15
RIGHT OUT OF HISTORY: THE MAKING OF
   JUDY CHICAGO'S DINNER PARTY   A
         16mm   Sd   C
         Phoenix Films, Inc.   75min
Follows the creation of the Judy Chicago Dinner Party--a monumental artistic tribute to women of achievement throughout Western history. It is the only record of a contemporary working community trying to transform their experience into a work of art.

Arts-D-16
BERT MORRIS   A
         35mm   1976
         Environmental Communications   30 slides
A controversial artist, whose career spans the sixties and seventies. Bert Morris is one of America's most productive and influential sculptors. This slide series attempts to document his work.

Arts-D-17
THE RON RESCH PAPER AND STICK THING FILM   A
         16mm   Sd   C   1976
         Environmental Communications   40min
This film documents Ron Resch's experiments in paper and stick constructions from 1961 and their development into his "folded mosaic domes." Many mathematical concepts of symmetry evolve into three-dimensional structures, toys and sculptures.

Arts-D-18
WOMEN ARTISTS: CLAY   SCA
         35mm   1978
         American Crafts Council   41 slides
Contemporary works by American women assembled by the Women's Caucus for Art and sponsored by the Bronx Museum of the Arts, New York.

            Arts - Decorative Arts and Household Furnishings

Arts-E-1
AMERICAN FIBER ART: A NEW DEFINITION   A
         35mm   1980
         American Crafts Council   50 slides
From the exhibition held at the Sarah Campbell Blaffer Gallery in Houston, Texas.

Arts-E-2
AMERICAN FOLK ART   SCA
         35mm   C   54
         Photo Lab, Inc.   45 slides
Shows shaving mugs, dowry chests, pitchers, carpets, figureheads, free-blown glass work and weathervanes.

Arts–E–3
AMERICAN GLASS, ITS ORIGINS AND DEVELOPMENT   SCA
       35mm   C   1969
       American Crafts Council   100 slides
Shows decorative glass panels for architectural use by artist–craftsmen from
1608–1969, from the collection of the Corning Museum of Glass in New York.

Arts–E–4
AMERICAN GLASS NOW   SCA
       35mm   C   1973
       American Crafts Council   54 slides
Exhibition of works by contemporary American glass craftsmen.

Arts–E–5
ANONYMOUS WAS A WOMAN   SCA
       16mm   Sd   C   1978
       Films, Inc.   28min
Presents an overview of 18th and 19th century American folk art created by
women. Looks at daily lives of those women in urban and rural America.

Arts–E–6
ART AMERICANA: QUILTS AND COVERLETS   SCA
       35mm   1975
       American Craft Council   61 slides
Rochester Institute of Technology exhibition of historical examples from private
collections.

Arts–E–7
ART DECO   SCA
       35mm   1971
       American Crafts Council   85 slides
Finch College Museum of Art exhibition of art and craft in the Art Deco style.

Arts–E–8
ARTISTS IN THE SCHOOLS: BOB AIKEN   SCA
       16mm   Sd   C   1972
       Film Production Unit   21min
Documents the activities of Bob Aiken as artist–in–residence during 1971–72 in
The South Tama Community Schools, Iowa. Illustrates value of the artists in the
school's program to the local community.

Arts–E–9
BANNERS   SCA
       35mm   1973
       Donars Productions   10 slides
Shows photographs of ten banners created by artist Norman Laliberte who explains
his intent in creating the banners and identifies the material and symbol expressed
in each one.

Arts–E–10
CALIFORNIA DESIGN '76   A
       35mm   C   1976
       Environmental Communications   10 slides
Design '76 is a juried California exhibition of well–designed manufactured products
and the work of artist–craftsmen, chosen from thousands of submissions.

Arts-E-11
CHRISTMAS ORNAMENTS   SCA
        35mm   1977
        American Crafts Council   42 slides
Christmas tree ornaments made by American craftsmen for the 1977 Christmas
tree of Vice President and Mrs. Walter Mondale.

Arts-E-12
CRAFTSMEN USA '66   SCA
        35mm   1966
        American Crafts Council   71 slides
Works from a national competition sponsored by ACC.

Arts-E-13
AN EAMES CELEBRATION: SEVERAL WORLDS
   OF CHARLES AND RAY EAMES   SCA
        16mm   Sd   C   1977
        INUAVC   90min
Profiles of Charles and Ray Eames, a creative couple renowned for their
communications of ideas through design.

Arts-E-14
FORMS FROM THE EARTH   SCA
        35mm   1962
        American Crafts Council   100 slides
One thousand years of pottery in America.

Arts-E-15
FUN AND FANTASY: CONTEMPORARY AMERICAN CRAFTS   SCA
        35mm   C   1974
        Art Now, Inc.   95 slides
Shows examples of work in a whimsical style by contemporary American artists
from an exhibition at the Xerox Gallery in Rochester, New York.

Arts-E-16
FURNITURE   SCA
        FS, Cassette   C   1975
        Photo Lab, Inc.   52 slides
Gives history of American furniture from colonial times to the 19th century.
Shows how particular pieces reflect the people who made and used them.

Arts-E-17
THE GOLDSMITH   A
        35mm   1974
        American Crafts Council   91 slides
Jewelry and other metalwork from an exhibition sponsored by the Renwick
Gallery/Minnesota Museum of Art/Society of North America.

Arts-E-18
INHERITANCE   SCA
        16mm   Sd   C   1976
        Doubleday and Co.   31min
Presents three craftsmen - a shovel carver, basketmaker, and tinsmith -
demonstrating their skills and talking about their lives and work. Contrasts their
craftsmanship with modern assembly lines producing a similar product pointing out
the lack of creative involvement in the factory system. Emphasizes that each of

these people are among the last skilled American craftsmen practicing their trades. Guide provides objectives, evaluation questions, and suggested activities.

Arts-E-19
NEW AMERICAN GLASS: FOCUS WEST VIRGINIA   SCA
          16mm   Sd   1976
          American Crafts Council   28min
Features Joel Philip Myers, Jamie Carpenter, Mark Peiser, Harvey Littleton, Fritz Dreisbach and Henry Halem participating in workshops held at six West Virginia glass factories.

Arts-E-20
THE NEW AMERICAN QUILT   SCA
          35mm   1976
          American Crafts Council   41 slides
Contemporary quilts of innovative design and techniques by 25 American craftsmen.

Arts-E-21
NEW HANDMADE FURNITURE: AMERICAN FURNITURE
  MAKERS WORKING IN HARDWOOD   A
          35mm   1979
          American Crafts Council   79 slides
Innovative statements in the design and construction of functional furniture.

Arts-E-22
OBJECTS FOR PREPARING FOOD   SCA
          35mm   1973
          American Crafts Council   80 slides
Co-sponsored with the Renwick Gallery; historical and contemporary examples.

Arts-E-23
OBJECTS USA   A
          35mm   1969
          American Crafts Council   128 slides
The Johnson Collection of Contemporary Crafts.

Arts-E-24
ROBERT SOWERS--STAINED GLASS   SCA
          35mm   C   1975
          American Crafts Council   11 frames
Documents part of the stained glass exhibition by the artist at the Museum of Contemporary Crafts in New York in 1975.

Arts-E-25
SENECA GLASS   A
          16mm   Sd   C   1975
          NAVC   24min
As documented for the Historical American Engineering Record, this film re-captures the production of early hand-blown glassware at Seneca Glass in Morgantown, West Virginia.

Arts-E-26
SPINET MAKING IN COLONIAL AMERICA   SCA
     16mm   Sd   C   1976
     Colonial Williamsburg Foundation   54min
Shows the stages involved in making a spinet using the tools and methods of 18th
century Williamsburg, Virginia.

Arts-E-27
WINTERTHUR, THE BENCHMARK OF EXCELLENCE   SCA
     35mm, Cassette   C   1982
     Winterthur Museum   122 slides
Photographs of furnishings from the original objects in the Winterthur collections.

Arts-E-28
WITH THESE HANDS   SCA
     UBV   Sd   C   1979
     Time-Life Video   53min
Film has footage of craftspeople at work; includes potters, sculptures, glassblower
and fiber artist.

Arts-E-29
WOMEN ARTISTS: CLAY, FIBER, METAL   SCA
     35mm   1978
     American Crafts Council   111 slides
Contemporary works by American women assembled by the Women's Caucus for
Art and sponsored by the Bronx Museum of Arts, New York.

Arts-E-30
WOMEN ARTISTS: METAL   SCA
     35mm   1979
     American Crafts Council   36 slides
Contemporary works by American women assembled by the Women's Caucus for
Art and sponsored by the Bronx Museum of the Arts, New York.

Arts-E-31
WOODENWORKS   SCA
     35mm   1972
     American Crafts Council   50 slides
Renwick Gallery/Minnestoa Museum of Art exhibition of furniture by Carpenter,
Castle, Esherick, Maloof, Nakashima.

Arts-E-32
YOUNG AMERICANS: AWARD WINNERS   SCA
     35mm   1982
     American Crafts Council   41 slides
Recent work by the 19 award-winning craftsmen in the 1977-78 American Crafts
Council-sponsored Young Americans competitions.

Arts-E-33
YOUNG AMERICANS: CLAY/GLASS   SCA
     35mm   1978
     American Crafts Council   90 slides
Winning entries of a competition sponsored by ACC.

Arts-E-34
YOUNG AMERICANS: WOOD   SCA
         35mm   1977
         American Crafts Council   24 slides
Winning entries from a national competition sponsored by ACC.

                        Arts - Ethnic Groups

Arts-F-1
AMERICAN INDIAN AND THE AMERICAN FLAG, THE   SCA
         35mm   C   1976
         American Crafts Council   60 slides
Documents an exhibition featuring American Indian crafts with patriotic motifs.

Arts-F-2
BEARDEN PLAYS BEARDEN   SCA
         16mm   Sd   C
         MTPS   28min
Shows black artist Romare Bearden's Southern roots and years in Harlem, and how
they have influenced his paintings and collages. James Earl Jones narrates.

Arts-F-3
THE BLACK EXPERIENCE   SCA
         35mm   1973
         SANDAK   60 slides
This exhibition visually documents the life and experience of the black American
from origins in slavery to the present day struggle for civil liberties and equality.
The works graphically illustrate such themes as: the slave trade, slave revolts and
the Underground Railroad, the Abolitionists, the Civil War, Reconstruction and
continuing violence, life in the rural south, life in the big city, the Black
Renaissance, socially conscious art, and the continuing struggle.

Arts-F-4
BLACK MODERN ART IN U.S.A.   SCA
         16mm   Sd   C   1976
         Tricontinental Film Center   22min
Presents three black artists, Dana Chandler, Valerie Maynard and Leroy Clarke,
discussing the origins and meanings of their painting and sculpture while examples
of their work are shown. Includes their views on the relationship between art and
social conditions of the oppressed.

Arts-F-5
CONTEMPORARY ESKIMO AND INDIAN ARTS AND CRAFTS   SCA
         35mm   C   1968
         American Crafts Council   60 slides
Presents a sampling of Eskimo and Indian crafts which emphasize the diversity of
tribal style.

Arts-F-6
GATECLIFF--AMERICAN INDIAN ROCK-SHELTER   SCA
        UBV   Sd   C   1974
        NGS
Archeologists attempt to discover the identity of ancient inhabitants of a shallow
rock-shelter located in Nevada.

Arts-F-7
INDIAN ARTISTS OF THE SOUTHWEST   SCA
        16mm   Sd   C
        EBEC   15min
Modern Southwest Indians have retained a remarkable measure of ancient art and
craft techniques as part of their cultural heritage. In this film, three Pueblo
Indian tribes, the Zuni, Hopi and Navajo introduce four of their major art forms;
stone and silverwork, pottery making, weaving, and kachina carving. As the
Indians deomonstrate their crafts, which comprise some of the oldest American art
forms, viewers see that the Indian's life-style and breathtaking surroundings are
reflected in their work.

Arts-F-8
INDIAN POTTERY OF SAN ILDEFONSO   SCA
        16mm   Sd   C   1972
        NAVC   27min
Maria Martinez, noted Indian pottery maker, demonstrates the traditional Indian
ways, beginning with the spreading of sacred corn before the clay is gathered.
Also shown are the mixing of clay, construction of pottery, hand decorating and
building of the firing mound.

Arts-F-9
MARIA OF THE PUEBLOS   SCA
        16mm   Sd   C
        Centron Films   15min
This motion picture offers a rare and final look into the artistry of this humble
woman who was perhaps the most famous and successful Indian potter of all times.
The film shows how Maria and her family formed, decorated, glazed and fired
their magnificent, iridescent black pottery.

Arts-F-10
MIRRORS, REFLECTIONS OF A CULTURE   SCA
        16mm   Sd   C   1980
        Churchill Films   16min
Murals by three Americans of Mexican descent offer images of the Chicano as
inheritor of a strong and important tradition.

Arts-F-11
MYSTERY OF THE ANASAZI, THE   A
        UVB   Sd   1976
        Life Multimedia   59min
Documents the attempts of archeologists in the southwestern United States to
determine who the Anasazi were and where they came from.

Arts-F-12
NATIVE AMERICAN ARTS   SCA
        16mm   Sd   C   1974
        NAVC   20min
Contemporary artists and craftsmen of Native American descent--Indian, Eskimo,

Aleut—are making unique and significant contributions to the cultural life of the United States. This film provides the viewer with a rich and vivid impression of the unique historic and esthetic values, images, and traditions that are being maintained and rigorously developed by Native Americans in virtually every art form today.

Arts-F-13
OSCAR HOWE: THE SIOUX PAINTER   SCA
          16mm   C   1973
          Centron Films   27min
Mr. Howe designs and executes the painting, Sioux Eagle Dancer—from addressing the blank canvas to signing the completed painting. As he works, Mr. Howe and Vincent Price comment upon his subject matter, technique and plhilosophy of art. Seventeen different paintings are explored by the camera, and the gradual changes in style in the most recent ones indicate a new movement and direction for Mr. Howe's future works.

Arts-F-14
SPIRIT CATCHER: THE ART OF BETYE SAAR   SCA
          16mm   Sd   C   1978
          Films, Inc.   30min
Explores the art, spirit, symbols and revelations of black American assemblage artist Betye Saar.

Arts-F-15
TWO CENTURIES OF BLACK AMERICAN ART   SC
          16mm   Sd   C   1976
          Pyramid Films, MTPS   26min
Traces the African influences in the first black art in America, the widening range of work produced in the slave era, the early struggles for serious recognition in the 19th century, and the cosmopolitan backgrounds and important work of modern black American artists.

Economic History

Richard Sylla

The economic history of the United States is interesting in part because so much economic change is compressed into a relatively brief historical period. The transformation from primitive settlement and economic organization to modern, industrial -- perhaps even post-industrial -- society has taken place in America in less than four centuries. The organization of this section of the audiovisual resources guide emphasizes the key economic sectors and time periods in which this transformation occurred.

After a section describing general accounts and surveys (EH-A), a fairly standard chronology of key periods follows. Section EH-B explores the seventeenth and eighteenth centuries, the period from first permanent settlement by Europeans to the birth of the United States. This is the "pre-modern" period of American economic history, but it was characterized by a very high rate of population growth and extensive economic development based on America's endowments of land and other natural resources. Economic modernization began in the 1800-1865 period covered by Section EH-C. Here the key themes are improvements in transportation, the ensuing westward movement across a continent, and the beginnings of modern, mechanized industry. Section EH-D covers the period of the United States' most rapid economic growth, from the end of the Civil War in 1865 to the beginning of the twentieth century. This was the era of the rise of big business (giant corporations), of great technological advance, of the railroadization of a continent, of a doubling of land in farms, and of a quickening of immigration from overseas and the emergence of organized labor. Finally, Section EH-E describes some of the more important audiovisual materials pertaining to the twentieth century economy. Here the main themes are the continuing economic dominance of the large corporation in the private sector along with a greatly enlarged role of government in the American nation's economic life. Both themes are related to the start of the automobile age, which created a need for public spending on roads. But the economic role of government became still greater during and after the Great Depression of the 1930s. Government, among other ventures, aided organized labor to become a co-equal partner with big business in the modern American economy. Fittingly, the section concludes with a large group of audiovisual materials on U.S. agriculture which, despite tremendous economic changes, remains --as it always has been-- a dynamic part of the American economy.

Any study or discussion of U.S. economic history can benefit greatly from the use of maps. The geographical expansion of the United States along with significant historical changes in the nature and location of economic activity as a continent was settled almost dictate a concern with time and place. Many types of historical maps are available but a particularly good series, available in both a standard atlas and trnsparencies for an overhead projector, has been issued by Hammond, Inc., of Maplewood, New Jersey. The Hammond -United States History Atlas- bears a Library of Congress Catalog Card Number Map 68-17, copyright 1968. The related overhead projector transparencies have a 1969 copyright. The

series of maps covers United States political and social as well as economic
history.

ECONOMIC HISTORY (EH)

EH-A   General Accounts and Surveys
                Agriculture and Natural Resources
                Population and Labor
                Organization and Innovation
                Transportation
EH-B   The Agrarian-Commercial Economy
            of the 17th and 18th Centuries
                General Accounts
                Government and Economy
                Community Studies and Agricultural Economy
                People and Occupations
EH-C   The Transition to Industry 1800-1865
                General Accounts
                Transportation Revolution
                The Westward Movement
                Industrialization
                Natural Resources
                Agriculture
                Immigration and Labor
EH-D   Rapid Industrialization, 1865-1900
                General Accounts
                Industry, Business Organization and Technology
                Transportation: The Railroad Age
                Agriculture
                Immigration and Labor
EH-E   The Corporate Economy, 1900 to Present
                General Accounts
                Business: Industry, Commerce, Finance
                The Changing Role of Government
                Transportation
                The Labor Force
                Agriculture

General Accounts and Surveys

Agriculture and Natural Resources

EH-A-1
COTTON BELT: YESTERDAY AND TODAY   SC
      16mm   Sd   C   1960
      INUAVC   17min
Tells the story of the changes that have taken place in the cotton–growing areas
of the southern United States. Describes the early importance of cotton, as a
money crop and the modern, less dominant cotton–growing activities.

EH-A-2
LAND--AMERICAN ENTERPRISE   SC
      UBV   Sd   C   1977
      Modern Video Center   30min
This program contrasts land availability from the time of the immigrants to the
present and develops the emergence of rural America to an urban nation.

EH-A-3
U.S. IS: RESOURCES, THE   S
      U   Sd   C   1979
      BFA   14min
This show demonstrates how the gifts which the United States has in such amazing
abundance enable it to produce so much and to be so successful as a nation.

EH-A-4
WESTWARD EXPANSION   SC
      16mm   Sd   C   1969
      MGHT   25min
Traces the westward growth of the United States from the first colonial rumbles
of discontent to the laying of the transcontinental railroad and the eventual
disappearance of the "Old West." Explores, through paintings and photographs, the
personality of the frontiersman. Follows the chain of events leading to the Indian
Removal Act, Manifest Destiny, the Civil War, and the Indian wars.

EH-A-5
YESTERDAY'S FARM   S
      16mm   Sd   C   1972
      BFA   16min
The ruggedness of life, the trials of the movement westward, the values that were
held by early settlers, and the hopes and ambitions of generations are reflected
in the abandoned buildings of yesterday's farms. Live action scenes interspersed
with old photographs and prints illustrate how each farm carries its own reminders
of the life and people of the past.
Population and Labor

Population and Labor

EH-A-6
HERITAGE OF SLAVERY   SC
      16mm   Sd   C   1968
      BFA   56min
Discusses the arrival of the first slaves in America and their importance in the
economic development of the South. Discusses the many slave revolts, the

underground railways, and the effects of the 1850 Fugitive Slave Law, allowing slave owners to reclaim runaway slaves. Points out that defacto slavery still exists in many southern states, particularly Mississippi. Contrasts the heritage of blacks and whites in the United States, and summarizes the black heritage of slavery as resurrection.

EH-A-7
OUR IMMIGRANT HERITAGE   SC
          16mm   Sd   C   1968
          MGHT   32min
Highlights many of the historical and characteristic events associated with the United States and its cultural and economic growth. Illustrates the various cultural groups from the Colonial period to the 20th Century, with emphasis on the reasons for these people coming to America and their many contributions to this country. Follows a Greek immigrant arriving in America and becoming a citizen.

EH-A-8
OUT OF SLAVERY: 1619-1860   SC
          16mm   Sd   B   1965
          MGHT   21min
Traces the history of the Negro in America from his first arrival to the outbreak of the Civil War. Pictures slavery in the ancient world and oulines the development of the slave trade in America. Depicts the life of the Negro as a slave in the South and as a free man in the North. Shows his role in the American Revolution and discusses slave labor as the foundation of Southern wealth.

EH-A-9
PEOPLE--AMERICAN ENTERPRISE   SC
          U   Sd   C   1977
          Modern Video Center   30min
The strong-willed American immigrants shaped and created the American economy and turned thirteen colonies into a country. This program depicts how they accomplished the task.

EH-A-10
U.S. IS: PEOPLE, THE   S
          U   Sd   C   1979
          BFA   15min
This program studies the population of the United States and illustrates the context and importance of people, a vital resource to any nation.

                           Organization and Innovation

EH-A-11
AMERICAN BUSINESS   S
          UBV   Sd   C   1979
          Dallas County Community College   29min
This program examines how American business developed into its present form.

EH-A-12
ENERGY - THE AMERICAN EXPERIENCE   S
          16mm   Sd   C   1978
          NAVC   29min
With the perspective of over 200 years of history, this film shows the development of different forms of energy under the unique conditions of the

American experience. We see the 60-year changing cycles of energy sources from wood to coal to oil and gas, producing the steam and electrical energy that helped make the U.S. the industrial giant of the world.

EH-A-13
GOVERNMENT--AMERICAN ENTERPRISE   S
           UVB   Sd   C
           Modern Video Center   30min
This program historically presents the effects of economic impact on American government by questioning the role of government. Defense, welfare, housing, and labor are discussed.

EH-A-14
HOW IT EVOLVED   S
           16mm   Sd   B   1962
           INUAVC   29min
Examines the influence of the industrial revolution on American technology, finance, and management, and traces the development of our business system from the handicraft economy of colonial times to the giant, diversified corporations of today.

EH-A-15
HOW TO CURE INFLATION   SC
           16mm   Sd   C   1980
           Penn Communications   30min
Milton Friedman presents his views on the causes and potential cures of inflation, views that are based on monetarist principles he says have worked in the past and will work now if given a chance. Using historical examples such as the inflation of the value of tobacco when it was used as money in early America, he states his case that the only soluton to inflation is the maintenance of a stable money supply.

EH-A-16
INNOVATION--AMERICAN ENTERPRISE   SC
           UVB   Sd   C   1977
           Modern Video Center   30min
This program features the great innovators--Edison, McCormick, Whitney, and Howe--who shaped American ingenuity.

EH-A-17
THE MAKING OF OHIO, CHAPTER I: INDUSTRY   S
           16mm   Sd   C
           Film Group, Inc.   29min
Recreations from the past combined with contemporary scenes tell the story of Ohio's agricultural and industrial beginnings and growth. From the past, we see blacksmiths, weavers, iron mills, and grist mills.

EH-A-18
ORGANIZATION   SCA
           16mm   Sd   C   1976
           MTPS   30min
Presents actor William Shatner portraying a dynamic entrepreneur who discusses how America's economic growth is based on organizational techniques, such as mass production and mass marketing. From the American Enterprise series.

EH-A-19
ORGANIZATION--AMERICAN ENTERPRISE   S
       UVB   Sd   C
       Modern Video Center   30min
The growth-organization process of American systems of the past and present is
the topic of this program.

EH-A-20
PATENT PENDING   S
       16mm   Sd   C   1973
       Lucerne   52min
Documents the history of the U.S. Patent Office and explains how it functions.
For the first 100 years of the U.S. Patent Office, a working model of each
invention had to be submitted. Despite two disastrous fires, a number of junkings,
and disbursement by sale, almost two hundred thousand models still exist,
scattered between the Smithsonian Institution and private collectors.

EH-A-21
STEEL AND AMERICA   S
       16mm   Sd   C   1966
       Disney   30min
A history of the steel industry in America stretches from the geological formation
of iron ore to innovations now being developed in research laboratores. Illustrates
the primitive steps of iron-making with Donald Duck as the original iron master,
traces the technological development of steel-making, and shows all stages of
contemporary steel production.

Transportation

EH-A-22
INLAND WATERWAYS IN THE DEVELOPMENT
   OF AMERICAN TRANSPORTATION   S
       16mm   Sd   C,B   1956
       EBEC   16min
Shows how the early American need for transportation started the use of
waterways to move people and goods and, where natural barriers existed, canals
were built. Depicts the growth of the waterways until the invention of the steam
engine and development of railroads threatened their usefulness.

EH-A-23
THE MAKING OF OHIO, CHAPTER II: TRANSPORTAION   S
       16mm   Sd   C
       Film Group, Inc.   27min
A mini-history of Ohio is told through its modes of transportation. Dramatic
re-creations and contemporary photography show water transportation, flatboats,
steamboats, barges, canals, and lake vessels. On land, covered wagons, stage
coaches, railroads, and automobiles are seen.

EH-A-24
MISSISSIPPI: ITS ROLE IN AMERICAN HISTORY   S
       16mm   Sd   C   1963
       BFA   22min
Focuses on the era in American history when the steamboat made the Mississippi,
Ohio, and Missouri rivers navigable for both cargo and passenger traffic and
opened the vast inland waterways of the United States. Uses maps, animation of

textbook pictures, authentic art prints, actual footage of a great steamboat race, scenes from areas described in Mark Twain's stories, and scenes of the modern Mississippi River.

EH-A-25
STEAM AGE, THE: HISTORY OF TRANSPORTATION
  IN THE UNITED STATES, PART I   S
          16mm   Sd   C,B   1958
          EBEC   17min
This film describes the swift development of transportation in the United States from the time of the Indians to the coming of the automobile. Utilizing historical re-enactments and unusual prints of the period, the film brings to life men's struggle to conquer the vast distances on the North American continent.

EH-A-26
TRANSPORTATION: FOOTPATH TO AIR LANE   S
          16mm   Sd   C   1965
          Churchill Films   16min
Animation and old graphic materials are used to present a history of transportation in the United States. Shows the varieties of transportation, their development during certain periods, their role in opening the continent, and their importance to the economy and everyday life.

EH-A-27
TRANSPORTATION REVOLUTION, THE:
  STORY OF AMERICAN GROWTH   S
          16mm   Sd   C   1970
          LCA   20min
Uses drawings, paintings, old newsreel footage, and live-action photography to survey the various modes of transportation that have shaped America's history. Film segments include the joining of the Union and Central Pacific Railroad lines in 1869, the Wright Brothers testing their flying machine in 1908, the horseless carriage and Henry Ford's Model T, and brief scenes of Lindbergh's solo flight across the Atlantic.

Economic History - The Agrarian-Commercial Economy of the Seventeenth and
                          Eighteenth Centuries

General Accounts

EH-B-1
AMERICANS, THE, 1776   S
          16mm   Sd   C   1978
          NAVC   28min
Presents a view of everyday life during the time of the American Revolution. Shows the crafts, ways of life, and the differences of attitudes among various types of people living in the colonies.

EH-B-2
COLONIAL AMERICA: THE BEGINNINGS   S
          16mm   Sd   C   1970
          MGHT   25min
Reviews economic and social conditions in England that caused men to immigrate to the New World and traces the history of the first hundred years of American colonization.

EH-B-3
COLONIAL AMERICA IN THE 18TH CENTURY   S
    16mm   Sd   C,B   1965
    MGHT   17min
This film illustrates life as it was lived in the 13 English colonies during the 75
years preceding the Revolutionary War. The film shows how people of the time
earned their living and the reasons for their differing moral and spiritual values.

EH-B-4
COLONIAL ECONOMY,THE   S
    16mm   Sd   C   1970
    MGHT   25min
Examines the unique solutions to the problems of capital, labor, and transportation
which developed in each of the three geographic regions: New England, the Middle
Colonies, and the South. Discusses economic growth and colonial discontent with
restrictions imposed by the British on trade, manufacturing, and the minting of
currency.

EH-B-5
ECONOMIC HISTORY   S
    Audio Cassette   Sd   1979
    NPR   58min
First historian Henry Steele Commanger and Henry Owen, former director of
foreign policy at the Brookings Institution, outline the economic system of
colonial America and analyze its effects on the U.S. Then, Dr. Commager and Mr.
Owen relate past to present, emphasizing our heritage of self-sufficiency,
mobility, inventiveness, and class systems. Produced by Rich Firestone.

EH-B-6
LOOK OF AMERICA, THE (1750-1800)   S
    16mm   Sd   C   1976
    Pyramid Films   27min
Uses still photography and motion picture footage to present a comparison of the
dominant lifestyles of early America. Contrasts the austere Puritan settlements of
New England with the luxury of plantation life in Virginia and the Carolinas. The
early colonies of Jamestown and Plymouth enjoyed some commercial success,
which spawned other colonies and settlements. The Carolinas thrived on crops of
indigo and rice, and later cotton. Virginia was the cultural and social center with
a lifestyle made possible by slave labor. Pennsylvania was established on the
principle of religious freedom, and by 1750 Philadelphia had grown into a thriving,
cultural city. To the west, pioneers were expanding our borders into the
wilderness and establishing new states.

Government and Economy

EH-B-7
ALEXANDER HAMILTON   SC
    16mm   Sd   B   1951
    EBEC   18min
Presents Alexander Hamilton as a boy-businessman in the West Indies, a student at
King's College, the author of -The Federalist Papers-, the first Secretary of the
Treasury, a reformer of the national economy, the champion of a strong,
aristocratic government, and a friend to Northern business. Concludes his life with
the fatal duel with Aaron Burr.

EH-B-8
AMERICAN HERITAGE: ALEXANDER HAMILTON   S
        16mm   Sd   B   1958
        Warner Bros.   7min
Against the background of the Grange, Alexander Hamilton's home in Manhattan,
a portrayal of Hamilton's life is given, his role in the Revolution, his leadership at
the Constitutional Convention, his statesmanship as Secretary of the Treasury,
and his tragic death.

EH-B-9
AMERICAN REVOLUTION: THE POSTWAR PERIOD   S
        16mm   Sd   C   1975
        Coronet   11min
Depicts the struggle to form the U.S. Constitution in a climate of conflicting
ideals and economic depression during the post-Revolutionary War years. Discusses
the difficulties caused by restrictions on trade, the poverty of the people, and the
lack of recognition by other countries of the Articles of Confederation, outlines
the convention called to allieviate conditions and emphasizes the compromise
necessary in forming the Constitution.

EH-B-10
BACKGROUND TO THE CONSTITUTIONAL CONVENTION   S
        16mm   Sd   B   1963
        NBC News   30min
There had been several attempts to achieve a greater centralization of
decision-making power among the colonies, beginning with the establishment of
the New England Confederation in 1643. The successful conclusion of the
Revolution did not put an end to the issue. The Articles of Confederation
government proved too weak to handle the major problems--inflation, an imbalance
of trade, demobilization of the army--that faced the new nation.

EH-B-11
GEORGE WASHINGTON AND THE WHISKEY REBELLION:
   TESTING THE CONSTITUTION   S
        16mm   Sd   C   1974
        LCA   27min
Dramatic, action-packed sequences capture the backwoods flavor of a fledgling
nation as the newly-formed law of the land meets its first challenge: enforcement
of the federally imposed whiskey tax. Farmers of western Pennsylvania rely on
whiskey for their livelihood, barter their liquor for goods and have no money to
pay the demanded tax. They band together in a reign of lawlessness. President
Washington leads the militia against the insurrectionists, and successfully defends
the principles of constitutional government.

EH-B-12
LAUNCHING THE NEW GOVERNMENT (1789-1800)   SC
        16mm   Sd   B   1958
        Coronet   14min
Presents problems that confronted the infant American government from 1789 to
1800 under the leadership of such men as Washington, Hamilton, Jefferson, and
Adams.

EH-B-13
THE PEOPLE VS. JOB SHATTUCK   S
        16mm   Sd   C   1974
        NGS   25min
At the close of the Revolutionary War, many veterans are deeply in debt with

creditors foreclosing. In 1876 Captain Job Shattuck leads a group of dissidents to the courthouse in Concord, Mass. to prevent the court from sitting, forestalling additional foreclosures. Shattuck is arrested and tried for treason.

Community Studies and the Agricultural Economy

EH-B-14
JAMESTOWN   SC
    16mm   Sd   C   1975
    NAVC   14min
Presents a story of Jamestown from the founding of the town to its gradual abandonment in the early 18th century. Uses art to illustrate the trials of the first settlers, the commerce attempted, and the various forms of government.

EH-B-15
BEGINNING AT PLYMOUTH COLONY, THE   SCA
    16mm   Sd   B   1964
    NEPAHC   15min
The failure of the socialist colonies established at Jamestown and Plymouth constituted a milestone in the development of America's structure. This film dramatizes the abandonment of Plymouth colony's communal storehouse and the principle of public ownership and her adoption of the principles of private ownership and individual self-reliance.

EH-B-16
COLONIAL WAY OF LIFE, THE   S
    16mm   Sd   C   1970
    MGHT   26min
A social history of the colonial period traces the growth of a common culture in America. Studies regional differences in religion, national origin, economy, and the lifestyle and then identifies the factors which gradually united the diverse colonies into one, uniquely American, culture.

EH-B-17
PURITAN FAMILY OF EARLY NEW ENGLAND   S
    16mm   Sd   C,B   1955
    Coronet   11min
Recreates a day in the life of a Puritan family. Shows the nature of work done, implements used, foods grown, hunting, fishing, trading, contacts with neighbors, and religious devotions.

EH-B-18
EIGHTEENTH CENTURY LIFE IN WILLIAMSBURG, VIRGINIA   S
    16mm   Sd   C   1956
    Colonial Williamsburg   44min
Pictures everyday life in Colonial Williamsburg, with emphasis on the activities of a well-to-do cabinetmaker and all the members of his household. The family and the slaves are shown using many imported and locally made objects. The role of the blacksmith in the community is also shown. Community life, social life, and methods of communication are dealt with more briefly. The background music is taken from the period.

People and Occupations

EH-B-19
ATLANTIC SLAVE TRADE   SCA
        16mm   Sd   C   1973
        Univ. of Minnesota   17min
The 17th century slave trade is explored from a new viewpoint as it seeks to
understand the African input into the trade. The film's thesis is that there is
much to be learned about the trade before any mention is made of European ships
or traders, and new questions are raised from an African perspective.

EH-B-20
AMERICA: A PERSONAL HISTORY OF THE UNITED STATES
  NO. 2 - HOME AWAY FROM HOME, PARTS 1 AND 2   SC
        16mm   Sd   C   1972
        Time-Life Films   52min
Cooke describes the diverse problems in England that prompted social dissenters
and merchant adventurers to leave and colonize America's East Coast. The
settling of Virginia by 126 colonists, led by Captain John Smith, is explained in
detail. Examines the emerging of a River Plantation System dependent on the
single crop, tobacco; the creation of the 'House of Burgess' as a form of
government in Virginia; and the use of the black man from Africa to do the heavy
labor.

EH-B-21
COLONIAL SHIPBUILDING AND SEA TRADE   SC
        16mm   Sd   B   1958
        Coronet   11min
Points up the focal position which New England shipbuilding held in the
commercial development of the American colonies in the seventeenth century and
relates those advances to the social and political growth of all the colonies.

EH-B-22
GUNSMITH OF WILLIAMSBURG   S
        16mm   Sd   C   1969
        Colonial Williamsburg   62min
A complete documentary on the manufacture of a flintlock rifle of the 1770
period by Master Gunsmith Wallace Gusler of Williamsburg, Virginia. The viewer
sees the step-by-step procedure as he forms and welds the barrel, then drills and
rifles it.

EH-B-23
HAMMERMAN IN WILLIAMSBURG:
  THE EIGHTEENTH CENTURY BLACKSMITH   SC
        16mm   Sd   C   1973
        Colonial Williamsburg   38min
In his shop, Williamsburg's present-day blacksmith and his journeymen re-create
the role of the blacksmith in colonial times.

EH-B-24
MAST MAKING FOR THE KING   S
        16mm   Sd   C   1977
        University of New Hampshire   17min
The history of mast making in New England goes back to 1634, when a shipment
of pines was sent to England to be hewn into masts for the ships of the King's
navy. Until the Revolutionary War, masts were the single most important product

England received from America. The film shows the process of selecting a mast tree, preparing the bed, building a platform for choppers, felling the trees, and hauling the 80-foot-long log with many yokes of oxen.

EH-B-25
SONG OF MOLASSES   S
        16mm   Sd   C   1974
        NGS   23min
In 1776 England imposed a tax of three pennies per gallon on molasses coming into the American Colonies--to be strictly enforced. Job Smith's sloop returning from Surinam carries twice as much molasses as declared. When the discrepancy is discovered, Smith offers to pay the tax, he is denounced and the cargo seized. Smith must decide whether to protest--as his fellow citizens demand--or submit to British officialdom.

Economic History - The Transition to Industry, 1800-1865

General Accounts

EH-C-1
BEGINNINGS AND GROWTH OF INDUSTRIAL AMERICA   SCA
        16mm   Sd   C,B   1960
        Coronet   10min
Views the growth of industrialization in the United States during the 1800s. The background of early manufacturing in this country is reviewed in the handicrafts and simple machines used to custom-make articles for each purchaser. Early industrial development is seen to rely upon proximity to water power and raw materials. The introduction of the tariff to protect infant industries and the improvment of transportation contributed to mid-1880 industrial growth.

EH-C-2
ERA OF THE COMMON MAN   SCA
        16mm   Sd   C,B   1965
        GRACU   25min
Reviews the principal aspects of the period 1828-1848 in the United States. Discusses the inauguration of Andrew Jackson, the "kitchen cabinet," Spoils System, the manufacturing North, agricultural South, and threats of recession. Describes the westward movement in terms of transportation, immigrant population, border problems, and territorial expansion.

EH-C-3
ERA OF GOOD FEELING   SCA
        16mm   Sd   B   1968
        GRACU   24min
After 1812, the United States was a nation divided economically into two sections, industrialization of the north and agriculture of the south. Economic independence gave the country a new status. A transportation system evolved, including the Erie Canal and 9000 miles of hard surface roads. The quarrel between the north and south over slavery began to cause concern.

EH-C-4
SECOND REVOLUTION   SCA
        16mm   Sd   C   1977
        BFA   28min
An exciting depiction of the Industrial Revolution in America and how it radically

changed the country during the century after the first revolution. Dramatizations of Samuel Slater, Eli Whitney and Francis Lowell show how the factory system, interchangeable parts, and mass production created a society that by 1876 celebrated its centennial with a gigantic industrial exposition in Philadelphia.

EH-C-5
THE INDUSTRIAL REVOLUTION   SCA
            16MM   SD   C
            MTPS
Three programs; each 30min in length.
The Great Discontinuity   What was the Industrial Revolution
and what distinguished it from other periods?
Freedom Under The Law   Why did it occur where and when it
did?
A Magnificent Century   What were the consequences for the
people who lived through the Inductrial Revolution?

                    The Transportation Revolution

PH-C-6
ERA OF WATER COMMERCE, 1750-1850   SCA
            16mm   Sd   C   1960
            MGHT   11min
Shows the influence of waterborne commerce and the demands of the growing economy for effective transportation during the early history of the United States. Uses animation to describe the dependence of the United States upon the sea lanes for economic survival; the settlements near coastal areas during colonial days; and the trade routes to the West Indies.

EH-C-7
ERIE CANAL   SCA
            16mm   Sd   C   1976
            Weston Woods   7min
When the Erie Canal was completed in 1825, the nation for the first time had a cheap, fast route through the Appalachian Mountains. This animated film takes the viewer on a trip along the Erie Canal that reveals the panorama of life along and on the historic waterway.

EH-C-8
ER-I-E (THE ERIE CANAL), THE   SCA
            UVB   Sd   1968
            BFA   17min
The history of the Erie Canal is traced through old photographs and drawings that depict its contribution to the growth of the United States.

EH-C-9
GIBBONS VS. OGDEN   SCA
            16mm   Sd   C   1979
            NAVC   36min
In this precedent-setting case, which linked states' authority to license steamboats in Federal waters with the seemingly unrelated issue of slavery, Chief Justice Marshall interpreted the Constitution to give the federal government the duty to determine the rules of commerce, thereby laying the foundation for an American "common market" nearly a century before Europe enjoyed it.

EH-C-10
PONY EXPRESS STORY, THE   SCA
        16mm   Sd   B   1963
        STERLED   22min
Relates how the pony express came into being, the problems encountered in its
establishment, and the cause of its passing. Explains that the idea was borrowed
from Asia. Dramatizes events leading to the selection of a route. Describes the
hardships of the riders and pictures the line in operation. Relates some of the
stories and legends which evolved from the pony express.

EH-C-11
STEAMBOAT ON THE RIVER   SCA
        16mm   Sd   C   1965
        IFB   18min
Old photos of famous steamboats, reenactments, and contemporary film footage
trace the history of the river steamboat, beninning with the first run of Fulton's
"Claremont" in 1807. Various types of river craft are shown serving their unique
purposes for transportation as bulk carriers, war ships, passenger packets,
excursion boats, show boats, and as a general means of communication. Lively
music and an introduction in the words of Mark Twain set the nostalgic tone of
the most romantic period in American transportation.

EH-C-12
RAILROAD BUILDERS, THE   SCA
        16mm   Sd   C,B   1971
        EBEC   14min
Uses live-action photography, illustrations, and art work of the period to present
an account of the building of the first transcontinental railroad and emphasizes
the role of the railroad builders in the westward expansion of the United States.
Reviews the problems and delays attending the building of the railroad.

                              The Westward Movement

EH-C-13
RAILROADS AND WESTERN EXPANSION: 1800-1845
        16mm   Sd   C   1978
        BFA   14min
Depicts the history and development of the early railroads and shows the effect
of the railroad on commerce, westward expansion, and jobs in the first half of the
1800s. After the War of 1812, immigration swelled the population, and settlements
pushed westward by stagecoach, canal boat and steamboat. But mud, frozen
water, and land-locked areas were barriers to effective transportation. The
Industrial Revolution was causing a whirlwind of inventions, and in 1830 America's
first rail passenger service began.

EH-C-14
RAILROADS AND WESTERN EXPANSION: 1845-1865   SCA
        16mm   Sd   C   1978
        BFA   16min
Illustrates how the growth of the frontier led to the growth of the railroad. In
the prairie wilderness devoid of roads and large rivers, railroads were the link to
eastern markets. Railroad towns sprang up all over, and cities like Atlanta,
Boston, Chattanooga and Chicago became major rail junctions. Government land
grants to railroads were sold to settlers, and many immigrants became tenant
farmers or worked on railroad construction crews.

EH-C-15
AMERICA: A PERSONAL HISTORY OF THE UNITED STATES
    NO. 5 - GONE WEST, PARTS 1 AND 2   SCA
        16mm   Sd   C   1972
        Time-Life Films   52min
Begins with the 1803 Louisiana Purchase in tracing the young nation's early
explorers and their westward journeys. Lewis and Clark are featured, along with
other river men and pioneers of the 1800s. Gold is doscovered in California and
the mad land rush begins. Expansionist whites forcibly drive Indian Nations from
their homelands.

EH-C-16
AMERICA: A PERSONAL HISTORY OF THE UNITED STATES
    NO. 7 - DOMESTICATING A WILDERNESS, PARTS 1 AND 2   SCA
        16mm   Sd   C   1972
        Time-Life Films   52min
Mormons enter and settle Utah. The desert blooms after years of strenuous work,
and modern Salt Lake City becomes the mecca for Latter-Day Saints the world
over. The first transcontinental railroad is begun and completed with the golden
spike ceremony at Promentary Point. A far-sighted realtor buys land and creates
the first cattle trail. The era of the cowboy begins and the West goes wild.

EH-C-17
DISCOVERY OF AMERICA, THE:
    THE WESTWARD MOVEMENT   SCA
        16mm   Sd   C   1975
        Handel Film Corp.   15min
Stills, motion pictures, drawings and paintings are used to depict events, and the
trials and tribulations of the men and women who opened up the West. Spanish,
English and French expeditions to claim the New World are briefly traced and
recounted. Focuses on Lewis and Clark, Daniel Boone, the Mountain Men (Jim
Bridger, Joe Walker, Jedediah Smith), the ill-fated Donner Party, Brigham Young
and the Mormons, John Charles Fremont and Kit Carson, and the part each played
in making history is told. The final links in settling the West are shown to be the
California Gold Rush and completion of the transcontinental railroad.

EH-C-18
WESTWARD MOVEMENT, NO 1 -
    SETTLERS OF THE OLD NORTHWEST TERRITORY   SCA
        16mm   Sd   C,B   1962
        EBEC   15min
Depicts the development of the Northwest Territory. Describes growth of
government, distribution of land, and formation of free education as set down in
the Northwest Ordinance of 1787.

EH-C-19
WESTWARD MOVEMENT, NO 2 -
    SETTLEMENT OF THE MISSISSIPPI VALLEY   SCA
        16mm   Sd   C,B   1962
        EBEC   16min
Traces the early 1800 settlement of the Mississippi Valley after the Louisiana
Territory purchase. Portrays the sturdy, self-sufficient people arriving by
flatboats and wagons, clearing the wilderness for farming, and developing
permanent communities. Shows the loyalty codes developed by men in claiming
their acreages and in bidding for claims at land association auctions.

EH-C-20
WESTWARD MOVEMENT, NO. 3 -
   THE SETTLING OF THE GREAT PLAINS   SCA
         16mm   Sd   C   1959
         EBEC   16min
Uses authentic photographs, documents, and illustrations of the period to
recapture the atmosphere and the spirit of "homesteading" on the Great Plains
during the period from about 1840 to about 1860. Describes the geographic and
climactic barriers and hostility of the Indians as major deterrents to earlier
settlement in the plains area.

EH-C-21
WESTWARD MOVEMENT, NO. 4 -
   TEXAS AND THE MEXICAN WAR   SCA
         16mm   Sd   C   1967
         EBEC   16min
Reveals the significance of the war with Mexico in the westward expansion of the
United States. Reviews the causes of the Texas settlers' revolt and the parts the
slavery issue and territorial expansion played in the annexation of Texas.
Identifies ill will in relations with Latin America and political crises within the
U.S. Federation as results of the United States' victory in Mexico.

EH-C-22
WESTWARD MOVEMENT, NO. 5 -
   THE GOLD RUSH   SCA
         16mm   Sd   C   1965
         EBEC   24min
Relates how the discovery of a few glittering particles of metal at Sutter's Mill
changed the history of California and the nation.

                          Industrialization

EH-C-23
AMERICA BECOMES AN INDUSTRIAL NATION   SCA
         16mm   Sd   C   1967
         MGHT   25min
Uses paintings to depict the industrialization of America during the period from
1776 to 1876. Describes the role of the Civil War in the industrial development.
Gives information on leading inventors, especially Eli Whitney. Discusses the
importance of transportation to city growth.

EH-C-24
ELI WHITNEY   SCA
         16mm   Sd   B   1951
         EBEC   18min
Dramatizes the life story of Eli Whitney, relating incidents which reveal his faith
in his ideas. Portrays his development of the cotton gin, which boomed the
economy of the South. Also describes Whitney's experiments in designing tools and
building machinery for the manufacture of muskets, which became the technical
basis for mass production.

EH-C-25
INDUSTRIAL REVOLUTION, THE BEGINNINGS
   IN THE UNITED STATES   SCA
         16mm   Sd   C   1967
         EBEC   23min

Traces the historical development of the industrial revolution in the United States, showing the rise of urban centers and the decline in the agricultural economy. Examines the reasons for change, the establishment of the first spinning mill and modern factory, and the development of new methods of transportation.

EH-C-26
MAN WHO TOOK A CHANCE, THE: ELI WHITNEY   SCA
        16mm   Sd   B   1952
        INUAVC   20min
Dramatizes events in the life of Eli Whitney, the Connecticut machinist and inventor, who postponed production of the cotton gin in 1798 to prove that his assembly line theory could be used in the mass production of muskets for the United States.

EH-C-27
SLATER'S DREAM: SLATERS COTTON SPINNER   SCA
        16mm   Sd   B   1953
        INUAVC   20min
Shows Samuel Slater, a young Englishman who came to America in 1790, struggling to reconstruct from memory the cotton spinner, the plan of which England guarded to insure a monopoly on cotton manufacture.

                            Natural Resources

EH-C-28
AMERICANA: YANKEE WHALING   SCA
        16mm   Sd   B   1968
        INUAVC   27min
Tours with Tony Saletan the last remaining 19th century whaling ship, preserved in Mystic, Connecticut, with insights into what took place in the days when the vessel earned its way by searching out, killing, and removing oil from the world's largest creatures. Presents the actual harpooning of a giant sperm whale from a small, six-man boat. Describes what the on-board life to the captain and the crew might have been like.

EH-C-29
BORN IN FREEDOM   SCA
        16mm   Sd   C
        American Petroleum Inst.   30min
Tells the story of Edwin L. Drake who, in the face of ridicule and failure, drilled the first successful oil well in northern Pennsylvania in 1859.

EH-C-30
CALIFORNIA AND GOLD   SCA
        16mm   Sd   C   1972
        Oxford Films   14min
Shows the first nugget of gold found by James W. Marshall at Sutter's Mill in 1848. Then recounts the story of the famous Gold Rush and subsequent events. Shows remnants of the culture which wealthy families developed. Contrasts ghost towns with mining communities which are still occupied. Points out that modern mining does not bring wealth, and that even Sutter and Marshall died in poverty.

EH-C-31
FUR TRADE, THE--BIG BUSINESS   S C A
        16mm   Sd   B   1954
        KUON-TV   30min
The map of the West was first drawn on a beaver skin. Shows how the fur trade
became the West's first big business, its effect on the Indians, and the fur
companies and fur trading posts.

EH-C-32
GOLDRUSH COUNTRY   S C A
        BVU   Sd   C   1974
        AIMS   18min
The development of western American civilization and the effects of the
discovery of gold beyond the Rocky Mountains.

EH-C-33
GOLD RUSH, THE...AND THE 49ERS   S C A
        16mm   Sd   C   1976
        BFA   22min
When the discovery of gold in California in 1868 was confirmed by President Polk,
it set of a rush to the west that was to transform the country. Prospectors
flocked to the western mountains by way of the Orregon Trail and the Old
Spanish Trail to establish communities where none had stood before.   The
four-month struggle over the trails was too much for some, who found it easier to
travel by boat around Cape Horn. San Francisco was born of the need for a port
for these pioneers.

                              Agriculture

EH-C-34
AMERICA'S HERITAGE: OUR FARMING PIONEERS   S C A
        16mm   Sd   B   1954
        Hearst-Metrotone News   10min
The Farmers' Museum at Cooperstown, New York, a crossroads community, shows
what life on the frontier was like. Here is a chance to look back across a century
and a half at a farm village in the early 1800s.

EH-C-35
ELI WHITNEY INVENTS THE COTTON GIN   S C A
        16mm   Sd   B   1956
        MGHT   26min
Uses a dramatized, "on-the-scene" news-type of interviewing and documentary
reporting to present the story of Eli Whitney's invention of the cotton gin. Shows
the struggle he had protecting his rights to the invention.

EH-C-36
PLANTATION SOUTH, THE   S C A
        16mm   Sd   C,B   1960
        EBEC   16min
Reviews the development of the agriculture and economics of the pre-Civil War
South, and traces this growth from the early Virginia colonies. An emphasis is
placed upon the English influence in architecture and customs upon the plantation
system and the pressure of the industrial revolution which caused a shift from
tobacco to cotton.

EH-C-37

PLANTATION SYSTEM IN SOUTHERN LIFE   SCA
    16mm   Sd   C,B   1950
    Coronet   11min
Contrasts Southern life before and after slavery was abolished and analyzes the
cause and significance of the plantation system. Pictures the one-crop economy,
poor transportation, cheap slave labor, and self-sufficiency of the plantation unit.

Immigration and Labor

EH-C-38

AMERICA: A PERSONAL HISTORY OF THE UNITED STATES
  NO. 6 - A FIREBALL IN THE NIGHT, PARTS 1 AND 2   SCA
    16mm   Sd   C   1972
    Time-Life Films   52min
For over 300 years, the Negro has been in turn, slave, lacky, hired help, and
licensed clown. He gave to America cheap labor and his melancholy music. Cooke
discusses the early history of the Negro slave, Slavery, called 'the peculiar
institution,' became even more profitable for the Northern shippers and vital for
the Southern economy with the invention of the cotton gin and the steamboat.
The North, meanwhile, participates more and more in the industrial revolution.

EH-C-39

BLACK PEOPLE IN THE SLAVE SOUTH, 1850   SCA
    16mm   Sd   C   1969
    EBEC   11min
In 1850 black slaves were imported in droves to provide cheap labor for the
cotton kings in Mississippi. Separated from their families at auction, they faced
harsh treatment from white planters and politicians who subjugated blacks for
profit and claimed them mentally inferior to their white brothers.

EH-C-40

A BOND OF IRON   SCA
    16mm,UBV   Sd   1979
    Ruth Sproat   60min
A Bond of Iron depicts the slave-master relationship at an antebellum ironworks
plantation in Virginia. Two narrators act as story tellers, describing the lives of
William Weaver, the iron-master, and Sam Williams, his slave. The film conveys a
sense of the reality of slavery from both perspecitves, and at the same time
provides insight into the broad economic and social tensions of the period.

EH-C-41

CHINESE AMERICAN, THE: THE EARLY IMMIGRANTS   SCA
    16mm   Sd   C   1973
    Handel Film Corp.   20min
Uses live-action sequences, paintings, prints and old photographs to illustrate the
history of the first Chinese immigrants to the United States. Reveals their role in
the California gold rush in the 1840s and 1850s, their contribution to the building
of the first transcontinental railroad in the 1860s, and their savage persecution
and unjust exclusion in the 1880s. Narrated by Sam Chu Lin.

EH-C-42
IMMIGRATION IN THE 19TH CENTURY   SCA
        16mm   Sd   B   1967
        Films, Inc.   12min
Describes the various waves of immigration to the United States during the 19th
century and the many contributions the immigrants made to the development of
the country. Documents with period drawings and photographs the treatment and
stereotyped attitudes which greeted the migrants. Considers wars, famine, and/or
tyranny as the reasons why many left their European homes for America.

EH-C-43
NEGRO SLAVERY   SCA
        16mm   Sd   C   1968
        MGHT   25min
Shows the beginning and development of slavery as an institution in the United
States and records the life of the slave. Describes the gradual division of
American society over the slavery issue and explains how this division contributed
as a cause for the Civil War. Traces slavery from the early colonists of the
seventeenth century to the election of Abraham Lincoln as president in 1861.

                Economic History - Rapid Industrialization, 1865-1900

                            General Accounts

EH-D-1
GROWTH OF BIG BUSINESS IN AMERICA   SCA
        16mm   Sd   B   1967
        Coronet   15min
Shows the growth and development of big business and its impact from 1865 to
1900. Discusses the roles of Andrew Carnegie, John D. Rockefeller, and J. P.
Morgan. Uses cartoons, still photos, and motion picture clips to portray the
influence of population growth, technology, and increasing capital.

EH-D-2
REBUILDING THE AMERICAN NATION   SCA
        FS, Cassette   C   1973
        Guidance Associates
Examines the history of the United States during the post-Civil War period,
including an explanation of the politics of Reconstruction, the enfranchisement of
Southern Blacks and the later restoration of white Southern rule.

EH-D-3
SETTLING THE WEST, 1853-1890   SCA
        16mm   Sd   C,B   1960
        Coronet   13min
Explains that in the period between 1853 and 1890 the largest frontier region of
the West was settled. Tracing this settlement of the area which extended
westward from Iowa and Missouri to the mountain ranges of California and
Oregon, the film shows how the frontier was developed by the early miners and
cattle ranchers, and later by the farmers and homesteaders.

EH-D-4
TOWARD A GILDED AGE   SCA
         16mm   Sd   C,B   1965
         GRACU   25min
Events in American history from 1876 to 1898 are re-created with views of
paintings, photographs, drawings, and present day film footage. Inventors
developed the telegraph, phonograph, electric light bulb and telephone. Business
and industry flourish, but farmers and laborers did not fare so well. There were
changes in architecture due to new uses of steel, and skyscrapers began to rise in
the large cities. The frontier was disappearing, and the first national parks were
formed. Touches on the Spanish-American war, and explains how the United States
acquired new territories.

Industry, Business Organization and Technology

EH-D-5
AMERICA: A PERSONAL HISTORY OF THE UNITED STATES,
   NO. 8 - MONEY ON THE LAND, PARTS 1 AND 2   SCA
         16mm   Sd   C   1972
         Time-Life Films   52min
Presents an historical view of the growth of Chicago, from a small village on the
prairie to an inland sea port that became the "grain center" of the world. Cooke
outlines the growth of cities in the Midwest as a result of the discovery of
minerals and the development of the mining industry. Discusses the contributions
to the growth of the United States made by such men as Edison, McCormick, and
Drake.

EH-D-6
ANDREW CARNEGIE   SCA
         16mm   Sd   B   1951
         EBEC   18min
Reviews the life of Andrew Carnegie from his poverty-stricken youth in Scotland
to his leadership in American industry. Depicts his trials and successes in
railroading and his development of the iron and steel works which made his huge
fortune. Then shows his decision to devote his fortune and energies to
philanthropy.

EH-D-7
ANDREW CARNEGIE: THE GOSPEL OF WEALTH   SCA
         16mm   Sd   C   1973
         LCA   26min
"In this fierce though voiceless contest, a peculiar type of manhood is developed,
characterized by vitality, energy, concentration, skill in combining numerous
forces for an end, and great foresight into the consequences of social events."

EH-D-8
CENTURY NEXT DOOR, THE   SCA
         16mm   Sd   C   1970
         BFA   25min
Life in New York City on June 30, 1870 is recalled through quotations from
newspapers and other primary source materials and visualized by paintings from
the Metropolitan Museum of Art's "19th Century America" exhibit. Issues of the
day included rising prices, union wages, child labor, women's rights, political
corruption, medicine and morality, fashions and the weather.

EH-D-9
CLOCKWORK   A
        16mm   Sd   C   1982
        California Newsreel   25min
One hundred years ago American management faced many of the problems it
confronts today - worker productivity, technological change, quality and inventory
control. -Clockwork- shows how Frederick Taylor and his followers attempted to
meet these challenges through "scientific management," a revolutionary attempt to
organize the workplace according to quantitative measures and systematic
planning. In so doing, Paylor gave birth to modern management and industrial
engineering—and left an indelible mark on the industrial culture of America.

EH-D-10
COKE MAKING IN THE BEEHIVE OVEN   SCA
        BVU   Sd   C   1975
        NAVC   18min
A documentation of an early American industry process of making blast furnace
coke, using techniques and equipment from the 19th century.

EH-D-11
HOPEDALE: REFLECTIONS ON THE PAST   SCA
        16mm   Sd   1977
        Merrimack Valley Textile Museum   28min
The film provides a record of daily life in the factory village of Hopedale,
Massachusetts, whose development remained linked to the paternalistic Draper
Company, producers of textile machinery, for over a century. Materials for the
film include a collection of 3,600 historic glass plate negatives owned by the
Merrimack Valley Textile Museum, interviews with Hopedale residents, and film
footage of the contemporary community planning and development that integrated
moral and economic goals. The film nostalgically recalls the lifestyle of the
company mill town, a way of life once characteristic of New England.

EH-D-12
RISE OF BIG BUSINESS   SCA
        16mm   Sd   C   1970
        EBEC   27min
Documents the rise of the large-scale, corporate type of business organization
that was to dominate many industries and shows how a changing economic
structure has affected the American people.

EH-D-13
THE WIZARD WHO SPAT ON THE FLOOR   SCA
        16mm   Sd   C   1974
        Time-Life Films   65min
A film biography of Thomas A. Edison, featuring interview sections with his
daughter, and historical footage of the inventor himself.

                    Transportation: The Railroad Age

EH-D-14
BALLAD OF THE IRON HORSE   SCA
        16mm   Sd   C   1970
        LCA   30min
A documentary stressing the parallel histories of the "iron horse" and the nation
it helped to transform from an agrarian to an industrial society. Highlights the

story of the first transcontinental railroad.

EH-D-15
COMPLETION OF THE FIRST
  TRANSCONTINENTAL RAILROAD, THE   SC
         16mm   Sd   C   1955
         MGHT   26min
Uses a dramatized, "on-the-scene" new type of interviewing and documentary
reporting to present the story of events leading up to the completion of the first
transcontinental railroad.

EH-D-16
ERIE WAR, THE   SC
         16mm   Sd   C   1978
         Films, Inc.   28min
Dramatizes the story of the tough, competitive and crooked world of high finance
in New York following the Civil War. In 1868, when Cornelius Vanderbilt, owner
of the New York Central Railroad, surreptitiously tries to buy control of the Erie
Railroad, its owners unload millions of dollars worth of phony stock certificates
on him. Realizing that he has been duped, Vanderbilt sets the law on Drew, Fisk
and Gould, who flee in a rowboat to Jersey City, taking along all of Erie's cash
and records. While planning their return to Wall Street, the Drew group bribes the
New York State legislature into bilking Vanderbilt. The two old pro's, Drew and
Vanderbilt, finally work out a deal, and the Erie war comes to an end.

EH-D-17
RAILROAD BUILDERS, THE   SC
         16mm   Sd   C,B   1971
         EBEC   14min
Uses live-action photography, illustrations, and art work of the period to present
an account of the building of the first transcontinental railroad and emphasizes
the role of the railroad builders in the westward expansion of the United States.
Reviews the problems and delays attending the building of the railroad.

EH-D-18
RAILROADS AND WESTWARD EXPANSION: 1865-1900   SCA
         16mm   Sd   C   1978
         BFA   17min
Focuses on the importance of the railroad in the settlement of the Great Plains
and the western states, and shows how the desire for resources of the West led to
building of the transcontinental.

                              Agriculture

EH-D-19
CATTLE: BIRTH OF AN INDUSTRY   SCA
         16mm   Sd   B   1954
         KUON-TV   30min
Shows the impact of cattle on the life of the West Overland Trail herds, Texas
cattlemen and the "long drive" north to market, Nebraska cow towns, range cattle
industry, its boom and bust, the romance of the roundup, life of the cowboy and
the homesteader-cattleman conflict.

EH-D-20
CIVIL WAR, THE: PROMISE OF RECONSTRUCTION   A
        16mm   Sd   C   1972
        LCA   29min
A dramatic re-creation of the Port Royal experiment during the Civil War shows
how the Sea Island plantation, abandoned by Southern planters to the pillage of
the Union Army, were turned over to former slaves under the supervision of
idealistic but ill-trained missionaries from the North.

EH-D-21
GROWTH OF FARMING IN AMERICA, 1865-1900   SCA
        16mm   Sd   B   1967
        Coronet   16min
Surveys the problems attending the changes in American farming in the period
preceding 1900. Details the decline of small farms and the increase in the scale of
farming as well as the introduction of farm machinery and its effects.

EH-D-22
SETTLERS AND THE LAND, THE   A
        16mm   Sd   B   1954
        KUON-TV   30min
Depicts the rapid settlement of the Great Plains after the Civil War, Union
veterans and government land policies, how railroads help the settlers, and
Nebraska's melting pot population.

EH-D-23
WHEN WE FARMED WITH HORSES   A
        16mm   Sd   C   1979
        Iowa State Univ.   25min
Today's world food supply depends on Midwest agriculture. From the opening of
the prairies to the coming of big equipment, we farmed with horses. The evolution
of equipment, the work year through the seasons, farm men and women
remembering the horses with "people" names, pride in craftsmanship, memories of
frustrations and fondness, a persistent sense of humor are included.

Immigration and Labor

EH-D-24
AMERICA: A PERSONAL HISTORY OF THE UNITED STATES
    NO. 9 - THE HUDDLED MASSES, PARTS 1 AND 2   SCA
        16mm   Sd   C   1972
        Time-Life Films   52min
Cooke explores the non-English origins of the immigration movements from the
post-Civil War period to the turn of the century. He describes the emigration
movements across Europe and explains how the political bosses in America
provided for the new arrivals to America.

EH-D-25
1876: LABOR AND VIOLENCE   SCA
        16mm   Sd   C   1975
        Films, Inc.   24min
Long hours, starvation wages, and crippling injuries were the rewards of coal
mining in the 1870s. In this realistic portrayal of the dehumanizing conditions of a
Pennsylvania coal mine, the despair and anger of the miners becomes readily
understandable. The degradation of their lives is impressed upon the miners at the

wake of an old man who doesn't even have a suit of clothes to be buried in. The Molly Maguires, a secret organization dedicated to worker protest and company sabotage, march to the company store to steal a decent suit for their comrade. Then, rage erupting at the futility of their lives, they gleefully wreck the store and finally burn it down.

EH-D-26
THE MASSES AND THE MILLIONAIRES -
   THE HOMESTEAD STRIKE   A
         16mm   Sd   C   1973
         LCA   27min
In 1892 at the Carnegie Steel Mill in Homestead, Pennsylvania, occurred a famous and tragic labor-management confrontation, the Homestead Strike. A dramatic and analytic re-creation of the event contributes to the understanding of labor-management problems.

Economic History - The Corporate Economy, 1900 to Present

General Accounts

EH-E-1
AMERICA IN THE DEPRESSION YEARS   A
         35mm
         Instructional Resources Corp.   450 slides
A collection of 450 slide images copied from the vast photographic collection of the Farm Security Administration, created in the 1930s and 40s by a group of America's greatest photographers. A 48-page Master Guide book provides captions, background information, and the index.

EH-E-2
AMERICA: A PERSONAL HISTORY OF THE UNITED STATES
   NO. 10 - THE PROMISE FULFILLED AND THE PROMISE
BROKEN, PARTS 1 AND 2   A
         16mm   Sd   C   1972
         Time-Life Films   52min
Discusses the events after World War I that helped shape the 1920s. Woodrow Wilson, hailed as the world's savior only to become a scapegoat later, protests. Race riots are shown, too.

EH-E-3
AMERICA: A PERSONAL HISTORY OF THE UNITED STATES
   NO. 13 - THE MORE ABUNDANT LIFE, PARTS 1 AND 2   A
         16mm   Sd   C   1972
         Time-Life Films   52min
The quality and staying power of the Republic has been productivity. The goal of productivity has been oriented to bringing well-being to the masses whether it be via Hoover Dam, the credit card, automobile, suburban housing, or contemporary rural communes.

EH-E-4
AMERICA: ON THE EDGE OF ABUNDANCE   A
         16mm   Sd   B   1965
         NET   55min
British television explores economic and social aspects of the automated and

computer-oriented society in the United States. America's growth from agricultural to industrial society is traced, with emphasis on automation, including the immense problem of retraining persons for new and different jobs. Suggesting that leisure is fast becoming a new business, the study implies that a re-examination of values is in order. Commentary by James Cameron.

EH-E-5
BOOM OR BUST - BETWEEN THE WARS (1925-1935)   A
            16mm   Sd   B   1966
            GRACU   24min
America tries isolation again. High tariffs are enacted: the plight of the farmer vs. the Golden 20s, the model T, the radio, refrigerators, vacuum cleaners, skyscrapers are part of the new scene. Lindy flies the Atlantic non-stop. The market crashes. Herbert Hoover is replaced. Adolf Hitler and Franklin Roosevelt become national leaders.

EH-E-6
GROWTH DILEMMA   A
            16mm   Sd   C   1979
            Churchill Films   20min
Continuing economic growth has become on one hand an essential to industrial societies and on the other hand the cause of environmental failure to those societies. Various experts comment (economists, bankers, biologists, environmentalists) to explain the concept of growth and its causes. The dangers and risks which result are exposed.

EH-E-7
LIFE IN THE THIRTIES   A
            16mm   Sd   B   1965
            MGHT   53min
Depicts significant social, political, and economic events of the thirties. Describes the depression and the actions of the Roosevelt administration in an effort to counteract it. Highlights the rise of Hitler and discusses other significant world events which were to lead to World War II.

EH-E-8
THE TWENTIES   A
            16mm   Sd   C   1968
            MGHT   25min
Presents the paradox and divisiveness of the decade which began with the rejection of Progressivism and the adoption of consumer capitalism. Examines the issues that divided Americans into hostile groups. Shows how the stock market crash led to the end of one era and the beginning of another.

Business: Industry, Commerce, Finance

EH-E-9
AMOSKEAG TRANSCRIPTS   A
            UBV   Sd   C   1978
            King Features Entertainment   29min
An historical look at what was once the largest mill in the world. The Amoskeag mill in New England went out of business in 1933 and its story is a classic biography of a mill town.

EH-E-10
ANATOMY OF A CRISIS   SCA
    16mm   Sd   C   1980
    Penn Communications, Inc.   30min
Milton Friedman presents his interpretation of the causes of the Great Depression.
Using dramatic film footage, Friedman reports on the big boom of the 20s, the
collapse that followed, and his views of what could have been done to head off
the Great Depression.

EH-E-11
BANK HOLIDAY CRISIS OF 1933, THE   A
    16mm   Sd   B   1957
    MGHT   26min
Uses a dramatized "on-the-scene" news type of interviewing and documentary
reporting to present the story of the quick collapse of American credit in 1933.
Discusses systems set to keep commerce temporarily active, government controls,
and measures taken to re-establish sound banking establishments. Points out the
unusual nature of the "bank holiday" declared by Franklin D. Roosevelt and
reviews many of the factors involved in strengthening the Federal Reserve
System.

EH-E-12
CORPORATION, THE   A
    16mm   Sd   C,B   1974
    Carousel Films   53min
A candid documentary which examines Phillips Petroleum, the 36th largest
corporation in the U.S. and reveals the corporate mind, its attitudes, goals and
ethics.

EH-E-13
DEPRESSION YEARS   A
    16mm   Sd   C   1975
    Films, Inc.   24min
Combines historic footage with modern sequences to discuss causes of the Great
Depression. Considers whether such an economic disaster could happen again.
Indicates safeguards have been built into the economic and political structure to
avoid a re-occurrence.

EH-E-14
MANUFACTURING MIDWEST   A
    16mm   Sd   C   1976
    MGHT
Describes the industrial nature of the Midwest by following iron ore from
Minnesota to the finished automobile in Michigan. Shows mining transporting new
materials, the steel mill, tool and die makers and assembly line workers.

EH-E-15
NEW INDUSTRIAL REVOLUTION, THE   A
    16mm,VB   Sd   C   1980
    NAVC   12min
This program allows us to observe the futuristic revolution taking place
today--the use of intelligent machines in industry.

EH-E-16
RISE OF INDUSTRIAL GIANTS, THE   A
          16mm   Sd   C   1967
          MGHT   26min
Covers the rise of the industrial giants, the growth of monopoly, and the
emergence of trusts. Deals with the serious social, economic, and political
problems that arose as the nation adapted itself to the rapid and far reaching
changes that were taking place.

EH-E-17
TRUSTS AND TRUST BUSTERS   A
          16mm   Sd   C   1967
          MGHT   25min
Presents, through the use of political cartoons, problems created by industrial
growth during the period after the Civil War. Explains why trusts were organized.
Notes the events which led Theodore Roosevelt to confront the trusts with
government international through enforcement of the Sherman Act.

EH-E-18
THE '29 BOOM AND THE 30s DEPRESSION   A
          16mm   Sd   B   1970
          MGHT   14min
Re-creating the events of this period in American history, the film examines the
prosperity and boom of the 1920s with special attention to the factors which
would later lead to the depression. Government legislation and regulation to end
the depression and to help future depressions are detailed.

EH-E-19
WHEN OUTPUT WAS LOW: THE 1930'S   A
          16mm   Sd   B
          INUAVC   29min
Attempts to recreate an image of the political, social, and economic effects of
the Depression of the 1930s for those who have always lived in times of
prosperity.

                    The Changing Role of Government

EH-E-20
EAGLE ON THE STREET   A
          16mm,UBV   Sd   C
          NAVC   22min
Traces the development of the securities industry and examines S.E.C. aims,
activities, and services available to the general public and investment
communities.

EH-E-21
FRANKLIN D. ROOSEVELT, PART 1: THE NEW DEAL   A
          16mm   Sd   B   1963
          MGHT   26min
Uses documentary footage to trace FDR's youth, family life, and political career
through the "New Deal" to his third term. Depicts his relationship with politicians
and voters, and analyzes his handling of the depression during the pre-war years.

EH-E-22
GOVERNMENT AND THE MARKET A
    16mm   Sd   B   1962
    INUAVC   29min
Shows that national resources can be allocated in two ways: either by individual interactions on a free market, or by deliberate action by the government, as a representative of the voting majority. States that the American business system shows a mixture of both influences, with some disagreement on the most effective blend.

EH-E-23
GREAT DEPRESSION A
    16mm   Sd   C   1976
    BFA   33min
Uses newsreel footage and interviews to analyze the 1930s depression in America. Discusses the New Deal, CCC, TVA, WPA, Bonus Army, farmer protests, union activities, and people's attitudes towards business and government.

EH-E-24
HUNDRED DAYS, THE A
    16mm   Sd   B   1966
    Films, Inc.   17min
Documents the conditions prevalent in the United States during the depression of 1929. Contrasts Herbert Hoover as a tired and disillusioned out-going President with President-elect Franklin Roosevelt who was full of promises and ideas. Describes the people hopefully awaiting the results of the activity of Roosevelt's first hundred days.

EH-E-25
MONEY ON THE MOVE - THE FEDERAL RESERVE TODAY A
    16mm   Sd   C   1963
    Federal Reserve Bank   27min
A detailed look at the Federal Reserve System and how it has influenced the economy. The developments since this film was produced do not negate the basic concepts of the Federal Reserve.

EH-E-26
NEW DEAL, THE A
    16mm   Sd   C   1971
    MGHT   25min
Uses stills and newsreel footage to reconstruct depression conditions and New Deal policies enacted by FDR.

EH-E-27
PROGRESSIVE ERA, THE: REFORM WORKERS IN AMERICA A
    16mm   Sd   B   1971
    EBEC   22min
Depicts social and economic conditions that prevailed during the Progressive Era (1890-1915), and demonstrates the continuity of reform movements in the United States. Shows the swelling effects of immigration on urban population, where political machines, dominated by the economic power of the trusts, controlled public life.

EH-E-28
REA STORY, THE   A
        16mm   Sd   C   1960
        NAVC   28min
Reviews the 25-year history of the Rural Electrification Administration. Stresses
the importance of electric power to farms and ranches to remote areas. Highlights
scenes showing farm life before and after electricity.

EH-E-29
ROOSEVELT AND HOOVER ON THE ECONOMY   A
        16mm   Sd   C   1976
        BFA   25min
In this dramatic and open-ended film the viewer is asked to evaluate the
conflicting views of Roosevelt and Hoover on the Great Depression, bureaucracy
and the role of the federal government in people's lives.

EH-E-30
TRADE AND AID   A
        16mm   Sd   B   1963
        NBC-TV   30min
The history of the American trade policy is reviewed with emphasis on
developments since 1934.

EH-E-31
TVA AND THE NATION   A
        16mm   Sd   C   1960
        Tennessee Valley Authority   20min
Portrays the developments of the Tennessee Valley and describes the benefits
accruing to the people of this valley and the entire nation from TVA. Conditions
in the valley before TVA are pictured and the actions needed to raise the area's
economy to that of the other regions of the nation are described. The various
changes that took place in the valley are enumerated in detail.

EH-E-32
WHO OWNS AMERICA?   SC
        Audio-cassette   1979
        NPR   59min
Lester Thurow, professor at M.I.T., talks about how wealth is distributed in
America and explores world economic policies in relation to equalizing income.
Comparing today's economic levels to those of the 60s, Dr. Thurow explores the
merits of social programs to redistribute the wealth.

                              Transportation

EH-E-33
AMERICAN AUTO INDUSTRY, THE:
    CURRENT PROBLEMS, POSSIBLE FUTURE   A
        Audio-cassette   Sd   1982
        NPR   79min
Beginning with a short history of the automobile industry, this series of reports
examines what has happened to the American system of manufacture. Topics
includea comparison of the Japanese and U.S. systems of
manufacture, an explanation of Japanese cost-cutting practices and techniques to
increase worker effeciency, and an examination of the manager-worker
communication problem, assembly-line conditions, and the human cost of
unemployment.

EH-E-34
AUTOMOBILES AND ROADS   A
   16mm   Sd   B   1960
   Newsweek   10min
A short history of the automobile from the time of the first horseless carriage
and the era of mud paths to the present super-highway of today.

EH-E-35
EVERYTHING RIDES ON THE ROADS   A
   16MM   SD   C   1978
   Allied Film Laboratory   28min
The story of America's roads—the backbone of our transportation system. Our
entire economy—food, clothing, shelter, goods—depends in one way or another on
roads.

EH-E-36
GASOLINE AGE: HISTORY OF TRANSPORTATION
  IN THE UNITED STATES, PART II   A
   16mm   Sd   C   1959
   EBEC   14min
Traces the developments in transportation in the United States. Illustrates how
the oil burning diesel engine extended the gasoline age to railroads, ships, and
other forms of heavy duty transportation. Maps and briefly surveys the three
inland waterway systems in the U.S. and traces the development of air
transportation.

EH-E-37
GOLDEN AGE OF THE AUTOMOBILE, THE   A
   16mm   Sd   C   1969
   LCA   30min
The introduction of the auto and the transformation of national life are traced in
this film.

EH-E-38
HENRY FORD   A
   16mm   Sd   B   1962
   MGHT   27min
Presents the life of Henry Ford, emphasizing his influence on modern industry.
Shows the development of the Model T, the assembly line, and the demand for
cars by ordinary working people. Discusses his troubles with labor unions, his
personal characteristics, and his role as a philanthropist.

EH-E-39
HENRY FORDS AMERICA   A
   16mm   Sd   C   1977
   CBC and NFBC   57min
Documents the turbulent history of the Ford dynasty, and the spawning and
evolution of the automotive age. Henry Ford I introduced the Model T and the
moving assembly line. He took the toy of the rich, made it the birthright of the
American masses and changed the course of history. He left America free to
move, and his grandson, Henry Ford II, makes sure it will move in the right
direction. "Is it any wonder," asks the narrator "that the captains and kings of
Detroit have assumed mythic proportions? Because of them, it has been argued,
the city of Detroit has had as great an influence on 20th century man as did
Rome in the time of Caesar and Athens in the age of Pericles."

EH-E-40
KITTY HAWK TO PARIS: THE HEROIC YEARS   A
    16mm   Sd   C   1970
    LCA   54min
The formative years of American aviation are recalled in the exploits of its
heroes: Wilbur and Orville Wright, World War I pilots, barnstormers and airmail
fliers, and Charles Lindbergh.

EH-E-41
MISSISSIPPI SYSTEM, THE: WATERWAY OF COMMERCE   A
    16mm   Sd   C   1970
    EBEC   16min
Traces the history of the Mississippi River, with emphasis on the rise and fall of
the steamboat, the "Big Flood" of 1927, and the development of the river into a
modern water transportation system. Explains the operation of barges and tow
boats as an economical alternative to railroad transportation of goods.

EH-E-42
ROAD TO HAPPINESS   A
    UBV   Sd   C   1980
    Films, Inc.   58min
Henry Ford's personal film collection leaves behind the story of a shy, nearly
illiterate farm boy who became an American legend. The history of his era is also
encompassed within his archives, the Ford Film Collection.

The Labor Force

EH-E-43
BETWEEN ROCK AND A HARD PLACE   SCA
    16mm   Sd   C   1981
    Blue Ridge Mountain Films   59min
Focuses on the changing meaning of life and work for three generations of
Appalachian coal miners.

EH-E-44
BLOOD OF BARRE, THE   A
    Audio-cassette   Sd   1979
    Vermont Public Radio   30min
The Blood of Barre traces the early history of the granite industry in Barre,
describing the process of quarrying and carving granite. It examines the
emergence of the industry within the national economy, the impact of ethnic
diversity on the Barre granite work force, the struggle of granite workers to
organize, and the impact on the labor force of the decline and partial restoration
of the industry in recent decades.

EH-E-45
CHALLENGE OF CHANGE   A
    16mm   Sd   B   1964
    NAVC   21min
Economic and social changes since the 1913 founding of the U.S. Department of
Labor. Improved working conditions from the horse and buggy era to the space
age; problems caused by the Depression and resultant social legislation; recent
technological changes and problems brought about by automation.

EH-E-46
FIRST PERSON AMERICA: VOICES FROM THE THIRTIES   A
                    Audio-cassette   Sd   1980
                    NPR
Based on actual interviews collected by the Federal Writers' Project during the
late 1930s. Through dramatized narratives, it recreates the experiences of
Americans from diverse walks of life in the decade of the Great Depression.
1. Troupers and Pitchmen: A Vanishing World. The program portrays a part of
American life which no longer exists: vaudeville palaces and carnival jammers,
purveyors of luck charms and patent medicine pitchmen.
2. When I First Came to This Land. By dramatizing narratives of a fish peddler
from Chicago, a Portuguese fisherman from Cape Cod, a Russian-Jewish itinerant
peddler, and a French-Canadian textile worker from New Hampshire, the program
describes how immigrants made their way in the new country and struggled to
preserve their ethnic identity as they adapted to the new life.
3. Making Ends Meet. The program suggests some of the ways women sustained
themselves during the hard times of the 1930s.
4. Talking Union. Through the dramatized narratives of Chicago packinghouse
workers, this program focuses on the fierce and dramatic struggles for
unionization in the 1930s.
5. Smoke and Steel. The human cost of building America is evoked through the
stories of an Oklahoma oilfield hand, a Missouri coal miner, a New York City
construction worker, a Penobscot Bay canoe maker, and a pair of Vermont granite
cutters.
6. Harlem Stories. The dramatized narrative of a Pullman porter who lamented his
move north to Harlem is the focal point of the program.

EH-E-47
GREAT DEPRESSION, THE: A HUMAN DIARY   A
                    16mm   Sd   B   1970
                    Mass Media Ministries   53min
Documents the depression years of the 30s, using photographs from the Library of
Congress, the Archives of the Farm Security Adminsitration, and the Office of
War Information. Depicts the plight of the unemployed, the breadlines, the Dust
Bowl, and the migrations to California.

EH-E-48
GREAT SIT-DOWN STRIKE, THE   A
                    16mm   Sd   C   1982
                    Films, Inc.   50min
In December 1936, the recently formed United Auto Workers Union was struggling
for recognition by the giants of the auto industry. The Pinkerton Detective
Agency had been hired by General Motors to "watch" its workers. In response, the
workers sat down--literally. For the first six weeks of 1937 they occupied the
plants, and nothing was built. This brilliant strategy resulted in recognition for
the union.

EH-E-49
IMMIGRATION IN THE 20TH CENTURY   A
                    16mm   Sd   B   1967
                    Films, Inc.   13min
Reviews the history of immigration to the United States during the 20th century,
discussing the reasons for the comparative trickle of immigrants and the national
origins quota system. Shows the problems facing those wishing to immigrate to
America in the 1900s, caused by the mood of isolationism and extreme prejudice
against "foreigners." Examines the changing attitude which ultimately led to the

end of the national origins quota system in 1965.

EH-E-50
INHERITANCE, THE   A
   16mm   Sd   B   1965
   MGHT   60min
Uses newsreels, still photographs, and silent film shots in illustrating the history
of the American labor movement for the past 50 years. Highlights visual
presentation with tunes and popular songs of that historical period. Emphasizes
that each generation must fight for its rights.

EH-E-51
LABOR COMES OF AGE   A
   16mm   Sd   B   1962
   Films, Inc.   19min
Surveys the strife between labor and management under the New Deal of the FDR
era and recalls Roosevelt's support of workers' rights--the first step toward the
protective labor legislation that followed.

EH-E-52
LABOR MOVEMENT, THE: BEGINNINGS AND
  GROWTH IN AMERICA   A
   16mm   Sd   C,B   1959
   Coronet   13min
Highlights the significant developments in labor's organization in the United States
from 1873 through the merger of the AFL and CIO. Depicts the role played by
Samuel Gompers in the development of American trade unions.

EH-E-53
MAD RIVER: HARD TIME IN HUMBOLDT COUNTY   SCA
   16mm   Sd   C   1982
   Fine Line Productions   54min
Unemployment, plant closures, environmental pressures--a portrait of a rural
community in the Redwood Region of Northern California. Here, where the
"tallest trees in the world" grow, there is today a shortage of timber.
Environmentalists and the timber industry blame one another for the economic and
environmental crisis.

EH-E-54
RISE OF LABOR   A
   16mm   Sd   C,B   1963
   EBEC   30min
Traces the history of government policy on trade unions and welfare legislation.

EH-E-55
ROOTS OF LABOR UNIONS, THE   A
   16mm   Sd   B   1962
   INUAVC   30min
Labor unions in the United States play an important role in economic life. In spite
of their influence, however, it has been in relatively recent years that unions
have become strong. Current issues involving labor cannot be understood, apart
from the story of its past.

EH-E-56
STATE OF THE UNIONS   A
        16mm   Sd   B   1966
        Carousel Films   56min
This film discusses the past, present, and future of labor unions. It discusses past
accomplishments and their present image amid charges of racial discrimination and
excessive power. The rising cost of living, automation, unemployment, and other
problems facing unions today are also explored.

EH-E-57
UNION MAIDS   A
        16mm   Sd   C,B   1975
        New Day Films   48min
Sitdowns, scabs, goon squads, unemployment, hunger marches, red baiting and
finally the energetic birth of the CIO--the 1930s were a landmark period for the
American Labor Movement. This turbulent period in American history is retold
through the personal history of three women as they give their accounts of the
changes they and their co-workers went through--a growing awareness of working
class oppression, of the second class status of women and minorities and of the
clear need for collective action to win change.

                                Agriculture

EH-E-58
AGRICULTURAL MIDWEST, THE   A
        16mm   Sd   C   1976
        MGHT   18min
The series examines eight principal regions of the U.S., conveying a sense of life
in each region. The Agricultural Midwest illustrates how many factors combine to
make the Midwest a region of major agricultural production.

EH-E-59
AGRICULTURE AND THE NEW DEAL   A
        16mm   Sd   B   1962
        Films, Inc.   16min
Surveys problems of U.S. Agriculture in the early 1930s and discusses reforms of
the New Deal, shows how Congressional approval of F.D.R.'s many programs from
the AAA in 1932 to the TVA in 1936 increased farmer's incomes, encouraged soil
conservation, resettled bankrupt farm families, established water conservation and
irrigation facilities, and provided power for rural electrification. Newsreels and
archive film records illustrate the film.

EH-E-60
CRISIS IN YANKEE AGRICULTURE   SCA
        16mm   C   1978
        Cambridge Media Resources   28min
A study of the decline of farming in industrialized, urban areas. Focuses on the
problems of rising land prices, competition from large corporate farms, the
shipping of food east from California and the marketing of local produce.

EH-E-61
FARMER IN CHANGING AMERICA, THE   A
        16mm   Sd   C   1973
        EBEC   25min
A documentary record of American farming, past, present, and future. The causes
and nature of change in American agriculture are portrayed.

EH-E-62
FROM THIS LAND   SCA
        16mm   Sd   C
        Vision Associates, Inc.   12min
Shows the importance of cooperatives in the American agricultural system with
particular emphasis on the family farmer throughout the country and across the
nation.

EH-E-63
THE GREAT PLAINS, PART 5, FARMING   A
        BVU   Sd   1976
        Adams County Historical Society   22min
Inspired by movie collections in the Adams County Historical Society Archives,
the series uses footage dating from the 1920s to the present which depicts the
social history and life of the Great Plains region.
The earliest farmers broke the sod, faced blizzards, grasshoppers, dust storms and
drought, and survived bitter adversity. This film traces the development of
farming methods, from the first primitive implements to modern large-scale
farming.

EH-E-64
THE GREAT PLAINS, PART 6, RANCHING   A
        BVU   Sd   1976
        Adams Country Historical Society   22min
Inspired by movie collections in the Adams County Historical Society Archives,
the series uses footage dating from the 1920s to the present which depicts the
social history and life of the Great Plains region.
From the days of the buffalo ranging across the grasslands, through the era of the
cattle trails up from Mexico through Texas and on to Montana, to the present
day, the Great Plains have always been cattle country. This film traces the
development of ranching from the early days on the trail, the era of the cattle
barons, to present day ranching.

EH-E-65
GREAT PLAINS, THE: FROM GREEN TO GOLD   A
        16mm   Sd   C   1965
        MGHT   15min
Dramatizes the development of the Great Plains from covered wagons to modern
multicombine harvesting. Pictures an early home of the region and shows how the
people lived. Shows a modern farm of more than 1,000 acres on which wheat is
grown. Shows modern farm machinery in use and explains something of the
economics of modern farming.

EH-E-66
GREAT PLAINS EXPERIENCE, THE:
        THE HEIRS TO NO MAN'S LAND   A
        16mm   Sd   C   1978
        GPITVL   30min
Examines the post-frontier modernization of the Great Plains. It considers the

technological innovations that encouraged people to believe that they had mastered the land. The main focus of the program is on the experiences and consequences of the Great Depression and Dust Bowl. The traumas of the era are captured in newsreel footage, photographs, and the words of the participants.

EH-E-67
LAND, THE   A
    16mm   Sd   B   1941
    NAVC   44min
Presents a deeply felt portrayal of American agriculture during the depression decade. Explores the grim agricultural unemployment that existed, the bleak vistas of eroded farms, and the desolate lives of migrant workers. Also expresses a wariness of the role of the machine as part of our lives.

EH-E-68
MAN OF WHEAT   SCA
    16mm   Sd   C   1981
    Pyramid Films   28min
Presents the life of a wheat farmer in eastern Washington state, following the course of a year on the boundless golden wheatfields. Starting to farm in 1943, Glen Miller now has sons and grandsons, and 20,000 acres to harvest.

EH-E-69
YELLOW TRAIL FROM TEXAS   SCA
    16mm   Sd   C   1978
    Time-Life Multimedia   50min
The harvesting of the North American wheat crop is one of the biggest farming operations in the world. For five months of the year, hundreds of combine harvesters chew their way over a 300-mile front. It is 18-hour-a-day back-breaking work. By the time it is through, the work of just one crew will feed the entire city of London for three months.

Folklore

John Vlach

The field of folklore study covers a wide variety of topics. As an intellectual pursuit, folklore combines the perspective and objectives of both the humanities and the social sciences. As a subject matter, folklore includes all manner of expressive and cognitive dimensions of traditional culture. Stories, songs, beliefs, customs, foodways, arts and crafts, dances, musical instruments, houses, and much more can all be studied as elements of folklore. Since the mid 1960s the term folklife has been joined with folklore to represent the interests of American folklorists. This move in nomenclature underscores the deliberate attempts to expand the definition of the discipline so that it can claim stewardship over not only the traditional performing arts but also over the material aspects of folk culture.

The selection of American folklore on film and other visual media presented here focuses mainly on music and oral literature. This particular dominance represents the continued interests of folklorists in singers and tale tellers. Tales and songs were the original "bread and butter" of folklore scholarship and they remain a central concern. Films depicting the work of fisherman, farmers, and various craftsmen along with films on arts and crafts and foodways, however, present a new direction for folklore research that encompasses the artifactual dimension of everyday life or the implementation of technology. Studies of such topics are more comfortably labeled as "folklife." Roughly forty percent of this selection of films can be described as folklife documents so that this list represents where folklore study has been and where, for the moment, it is going.

FOLKLORE (F)

F-A	Communities (See also An-H, Anthropology)
F-B	Music
F-C	Oral Traditions
F-D	Occupations
F-E	Arts and Crafts
F-F	Food
F-G	Religion
F-H	Dance
F-I	Festivals and Fairs

Folklore - Communities

F-A-1
ALUMINUM TOWN   A
                U   Sd   C   1980
        Univ of N.C., N.C. Office of Folklife Programs   26 min
A documentary about Badin, North Carolina, a small industrial town created by
the aluminum industry.

F-A-2
AMERICAN CIVILIZATION 1840-1876   SCA
        FS, Cassettes - 4 Parts   C
        Sunburst Communications
        Part 1: 74 frs, 14 min
        Part 2: 80 frs, 15 min
        Part 3: 80 frs, 15 min
        Part 4: 80 frs, 15 min
Examines the mood and tone of American society preceding, during and after the
Civil War.

F-A-3
AMISH, THE — A PEOPLE OF PRESERVATION   A
        16mm   Sd   C   1975
        Heritage Productions, Inc.   52 min
Based on the Old Order Amish community of Lancaster County, Pennsylvania,
their beliefs, history, world view, schooling.

F-A-4
EVERYTHING CHANGE UP NOW:
 A VIEW OF THE SOUTH CAROLINA SEA ISLANDS   A
        16mm   Sd   C   1976
        Gretchen Robinson   43 min
The life-style of South Carolina Sea Islanders is seen, with the issues facing them
and their culture. Interviews with Gullah basketmakers, net makers, fishermen,
educators, farmers and "witch doctors."

F-A-5
LOW RIDERS   A
        16mm, UBV   Sd   C   1976
        Image Associates   22 min
Two young Mexican-Americans pool their time, talent and resources to transform
a 1969 Chevy Impala into a "low rider" car. The steps of stripping, repairing and
painting are shown.

F-A-6
NEW AMERICANS, THE   SCA
        UBV   Sd   1981
        GPN Educational Media   30 min
Four 30-minute programs on Indochinese history and culture, including the
Vietnamese, ethnic Chinese from Vietnam, Laotian, Lao-Hmong from Laos and
Cambodian.

F-A-7
SPARK, THE   A
        16mm   Sd   C   1974
        Jewish Media Service   28 min
A portrait of Brooklyn's Satmarer and Lubavitcher Hasidim. It describes the
history of Hasidism, its values and way of life.

F-A-8
YES, MA'AM   A
        16mm   Sd   C   1980
        Gary Goldman   48 min
The gracious life within the stately mansions and gardens of New Orleans is
maintained by black household workers. Many have spent their whole working life
in one family's employment, and strong attachments have developed on both sides.
The whole issue of the "mammy" is subtly explored. This is a rare social document
whose insights will be useful in many areas.

                              Folklore - Music

F-B-1
AFRO-AMERICAN WORKSONGS IN A TEXAS PRISON   A
        16mm   Sd   B   1966
        Film Images   29 min
Afro-American work songs in prison farms. This film records seven of them at the
Ellis Unit of the Texas Department of corrections, near Huntsville.

F-B-2
AND THIS IS FREE   A
        16mm   Sd   B   1976
        New Yorker Films   47 min
Chicago's Maxwell Street Market, with hawkers, vendors and a great variety of
Afro-American musical forms.

F-B-3
ARTHUR CRUDUP: BORN IN THE BLUES   A
        16mm   Sd   C   1973
        David Deutsch   29 min
A biography of blues performer Arthur "Big Boy" Crudup filmed on location at his
home in Exmore, Virginia.

F-B-4
BANJO MAN   A
        16mm, U   Sd   B   1978
        Texture Films   26 min
A portrait of the life and music of John "Uncle" Homer Walker -- steel driver,
coal miner, railroad worker, tenant farmer. Walker's story leads to the neglected
history of black Appalachian people. He performs work songs and folk songs.

F-B-5
BLUES ACCORDIN' TO LIGHTNIN' HOPKINS, THE   A
        16mm   Sd   C   1969
        Flower Films, Grove Press   31 min
A portrait of Texas blues singer Lightnin' Sam Hopkins. Includes scenes of life in
Hopkins' hometown of Centerville, Texas.

F-B-6
CHICAGO BLUES   A
        16mm, UBV   Sd   C   1979
        Time Life Multimedia   49 min
Chicago blues music is seen through interviews, performances at home and
southside club appearances. Features Muddly Waters, Junio Wells, Floyd Jones,
J.B. Hutto, Dick Gregory and many others.

F-B-7
CHULAS FRONTERAS   A
        16mm   Sd   C   1976
        Flower Films, Unifilm   58 min
An introduction to the Nortena ("Northern" Texas-Mexican border) music of the
Southwest. Musicians who appear include Los Alegres de Teran, Lydia Mendoza,
Flaco Jimenez and others.

F-B-8
DID YOUR MOTHER COME FROM IRELAND?   A
        16mm, UBV   Sd   C   1981
        Mick Molony   53 min
Film of Irish-American children in the Bronx, New York, expressing their ethnicity
in their community by learning and performing traditional Irish music.

F-B-9
DINK: A PRE-BLUES MUSICIAN   A
        16mm   Sd   B   1975
        Cecilia Conway   25 min
Dink Roberts is an 80-year-old black banjo player from Haw River, North
Carolina. His wife, Lily, and son, James, are dancers. Mike, the grandson, plays
guitar.

F-B-10
DRY WOOD AND HOT PEPPER   A
        16mm   Sd   C   1973
        Flower Films   91 min
Two-part documentary about the life and music of French-speaking blacks in
southwestern Louisiana's Cajun country.

F-B-11
LAND WHERE THE BLUES BEGAN   A
        16mm, UBV   Sd   C   1980
        Phoenix Films   58 min
An examination of black folk culture in Mississippi: musical traditions and
community events, country picnics, a revival, work songs and other blues forms.

F-B-12
MUSIC MAKERS OF THE BLUE RIDGE   SCA

        UBV   Sd   1966
        INUAVC   48min
A sampling of traditional melodies and verses indigenous to the Blue Ridge
Mountains of North Carolina.

F-B-13
NASHVILLE SOUND, THE   A
        16mm   Sd   C
        Joseph Green Pictures   90 min
A musical about singer Herbie Howell arriving in Nashville to break into the music
business. Includes appearances by Roy Acuff, Johnny Cash, Lester Flatt, Doug
Kershaw, Loretta Lynn, Bill Monroe, Tracy Nelson and Mother Earth, Dolly
Parton, Charley Pride, Tex Ritter, Earl Scruggs, Hand Snow, the Stoney Mountain
Cloggers, Porter Wagoner and many others.

F-B-14
SPROUT WINGS AND FLY   A
        16mm, UBV   Sd   C   1982
        Flower Films   35 min
Old-time North Carolina mountain fiddler, humorist and storyteller Tommy Jarrell
is portrayed.

F-B-15
ZODICO: CREOLE MUSIC AND CULTURE   A
        16mm   Sd   C
        Gulfsouth Films   30 min
The music and social life of rural French-speaking blacks in St. Landry Parish,
Louisiana. Scenes of home life, clubs, festivals and religious activities. In English
and subtitled French.

F-B-16
FACTS OF LIFE, THE   A
        16mm, UBV   Sd   C   1982
        Beacon Films   28 min
Highlights of the film include a performance by Mr. Dixon and his band at
Theresa's Lounge in Chicago, and dramatic reenactments both humorous and
poignant, from his life.

F-B-17
FOLK SONGS IN AMERICA'S DEVELOPING YEARS   S
        FS, Cassettes (Series of 6 FS)   C   1976
        Coronet
        :Songs of Hope   62 frs
        :Songs of Love   53 frs
        :Songs of Politics   57 frs
        :Songs of Protest   56 frs
        :Songs of War   57 frs
        :Songs of Work   59 frs

F-B-18
GIVE MY POOR HEART EASE   A
        16mm   Sd   C   1975
        Center for Southern Folklore   20 min
Shows how the experiences of bluesmen who lived and worked in the Mississippi
Delta are expressed in their music.

F-B-19
GRAVEL SPRINGS FIFE AND DRUM   A
        16mm   Sd   C   1971
        Center for Southern Folklore   10 min
This is a documentation of traditional fife and drum music. It follows Othar

Turner and his family in the performance of their daily household and farm chores, and ends with Turner and his friends performing at a community picnic.

F-B-20
YONDER COME DAY   A
        16mm, UBV   S   1976
        MGHT   26 min
Through the songs and words of Bessie Jones, this program gives an anthology of slave culture.

Folklore - Oral Traditions

F-C-1
BEING A JOINES; A LIFE IN THE BRUSHY MOUNTAINS   A
        16mm, UBV   S   C   1980
        Tom Davenport Films   55 min
John E. "Frail" Joines is a master traditional tale teller who has lived almost all his life on the eastern slope of the Blue Ridge in North Carolina. The film portrays his tall tales, local anecdotes, stories of World War II and religious narratives.

F-C-2
CHESTER GRIMES   A
        16mm   Sd   C   1971
        Vermont Ctr for Cultural Studies   30 min
Chester Grimes, a 70-year-old logger, still works in the northern Vermont woods with his team of horses. His co-workers are dead, the logging camps are gone, the land grown up to brush or sold to summer outsiders. Chet camps on land not his own and laments the loss of community, the good farms gone by, the wrong of land bought up and left unused beyond the reach of those who feel "the land was put here for us to get a living with."

F-C-3
FOLKTALES OF BLACK AMERICA   A
        FS, Cassettes(4)   C   1977
        IFB
Presents 4 folk poems from the black oral tradition.

F-C-4
FREE SHOW TONITE   A
        16mm   Sd   C   1981
        Smithsonian Inst. Office of Folklife Programs   60min
A documentary about the recreation of a medicine show in North Carolina by a group of actual medicine show performers.

F-C-5
HARMONIZE: FOLKLORE IN THE LIVES OF FIVE FAMILIES   A
        16mm   Sd   C   1981
        Center for Southern Folklore   21min
In their day-to-day lives families create the stories, expressions and traditions which comprise their family folklore. The love of a family is born of the interrelationships among its members. The members of a family are like the singers in a barbershop quartet--their art is in the way they harmonize.

F-C-6
MERMAIDS, FROGLEGS AND FILLETS   A
    16mm   Sd   C   1980
    Pennsylvania State University   20min
The work and backgrounds of two "fish criers" -- one a black man from the inner
city of Washington, D.C., the other a white man from the rural Eastern Shore of
Virginia.

F-C-7
MR. STORY   A
    16mm   Sd   C   1973
    Phoenix Films   28min
Portrait of Albert Story, 86-year-old resident of Bloomingsburg, New York, ably
coping with the problems of old age in our society. Shows Mr. Story pumping his
own water, mowing his lawn, planting a garden, driving a car, shopping and
cooking his meals. He canes chairs, a dying craft, and he articulates some basic
contradictions in American moral life: the conflicts between his independence and
his loneliness, sexuality and his puritanical code of behavior.

F-C-8
PERFORMED WORD, THE   A
    16mm   Sd   C
    Center for Southern Folklore   56 min
The film examines a wide variety of performance situations and then relates them
to forms of Afro-American religious expression. Concludes with a display of
sermon music contrasting the preaching style of Berkeley, California's E.E.
Cleveland with that of his daughter, Pastor Ernestine Cleveland Reems.

F-C-9
RAY LUM: MULE TRADER   A
    16mm   Sd   C   1973
    Center for Southern Folklore   18min
Documents the life of Ray Lum, a unique storyteller and auctioneer. His stories
and life reflect the shift from an agricultural to an industrial society.

F-C-10
WE AIN'T WHAT WE WAS   SCA
    UBV   Sd   C   1978
    Maryland Center for Public Broadcasting   60min
Progressive look at the epic struggle of blacks to achieve freedom and equality in
American society.

F-C-11
YUDIE   A
    16mm   Sd   B   1974
    New Day Films   20min
A delightful old woman guides us through her past with insight, humor and
authority. Interwoven themes are Jewish immigration and life on New York's lower
East Side, living alone and aging.

Folklore -- Occupations

F-D-1
ARABIN' WITH THE HUCKSTERS OF BALTIMORE   A
      16mm   Sd   1977
      Brainstorm Films   25min
Using horse drawn wagons, the street hucksters of Baltimore, known as "Arabbers," h ve carried fresh produce and other wares to the city's neighborhoods for generations. Today, Baltimore is the only city where this traditional occupation survives. The film explores the streets of Baltimore by horse-drawn wagon. We hear the songs and witness the art of street hawking.

F-D-2
CATTLE DRIVE   A
      16mm   Sd   C   1981
      Jacques Bailhe   27 min
Cowboys, cattle trails, ranch life, social life and customs.

F-D-3
COWBOY HEAVEN   A
      UBV   Sd
      PBS Video   28min
A visual essay on the life of the cowboy. Emphasis is on the romance and camaraderie of the cowboy life.

F-D-4
THE FORGOTTEN WEST   A
      16mm   Sd   C   1973
      NGS   24min
Cowboy Bruce Shepherd and miner Billy Varga continue the tradition of roaming from town to town and job to job. Explore their life-styles by joining a cattle drive and by descending into the deepest hard-rock mine in the United States.

F-D-5
HOBO: AT THE END OF THE LINE   A
      16mm, V   Sd   C   1978
      EBEC   24min
The hobo as symbol of an American romantic tradition - living on the road, riding freight trains, and going to skid row missions for meals.

F-D-6
THE LAST FISHERMAN   A
      UBV   Sd   C
      PBS Video   29min
A film essay about the commercial fishers of the Great Lakes. Mavin Weborg, a third-generation northern Wisconsin fisher, and his sons are followed as they fish the waters of Lake Michigan from their gill-net tug.

F-D-7
THE LOBSTERMAN   A
      16mm   Sd   C   75min
      Preservation Ventures, Inc.   25.5min
Documentation of the history of lobster fishing, trap building, and lobster lore.

F-D-8
ROOT HOG OR DIE   A
          16mm   Sd   B
          Documentary Educational Resources   59min
A documentary, shot in western Massachusetts and southern Vermont, about farm
life in rural New England.

F-D-9
THOUGHTS ON FOX HUNTING   A
          16mm, V   Sd   C
          Tom Davenport   30min
The art of an American huntsman in traditional English-style fox hunting, filmed
near Middleburg, Virginia.

                    Folklore - Arts and Crafts

F-E-1
THE AFRO-AMERICAN TRADITION
   IN THE DECORATIVE ARTS   A
          UV   Sd   C   1978
          North State Public Video   13min
The rich Afro-American tradition in such folk arts as pottery, quilting,
metalworking, basketry and wood carving is revealed.

F-E-2
ANATOMY OF A MURAL   A
          16mm   Sd   C   1982
          Rick Goldsmith   15min
Documents the creation, from conception to completion, of a large mural painted
on the face of a Latino community cultural center in San Francisco.

F-E-3
THE BIRCH CANOE BUILDER   A
          16mm   Sd   C   1971
          ACI Media, Inc.   23min
Bill Hafeman, in his 70s, lives with his wife in the woods of northern Minnesota.
He talks of how he came to the woods in the 1920s, how he built a succession of
cabins, made a living through hunting, and how he builds authentic reproductions
of the traditional Indian birch canoe.

F-E-4
BIRTH OF A BUGEYE   A
          UBV   Sd
          Maryland Center for Public Broadcasting   30min
A documentary about the craftsmanship of a master shipwright from the Eastern
Shore of the Chesapeake Bay.

F-E-5
DUCK CARVERS   A
          16mm   Sd   C   1974
          Maryland Center for Public Broadcasting   24min
Duck carvers from Maryland's Eastern Shore explain their craft and show why this
particualar folk art is popular among collectors.

F-E-6
FINAL MARKS: THE ART OF THE CARVED LETTER   A
     16mm   Sd   C   1979
     Skylight Films   50min
A look at the work of the John Stevens Shop in Newport, Rhode Island, where
letters are still cut into stone by hand with hammer and chisel.

F-E-7
THE KENNEDY BRIDGE BUILDERS:
  COVERED BRIDGES OF SOUTHERN INDIANA   A
     UBV   Sd
     Monroe County Public Library   60min
The life and work of the covered bridge builder. The story of covered bridges is
told in relation to pioneer life, folk architecture and engineering skills.

F-E-8
LEARNED IT IN BACK DAYS AND KEPT IT   A
     UV   Sd   C   1981
     Florida Folklife Program   30min
Lucreaty Clark was born in 1904 on the Randall Plantation in North Florida. The
videotape documents her basketmaking, as well as her views on family, food
customs and religion.

F-E-9
LEON "PECK" CLARK: BASKETMAKER   A
     16mm   Sd   C   1980
     Center for Southern Folklore   15min
Leon "Peck" Clark and his wife, Ada, live in the rural community of Sharon,
Mississippi. The film follows Clark as he goes through his daily routine. He plows
a field with his mule, puts a new pig in a pen, walks into the woods and cuts
down a white-oak tree with his ax. Clark then tells stories of his youth. While
telling these stories, Clark is following the step-by-step processes of splitting
wood and running up a basket. The film concludes with the completion of the
basket and the knowledge that craftsmen like Clark are part of a passing
generation.

F-E-10
MADE IN MISSISSIPPI: BLACK FOLK ART AND CRAFTS   A
     16mm   Sd   C   1975
     Center for Southern Folklore   20min
Presents folk art, crafts, and architecture through interviews with a builder, an
artist, and craftspeople in rural Mississippi.

F-E-11
MARSHALL ABEL: BLACKSMITH   A
     UBV   Sd
     Monroe County Public Library   30min
T.M. "Marshall" Abel and his father were blacksmiths in the Bedford, Indiana,
area for over 50 years. In addition to traditional blacksmithing, they were also
involved in forging stone-carving tools for use in the limestone mills.

F-E-12
THE MEADERS FAMILY: NORTH GEORGIA POTTERS   A
     16mm, UBV   Sd   C   1980
     Pennsylvania State University   31min
A study of four members of the Meaders family of Cleveland, Georgia, as they
work at their kiln site. The family is seen working at every step in the process.

F-E-13
MURALS OF EAST LOS ANGELES, THE   A
    16mm   Sd   C   1977
    Cinetronics   37min
This film explores the murals and artists--both professional and amateur--who
create them.

F-E-14
QUILTS IN WOMEN'S LIVES   A
    16mm   Sd   C   1980
    New Day Films   28min
A series of portraits of traditional quiltmakers who describe their inspirations and
the meaning quilts have in their lives.

F-E-15
SERMONS IN WOOD   A
    16mm U   Sd   C   1976
    Center for Southern Folklore   27min
The life and art of Elijah Pierce, a black man born in Mississippi, who now lives
in Columbus, Ohio. Pierce carves both relief and free standing wood sculptures.

F-E-16
STONEY KNOWS HOW   A
    16mm, BV   Sd   C   1982
    Flower Films   29min
A portrait of tattoo artist Leonard L. "Stoney" St. Clair, who is a paraplegic and
a dwarf. He is seen with customers, friends, and another tattoo artist.

Folklore - Food

F-F-1
GUMBO--THE MYSTERIES OF CREOLE
  AND CAJUN COOKING   A
    16mm, U   Sd   C   1978
    Bayou Films, Gulfsouth Films   29min
The food and foodways of south Louisana, from New Orleans to the Cajun
country.

Folklore - Religion

F-G-1
COME DAY, GO DAY, GOD SEND SUNDAY   A
    16mm   Sd   C   1974
    NGS   52 min
Focuses on black church in rural Rappahannock County, Virginia.

F-G-2
IN THE RAPTURE   A
    16mm   Sd   C
    INUAVC   60 min
A traditional black church musical drama portraying the human struggle to resist
the temptations of Satan and follow Jesus.

F-G-3
OLD BELIEVERS   A
        16mm   Sd   C   1981
        Media Project   29 min
The Old Believers, or Starovery, are descendents of Russians who refused to
accept changes made by the patriarch Nikon in the Russian Orthodox Church in
1666. Those who survived torture and execution eventually migrated to many parts
of the world, including Oregon, where there is a community of 5,000.

F-G-4
PEOPLE WHO TAKE UP SERPENTS, THE   A
        16mm   Sd   C   1974
        Independent Southern Films, Inc.   53min
Examines personalities of believers in the Holiness Church of God in Jesus' Name.
Film includes scenes of the members handling a deadly cobra, the feeding of
snakes used in the church and a snake hunt.

F-G-5
SHAKERS, THE   A
        16mm   Sd   C   1974
        Tom Davenport Films   29min
This film traces the growth and decline of this remarkable religious sect through
memories and songs of the surviving Shakers themselves.

                        Folklore – Dance

F-H-1
NO MAPS ON MY TAPS   A
        16mm   Sd   C   1979
        Direct Cinema Ltd.   58min
The spirit of tap is shown in photos and Hollywood film clips of the 1930s. Three
surviving dancers—Sandman Sims, Chuck Green and Bunny Briggs—talk about their
lives, rehearse and perform.

                    Folklore – Festivals and Fairs

F-I-1
ALWAYS FOR PLEASURE   A
        16mm   Sd   C   1978
        Flower Films   58min
A view of public celebrations in New Orleans. The first section contains a jazz
funeral, Mardi Gras Activities and St. Patrick's Day parade. In the second part
Mardi Gras festivities in the black community are observed.

F-I-2
CHOCTAW: CHOCTAW INDIAN FAIR   A
        BVU   Sd   B   23min
        Native Amer. Videotape Archives   1976
Choctaw dancing and singing are presented, as well as a demonstration of making
stickball racquets and then the game itself.

F-I-3
LA DOLCE FESTA   A
        16mm   Sd   C   1978
        Cecropia Films   31min
Documents the Italian-American San Gennaro festival in New York City, which
lasts for 10 days and celebrates the patron saint of Naples. The festival is alive
with music, gambling, food, dancing, floats and saints being carried in the streets.
The film uses the festival as a window on New York's" Little Italy."

F-I-4
MORRIS FAMILY OLD TIME MUSIC FESTIVAL   A
        16mm   Sd   1980
        Omnificent Systems   30min
A film about the 1972 music festival held by the Morris Brothers at their home in
Ivydale, West Virginia. The festivals were held from 1969 to 1973, attracting
many traditional musicians.

F-I-5
RAMSEY TRADE FAIR, THE   A
        16mm   Sd   1973
        Appalshop Films   18min
Ramsey Day is a weekly flea-market in the small coalfield community of Ramsey,
Virginia, a microcosm of rural Appalachian life and values. Appearing in the film
are Bill Burleson, a 76-year-old trader of guns and knives, and the folk poet and
singer, blind Bill Denham, who plays a guitar and harmonica.

F-I-6
WELCOME TO SPIVEY'S CORNER, N.C.   A
        16mm   Sd   C   1979
        Perspective Films   16min
Spivey's Corner, N.C., is aptly named the "Hollerin' Capital of the World." A
serene farm community, it becomes a gigantic, ear-splitting festival each June as
it hosts the National Hollerin' Contest.

Geography

John B. Garver, Jr.

This section of the catalog relates primarily to Geography. For the purposes of this work, Geography may be viewed as an orderly presentation of the diverse physical and man-made landscape of the United States. It provides a special geographic perspective on the American people and their habitat, on the human and non-human activities which occur in varied regional environments, and on the interrelationships between places. The list contains items whose content and treatment are either topical or regional. Examples of topical treatment are: Agricultural America, America's Wetlands, Industrial America, and The River. Examples of regional coverage are: The Appalachian Highlands, Hawaii: The 50th State, The Great Plains Experience, and The Middle Atlantic Region. Most of the materials listed deal with contemporary America, although some films begin with historic treatment of the region so the audience can better appreciate how the region evolved into its present day form. The majority of these resources are appropriate for the secondary level, while some also relate to adult audiences. This list is an attempt to select from hundreds of choices those films, filmstrips and cassettes that best portray the contemporary American landscape to people who live in other parts of the world. Sources for other materials dealing with geography can be found in the audiovisual libraries at major universities in the United States and other agencies listed in the front of this catalogue.

GEOGRAPHY (G)

G-A	General
G-B	Agriculture
G-C	Natural Resources
G-D	Regions
G-E	Sites and National Parks
G-F	States
G-G	Urbanization and Cities

Geography - General

G-A-1
AGRICULTURAL AMERICA: UNITED STATES GEOGRAPHY   SCA
          FS, 4 Cassettes   C   1979
          SSSS
America has been blessed with fertile land and beneficent climate; nevertheless,
American small farmers are facing harder and harder times financially. This
program focuses on these problems through case studies and historical
illustrations. The role of the U.S. as a major world food supplier is examined, as
are the effects of terrain on agriculture, climate, industrialization, and
technology.

G-A-2
AMERICAN SPECTACLE   A
          16mm   Sd   C   1964
          NBC News   34min
A scenic tour of the United States, from Cape Cod to glacial Lake George in
Alaska, views many natural spectacles such as Niagara Falls, Yellowstone National
Park, Grand Canyon, Death Valley, Yosemite, and others. The journey ends in
Hawaii with scenes of rare and beautiful flowers, and of Mauna Loa, an active
volcano. Narrated by Van Heflin.

G-A-3
AMERICAN TIME CAPSULE   A
          16mm   Sd   C   1968
          Pyramid Films   3min
Condenses two hundred years of American history into three minutes. Using a
"flash frame" technique, 1,300 pictures are photographed at rates ranging from
one-twelfth to two-thirds of a second. Youthful audiences will find this film an
especially attractive discussion-starter that graphically demonstrates the speed
with which America and the idea of the "frontier" have changed.

G-A-4
GEOGRAPHY OF THE UNITED STATES   A
          UBV   Sd   C   1973
          BFA   15min
The diverse aspects, life styles, resources, and business characteristics of the five
major regions in the USA are analyzed. The five programs in the series are
available individually: 1. Great Plains, 2. Middle West, 3. Northeast, 4. Pacific
States, 5. South.

G-A-5
INDUSTRIAL AMERICA   A
          FS, 5 cassettes   C   1980
          SSSS
Abundant resources, a continent-wide mass market, and an ambitious population
are key factors that have spurred tremendous industrial growth in the United
States. This program outlines the geographic factors that determine the location
of specific industries, and shows how this pattern is changing as a result of
energy requirements, technological developments, and foreign competition.

G-A-6
LIVING IN THE UNITED STATES   S
    16mm,UBV   Sd   C   1974
    Coronet   13min
From Hawaii to New England, from Alaska to the Southern States, this sweeping
overview of the nation, its people, and their work introduces each of the nine
state groupings treated in depth in the related series. This second edition shifts
emphasis from physical geography to human geography and reflects current social
studies directions.

G-A-7
MISSION TO EARTH: PART 1, PHYSICAL GEOGRAPHY   A
    U   Sd   C   1977
    Barr Films   15min
The crew of a spaceship from an unknown galaxy gathers data on the physical
terrain of Earth and how it is affected by external forces.

G-A-8
PANORAMA: THESE UNITED STATES   S
    FS, Cassettes(8)   C   1980
    SSSS
The unique character of the American landscape is portrayed in this sweeping
view of our diverse nation. Color filmstrips tour eight regions of the country to
explore our cultural and physical habitats—from breathtaking national parks,
scenic deserts, and endless rural plains to the hum of industry and commerce in
urban centers. The emphasis on people and the American quality of life gives
students a taste of each region's special charm, proud past, and future promise.

G-A-9
PHYSICAL HABITAT   S
    FS, Cassettes(4)   C   1980
    SSSS
Americans have found uses for most of their varied physical habitats, minimizing
deficiencies where they exist. This program looks at the changing environment and
the development of land usage from the times of early settlement to projected
future development. Regional characteristics such as size, boundaries, physical
features, climate, and resources are examined light of natural and human impact
on the land.

G-A-10
REDISCOVERING AMERICA   A
    U   Sd   C   1979
    Dallas County Community College   29min
This program recalls the first travelers from the east to rediscover and explore
the various parts of the American continent in a dramatization by the Black
Ghetto Theater.

Geography - Agriculture

G-B-1
GREEN ECHO OF SNOW   A
    16mm,UBV   Sd   C   1977
    NAVC   25min
What was once known as part of the "Great American Desert" in northern
Colorado is now 1.5 million acres of lush farm land. This imaginative

dramatization traces the development of the region known as the Northern Colorado Water Conservancy District, from its arid, inhospitable beginning to its present state—thanks to a planned program of irrigation, channel construction, and reservoir building—pro ucing hydroelectric power, abundant crops and sparkling water.

G-B-2
MAKING THE DESERT GREEN   A
    16mm   Sd   C   1966
    EBEC   16min
A case study for the Pacific Southwest region, this film introduces the concept of water management and scientific farming to children. Shows the method of irrigation used in the Coachella Valley, California, which has changed this dry soil into the richest farm land acre for acre in the world today.

G-B-3
TWO FARMS: HUNGARY AND WISCONSIN   A
    16mm   Sd   C   1973
    LCA   22min
Two Farms provides an incisive comparison of the lifestyles of an independent Wisconsin farmer and a collective farm family in southeastern Hungary. At first glance, the two seem as far apart culturally as they are geographically, but both share an abiding love of the land, a joy in the growing cycle and close family ties.

G-B-4
TWO GRASSLANDS: TEXAS AND IRAN   A
    16mm   Sd   1971
    LCA   21min
The Edwards Plateau in Texas and the steppes of Iran are regions similar in rainfall pattern and sparsity of vegetation. By exploring the lifestyles of the ranchers of Texas and the Qashqai herdsmen of Iran, the relationship between man and his environment is stressed.

Geography – Natural Resources

G-C-1
AMERICA'S WETLANDS   A
    16mm   Sd   C
    NAVC   28min
America's Wetlands, from the Atchafalaya River Swamp in lower Louisiana to Alaska's arctic tundra, have been traditionally viewed as worthless and dispensable; they, however, have their hidden values which are beneficial to man and wildlife. This film conveys these benefits and the potential impact of the loss of these Wetlands.

G-C-2
COLORADO RIVER, THE   S
    16mm,UBV   Sd   1968
    Coronet   12 1/2min
High in the Rocky Mountains begin the headwaters of the Colorado River and its tributaries. Draining an area almost one-quarter million square miles in the southwestern United States, the river system provides water to a semi-arid yet

developing region. Its dams provide electric power, recreation and help eliminate floods and drought.

G-C-3
COLUMBIA RIVER, THE   S
    16mm,UBV   Sd   1966
    Coronet   11min
Colossal, multi-purpose dams introduce us to the importance of the Columbia River system, the world's largest single source of hydroelectric power. Historical footage of floods, the initial construction of Grand Coulee, and the U.S.-Canadian agreements for further development detail man's triumphs in harnessing the great waterway.

G-C-4
GREAT LAKES   A
    UBV   Sd   C   1972
    EBEC   17min
Demonstrates the importance of the Great Lakes to the development and economy of mid-America. Also stressed is the need for conservation.

G-C-5
GREAT WEB OF WATER, THE:
  THE CENTRAL VALLEY PROJECT   A
    16mm   Sd   C   1982
    NAVC   28min
Describes the federal Central Valley Project (CVP) in California, one of the world's largest water management developments. Depicts the physical structures of the CVP, the flow of water from north to south, the changing seasons—in nature, in agriculture, in industry, in human activities, and the 500-mile water control and distribution system in Central Valley.

G-C-6
GULF ISLANDS BEACHES, BAYS, SOUNDS AND BAYOUS   SCA
    16mm,UBV   Sd   C   1982
    NAVC   28min
Shaped by waves and wind, several hundred barrier islands rim the Atlantic and Gulf Coasts. Viewers of all ages will enjoy learning about the composition, features, and living organisms of these islands and surrounding waters. The film shows fascinating close-ups of tiny shellfish, ghost crabs, carnivorous snakes and sea milkworts...defines geographical terms...reviews the history of the islands...and examines mankind's impact on the Gulf Islands' delicate balance of life.

G-C-7
MISSISSIPPI RIVER, THE   S
    16mm,UBV   Sd   C   1977
    Coronet   14 1/2min
A fascinating examination of the river and its people—the ndians who named it, the European explorers who charted it, the settlers who developed the basin, and the people today who use the Mississippi for commerce and industry.

G-C-8
MISSISSIPPI SYSTEM: WATERWAYS OF COMMERCE, THE   A
            UBV   Sd   C   1970
            EBEC   16min
Traces the development of river traffic that started soon after DeSoto discovered
the Mississippi in 1541 until the present. The program also explores the Big Flood
of 1927.

G-C-9
MISSOURI RIVER, THE:
  BACKGROUND FOR SOCIAL STUDIES   S
            16mm,UBV   Sd   C   1971
            Coronet   12 1/2min
Lewis and Clark began exploring the Missouri River in 1804 and were followed by
settlers who founded communities like Omaha and Kansas City. The river and its
tributaries were a serious threat until 1944 when construction of dams and levees
began to control the river. Today, problems like water pollution must still be
solved.

G-C-10
OHIO RIVER, THE: BACKGROUND FOR SOCIAL STUDIES   S
            16mm,UBV   Sd   C   1967
            Coronet   10 1/2min
Colonists floating down the Ohio River helped to settle many present- day cities.
Its enormous volume of water and nearby coal fields have attracted steel,
chemical, aluminum, and atomic energy plants, and efforts are being made to solve
problems of water pollution, flood control and increasing traffic.

G-C-11
OHIO RIVER--UPPER VALLEY   A
            UBV   Sd   C   1971
            Academy Films   11min
Examines the Upper Valley of one of the most important "commercial" rivers in
the United States.

G-C-12
RIO GRANDE IN NEW MEXICO, THE   A
            U   Sd   C   1976
            Blue Sky Productions   40min
Follows the history of the Rio Grande from the San Juan Mountains of Colorado
to El Paso. Covers New Mexico's people, culture, and landscape.

G-C-13
RIVER, THE   A
            16mm   Sd   B   1937
            NAVC   32min
Classic documentary story of the Mississippi River and its reflection of the
conservation needs of the nation. Produced and written by Pare Lorentz for the
U.S. Department of Agriculture. Music by Virgil Thomson.

G-C-14
STORY OF THE GREAT LAKES   A
            16mm   Sd   B   1954
            NAVC   25min
Depicts the overall economic significance of the Great Lakes and the important

role played by the coast guard thereon. A cycle of one full year is covered.

G-C-15
TWO DESERTS: SAHARA AND SONORA   S
          16mm   Sd   C   1971
          LCA   17min
Separated by ten thousand miles, the Sahara Desert in Africa and the Sonora
Desert in America are geologically identical but they look, and are, utterly
different. Looking at the sharply contrasting lifestyles, the film reveals why in
one desert man changed the land, and in the other adapted himself to it.

G-C-16
WHERE DID THE COLORADO GO?   A
          16mm   Sd   C   1976
          Time-Life Multi-Media   59min
The Colorado River used to flow into the ocean, and once there were paddlewheel
steamers that went up the river between Colorado and Arizona for 500 miles to
the Nevada border. The changes made by man on this once great river are
discussed over motion pictures made from its point of origin in the Rockies to
Mexico, where the last of its waters disappears into sand about 20 miles inland
from the sea. The vast lakes, gigantic dams, irrigation ditches, canals, and Glen
Canyon are all part of man's achievements. What each of these projects
contributed to the fate of the river is pointed out. Closing sequence covers the
possibility that water from the Columbia and Mississippi Rivers may have to be
diverted to save the Colorado. Several alternatives are presented and the pros
and cons of their feasibility are compared.

G-C-17
YUKON PASSAGE   A
          16mm,UBV   Sd   C   1977
          NGS   59min
Join four adventurers who run the Yukon River and sample life along its course.

                        Geography - Regions

G-D-1
AMERICAN SOUTHWEST--LAND OF ENRICHMENT, THE   A
          UBV   Sd   C   1968
          RMI Media Productions   9min
Features Monument Valley, the Grand Canyon, Arches National Monu- ment.
Prairie dogs, horned toads, rattlesnakes and deer are shown in their natural
habitat.

G-D-2
APPALACHIA: RICH LAND, POOR PEOPLE   A
          16mm   Sd   B   1969
          INUAVC   59min
A detailed, revealing study of Appalachian poverty; the reasons behind it and its
effect on the people of this region of eastern Kentucky. Includes interviews with
a family, mine owners, and other members of the community.

G-D-3
APPALACHIAN HIGHLANDS, THE   A
        16mm   Sd   C   1967
        Coronet   13min
Stretching from northeastern Canada to southern Alabama, the Appalachian
Highlands are characterized by an extensive mountain system, flowing waters, and
large and small valleys. Light manufacturing, cash crop farming, and mining have
been traditional, but the area is being changed by conservation, public works
projects, and new industries.

G-D-4
DENALI WILDERNESS   S
        16mm,UBV   Sd   C   1982
        NAVC   30min
Carved out of a sub-arctic region of Alaska, Denali National Park and Preserve is
home to a wide variety of animal life including caribou, moose, Dall sheep, grizzly
bears, wolves, and red foxes. In this land of the eight month winter, the cycle of
life dictates that only the fittest of species survive.

G-D-5
GEOGRAPHY, CLIMATE, AND NATURAL RESOURCES
    IN THE NORTHCENTRAL REGION   A
        FS, Cassette   C   1972
        Eye Gate House   41 frs
Title describes content.

G-D-6
GEOGRAPHY, CLIMATE AND NATURAL RESOURCES
    IN THE NORTHEAST   A
        FS, Cassette   C   1972
        Eye Gate House   40 frs
Title describes content.

G-D-7
GEOGRAPHY, CLIMATE, AND NATURAL RESOURCES
    IN THE SOUTH   S
        FS, Cassette   C   1972
        Eye Gate Housc   48frs
Title describes content.

G-D-8
GEOGRAPHY OF THE FIVE PACIFIC STATES   A
        U   Sd   C   1966
        Barr Films   15min
Surveys the physical and cultural geography of the five Pacific states and
explains how the physical geography affects man's activities.

G-D-9
GRASSLAND REGIONS: FARMERS AND HERDERS   A
        UBV   Sd   C   1980
        BFA   15min
The environmentalists and cultures of herdsmen in the Kenyan grasslands and
farmers of the Midwest are depicted. Similarities and differences are drawn and
the effects of culture on life-styles are indicated.

G-D-10
GREAT PLAINS, THE   A
    16mm,UBV   Sd   C   1976
    Adams County Historic Society   22min
This film describes the geography of the area. It tells of early Indian history; the
Spanish, French and American explorations; the fur traders, missionaries and
military forts; the Oregon, Santa Fe and other trails that took people through the
area; and the early days of settlement.

G-D-11
GREAT PLAINS EXPERIENCE, THE   A
    U   Sd   C   1975
    NETCHE   30min
No matter how the Great Plains is defined, the region in large measure has
defined the lives of the people who inhabit it. There is special ecology, culture,
and a special experience on the Great Plains.

G-D-12
INDUSTRY, AGRICULTURE, AND COMMERCE IN
  THE NORTH CENTRAL REGION   S
    FS, Cassette   C   1972
    Eye Gate House   41 frs
Title describes content.

G-D-13
INDUSTRY, AGRICULTURE, AND COMMERCE IN
  THE NORTHEAST   S
    FS, Cassette   C   1972
    Eye Gate House   36 frs
Title describies content.

G-D-14
INTERIOR WEST: THE LAND NOBODY WANTED, THE   A
    UBV   Sd   C   1966
    EBEC   20min
Presents the different points of view as to how the land and its resources should
be used, now that irrigation and water control make it possible to farm and build
modern cities there.

G-D-15
LIVING IN THE MIDDLE ATLANTIC STATES:
  URBAN COMPLEX   S
    16mm,UBV   Sd   1974
    Coronet   15min
Together, New York, Pennsylvania, New Jersey, Delaware, Maryland and West
Virginia contain more than one-quarter of the nation's population with many urban
centers reflecting the essence of modern metropolitan life. A department store
worker, factory foreman, truck farmer, toll-collector, and railroad yard master
talk about living and working in megalopolis.

G-D-16
LIVING IN THE MIDWESTERN STATES:
    THE NATION'S HEARTLAND   S
        16mm,UBV   Sd   C   1974
        Coronet   12 1/2min
The Midwestern states of Ohio, Indiana, Michigan, Illinois and Wisconsin integrate
transportation, manufacturing, marketing and farming to create a highly
productive industrial and agricultural region. A farmer, secretary, commodities
trader, and automobile assembler show how their jobs relate to their section of
the Midwest and to the rest of the nation.

G-D-17
LIVING IN THE NEW ENGLAND STATES:
    BIRTHPLACE OF A NATION   S
        16mm,UBV   Sd   C   1974
        Coronet   12 1/2min
The people of Maine, Vermont, New Hampshire, Massachusetts, Connecticut, and
Rhode Island live amid reminders of American tradition and history. People in
lobstering, innkeeping, shoemaking, and electronic research reflect some of the
changes from colonial New England to the resort and commercial regions of today.

G-D-18
LIVING IN THE PACIFIC STATES:
    VARIETY AND CHANGE   S
        16mm,UBV   Sd   C   1974
        Coronet   14min
Washington, Oregon, and California enjoy a wide range of history, geography,
resources, and lifestlyes. Five people in various occupations in the fields of
logging, aerospace, fishing, recreation, and farming talk about their work and
their reasons for living in the Pacific States.

G-D-19
LIVING IN THE PLAINS STATES:
    MEAT AND GRAIN   S
        16mm,UBV   Sd   C   1974
        Coronet   12 1/2min
From raising livestock to processing food, feeding the nation is the main business
of North Dakota, South Dakota, Nebraska, Kansas, Minnesota, Iowa, and Missouri.
A corn belt farmer, wheat belt farm implement dealer, and cereal mill worker
give their impressions of the Plains States.

G-D-20
LIVING IN THE ROCKY MOUNTAIN STATES:
    CHANGING FRONTIER LANDS   S
        16mm,UBV   Sd   C   1974
        Coronet   15min
The people of Montana, Idaho, Wyoming, Colorado, Utah, and Nevada live in a
region of spectacular natural beauty. Mountains, deserts, salt flats, and glaciers
make this one of the nation's most majestic areas. A park ranger, mining foreman,
meat inspector, engineer, and geology student talk about living and working there.

G-D-21
LIVING IN THE SOUTHERN STATES:
  HISTORIC LANDS, NEW IDEAS   S
          16mm,UBV   Sd   C   1974
          Coronet   13 1/2min
Virginia, Kentucky, Tennessee, North Carolina, South Carolina, Georgia, Florida,
Arkansas, Alabama, Mississippi and Louisiana share a splendid heritage of
American history. Voices of the new south are heard as a tugboat captain, a
geneticist, workers at a poultry farm, peanut butter factory, and textile mill talk
about life and work.

G-D-22
LIVING IN THE SOUTHWESTERN STATES:
  GROWTH IN THE DESERT   S
          16mm,UBV   Sd   C   1974
          Coronet   15min
The climate and vast open spaces of the southwest continue to attract new
residents at a phenomenal rate to Arizona, New Mexico, Oklahoma, and Texas. A
cowboy, Indian, prospector, oil man, and tour guide talk about the advantages of
living in the Southwestern States.

G-D-23
MANUFACTURING MIDWEST, THE   A
          UBV   Sd   C   1976
          CRM/McGraw Hill   18min
This program looks at the resources, transportation, and great industrial centers
of the Midwest and then explores all the problems that go with these things.

G-D-24
MIDDLE ATLANTIC REGION, THE   A
          UBV   Sd   C   1976
          CRM/ McGraw Hill   17min
This program looks at the cities that span the mideastern seaboard. These cities
provide services for many people. Often there are problems and advantages
involving the cities' functions. Pi River in 1804 and were followed by
settlers who founded communities like Omaha and Kansas City. ems.

G-D-25
MIDDLE WEST, THE   A
          UBV   Sd   C   1973
          BFA   13min
The Middle West--its history, industries, and physical features--is presented in
this show.

G-D-26
NEW ENGLAND REGION, THE   A
          UBV   Sd   C   1976
          CRM/McGraw Hill   15min
Today New England enjoys a thriving technology-based business. This program
from the "United States Geography" series shows how traditions have given the
people of this region respect for their past and an adaptability to their changing
present.

G-D-27
NORTHEAST   A
            UBV   Sd   C   1972
            BFA   15min
The Northeastern seacoast--its history, industries, and physical features--is
presented in this program.

G-D-28
NORTHWEST USA   A
            16mm   Sd   B   1945
            NAVC   22min
Reviews the resources, industries, and people of Oregon and Washington.

G-D-29
PACIFIC NORTHWEST, THE   A
            UBV   Sd   C   1976
            CRM/McGraw Hill   17min
This program shows how the Pacific Northwest combines development with
preservation. The area has plans to encourage industrial development while
remaining a place where people want to live.

G-D-30
PACIFIC WEST, THE   S
            16mm   Sd   C   1969
            EBEC   24min
Presents an overview of the Pacific West--its people, resources, industries, cities,
and opportunities. Focuses on the lives of four men who live and work in the
Pacific West. Reviews some of the history of the Pacific West and speculates on
the future of this region.

G-D-31
PLAINS PEOPLE   A
            UBV   Sd   C   1971
            STERLED   14min
The Masai, nomadic herdsmen of Kenya and Tanganyika, and the Indians of the
North Cheyenne Reservation in Montana are seen in this program. Non-narrative.

G-D-32
PLOW THAT BROKE THE PLAINS, THE   A
            16mm   Sd   B   1936
            NAVC   25min
A classic documentary from the 1930s which depicts the social and economic
history of the Great Plains from settlement of the prairies by cattlemen and
farmers through the World War I boom to drought and Depression.

G-D-33
SEEING THE SOUTHEASTERN STATES- LAND AND CLIMATE   S
            FS   Sd   1972
            Coronet   53 frs
Explores the diversity of the land and climate found in the southeastern part of
the United States, from the red clay soil of the Piedmont to the white sands of
Florida.

G-D-34
SOUTH   A
     UBV   Sd   C   1972
     BFA   14min
The southeastern part of the United States is one of the most rapidly changing
areas in the country.

G-D-35
SOUTH ATLANTIC REGION   A
     UBV   Sd   C   1976
     CRM/McGraw Hill   14min
A look at the new South--emerging hopefully with the best of the old intact.

G-D-36
SOUTH CENTRAL REGION, THE   A
     UBV   Sd   C   1976
     CRM/McGraw Hill   15min
This program examines the South Central region where some states are heavily
into oil and energy, yet still searching for new fuel sources.

G-D-37
SOUTHERN APPALACHIA   S
     FS, Cassette   C   1972
     SVE   99 frs
Examines poverty, unemployment and other problems of southern Appalachia.
Investigates their causes and relationship to mountain geography. Features the
area's mining activity and discusses problems associated with strip mining. Profiles
a variety of regional life-styles including the detailed study of a West Virginia
dairy farmer.

G-D-38
SOUTHWEST, THE   A
     UBV   Sd   C   1976
     CRM/McGraw Hill   17min
This program from the "United States Geography" series looks at how the scenic
surroundings and warm, dry climate make the Southwest the fastest growing
region of the country.

Geography - Sites and National Parks

G-E-1
AMAZING GRACE   A
     16mm   Sd   C   1979
     NAVC   10min
Exquisite photography and an enchanting score convey the essence of the majestic
trees of the Sequoia National Park in California. Communicating through images
alone, this program is well-suited for viewing by hearing-impaired students. Among
the towering perennials of the park is the General Sherman tree--the largest
living thing in the world.

G-E-2
FANTASTIC YELLOWSTONE   A
        16mm,UBV   Sd   C   1979
        NAVC   25min
Old Faithful, the Grand Canyon, abounding wildlife...for years, Yellowstone
National Park has offered the country a truly fantastic collection of natural
wonders. But it has also given the world another kind of gift, one as special as
any of its physical offerings: the concept of a "national park." Following
expeditions through the breathtaking wilderness, Congress in 1872 made
Yellowstone the first national park. This visual account documents vital phases in
Yellowstone's history.

G-E-3
FLAMING GORGE--A STORY WRITTEN IN WATER   A
        16mm,UBV   Sd   C   1979
        NAVC   22min
The story of Flaming Gorge, Utah, "begins and ends with water." Scenes of
rushing water, dramatic rocky cliffs, and peaceful wildlife, counterbalance man's
use of the Gorge for agriculture, industry, and recreation. Here we learn the
history of the area, from early Indian settlers to fur trappers, and from
observations of explorer-geologist John Wesley Powell.

G-E-4
GIANT SEQUOIA   A
        16mm,UBV   Sd   C   1979
        NAVC   17min
The Sequoia trees are monuments of nature--monuments that cover 850,000 acres
of the Sequoia National Park located between San Francisco and Los Angeles.
Here is the natural science story of these giant trees, including new material on
the roles played by animals in the reproduction of the Sequoia species and on the
effects of forest fires.

G-E-5
HOOVER DAM STORY, THE   A
        16mm,UBV   Sd   C   1962
        NAVC   28min
Hailed by the American Society of Civil Engineers as one of the seven modern
civil engineering wonders, the Hoover Dam transformed the Pacific southwest by
relieving the area of periodic flooding and drought, and providing hydroelectric
power as well. Through the use of fascinating archival footage, viewers follow the
planning, construction, and completion of this huge and complex dam, built nearly
50 years ago.

G-E-6
LIVING WATERS OF THE BIG CYPRESS   SCA
        16mm   Sd   C   1980
        NAVC   14min
Viewers are given the rare opportunity to observe the activities and lifestyles of
the inhabitants of the wilderness--the plants and animals that live
interdependently in the Big Cypress National Preserve--the first national preserve
located in the Everglades. In addition to close-up views of various life forms, we
learn about the geography and seasonal change of the estuaries.

;-E-7
*ARK TWAIN: WHEN I WAS A BOY   A
    16mm   Sd   C   1977
    NGS   25min
*ark Twain's best writing always seems to start with, "When I was a boy..."
wain spent his youth along the mighty Mississippi River. Uses Twain's own words
⊃ demonstrate the river's formative influence on his imagination. A major focus
& Twain's passage to maturity—from cub to master pilot of a Mississippi
teamboat. During his apprenticeship to the great pilot Bixby, Twain must "learn"
,000 miles of river, and himself as well.

;-E-8
ATIONAL PARKS: A PLAYGROUND OR PARADISE   A
    16mm   Sd   C   1981
    NGS   59min
'an we both use and preserve our national parks? Visits to Yellowstone,
osemite, and the Grand Canyon point out the dilemma. Alaska has set aside land
is a wilderness reserve, while urban parks are emerging as a new park frontier.

;-E-9
A-HAY-OKEE   A
    16mm   Sd   C   1982
    NAVC   18min
n artistic look at the creatures and qualities of the Everglades National Park
*hich demonstrates a tolerable balance between man and natural resources.

;-E-10
ANCTUARY—THE GREAT SMOKY MOUNTAINS   SCA
    16mm,UBV   Sd   C   1979
    NAVC   10min
he incredible diversity of geography and wildlife make the Great Smoky
ountains National Park a sanctuary worth preserving for all time. Lush, lyrical
limpses of nature in all seasons give the viewer several moments to ponder the
eauty...experience the exhilaration...and nourish the imagination. This special
rogram will enrich curricula from elementary through adult education.

-E-11
EARCH FOR ACADIA, THE   A
    16mm,UBV   Sd   C   1980
    NAVC   15min
he pounding surf of Maine's Acadia National Park symbolizes the struggle
etween land and sea. Here, an array of images are contrasted: a quiet fog and
he awesome power of a stormy sea...tales of the schooners that once scuttled
long the coast of Mt. Desert Island and the tourists enjoying the park's inviting
andscape today.

Geography - States

-F-1
LASKA: THE 49TH STATE   SC
    16mm   Sd   C   1960
    EBEC   17min
isualizes the natural beauty of Alaska, and developments of the five geographic

areas, showing the land, resources, the people and their work. Surveys the rapidl
growing cities, the homesteads, farmlands and major industrial development.

G-F-2
GEOGRAPHY OF ALASKA AND HAWAII   SA
    16mm,UBV   Sd   1970
    Coronet   15 1/2min
The story of our two newest states is one of continuing change and development
Alaska, with its rich and colorful history, is a vast area with resources not ye
fully developed. Hawaii, with its exotic past, its sugar and pineapple industries
and its military bases, is growing rapidly as a tourist attraction.

G-F-3
HAWAII: THE 50TH STATE   SCA
    16mm   Sd   C   1059
    EBEC   17min
Presents an overview of Hawaii and a brief history of the volcanic formatior
Reviews the history of early Polynesian settlement and the influence of divers
cultures on the present way of life in Hawaii.

G-F-4
ONE MAN'S ALASKA   A
    16mm,UBV   Sd   C   1977
    NAVC   27min
A documentary profile of Dick Proenneke (conservationist, wildlife photographer
at his home in the Lake Clark area of Alaska features closeup scenes of nativ
wildlife, dramatic panoramas of the change of seasons, and clips of Proennek
carving his log cabin out of the wilderness. This man's singular harmony with h
environment and with the wildlife he photographs is demonstrated both i
commentary and in picture.

Geography - Urbanization and Cities

G-G-1
AMERICAN CITY, THE: PROBLEMS AND PROMISE   S
    FS, 5 Cassettes   1975
    NGS   12-14min
The past, present and future of American cities: The Growth of the City; Th
City at Work; Living in the City; Governing the City; Toward a Better City.

G-G-2
MEGALOPOLIS   A
    16mm   Sd   C   1972
    INUAVC   29min
Observes that cities are growing into one huge, man-made environment,
megalopolis, which devotes too much land to the automobile and looks at on
solution to the problem. Focuses on the new city of Park Forest South, Illinois,
which paths were constructed to allow pedestrians and cyclists to trav
throughout the city without crossing the main streets. Points out that ci
planners believe the technology is available to build cities which provide f
varying life styles.

G-G-3
TWO CITIES: LONDON AND NEW YORK   A
     16mm   Sd   C   1973
     LCA   23min
Two international capitals--one fast-paced, restless, multi-national, the mecca for
success to many Americans--the other, a busy financial and cultural center of
British life, yet predominantly people-oriented.

G-G-4
TWO FAMILIES: AFRICAN AND AMERICAN   A
     16mm   Sd   1974
     LCA   22min
The film confronts two contemporary family structures; an interdependent African
tribal family and an independent space-age family in New York City. Members of
the American family pride themselves on being individuals, while the African clan
is governed by a sense of unity.

G-G-5
TWO TOWNS: GUBBIO, ITALY AND CHILLICOTHE, OHIO   A
     16mm   Sd   1973
     LCA   22min
Chillicothe, in southeastern Ohio, and Gubbio, located north of Rome, are both
agricultural centers. Yet, one lifestyle looks to the future, while the other recalls
the past. For all their differences, the film uncovers a civic pride and
responsibility that may be a common bond of all small towns.

History

John W. Larner

The United States history audiovisual teaching materials included in this list reflect a range of topics, formats, philosophical bents and resulting historical interpretations. The emphasis in selecting these materials has been on diversity. It is hoped that teachers working in many different settings can find included here some materials suited to a variety of teaching styles and a host of student needs and interests.

It will be evident that the number of items appearing under the History headings varies from one topic to another. As might be the case with any of the communications media, the volume of materials on any given historical subject is largely dependent on popular and professional interest as well as availability of suitable pictorial and aural source material. Where such audiovisual primary sources are lacking, historical dramatizations simulate events described mainly in written accounts. Clearly, some themes better lend themselves to audiovisual communi- cation than others -- a fact obviously surfacing in this list.

It must be recognized that the same canons of historical reasoning that we encourage students to develop with written presentations apply equally well to audiovisual materials. Whether the piece be a classic period film or recording, a contemporary dramatization of an historical episode, or a thematic collage of primary source visuals and sounds, it is urgent that students not allow themselves to be lulled or enthralled to uncritical acceptance. Students of this era possess unparalleled sensitivities to sights and sounds; yet the potency of their powers to decode, reflect, select and reason still largely depends on effective classroom analysis and critique of what is viewed and heard.

HISTORY (H)

H-A	Native Americans
H-B	Women/Minorities
H-C	Regional History
H-D	Intellectual
H-E	Legal
H-F	Longterm Views and Special Syntheses
H-G	Religious
H-H	17th Century
H-I	18th Century
H-J	19th Century
H-K	20th Century

History – Native Americans

H-A-1
EXCAVATION OF MOUND   A
        16mm   Sd   C   1973
        NAVC   44min
Describes the mysteries of the Indian Pueblo de las Humanas at Gran Quivira
National Monument, New Mexico.

H-A-2
INDIAN REORGANIZATION ACT, THE   A
        Audio-Cassette   1981
        NPR   29min
The Indian Reorganization Act, approved by President Franklin Roosevelt in 1934,
recognized the right of Indian tribes to exist perpetually as culturally and
politically distinct sovereigns.

H-A-3
INDIAN POTTER OF SAN ILDEFONSO   A
        16mm   Sd   C   1972
        NAVC   27min
Maria Martinez, a noted Indian potter, demonstrates the traditional Indian ways.
Shows mixing of clay, construction of pottery, hand decorating, and building of
the firing mound.

H-A-4
IOWA'S ANCIENT HUNTERS   A
        16mm   Sd   C   1976
        University of Iowa Audiovisual Center   28min
In 1976, a team of specialists including archaeologists, geologists, climatologists
and anthropologists attempted to reconstruct the climate, environment and culture
of a prehistoric site located near Cherokee, Iowa.

H-A-5
I WILL FIGHT NO MORE FOREVER   A
        16mm   Sd   C   1975
        LCA   106min
Chief Joseph of the Nez Perce was a peace-loving man who counseled patience
with the white man. When this course failed, he attempted to fight his way to
freedom in Canada.

H-A-6
SEEKING THE FIRST AMERICANS   A
        16mm   Sd   C
        Documentary Educational Resources   58:30min
Archeologists search from Texas to Alaska for clues to the identity of the first
people to tread the American continent.

H-A-7
WHITE MAN AND INDIANS, FIRST CONTACTS, THE   SCA
        FS,Cassette   Sd   C
        SSSS
Narratives of Jacques Le Moyne and Robert Harriot which describe their travels
along the Eastern coast of North America in the 16th century.

History - Women/Minorities

H-B-1
AMERICA, THE MELTING POT: MYTH OR REALITY?   A
          FS, Cassette   C   1971
          SSSS
Explores the slow assimilation into American life of Blacks, Puerto Ricans and
Mexican-Americans.

H-B-2
BLACK SHADOWS ON A SILVER SCREEN   SCA
          16mm   Sd   B,C   1976
          Lucerne Films   53min
A documentary, with original feature film clips of the period between 1915 and
1950 when there were two film industries in the United States: Hollywood—and a
parallel black film industry making feature films for segregated theatres in black
communities.

H-B-3
ELIZA   SCA
          16mm   Sd   C   1976
          Films,Inc.   27min
Story of Eliza Lucas, who managed a South Carolina plantation in the 18th
century. Through her efforts, indigo was exported in large quantities.

H-B-4
FAMOUS WOMEN OF THE WEST   SCA
          FS, Cassette   1983
          SSSS
This program reviews the contributions of many outstanding western women,
including politicians, entertainers, teachers, and guides.

H-B-5
HEARTLAND   A
          16mm   Sd   1981
          Wilderness Women Prod.   90min
A stirring and unromaticized picture of life on the prairie. Based on the
experiences of Elinore Pruitt Stewart and Clyde Stewart, turn-of-the-century
pioneers near Burntford, Wyoming.

H-B-6
HOW WE GOT THE VOTE   SCA
          16mm   Sd   C   1975
          Lucerne Films   53min
The saga of how women achieved suffrage with determined, organized willpower.
The film features the voices of pioneers in the movement.

H-B-7
IMMIGRANT AMERICA   A
          FS, Cassettes (2)   1974
          SSSS
Looks at the immigrants who came to America between 1903 and 1913 and a
present day immigrant community. Part II examines, through contemporary color
photographs and interviews with residents, a Polish/Mexican community in
Chicago, where a long time Polish neighborhood is gradually acquiring Mexican

shops, restaurants and murals as the population changes.

H-B-8
IMMIGRATION: THE DREAM AND THE REALITY   A
      FS, Cassettes (6)   C   1974
      SSSS
Tells the story of immigrants and their confrontation with the harsh and disillusioning realities of life in America around the turn of the century.

H-B-9
IRISH, THE   SCA
      16mm   Sd   C
      Films, Inc.   30min
The story of the role of the Irish in building cities, canals, railroads and politics in America.

H-B-10
ITALIAN AMERICAN   SCA
      16mm   Sd   C
      Films, Inc.   26min
The father and mother of Martin Scorsese recollect their early immigrant experience from their home in New York's "Little Italy."

H-B-11
JEWISH AMERICAN   SCA
      16mm   Sd   B
      Films, Inc.   26min
A moving narrative of the Jewish experience in America, including the rich texture of life on Hester Street, the persecutions fled and the sufferings encountered.

H-B-12
KLAN, THE: A LEGACY OF HATE IN AMERICA   CA
      16mm   Sd   C
      NFL Films   28 1/2min
The beginnings of the Klan immediately after the Civil War; its growth and prestige in the 1920s and its resurgence in the 1960s.

H-B-13
LIFE AND TIMES OF ROSIE THE RIVETER, THE   A
      16mm   Sd
      Clarity Educational Productions   60min
Studies five women's experience during World War II, in the factories and plants. They were welders, foundry and ammunition workers.

H-B-14
LIVING ATLANTA: KKK   A
      Audio-Cassette   Sd   1979
      NPR   29min
History of the KKK in Atlanta in the 1920s and 1930s. Klan philosophy is explored.

H-B-15
MARTIN LUTHER KING, JR. (Second Edition)   A
      16mm   Sd   C   1971
      EBEC   24min
Traces King's career and examines his belief in nonviolent protest.

H-B-16
MEN OF BRONZE   A
        16mm   Sd   C   1977
        Films, Inc.   58min
Story of the 369th Combat Regiment made up of Black Americans in World War I.

H-B-17
MILES OF SMILES, YEARS OF STRUGGLE   SC
        16mm   Sd   C   1981
        Benchmark   59min
Story of the Black Pullman Porters and the founding the of black Trade Union in
1925.

H-B-18
A NATION OF IMMIGRANTS   SCA
        FS, Cassette   Sd
        Guidance Associates
This program traces the history of immigration in the United States from the
Pilgrims' landing to the signing of the Immigration Act of 1965, and the
immigrants' continuing contributions to the development of our culture.

H-B-19
NEVER TURN BACK: THE LIFE OF FANNY LOU HAMER   SCA
        16mm   Sd   C   1983
        Rediscovery Productions   58min
Through the eyes of Fannie Lou Hamer, a black sharecropper from Mississippi, we
see the growth of unprecedented political participation by black Americans. She
shows us the past; today's legislators and educators show us the new South which
Mrs. Hamer helped create.

H-B-20
RELOCATION OF JAPANESE-AMERICANS:
  RIGHT OR WRONG?   CA
        FS, Cassettes (2)
        SSSS
Two parts. Explores the history of the Japanese-Americans, and their adaptation
to a new life and their life after Pearl Harbor in the internment camps.

H-B-21
REMEMBER THE LADIES   SCA
        16MM,U   SD   C   1979
        MTPS   25MIN
Depicts the extraordinary achievements of America's women during the period
1750-1815. Through letters, diaries, crafts and artifacts we see women at work
and at war. Narrated by Celeste Holm.

H-B-22
ROOTS   A
        16mm   Sd   C   1977
        Films, Inc.   47-52min
                                                       each film
Traces the life and times of the family of Alex Haley from 1750 to pre-Civil War.
There are twelve (12) episodes.

H-B-23
SILVER WINGS AND SANTIAGO BLUE   A
        16mm   Sd   C,B   1979
        Adams/King Prod.   59min
This film tells the true story of the Women Air Force Service Pilots, the WASP.

H-B-24
SLAVE'S STORY, A   A
        FS, Cassettes (2)   C   1977
        SSSS
Based upon the true story of William and Ellen Craft, this drama shows the
extremes to which slaves went to escape from the South before the Civil War.

H-B-25
"THERE WAS ALWAYS SUN SHINING SOMEPLACE"-
    LIFE IN THE NEGRO BASEBALL LEAGUES   SCA
        16mm   Sd   B   1984
        Refocus Films   58min
Chronicles the history of black baseball (1887-1950) and examines Jackie
Robinson's pioneering role in reintegrating the game. Has rare historical footage
of former Negro Leaguers who have been immortalized in baseball's Hall of Fame.
Shows Negro Leaguers in the winter leagues of the Carribean, Mexico and Latin
America. Narrated by James Earl Jones.

H-B-26
VILLAGE IN BALTIMORE, A   A
        16mm   Sd   C   1981
        Hellenic American Neighborhood Action Committee   58min
Set in the ethnic neighborhood of "Greek Town" in Baltimore, Maryland, deals
with the assimilation levels of four young Greek-American women—their personal
and professional goals, and the importance of their families.

H-B-27
WAR STORY, A   SCA
        16mm   Sd   C   1982
        NFBC   58min
The story of Dr. Ben Wheeler, who was a P.O.W of the Japanese during World
War II. An account of his will to live in spite of mental and physical suffering.

H-B-28
WE ALL CAME TO AMERICA   SCA
        16mm   Sd   C   1976
        Lucerne Films   53min
The film uses interview, photographs, and motion pictures to document the
incredible story of millions of people who left their homes to travel thousands of
miles to an unknown country that symbolized freedom and opportunity.

H-B-29
WOMEN OF CANE RIVER   CA
        16mm   Sd   1980
        Southwest Film Labs   20min
Women of Cane River is a portrait of four women who lived and created in the
Natchitoches Country area in Louisiana.

H-B-30
WOMEN IN THE CIVIL WAR   A
          FS, Cassette   Sd   C   1979
          SSSS
During the Civil War, women are shown at work in factories and on the
plantation, caring for the sick and wounded in hospitals, acting as spies, and
running the volunteer organizations.

History – Regional History

H-C-1
THE AMERICAN WEST, MYTH AND REALITY   CA
          FS, Cassettes (3)   C   1976
          SSSS
The filmstrips in this series examine our varied images of the American West. The
first filmstrip presents a vivid chronicle of the historical development of the
media West, from James Fenimore Cooper to John Wayne. The second filmstrip
gives a more realistic portrait of Western expansion and the hardships of pioneer
life. The third filmstrip shows how more than 100 years of fantasy have blended
with reality to make it extremely difficult to distinguish between Western myth
and facts. The narration uses soundtracks from radio, TV, films, contemporary
popular movies, and quotations from historical figures.

H-C-2
CASTLE ON THE PLAIN   CA
          16mm   Sd   C   1976
          NAVC   31min
The epic story of one family's involvement in the tumultuous past of the
Southwest. A story of traders, of Indians, of mountain men, of Texas and Mexico,
of war and peace.

H-C-3
COKE MAKING IN THE BEEHIVE OVEN   CA
          16mm   Sd   C   1975
          NAVC   18min
The early American industrial process of making blast furnace coke using
techniques and equipment from the 19th century.

H-C-4
DREAM COME TRUE, A   CA
          16mm   Sd   C   1980
          WAVE-TV   28 1/2min
Shows the social changes brought to Eastern Kentucky's coal region at the turn of
the century.

H-C-5
FRONTIER AMERICA: THE FAR WEST   SCA
          16MM   Sd   C   1977
          MTPS   26min
Story of the pioneer and the Indian, told through the paintings, crafts, drawings
and photographs that capture the frontier era.

H-C-6
GRANITE LADY, THE   C A
    16mm   Sd   C   1974
    NAVC   28min
The excitement of the Gold Rush, the terror of the San Francisco earthquake and fire, and the impact of the Old Mint--the Granite Lady--on America's history can again be experienced through this entertaining and educational film. Actress Mercedes McCambridge dramatically narrates the story of the creation, abandonment, preservation and restoration of the Old Mint, which was reopened in 1973 as a national landmark. Restored to its original 1874 grandeur, the Old Mint houses exhibits such as a miner's cabin, early minting equipment, and a 1869 coin press.

H-C-7
HAGLEY MUSEUM, THE: A 19TH CENTURY
  INDUSTRIAL COMMUNITY   C A
    16mm   Sd   1978
    Hagley Museum   15min
An interpretive documentary film about Delaware's Brandywine River area, one of the most important industrial communities in the 19th century. The film places the Hagley Museum's restoration exhibits in cultural and historical perspective.

H-C-8
HOPEDALE: REFLECTIONS ON THE PAST   C A
    16mm   Sd   1977
    Merrimack Valley Textile Museum   28min
The film provides a record of daily life in the factory village of Hopedale, Massachusetts, whose development remained linked to the Draper Company, producers of textile machinery, for over a century.

H-C-9
JOHNNY APPLESEED AND THE FRONTIER WITHIN   S
    16mm   Sd   C
    MTPS   28min
Stars Lillian Gish in a dramatic reenactment of the life and times of Johnny Appleseed (John Chapman), a naturalist and early conservationist. Explores the concern for living things and spiritual convictions he developed during a lifetime in the wilderness.

H-C-10
LAST OF THE LOG DRIVES   C A
    16mm   Sd   C   1981
    Film Distribution Centers, Inc.   20min
Traces the colorful history of river log drives in America. The drive on the Clearwater in Idaho.

H-C-11
LEGACY OF THE MOUNTAIN MEN   C A
    16mm   Sd   C   1981
    Brigham Young University   29min
What life as a mountain man was really like in the 19th century.

H-C-12
LEGENDARY WEST, THE   SCA
    16mm   Sd   C   1976
    Lucerne Films   53min
Using Hollywood motion pictures and archive material, this film traces the
creation of the legend of the West. The popular image of bandits, badmen, law
officers and the American Indian with respect to the way it really was, is
documented.

H-C-13
LIFE AND ASSASSINATION OF THE KINGFISH, THE   CA
    16mm   Sd   C   1979
    LCA   97min
Life and times of Huey Long.

H-C-14
LINCOLN'S SPRINGFIELD   A
    16mm   Sd   C   1977
    NAVC   23min
Traces 20 years in Lincoln's career.

H-C-15
MOLDERS OF TROY   CA
    16mm   Sd   1979
    WMHT-TV   90min
The story of an Irish family torn by the changing tides of the American Industrial
Revolution. Traces the triumphs and failures of an iron molder's son, Brian Duffy,
from 1859 to 1876.

H-C-16
NUMBERS START WITH THE RIVER, THE   A
    16mm   Sd   C   1971
    NAVC   15min
Gives a poignant and personal view of the quality of life in a small mid-western
town--representative of 16,000 such towns across the United States. The small
town experience is documented with scenes of work, play, and family life.

H-C-17
PITTSBURGH: AN AMERICAN INDUSTRIAL CITY   A
    16mm   Sd   C
    Magic Lantern Films   43min
A chronological introduction to over two hundred years of Pittsburgh's past to
understanding its roots, interpret the present and find clues to the future.

H-C-18
QUEEN'S DESTINY, THE   SCA
    16mm   C   1976
    Films, Inc.   27min
Examines the circumstances behind Hawaii's move toward American- ization and
ultimate statehood, a move many Hawaiians opposed. Dramatizes the downfall of
Queen Liliuokalani, who ruled Hawaii as a divine monarch until 1893, when she
was overthrown by American businessmen.

H-C-19
SEGUIN   A
        16mm   Sd   C   1981
        KCET-TV   60min
Juan Seguin was a Mexican born in Texas before it was annexed to the United
States. He and his father, Don Erasmo, helped Anglo-American colonists settle in
Texas from 1821 to 1836. Seguin fought on the American side against his
countrymen at the Alamo, and he was a hero at the battle of San Jacinto where
Mexican President Santa Anna was captured. Soon after, Seguin was elected as a
senator of the Texas Congress and mayor of his home town, San Antonio. His
political success was short-lived, however, for too many Texans felt that as a
Mexican he could not be trusted in office; he was forced to resign and was
banished from Texas, the only home he had ever known. Seguin moved to Mexico
where he joined the forces of President Santa Anna and for two years fought on
the Mexican side of the Mexican-American War, at times fighting against the very
neighbors he led in the past. The film was shot on location in Bracketville, Texas.

H-C-20
SPIRIT OF AMERICA, THE   SCA
        16mm   Sd   C   1976
        BFA   18min
A travel to the hill country of the United States.

H-C-21
TIME EXPOSURE: WILLIAM HENRY JACKSON
  PICTURE MAKER OF THE OLD WEST   CA
        16mm, UBV   Sd   1979
        Crystal Productions   28min
Portrays the development and history of the American West in the last half of the
19th century through the photography of William Henry Jackson.

History - Intellectual

H-D-1
ANARCHISM IN AMERICA   A
        16mm   Sd   C   1981
        Pacific Street Film Library   90min
Explores the history of anarchism in the United States, its philosophy and its
place in contemporary political theory and practice.

H-D-2
ANDREW CARNEGIE: THE GOSPEL OF WEALTH   A
        16mm   1974
        LCA   26min
Actor Bramwell Fletcher stars as the fiery and paradoxical Andrew Carnegie in a
drama which provides both a fascinating portrait of the legendary tycoon and a
remarkable insight into the power games of big business.

H-D-3
COMICS, THE: A CULTURAL HISTORY   SCA
        FS, Cassettes (5))   C   1976
        SSSS
The comic strip pages in the daily newspaper are a 20th century phenomenon. This
series of color sound filmstrips traces the emergence of the comics as a popular

art form, the special language and literary forms incorporated into comics, how comics reflect the times and change as society changes, and the comics as art. The visuals draw upon documentary sources that show the origins of comics in 18th and 19th century art, illustrate the development of the comic book, and the emergence of "intellectual" comic strips in the 1960s.

H-D-4
DRAWINGS: A PLURALIST DECADE   A
            16mm   Sd   C   1980
            USIA   19min
Examines the drawings of 66 American artists that compose the American Exhibit at the 1980 Venice Biennale.

H-D-5
GOLDEN AGE OF HOLLYWOOD, THE   SCA
            16mm,UBV   Sd   C   1977
            Time-Life Films   34min
Examines Hollywood as it became the ultimate dream factory.

H-D-6
MOBILE BY ALEXANDER CALDER   A
            16mm   Sd   C   1980
            NAVC   24min
Shows the American artist Alexander Calder's work of art in the National Gallery of Art. Documents the mobile from idea through completion.

H-D-7
POP MUSIC IN THE TWENTIETH CENTURY   A
            FS, Cassettes (6)   C   1973
            EAV
A filmstrip series examining the relationship of pop music to the social history of America in the 20th century. The set concentrates on the music: how it became "Americanized" in the early years of the century as the country grew to world power; the jazz sounds of Prohibition; the "swing" sounds of the Depression; the "sing" era of the 1940s; the origins of rock and roll in the 1950s; the folk song movement and age of rock in the 1960s and 1970s.

H-D-8
REFLECTIONS   A
            16mm   Sd   C   1976
            NAVC   58min
Presents Margaret Mead discussing her own studies of the primitive people in Samoa, children, the family, and other subjects.

History - Legal

H-E-1
AN ACT OF CONGRESS   SCA
            16mm   Sd   C   1979
            LCA Films   58min
Documentary film showing how a law is made by Congress. It shows the drama and dynamics involved in translating the issues and the conflicting desires of people into the law of the land.

H-E-2
CABINET, THE   S C A
        FS, Cassettes(2)   C   1982
        SSSS
The origin and function of the Cabinet and the role of the President's advisory
council.

H-E-3
TRAVELLING HOPEFULLY   S C A
        16mm   Sd   C   1981
        Films, Inc.   28min
A profile of Roger Baldwin, founder of the American Civil Liberties union.

H-E-4
YEARS BETWEEN, THE   A
        16mm   Sd   C
        Films, Inc.   56min
This is the story of the dissenters who made the Bill of Rights work. Under the
Alien and Sedition Act of 1875 it was treason for the opposition party to attack
the rulings of the party in power. Mary Lyon went to jail to change this rule.
Henry David Thoreau fought the Poll Tax with civil disobedience, Susan B.
Anthony fought for women's rights, Eugene V. Debs painfully launched the Union
movement.

H-E-5
TRUST-BUSTING: TURNING POINT   A
        FS, Cassette   Sd   C   1982
        SSSS
This program examines the judicial and legislative action taken against industrial
monopolies during the trust-busting era, a period which began under the
presidency of Theodore Roosevelt and continued throughout the administrations of
William Howard Taft and Woodrow Wilson. The program fills in the background to
the growth of the big monopolies, recounts some of the most famous cases, and
explores the effect of trust-busting on the future development of the U.S.
economy.

History - Longterm Views and Special Syntheses

H-F-1
THE AGE OF EXPLORATION   A
        16mm   Sd   C
        EBEC   15min
This film describes the first stages in Europe's expansion—the growth of trade,
the rise of a strong merchant class, and the birth of new ideas about man and his
world. It explains why the first explorers were anxious to discover a new sea
route to India.

H-F-2
AMERICA - A PERSONAL HISTORY OF THE U.S.   S C A
        16MM   Sd   C
        Time-Life Films   26min
This 26-part series presents Alistair Cooke taking a look at the best of American
history, with reminders of the worst, shaking up the myths and sentimentalities of
high school textbooks. Each part is 26 minutes in length.

H-F-3
EUROPE AND THE AGE OF DISCOVERY   SCA
        FS, Cassette (2)
        Guidance Associates
By examining the technological, economic, intellectual and religious facets of the
Age of Discovery, this program builds understanding of historical cause and
effect. The expeditions of early Norsemen, Columbus, Vasco da Gama and
Magellan are considered in light of their social and economic impact on Europe
and the rest of the world.

H-F-4
PURITAN LEGACY, THE   SCA
        FS, Cassettes (2)
        Guidance Associates
This program examines the impact of Puritan values and ideals on the growth of
American culture. From the Puritan belief that New England was divinely favored
and its people were the elect of God has come the American sense of national
pride, purpose and infallibility; and the Puritan work ethic has evolved into thrift,
self-reliance and success. Quotations from Mather, Thoreau, Franklin, Lewis, and
Franklin Delano Roosevelt trace this development.

H-F-5
AMERICAN REVOLUTION, THE   SCA
        FS, Cassettes (2)
        Guidance Associates
This program offers a chronological overview and thematic analysis of the main
war events and issues which led to American independence. After prewar events
are discussed, the program focuses on the shaping of the Declaration of
Independence, the spread of war and the military campaigns.

H-F-6
CREATING A FEDERAL UNION (1783-1791)   SCA
        FS, Cassettes (2)
        Guidance Associates
Facing a common enemy, Americans of different regions, beliefs and interests
developed a sense of nationalism that drew them toward the creation of a federal
union. This program explores the problems which forced Americans to assemble
the Constitutional Convention of 1787 and examines the causes and impact of the
whiskey rebellion.

H-F-7
WESTWARD EXPANSION   SCA
        FS, Cassettes (2)
        Guidance Associates
The historic interactions of economic, social and technological changes that
evolved into the American Industrial Revolution are explored in this program. It
reviews the traditional distrust of manufacturing in agrarian societies and
identifies inventions and cultural shifting which changed this attitude in America.

H-F-8
VOICES OF BLUE AND GREY: THE CIVIL WAR   SCA
        FS, Cassettes (3)
        Guidance Associates
Readings from primary sources, early photography and detailed photo essays
depict the Civil War era and its people. The words of statesmen, former slaves,
newsmen, soldiers and civilians bring students into the center of the prewar

slavery debate, Civil War battle experience, and regional feelings about the war, surrender, emancipation and the war's aftermath.

H-F-9
REBUILDING THE AMERICAN NATION   SCA
         FS, Cassettes (2)
         Guidance Associates
Our nation's political and economic structures have been strongly influenced by events which followed the Civil War. This program helps students understand those influences and see how the same social forces interacted to create Reconstruction and to overthrow it.

History - Religious

H-G-1
BISHOP HILL   SCA
         16mm   Sd   C   1979
         Bishop Hill Heritage Association   27min
Traces the Jansenist religious dissidents from their rural Swedish homes to their 1846-1861 farming and manufacturing commune in Illinois, Bishop Hill Country.

H-G-2
WORKING FOR THE LORD   SCA
         16mm   Sd   C   1976
         Lucerne Films   52min
Many communal religious societies, having originated because of dissatisfaction with greater society, survived by vigorous enterprise and commerce. Drawing from photos, film clips and interviews, the film shows how their skills benefitted the world from which they withdrew.

History - Seventeenth Century

H-H-1
COLONIAL AMERICA: THE ROOTS OF REVOLUTION   A
         FS, Cassettes (2)   C   1979
         Benchmark Films
The desire for independence from England varied in the American colonies by region, and loyalties to the mother country were affected by religious, economic, ethnic, and cultural factors.
Part 1. The Southern Colonies were the most closely tied to England and would reman loyal to England the longest. The Middle Colonies were settled by immigrants of many countries and religions. They had a well-balanced and self-sufficient agricultural and manufacturing economy. Religiously, culturally, and economically, they had the loosest ties with England.
Part 2. American and English military forces joined to defeat the French in the French and Indian War.

H-H-2
JAMESTOWN   A
         16mm   Sd   C   1975
         NAVC   14min
Story of Jamestown and its abandonment in the 18th century.

H-H-3
MAYFLOWER COMPACT, THE   CA
        FS, Cassette   C   1983
        SSSS
The first written agreement establishing self-government in America was signed
by the men aboard the Mayflower in 1620. This program describes this event, the
background and its meaning to democracy.

H-H-4
MAYFLOWER STORY, THE   SCA
        16mm   Sd   C   1957
        MTPS   25min
Depicts how the Mayflower II, a faithful replica of the ship that carried the
Pilgrims to Plymouth, Massachusetts, in 1620, was built and sailed across the
Atlantic in 1957.

H-H-5
PURITAN EXPERIENCE, THE: FORSAKING ENGLAND   SCA
        16mm, UBV   Sd   C   1975
        LCA   28 min
This film examines the reasons the immigrants left their native homes for the
wilderness of North America.

H-H-6
PURITAN EXPERIENCE, THE: MAKING A NEW WORLD   SCA
        16mm, UBV   Sd   C   1975
        LCA   31 min
This film focuses upon the conflict of cultures which occurred as the English
displaced the Indians.

H-H-7
SEARCH FOR A CENTURY   A
        16mm, UV   Sd   C
        Colonial Williamsburg   59 min
The lost settlement of Wolstenholme on the James River has been located and
documented, including the first known physical evidence of the 1622 Indian
massacre.

H-H-8
THE WITCHES OF SALEM   SCA
        16mm, UBV   Sd   C   1972
        LCA   34 min
This dramatic film portrays the causes and events of the 1692 witch hunt.

                        History - Eighteenth Century

H-I-1
ADAMS CHRONICLES, THE   A
        16mm,U   Sd   C   1976
        Films, Inc.   60min
The drama and history of the Adams family from the pre-Revolutionary period to
the Industrial Revolution unfolds in eight parts.
1. John Adams, Diplomat (1776-1783)
2. John Adams, Minister to Great Britain (1784-1787)

3. John Adams, Vice-President (1788-1796)
4. John Quincy Adams, Diplomat (1809-1815)
5. John Quincy Adams, Secretary of State (1817-1825)
6. John Quincy Adams, President (1825-1829)
7. John Quincy Adams, Congrssman (1830-1848)
8. Charles Francis Adams, Minister to Great Britain (1861-1864)

H-I-2
AGE OF REVOLUTIONS, AN   A
         16mm   Sd   C   1971
         NAVC   30min
Traces U.S. foreign relations from the diplomacy of the American Revolution
through the early federal period.

H-I-3
ALEXANDER HAMILTON   SC
         16mm   Sd   B   1951
         EBEC   18min
Shows Hamilton's boyhood: his contributions to the formation and growth of our
nation; and his death at the hands of Aaron Burr.

H-I-4
THE AMERICANS, 1776   CA
         16mm   Sd   C   1975
         NAVC   28min
Here is an authentic view of everyday life during the time of the American
Revolution. The crafts, ways of life, and differences of attitudes among various
types of people living in the Colonies.

H-I-5
AMERICAN REVOLUTION, THE   SCA
         16mm   Sd   C
         EBEC   16min
Explains the strategy, struggle, movement for forces, important military
engagements and the meaning of the War of Independence.

H-I-6
AMERICAN REVOLUTION: THE CAUSE OF LIBERTY   SCA
         FS, Cassettes (2)   C
         SSSS
Examines the British attitude to American aspirations and actions and the
difficulty slave-owning Americans had in justifying that institution.

H-I-7
AMERICAN REVOLUTION: THE IMPOSSIBLE WAR   SCA
         FS, Cassettes (2)   C
         SSSS
The program covers the long, discouraging years of war, the suffering of the army
at Valley Forge, the problems of Congress, the possibility of a military takeover
of government, the victory at Yorktown, and John Laurens' death in the final
skirmishes of the war.

H-I-8
THE AMERICAN REVOLUTION: TWO VIEWS   SCA
          FS, Cassettes (4)   C
          SSSS
A four part color sound filmstrip program which examines the causes, events, and
aftermath of the American Revolution, from both American and British
viewpoints.

H-I-9
BENJAMIN FRANKLIN   CA
          16mm   Sd   C   1949
          EBEC   11min
Highlights of Benjamin Franklin's life and his role in American history.

H-I-10
BENJAMIN FRANKLIN:
  SYMBOL OF THE AMERICAN REVOLUTION   CA
          FS, Cassettes (2)
          Guidance Associates
Extensive selections from Franklin's writings and a rich sampling of early
American art.

H-I-11
CHECKMATE ON THE HUDSON   SCA
          16mm   Sd   C   1975
          NAVC   20min
Depicts the two battles of Saratoga and the surrender of a British army to
American forces there.

H-I-12
CONSTITUTION, THE   SCA
          16mm   1975
          LCA   27 min
Traces the events of the Constitutional Congress of 1789 and the people who
participated.

H-I-13
CONSTITUTION OF THE UNITED STATES, THE   SCA
          16mm   Sd   C   1982
          EBEC   19min
Constitutional Convention, as seen through the eyes of James Madison. Shows how
the delegates resolved the major issues confronting the states as they struggled to
maintain their individual sovereignty in the face of the need to create a strong
national government.

H-I-14
DECLARATION OF INDEPENDENCE, THE   SCA
          FS, Cassettes (2)   C
          SSSS
Analyzes the origins, major events and philosophies involved in the formulation
and signing of this landmark document.

H-I-15
DECLARATION OF INDEPENDENCE BY THE COLONIES, THE   SCA
     16mm   Sd   C   1956
     EBEC   20min
Relates the story of the writing and adoption of the Declaration of Independence, and the conditions which led American colonists to embark on a struggle for national freedom.

H-I-16
GEORGE WASHINGTON AND THE WHISKEY REBELLION   SC
     16mm   Sd   1975
     LCA   27min
Judson Lair portrays a very human President Washington, reluctantly leading the military to enforce the federally imposed whiskey tax opposed by Pennsylvania farmers.

H-I-17
INDEPENDENCE   A
     16mm   Sd   C   1975
     NAVC   30min
John Huston directs Eli Wallach as Benjamin Franklin and Anne Jackson as Abigail Adams in an epic portrayal of the dramatic events that led to the signing of the Declaration of Independence on July 4, 1776.

H-I-18
KOSCIUSZKO   SCA
     16mm   C   1976
     Pyaramid Films   21min
Kosciuszko, a young Polish military engineer who came to assist in the American Revolution twice made decisive contributions to the American victory over the British Army. His fortification of Philadelphia deterred their attack, and after the fall of Fort Ticonderoga his strategy won the 16-day battle.

H-I-19
LOYALISTS IN THE AMERICAN REVOLUTION, THE   SCA
     FS, Cassette   C
     SSSS
Thousands of people living in the American colonies refused to forsake their old loyalty to England. These "loyalists" were abused during the Revolution, driven from their homes, and never reimbursed by the American government for the losses they suffered. This filmstrip traces the events of the Revolution as they affected the loyalists, attempts to define what colonists were loyalists, and shows what happened to them after independence.

H-I-20
MAN AND THE STATE   A
     16mm, UBV   Sd   C   1974
     BFA   26min
Hamilton and Jefferson are forced to react to various crises in American History.

H-I-21
MR. JEFFERSON'S LEGACY   A
    16mm   Sd   C   1976
    Guggenheim Productions   28 1/2min
Using 18th century homes, taverns, meeting places and artifacts--as well as
Monticello and the Univ. of Virginia--this historical documentary traces the
influence of Thomas Jefferson's birthplace, Albermarle County, on his life.

H-I-22
OTHER SIDE OF VICTORY, THE   A
    UBV   Sd   1976
    Bill Jersey Productions   58min
"The Other Side of Victory" explores the struggles of common American soldiers
during the Revolutionary War. The incompetence of the officers, food and supply
shortages, the inclement weather and the resulting loss of morale.

H-I-23
PRELUDE TO REVOLUTION   S
    16mm   Sd   C   1975
    EBEC   12min
This animated film portrays the tug-of-war between radicals and conservatives as
the colonies struggled first to keep their ties with England and, finally,
reluctantly to break them.

H-I-24
RELIVING THE AMERICAN REVOLUTION   S
    FS, Cassettes (2)   C
    SSSS
A two-part sound filmstrip traces the history of the American Revolution, its
origins in the worldwide contest for land among European powers, and the
consequences of independence for America.

H-I-25
THOMAS JEFFERSON: ARCHITECT OF LIBERTY   S
    FS, Cassettes (2)   C
    Guidance Associates
This program offers students a detailed portrait of Jefferson's work as a diplomat,
political philosopher and president.

H-I-26
WORLD OF FRANKLIN AND JEFFERSON, THE   SC
    16mm   Sd   C   1976
    MTPS   27min
Traces the interlocking careers of the two men who largely shaped American
history. Spans 120 years before and after independence, presenting lifestyles of
city and town in early America. Good coverage of the fine arts and handicrafts of
colonial life.

H-I-27
WORLD TURNED UPSIDE DOWN, THE   SC
    16mm   Sd   C   1974
    Films, Inc.   54min
A legend is put to rest and a human being emerges in this story of George
Washington and our Revolution. For six frustrating years he drove his ragtag army
relentlessly until, in a bold move to trap Cornwallis at Yorktown, he gambled all
on the outcome of a single battle, and won. In the flush of victory, there was an

attempt to make him King, but he refused and by this rejection achieved his greatest glory.
Part 1. Washington: Years of Trial - 32min
Part 2. Washington: Time of Triumph - 22min

History - Nineteenth Century

H-J-1
ABE LINCOLN IN ILLINOIS   SCA
          FS, Cassettes (3)   C
          SSSS
Depicts Abe Lincoln's formative years, from his life in New Salem and Springfield to his election as President. An emerging frontier America provides the backdrop for the experiences of young Lincoln with Stephen A. Douglas, John Brown, Elijah Lovejoy, and Mary Todd.

H-J-2
AMERICA'S 19TH CENTURY WARS   SCA
          FS, Cassettes (6)   C
          SSSS
This companion program to the "America's 20th Century Wars" treats the conflicts of an earlier era which show the emergence of an isolated agrarian nation into an industrial power.
1. The War of 1812   4. The Civil War, Part II
2. The Mexican War   5. The Indian Wars
3. The Civil War, Part I   6. The Spanish-American War

H-J-3
ANTIETAM VISIT   SCA
          16mm, UBV   Sd   C   1982
          NAVC   27min
Return to Antietam in 1862—and witness the bloodiest battle of the Civil War. Reenactments of the battle at this tributary of the Potomac River near Sharpsburg, Maryland, and President Lincoln's secret visit with Union General George McClellan.

H-J-4
ASSASSINATION OF PRESIDENT WILLIAM MCKINLEY   A
          FS, Cassettes (2)   C
          SSSS
Details the retaliatory actions of the courts and government in response to the assassination of William McKinley.

H-J-5
CELEBRATING A CENTURY: THE 1876
    PHILADELPHIA CENTENNIAL EXHIBITION   SCA
          16mm   Sd   C   1976
          NAVC   28min
Shows the dramatic preparations for the 1876 Centennial Exposition in Philadelphia from early planning stages to the colorful opening day ceremonies led by President Grant and Dom Pedro, the Emperor of Brazil.

H-J-6
CIVIL WAR, THE   SCA
          FS, Cassettes (6)   C
          SSSS
Describes the war strategies of the North and South, and discusses economic and
cultural factors which led to the war and determined its outcome.

H-J-7
CIVIL WAR AS IT HAPPENED, THE   SCA
          FS, Cassettes (6)   C
          SSSS
Actual Civil War photographs from the collections of Mathew Brady.
1. How We Know About the Civil War
2. The Foot Soldier in the Civil War
3. The Artillery in the Civil War
4. Supporting Services in the Civil War
5. The War on the Water
6. The Toll of the Civil War

H-J-8
CIVIL WAR, THE: THE ANGUISH OF EMANCIPATION   A
          FS, Cassettes (2)   C
          SSSS
The Emancipation Proclamation has been remembered as Lincoln's instrument to
free the slaves. This two-part sound filmstrip examines the Emancipation
Proclamation as it fit into the strategy of the war, the feelings of abolitionists,
and Lincoln's own ideas of his constitutional responsibilities. All dialogue is drawn
verbatim from speeches, letters, and diaries of the period.

H-J-9
CIVIL WAR, THE: PROMISE OF RECONSTRUCTION   A
          FS, Cassettes (2)   C
          SSSS
The plight of the Blacks during Reconstruction. Using the government experiment
with the Sea Island plantations as an example, the two-part sound color filmstrip
shows how Blacks were forced back into raising cotton when food crops would
have been more profitable to them, how efforts to give Blacks land were aborted,
and how the failure to make the Blacks self-sufficient led the way to a rebuilding
of the plantation system.

H-J-10
EXECUTIVE VS. LEGISLATIVE:
   THE IMPEACHMENT OF ANDREW JOHNSON   SCA
          FS, Cassettes (2)   C
          SSSS
Presents the dilemma faced by Andrew Johnson, whose inflexible stand on his
idealistic program of a reconstructed South brought about his impeachment trial
by a hostile congress.

H-J-11
GHOSTS OF CAPE HORN   SCA
          16mm   Sd   C   1980
          Actuality Films, Ltd.   54 min
The American sailing history from 1847 until the turn of the century is portrayed
through man's attempt to round Cape Horn and make westing.

H-J-12
GOLDEN SPIKE   A
     16mm,UBV   Sd   C   1969
     NAVC   21 min
Struggling against Indians, blizzards, and rugged terrain, laborers drove the final
spike of America's first transcontinental railroad at Promontory Point, Utah, in
1869

H-J-13
GREAT AMERICANS: ABRAHAM LINCOLN   A
     16mm   Sd   C
     EBEC   23 min
With the aid of historical photographs and on-location filming, the life of
Abraham Lincoln unfolds in this story of his rise from a humble farm boy to the
16th President of the United States.

H-J-14
HONORABLE SAM HOUSTON, THE   SCA
     16mm   Sd   C   1975
     Films, Inc.   52 min
This film focuses on the eventful and trying period of 1860 when, as governor of
Texas, Sam Houston led a courageous but losing fight to keep Texas from seceding
from the Union.

H-J-15
JACKSONIAN DEMOCRACY   A
     FS, Cassettes (2)   C
     SSSS
Two color sound filmstrips chronicle and evaluate the changes that centered upon
the presidency of Andrew Jackson. The program analyzes the political changes
which have had permanent effects upon American government and the social
changes which reshaped American attitudes.

H-J-16
JACKSON YEARS, THE: THE NEW AMERICANS   SCA
     16mm   Sd   C   1971
     LCA Films   27 min
Vivid action dramatizations of episodes in the life of Andrew Jackson. Narration
is in the authentic words of Alexis de Tocqueville.

H-J-17
JACKSON YEARS, THE: TOWARD CIVIL WAR   SCA
     16mm   Sd   C   1971
     LCA   27 min
From the exuberant White House party celebrating his inauguration, this film
covers the major events of the Jackson administration. "Old Hickory's" forceful
personality dominates the scene -- South Carolina's threat of succession; Nat
Turner's rebellion; John Quincy Adams' struggle to debate the question of slavery
before the House -- as America relentlessly marches toward civil war.

H-J-18
JOHN BROWN: VIOLENCE IN AMERICA   S
     FS, Cassette   C
     SSSS
The life of John Brown is analyzed in terms of his hatred of slavery and
inequality.

H-J-19
JOURNALS OF LEWIS AND CLARK   A
    16mm   Sd   C   1965
    EBEC   27 min
The film is faithful to the journals and covers the same terrain traveled by Lewis
and Clark. It captures the wonder of the virgin west.

H-J-20
LAST BALLOT, THE   SCA
    FS, Cassette   C
    SSSS   16 min
A WNET-TV production. In the presidential election of 1800 Jefferson and Burr
have 73 electoral votes each, throwing the election into the House of
Representatives.

H-J-21
LURE OF THE EMPIRE: AMERICA DEBATES
  IMPERIALISM   SCA
    16mm   Sd   1974
    LCA   27 min
The U.S. is plunged into national controversy over her occupation of the
Philippines. All dialogues in this authentic recreation of a significant period in
our history are based on official records -- presenting the viewpoints of U.S.
military and political figures, as well as Filipino leaders and finally, the decision
of President McKinley that catapults America into a twentieth century world
power.

H-J-22
MANIFEST DESTINY   A
    FS, Cassette   C
    SSSS
Traces the history and rationale of United States expansion from colonial times to
the Spanish-American War. American savagery against Indians, and other
consequences.

H-J-23
MASSES AND THE MILLIONAIRES: THE HOMESTEAD STRIKE   SCA
    16mm   Sd   1974
    LCA   26 min
A startlingly realistic film recreates the bloody strike at the Carnegie Steel
Company in 1982 through the experiences of an Irish labor organizer and a Slav
coal heaver. From the stark portrayal of the workers' living and working
conditions to the dramatization of their final defiant stand against overwhelming
odds at the Homestead plant. Graphically relates a significant chapter in the
history of organized labor.

H-J-24
RAILROADS WEST: AMERICA COMES OF AGE: 1870-1917
    FS,Cassette   B   1974
    SED
Presents an overview of America's railroads and their accomplishments.

H-J-25
THEY'VE KILLED PRESIDENT LINCOLN   SCA
    16mm   Sd   1972
    Films Inc.   52min
Matthew Brady photographs skillfully integrated with "antiqued" footage results in
a rare "vintage documentary" that involves the audience in the immediacy of the
events surrounding the assassination of President Lincoln and the intrigues leading
to that event.

H-J-26
WAR WITH MEXICO, 1846-1848   A
    FS, Cassette   C
    SSSS
Two sound color filmstrips show the factors which led to the decision for war, the
far-reaching impact of the war, and the internal differences within each country.

History - Twentieth Century

H-K-1
AGE OF BALLYHOO, THE   A
    16mm   Sd   C   1976
    Lucerne Films   52 min
A documentary of the roaring twenties. Everyone moved to the city, skirts went
up, speakeasies flourished, Clara Bow became "It," Lindbergh crossed the Atlantic,
and Calvin Coolidge and Warren G. Harding hit the campaign trail.

H-K-2
AMERICA BETWEEN THE WORLD WARS   A
    FS, Cassette   C   1980
    SSSS
Historical photos, period artwork and music provide vivid images of American life
in the twenties and thirties. The heroes of the time -- Henry Ford, Babe Ruth,
Charles Lindbergh -- the great technological advances, the economic boom and
bust, the growth of organized labor, the migration westward, the Depression and
the social legislation designed to combat it are among the topics covered.
Separate filmstrips focus on the booming twenties, the crash of '29, industrial
strife, the New Deal, the Dust Bowl, and politics and mass media. A fascinating
look at the major events and changes of two crucial decades in American history.

H-K-3
AMERICA IN SEARCH OF ITSELF   A
    UBV   Sd   C   1982
    Films, Inc.   43 min
How Ronald Reagan won the 1980 Presidential election -- based on the social and
political trends of the past 25 years. Reported by John Chancellor and Theodore
H. White.

H-K-4
AMERICANISM, AN: JOE MCCARTHY   SCA
    16mm, UBV   Sd   C   1979
    Films, Inc.   82 min
The story of his life and rise to power is told by friends, business associates and
fellow politicians.

H-K-5
AMERICA LOST AND FOUND   A
      16mm, UBV   Sd   B   1980
      Direct Cinema Ltd   60 min
A study of life in the United States during the decade of the 1930's.

H-K-6
AMERICA'S 20TH CENTURY WARS:
  THE INTERNATIONAL CHALLENGE   A
      FS, Cassettes (6)   C   1979
      SSSS
During this century, the USA has reluctantly entered into four major wars --
World War I, World War II, the Korean conflict, and Vietnam. These six color
filmstrips follow the course of each of these wars and attempt to explain why and
how each took place. The events of the wars -- at such famous and infamous
locations as Verdun, Normandy, Nagasaki, Panmunjon, and Saigon -- are vividly
portrayed. Treating each of these wars separately, the filmstrips survey prewar
disputes, military tactics, technology, turning points, and the results of each
conflict. A teacher's guide provides discussion questions and activities.

H-K-7
ATOMIC CAFE, THE   S,C,A
      16mm, UBV   Sd   C,B   1982
      New Yorker Films, SSSS   88 min
Created entirely from American atomic propaganda films of the 1940's and 1950's.
With no narration, it tells its story by juxtaposing excerpts from newly-discovered
and rarely seen government and military propaganda, television and radio shows,
cartoons and the "bomb songs" that saturated the airways. This material reveals
15 years of concerted efforts by the U.S. government and media to mislead the
public about the dangers of nuclear war.

H-K-8
DECEMBER 7TH   A
      16mm,UBV   Sd   B   1943
      Films, Inc.   34 min
An authentic record of the attack on Pearl Harbor.

H-K-9
DECISION TO DROP THE BOMB, THE   A
      16mm, UBV   Sd   B   1965
      Films, Inc.   82 min
The decision in 1945 to drop the bomb and end World War II.

H-K-10
EMERGING GIANT, THE: THE U.S. IN 1900   SCA
      FS, Cassettes (2)   C
      SSSS
From the pages of Puck magazine in the early 20th century, a panorama of life
and attitudes is presented, sometimes in satirical form and sometimes as social
commentary during period when the U.S. suddenly realized it was the leading
power in the world.

H-K-11
EL SALVADOR: ANOTHER VIETNAM   SCA
     16mm   Sd   C   1981
     ICARUS Films   53 min
Examines the civil war in El Salvador in light of the Reagon administration's
decision to "draw the line" against "Communist interference" in Central America.
Offers an overview of U.S. military and economic policy in Central America since
1948, with extensive background to the current political crisis. Includes scenes
with both government and guerilla forces, and discusses U.S. aid to the junta. Is
this the beginning of a "new Vietnam?"

H-K-12
FDR: A PORTRAIT OF POWER   SCA
     FS, Cassette   C
     SSSS
A portrait of the man who dominated American politics for two decades.

H-K-13
GREAT DEPRESSION, THE:
 A CHRONICLE OF THE LEAN YEARS   A
     FS, Cassettes (2)   C   1982
     Educational Enrichment Materials
Presented in a two-part format, this program brings to life the social and political
events of the Depression.

H-K-14
GREAT DEPRESSION, THE   A
     FS(2), Cassette   C
     SSSS
The impact of the depression on individual security and purpose, told through the
words of participants, political cartoons, photographs by Dorothea Lange, and
other contemporary sources.

H-K-15
GROWTH OF CITIES, MUNICIPAL CORRUPTION,
 AND BOSS TWEED   CA
     FS, Cassette   C
     SSSS
Examines how the decline of public morality and the willingness of politicians to
use corrupt methods led to the rise of political machines and corruption in big
cities during the 1880's. The program describes the rise of the Boss Tweed ring
and its use of electoral manipulation, patronage, favors, and graft to remain in
power.

H-K-16
HARLAN COUNTY, USA   CA
     BV   Sd   1976
     SSSS   103 min
Chronicles the efforts of 180 Kentucky coal mining families to win a United Mine
Workers of America contract.

H-K-17
HARRY S. TRUMAN: PORTRAIT OF POWER   SCA
     FS, Cassette   C   1976
     SSSS
This filmstrip shows us who he was, where he came from and events as he saw
them.

H-K-18
HERBERT HOOVER: PORTRAIT OF POWER   CA
          FS, Cassette   Sd   1981
          SSSS
The Depression's effect on the country.

H-K-19
HISTORY AS THE NEWS CAMERA SAW IT   CA
          FS, Cassettes (4)   C
          SSSS
The six decades from 1910 to 1970. Set 1: 1910-1950. Set 2: 1950-70.

H-K-20
IKE: A PORTRAIT OF POWER   A
          FS, CASSETTE   C   1979
          SSSS
A portrait of his life from WW II to the White House.

H-K-21
JIMMY THE C   A
          16mm   Sd   C   1979
          Pyramid Films   3min
Jimmy Carter, in clay animation, is seen sitting in the Oval Office late at night,
singing nostalgically of the simpler days prior to his presidency. The action is in
sync with the voice of Ray Charles singing "Georgia On My Mind."

H-K-22
JOHN F. KENNEDY: PORTRAIT OF POWER   SCA
          FS, Cassette   C   1979
          SSSS
Sound filmstrip that documents his life and times.

H-K-23
JUST AROUND THE CORNER   SCA
          16mm   1976
          Lucerne Films   53min
That's where the good times were supposed to be during the depression of the
Thirties. The film draws from archives of motion pictures, radio, magazines,
recordings, and newspapers to recreate the social experiments that flooded the
desperate American people, and concludes with the beginnings of World War II.

H-K-24
LAWRENCE 1912: THE BREAD AND ROSES STRIKE   A
          FS, Cassette   1980
          SSSS
The turbulent events of the strike are recounted, and an outline of the labor
movement in America is presented.

H-K-25
LYNDON B. JOHNSON: A PORTRAIT OF POWER   SCA
          FS, Cassette   C   1979
          SSSS
Focuses on his five years as President.

H-K-26
THE MEXICAN PUNITIVE EXPEDITION:
  VILLA VS. PERSHING?   SCA
        FS, Cassette   1982
        SSSS
Summary: The conflict between America and Mexico in 1916 because of "Pancho"
Villa's raid on a new Mexico town; how war was averted and a portrait of
General Pershing are explored.

H-K-27
THE MIGRANTS, 1980   A
        16mm   Sd   C   1980
        Films, Inc.   52min
Tells the plight of the migrant worker, the poverty and misery.

H-K-28
MY FATHER THE PRESIDENT   A
        16mm   Sd   C   1981
        Sidney Kirkpatrick   23min
A documentary about Theodore Roosevelt, his life at Sagamore Hill, and his home
in Oyster Bay, Long Island. Narrated by his daughter, Mrs. Ethel Roosevelt Derby.

H-K-29
NEW DEAL, THE   A
        FS, Cassettes (2)   Sd   C
        SSSS
Is it possible to make changes within the system? The New Deal is examined as a
compromise between those who demanded radical change and those who tried to
keep the lid clamped down.

H-K-30
NO PLACE TO HIDE   A
        16mm   Sd   C,B   1981
        Direct Cinema   29min
From Hiroshima to the Cuban Missile Crises, government films, newsreels,
cartoons, popular TV programs and celebrities sold America on personal and
community fallout shelters. School children were told to save themselves from
nuclear annihilation by ducking underneath their desks.

H-K-31
NOTHING TO FEAR--THE LEGACY OF FDR   SCA
        16mm, UBV   Sd   C   1982
        Films, Inc.   52min
Explores the legacy of Franklin Delano Roosevelt by combining present-day
interviews with extensive historical material. The Roosevelt legacy includes Social
Security, collective bargaining, unemployment compensation, and control of
financial institutions.

H-K-32
PANAMA CANAL: THE LONGEST SHORTCUT   SCA
        16mm   Sd   C   1981
        Mar-Chuck Film Industries   28min
The problems of building the canal are brought to life by photos, color maps, live
footage and animation.

H-K-33
PEARL HARBOR:TURNING POINT   SCA
       FS, CASSETTE   C   1982
       SSSS
The attack on Pearl Harbor results in death, destruction, and all out war.

H-K-34
PRAIRIE FIRE   SCA
       16mm   Sd   C   1977
       Cine Manifest   30min
The history of the Non-Partisan League, a grassroots farmers' organization
founded in 1915 on the North Dakota Plains which sought to combat abuses by the
Eastern business trusts.

H-K-35
THE PROGRESSIVE ERA, REFORM WORKS IN AMERICA   SCA
       16mm   Sd   B   1971
       EBEC   22min
Describes the years spanning 1890-1915 and how they marked this period of
American history as one of great turmoil and violence.

H-K-36
THE PUBLIC PRESIDENT:
  WIT AND WARMTH IN THE WHITE HOUSE   SCA
       16mm   C   1976
       Lucerne Films   50min
The Presidents who served between 1933 and 1963 are featured. Roosevelt,
Truman, Eisenhower and Kennedy. Despite the gravity of their times, their ability
to communicate with warmth and charm endeared them to the Nation.

H-K-37
RIVER, THE   A
       16mm   Sd   B   1937
       Films, Inc., NAVC   32min
"This is the story of a river,
A record of the Mississippi;
Where it comes from, where it goes;
What it has meant to us-
And what it has cost us."

H-K-38
SINKING OF THE MAINE, THE   SCA
       FS, Cassette   C   1982
       SSSS
With the sinking of the Maine and entry into the Spanish American War, America
changed from the isolationist nation of the Monroe Doctrine to a world power
with control over Cuba, Puerto Rico, Guam, and the Philipines.

H-K-39
SPANISH-AMERICAN WAR, THE   SCA
       FS, Cassette   C
       SSSS
Traces the combination of yellow journalism, U.S. interest in Cuba, and her desire
for recognition as a world power, which led to war with Spain.

H-K-40
TEDDY ROOSEVELT: THE RIGHT MAN AT THE RIGHT TIME   SCA
            16mm   Sd   C   1974
            LCA   28min
The film highlights his vigorous leadership in breaking up big business trusts,
forcing arbitration between business and labor, and instigating social and
economic reforms.

H-K-41
TRUE GLORY, THE   A
            16mm,UBV   Sd   B   1945
            Films, Inc.   85min
The teamwork of British and American troops from the Normandy Invasion to the
occupation of Germany.

H-K-42
VICTORY AT SEA EPISODES   SCA
            16mm   Sd   B   27 min each
            Lucerne Films
      The taut and dramatic story of World War II on the sea, over the sea, and
under the sea is depicted in this documentary series.

DESIGN FOR WAR
            The battle of the Atlantic, 1939-1941
THE PACIFIC BOILS OVER
            Pearl Harbor, December 7, 1941
SEALING THE BREACH
            Anti-Submarine Warfare, 1941-1943
MIDWAY IS EAST
            Japanese Victories and the Battle of Midway
MEDITERRANEAN MOSAIC
            Gibraltar, Allied and Enemy Fleets, Malta
GUADALCANAL
            The Battle for Guadalcanal
RINGS AROUND RABAUL
            Struggle for the Solomon Islands
MARE NOSTRUM
            Command of the Mediterranean, 1940-1942
SEA AND SAND
            Invasion of North Africa, 1942-1943
BENEATH THE SOUTHERN CROSS
            War in the South Atlantic
MAGNETIC NORTH
            War from Murmansk to Alaska
THE CONQUEST OF MICRONESIA
            Fast Carrier Warfare in the Gilberts and Marshalls
MELANESIAN NIGHTMARE
            New Guinea Campaign
D-DAY
            Normandy
ROMAN RENAISSANCE
            Sicily and the Italian Campaign
KILLERS AND THE KILLED
            Victory in the Atlantic, 1943-1945
THE TURKEY SHOOT
            Conquest and Development of the Marianas

TWO IF BY SEA
          Peleliu and Angaur
THE BATTLE FOR LEYTE GULF
          The Battle for Leyte Gulf
RETURN OF THE ALLIES
          Liberation of the Philippines
FULL FATHOM FIVE
          Submarines, 1941–1945
THE FATE OF EUROPE
          Black Sea, South of France, Unconditional Surrender
TARGET SURIBACHI
          Iwo–Jima
THE ROAD TO MANDALAY
          China, Burma, India, and the Indian Ocean
SUICIDE FOR GLORY
          Okinawa
DESIGN FOR PEACE
          Surrender of Japan and Aftermath of War

H–K–43
VIETNAM: AN AMERICAN JOURNEY   SCA
          16mm   Sd   C   1979
          Films, Inc.   85min
Robert Richter's trip from Hanoi to Saigon and his interviews with survivors.

H–K–44
VIETNAM REQUIEM   A
          16mm   Sd   C   1982
          Direct Cinema Ltd.   58min
Focuses on five Vietnam veterans who are now serving time in prison. All five
men enlisted––each fought honorably and was heavily decorated for heroism.
Provides stock footage of the war, intercut with the men recalling their personal
experiences during and after their service in Vietnam.

H–K–45
WOODROW WILSON: A PORTRAIT OF POWER   CA
          FS, Cassette   C
          SSSS
Woodrow Wilson's efforts to bring about a "just and lasting" peace are highlighted
in this presentation of his life. Depicting Wilson's tireless cross–country campaign
to build support for the League of Nations, the filmstrip also explores his role in
leading the country through World War I. Exploring how Wilson's character traits
determined his actions in office, this program covers his domestic
accomplishments––establishment of the Federal Trade Commission, passage of the
Child Labor Law and Women's Suffrage––as well as his renowned efforts in the
field of international relations.

International Relations

William D. Coplin

Selecting audio-visual materials representative of what is available to American audiences in the field of international relations is a difficult task. First, the vast majority of events that constitute international relations are symbolic in nature. They involve communi- cations between governments, documents specifying relationships among states, and decisions taken behind closed doors. For the most part, they cannot be easily captured by audio-visual materials. Except for warfare, there is not much to present visually. As a result, the materials selected over-represent war and the instruments of war, and under-represent the critical role that diplomacy and economic relationships play in contemporary international relations. They also tend to take the form of historical documentaries or panel discussions among experts -- both of which are not very imaginative when it comes to the effective use of audio-visual materials.

Second, the materials tend to be ideologically biased. The large expense required to produce audiovisual materials and the relatively small market for them means that ideological motivation is frequently the determining factor in the construction of a given piece of material. Even when it is not the main motivation, it frequently permeates the material developed. As a result, if absence of ideological bias were a primary criteria in the selection of material, there would be very little left in the list. Instead, the selected materials are not ideologically extreme and include as many ideological perspectives as are available.

Despite these difficulties, however, a large number of materials are included in our list. Some of these come from movies and television productions. Others are produced as a result of carefully planned panel discussions. Still others are the result of formal theoretical or historical material presented in the audio-visual format.

The materials could have been classified in any number of ways. The lack of agreement on the organization of the field among international relations scholars and the lack of broad coverage of many areas of the international relations discipline by producers of audio-visual material make it impossible to use a traditional academic outline. Instead the developed set of categories should be helpful to prospective users.

INTERNATIONAL RELATIONS (IR)

IR-A   Foreign Policy History - Contains the largest number of items. It includes general surveys of U.S. foreign policy at global and regional levels as well as specific events like the Cuban Missile Crisis.

IR-B   Contemporary Foreign Policy – Contains materials that explore
            contemporary foreign policy issues like human rights, U.S.
            intervention in the third world, and policies toward specific
            areas of the world. It does not include issues related to war
            and peace.

IR-C   Defense – Includes materials related to war and peace ranging
            from discussion of defense policies to the threat of nuclear war.

IR-D   Economics – Includes materials that cover economic topics such as
            environmental concerns, the role of multinationals and the use
            of resources.

IR-E   Decision-Making – Covers discussion of United States foreign
            policy decision-making and the organization of the American
            government to conduct foreign policy. It includes topics like
            the CIA, the Ambassador and the role of the White House and
            State Department.

IR-F   Concepts – Includes a diverse set of subjects that are treated
            as organizing concepts in international relations courses. It includes
            the balance of power, international terrorism, and revolution.

International Relations - Foreign Policy History

IR-A-1
AGE OF REVOLUTIONS   A
            UBV   C   1976
            IFB   26 MIN
Begins with the "militia diplomacy" of the American Revolution and ends with the
issuance of the Monroe Doctrine. Highlights include Benjamin Franklin's diplomatic
mission to Paris, early American concern with the rights of neutrality and
freedom of the seas, the Louisiana Purchase, and the War of 1812.

IR-A-2
AMERICA'S 20TH CENTURY FOREIGN POLICY:
Crises In Diplomacy   SCA
            FS, Cassettes, guide   C   1981
            New York Times
Dramatic foreign policy developments from the days of McKinley to Reagan are
chronicled with archival and news photos supplemented with modern re-creations.
An inquiry-oriented format invites students to participate vicariously in the
age-old debates between isolationists and interventionists. The first three
programs show how America struggled to remain free of foreign entanglements
despite growing economic power on the world market. The fourth filmstrip shows
the emergence of the cold war from the ashes of World War II, leading the United
States into two Asian wars to "contain" communism. The growing influence of the
Third World and current crises in Latin America and the Persian Gulf are
highlighted in the final two programs. A separate cassette featuring dramatic
excerpts from realistic debates of the past is included.

            1. Isolation and Expansion   4. Evolution of the Cold War
            2. From Neutrality to War   5. Third World Rumblings
            3. Between World Wars   6. The World Arena

IR-A-3
AMERICANS IN THE RUSSIAN REVOLUTION:
An Army in the Middle   SCA
            Filmstrip, guide, cassette   1982
            SSSS
Russia had been an ally of Great Britain, France, and the United States against
Germany in World War I until the 1917 Communist Revolution. Fearing that Allied
supplies to Russia would fall into German hands, the Allies sent troops to take
the port cities of Archangel in the north and Vladivostak in the Far East.
President Wilson gave the Americans strict orders not to interfere in the civil
war between the Red and White armies, while the British and French actively
supported the Whites. This program uses extensive archive photography to
recreate the American experience in revolutionary Russia, and to comment on how
this nearly forgotten affair was to affect Soviet-American relations.

IR-A-4
AMERICAS IN TRANSITION   SC
            16mm film   C   1981
            Americas in Transition, Inc.   29 min
Documentary tracing US involvement in Latin American affairs in this century.
Concentrates on the roots of dictatorship, its effects on citizens, movements
toward majority rule, Communist influences, and the role of the United States.
Covers Nicaragua, Guatemala, Cuba, Dominican Republic, Chile, and El Salvador.

Narrated by Ed Asner.   Characters include writer Carlos Fuentes, a former CIA executive, a Maryknoll nun, and a former ambassador to El Salvador.

IR-A-5
THE ARSENAL   SCA
        16mm   Sd   C   1973
        Time-Life Multi-Media   52 min
In this episode of the American series Alistair Cooke traces "the American way of war" from the civilian militia of the Revolution through World War II, Korea, and present-day military power centers: the United nations' Security Council, the Los Alamos atomic laboratories, the underground Strategic Air Command War Room.

IR-A-6
THE BERLIN AIRLIFT: TURNING POINT   SCA
        FS, Cassette   C   1981
        SSSS
 In 1948 the Soviet Union attempted to drive the Western occupation powers from Berlin by blockading the city. The blockade was broken by a dramatic, massive airlift operation which lasted nearly a year. This program re-creates the tense atmosphere of this confrontation and explains its importance within the context of the cold war and the development of postwar relations between the Soviets and Western powers. 1981.

IR-A-7
CHINA'S CHAIR   SCA
        16mm   Sd   C   1971
        MGHT   29 min
Examines the relations between the United Nations and the two Chinas (Nationalist vs. Communist) since the end of World War II, and the role of the United States in preventing the seating of Communist Chinese delegates as the official representatives of China to the Unitd Nations.

IR-A-8
CRISIS IN ASIA   SC
        16 mm   Sd   B   1957
        Time-Life Multi-Media   20min
Traces the history of America's role as a Pacific power since WW II. Explains that U.S. did not intervene in the Chinese Civil War; Peoples' Republic of China becoming a seemingly implacable enemy and Formosa giving it strategic importance. Outlines events of the Korean War and discusses the Vietnam War.

IR-A-9
MISSION TO YENAN   SCA
        16mm   Sd   C   1973
        Films, Inc.   32 min
Presents an historical re-evaluation of America's China policy.

IR-A-10
ONE SMALL STEP   SCA
        16mm   Sd   C   1972
        Hearst Metrotone News   17 min
Captures the momentous events of President Nixon's visit to the Peoples Republic of China.

IR-A-11
CUBA: BAY OF PIGS   C A
    16mm   Sd   B   1964
    Films, Inc.   30 min
Traces the events leading to the abortive attempt by US trained and financed
Cuban exiles to invade Cuba in 1960. This was a "failure of U.S. policy which led
to a failure of U.S. power." A searching historical review which attempts to shed
light on this failure by examining the attitudes of the CIA, the Cuban
underground, and Fidel Castro.

IR-A-12
CUBA: BALANCE SHEET OF A REVOLUTION   SCA
    FS, Cassette   Sd   C   1975
    Current Affairs Films   68 frs
Examines what has happened to Cuba under the Castro government. Tells how
social institutions, the economy and people's lifestyles changed and discusses the
possible effect of improved relations with the U.S.

IR-A-13
THE CUBAN MISSILE CRISIS; Turning Point   SCA
    FS, Cassette   C   1981
    SSSS
The 1962 Cuban missile crisis brought the world's two superpowers to the brink of
nuclear war. This filmstrip re-creates the events of that momentous week,
explaining how the installation of Soviet missile sites a few hundred miles off the
coast of Florida led the U.S. to order a blockade of all military shipments to
Cuba. The timing, bluffs, and maneuvering of President Kennedy and Soviet
Premier Khrushchev are recounted in this absorbing account of a historic
confrontation.

IR-A-14
THE DECISION TO DROP THE BOMB   C A
    16mm   Sd   B   1965
    Films, Inc.   81 min
A revealing overview of the events that led to a nuclear bomb's first use in war.
As 1945 began, President Truman had no idea that the U.S. government was
engaged in atomic research, but by August of that year he had decided to drop
the bomb that obliterated countless Japanese and brought World War II to a
stunning end. The controversy his decision stirred has gone on ever since. Truman
accepted full responsibility for his choice, saying, "I never suffered one moment
of regret."

IR-A-15
DEVELOPING THE A-BOMB: A Decision of Destiny   S
    FS, Cassettes (2)   C   1982
    SSSS
This two-part color filmstrip program documents the events surrounding the
dropping of the A-bomb on Hiroshima. Part I provides the background: initial
fission discoveries, further bomb research, and the work of the Manhattan
Project. Part II details the flight of the Enola Gay and its terrible aftermath. The
epilogue and prologue portions of these filmstrips confront the issues of nuclear
proliferation, current U.N. efforts to control arms stockpiling, and the role of the
atom bomb in the evolution of the cold war. A teacher's guide is included.

IR-A-16
TO DIE, TO LIVE: THE SURVIVORS OF HIROSHIMA   SCA
          16mm   C   1982
          Films, Inc.   63min
The dropping of the first atomic bomb on Hiroshima was the greatest single
catastrophe man has ever inflicted on man. This film presents the thoughts and
feelings of survivors of the tragedy, their guilt at being alive when their friends
and families are dead, and the still-remaining dangers of radiation effects. The
film suggests that in a sense, we are all survivors of that cataclysmic event at
Hiroshima.

IR-A-17
EGYPT   SCA
          16mm   C
          Films, Inc.   16 min
Spurred on by overwhelming poverty, Anwar Sadat took a tremendous gamble when
he launched his peace initiative to Israel, a move which made him an outcast, a
traitor, to the Arab world. The assumption that moderate Arab countries would
accept the Camp David agreement was a serious miscalculation. The U.S. is caught
in the three-sided dispute between Israel, Egypt and Saudi Arabia.

IR-A-18
EUROPE'S NEW LOOK   S
          FS, Cassette   B   1974
          Educl Enrichment Materials   65 frs
Discusses what the new climate of conciliation between Western Europe and the
Communist Block means to the U.S.

IR-A-19
HIROSHIMA DECISION: Was the Use of the A-Bomb Necessary?   SCA
          FS, Cassette   C
          SSSS
This sound filmstrip with accompanying photo aids focuses on the presidential
decision to drop the atomic bomb on Japan in 1945, while providing a background
on its development. The program offers an opportunity to evaluate and examine
the process of decision making in government, at the same time establishing a
feeling for the destructive power of the bomb and its devastating effects on life
and property. Why was the decision made? This filmstrip provides much of the
background information needed to discuss these issues. Ten 11" x 14" glossy stock
photo aids are included, and are also available separately.

IR-A-20
THE HISTORY OF U.S. FOREIGN RELATIONS   SCA
          16mm   Sd   C
          NAVC   29 min
Series highlights the major events and principal themes at pivotal times in
American history.Transports viewers into four historical contexts. Lets them learn
for themselves the diplomatic lessons which are still relevant to foreign relations
decisions and policies today.

                    Part 1: An Age Of Revolutions   1973
                    Part 2: Youth To Maturity   1971
                    Part 3: The Reluctant World Power   1973
                    Part 4: The Road To Interdependence   1976

IR-A-21
IRAN   SCA
        16mm   Sd   C   1979
        Films, Inc.   22min
This overview of American policy in Iran includes our part in the coup of 1953
and the Nixon Doctrine of 1972, defended by Henry Kissinger. The seeds of
revolution sown by the Shah, the rise of anti-Americanism exploited by the
Ayatollah Khomeini, and the current state of Iran under the Ayatollah are seen
within the context of the revolution itself.

IR-A-22
THE JAPANESE AMERICAN   SCA
        16mm   Sd   C   1974
        Handel Film Corporation   30 min
A graphic and objective summary of the history of U.S. interrelationships with
Japan, and of its effects on those who embody both cultures.

IR-A-23
JUDGMENT AT NUREMBERG: Films Into Filmstrips   SCA
        FS, Cassette   1979
        SSSS
The all-star cast of this award-winning production includes Spencer Tracy, Burt
Lancaster, Judy Garland, and Maximilian Schell. Based on the Nuremberg War
Crimes Tribunal, the filmstrips raise important issues concerning national loyalty
vs. moral responsibility to humanity. Discussions can be centered on the meaning
of international law, the notion of "crime" during wartime, and issues of morality
and human rights that transcend "obeying orders." A copy of The Holocaust Years:
Society On Trial is included.

IR-A-24
KENNEDY VS. KRUSCHEV   SCA
        16mm, UBV   B
        Films, Inc.   25 min
How we survived an impending nuclear crisis! The film examines the confrontation
between the U.S. and the Soviet Union over the construction of missile bases in
Cuba in 1962. It provides an almost day-to-day account of the dramatic events
that occurred and pays particular attention to the two world leaders in crisis as
they consider alternative courses of action. A study of how President Kennedy
secured victory from the brink of disaster.

IR-A-25
MR. KENNEDY AND MR. KRUSHCHEV   SCA
        16mm, UBV   C   1981
        Films, Inc.   20min
In the early Fifties, Cuba was a military dictatorship led by Fulgencio Batista. In
1956, Fidel Castro overthrew that government. This film documents that period
together with the rise to power of Nikita Krushchev in the Soviet Union and John
Kennedy's election. These two powerful leaders would later confront each other
in 1963 over the establishment of Soviet nuclear missile sites on Cuba.

IR-A-26
KOREA: THE 38TH PARALLEL   SCA
        16mm   B   1964
        Films, Inc.   50min
Written, produced, and directed by Irwin Rosten, this is a personal view of the
United States involvement in the Korean "police action." A strongly

anti-communist, yet anti-war presentation, it reviews U.S. entry into the Korean conflict as part of the United Nations peace-keeping force; the conflict between General Douglas MacArthur who wanted to fight an all-out war and President Truman who was committed to a limited police action; and the prisoner of war issue which prolonged a resolution of the conflict. Narrated by Richard Basehart.

IR-A-27
DEMOCRACY AND LATIN AMERICA   S
        FS, Cassette   C   1975
        SVE   60 frs
Shows the role of the U.S. in the Latin American independence movements in the early 19th century.

IR-A-28
LURE OF EMPIRE: AMERICA DEBATES IMPERIALISM   SCA
        16mm   Sd   C   1974
        LCA   27 min
Following the Spanish-American War, the United States was plunged into an internal debate over the disposition of the Philippine Islands and whether the U.S. should embark on a course of imperialism. The testimony and speeches in this dramatized documentary are taken verbatim from official records, and the dialogue is also closely based on those records.

IR-A-29
ORDEAL OF WOODROW WILSON   SCA
        16mm   B   1965
        Films, Inc.   26 min
Following World War I, President Woodrow Wilson was the principal architect of a League of Nations which he believed would prevent the reoccurrence of another worldwide debacle. But, ironically, a renewal of isolationist sentiment made it impossible for him to convince Congress to approve U.S. entry into the League. Compiled from newsreel footage of the era, this film traces Wilson's hearbreaking struggle on behalf of the League. Includes commentary by Herbet Hoover on Wilson's ordeal, and glimpses of the Senators who opposed Wilson.

IR-A-30
OUR IMAGE ABROAD: New Tests of America Foreign Policy   SCA
        FS, Cassette   C   1981
        SSSS
Recent events in Iran and Afghanistan have led to a reevaluation of our country's global peacekeeping strategy. Did the Carter administration's responses — increased defense spending, military aid for Pakistan, an Olympic boycott, and postponement of SALT talks — form the nucleus of a new America foreign policy? This program examines our commitment and capability to protect Western interests in the Persian Gulf. Concise analyses of our military strength, anticipated allied support, and likely alignments of Third World powers provide background information for classroom discussion and debate. A student handout reinforces key concepts.

IR-A-31
BOTH SIDES OF THE PANAMA CANAL   S
        Fs, Cassette   C   1978
        Educational Enrichment Materials   95 frs
Deals with issues surrounding the decision by the U.S. Senate to give Panama control of the Panama Canal by the year 2000.

IR-A-32
THE RELUCTANT WORLD POWER   CA
        UBV   C   1977
        NAVC   29 min
America's participation in two world wars and its futile attempts at isolationism
between these conflicts are portrayed in this segment. Highlights include Wilson's
efforts to keep us out of war, the Senate's rejection of the Versailles Treaty, the
rise of dictatorships and the collapse of economic security in the 20s and 30s, and
the dilemma of "neutral" America facing a world at war prior to the awakening
shock of Pearl Harbor.

IR-A-33
THE ROAD TO INTERDEPENDENCE   CA
        UBV   C   1977
        NAVC   30 min
Outlines the development of U.S. foreign policy from the end of World War II to
1976. The onset of the Nuclear Age, the cold war in Europe and Asia, NATO and
the Warsaw Pact, the Marshall Plan, the Cuban missile crisis, the controversy
over our involvement in Vietnam, and attempts at detente and improved relations
with China, the Soviet Union, and emerging Third World nations are all depicted.
The program concludes with a discussion of the energy crisis and the Middle East,
stressing the economic interdependence of all nations.

IR-A-34
ROSES IN DECEMBER: THE STORY OF JEAN
    DONOVAN   SCA
        16mm   Sd   C   1982
        First Run Features   55 min
A documentary study concerning the brutal murder of four women missioners in El
Salvador on December, 2, 1980. Examines the circumstances surrounding the
deaths, the aftermath, and the political situation currently surrounding the events.
Much of the story is told in the words of Jean Donovan, the one lay missioner,
whose life is the focus of the film.

IR-A-35
AEF IN SIBERIA   SC
        UBV   Sd   B   1979
        NAVC   29 min
Shows mission and activities of expeditionary force which journeyed into Russia
following WW I.

IR-A-36
THE COLD WAR   SC
        16mm   Sd   B   1981
        Time-Life Films   20 min
Discusses the emergence of Russia as a world power following WW II, increasing
the Allies' fear of communism. Considers the Truman Doctrine, the Brussels Pact
and the Atlantic Pact. Tells how the Cold War hardened when Stalin tried to
isolate Berlin and shows how the Korean War led to the formation of the
Southeast Asia Treaty Organization. Discusses the Cuban missile crisis.

IR-A-37
SOUTHEAST ASIA SINCE VIETNAM:
  TERRITORIAL TURMOIL   SC
    FS, Cassette   C   1980
    SSSS
In 1975 both Vietnam and Cambodia fell to Communist forces, bringing U.S.
Involvement in the area to an abrupt end — or did it? This color filmstrip program
agonizingly describes the turmoil after 1975 that still embroils Southeast Asia
today — the Boat People, the expelled Chinese of Vietnam, the inhuman "utopia"
of Pal Pot in Cambodia, the Sino-Soviet struggle for influence, and the teeming
refugee camps in Thailand. What roles and obligations does the U.S. still have in
Southeast Asia?   A teacher's guide with discussion questions and a map of
southeast Asia on a spirit duplicating master are included in the program to aid
students in analyzing these questions.

IR-A-38
TEN SECONDS THAT SHOOK THE WORLD   SC
    16mm   B   1963
    Films, Inc.   50 min
The event that forever changed the course of war and peace: At 8:15 on the
morning of August 6, 1945, the B-29 bomber, "Enola Gay", dropped an atomic
bomb over the city of Hiroshima, Japan. In less than a minute, the city withered
under the fireball and crumbled before the shock wave.   This unnerving
documentary relates the story of destruction, of fear, of bewilderment — and of
hope. It is the story of a discovery that could bring the greatest good or the
ultimate evil.

IR-A-39
THE UNITED STATES AS A WORLD LEADER   SCA
    FS, Cassettes (8)   C   1976
    SSSS
An overview of the events and governmental attitudes that shaped United States
foreign policy ... from George Washington's belief in inward focus to John
Kennedy's reexamination of the American role in international affairs. Included
are photographs, political cartoons, documents and newspaper items of historic
importance. The set includes teacher's notes and printed copies of selected texts
of key documents.

        1. World Scene: to 1913   5. Gathering Storm: 1933-41
        2. Road to War: to 1917   6. World War II: 1941-45
        3. War and Treaty: 1917-19   7. Responsibility: 1945-53
        4. Isolationism: 1919-33   8. Coexistence: 1953-63

IR-A-40
THE UNITED STATES AS A WORLD LEADER:
Johnson to Ford   SCA
    FS, Cassettes (3)   C   1976
    SSSS
An exploration of the eroding position of the United States in world affairs, with
major emphasis on involvement in Southeast Asia. Also included are discussions of
the renewal of relations with China, the Middle East, the impact upon presidential
power of the Watergate affair, and changing American attitudes toward the
nation's responsibilities as a world leader.

IR-A-41
VIETNAM: CHRONICAL OF A WAR   SCA
      UBV   Sd   C   1981
      SSSS   56 min
This program presents a retrospective portrait of American military involvement
as witnessed by on-the-scene correspondents and camera crews. Some portions are
in black and white.

IR-A-42
VIETNAM -- THE TONKIN GULF RESOLUTION: TURNING POINT   SC
      FS, Cassette   C   1982
      SSSS
A color filmstrip program recalling the events of the 1964 Tonkin Bay attack on
two United States destroyers by North Vietnamese PT boats, and the consequent
Tonkin Gulf Resolution which supplied the legal basis for American military action
in Vietnam. The program places these events in the context of the Vietnam War
up to that point, traces the results of the attack and the congressional resolution,
and follows the course of America's deepening involvement in the war. Teacher's
guide.

IR-A-43
WHY VIETNAM   CA
      UBV   B   1966
      DUART   25 min
A history of U.S. support in Southeast Asia, including speeches by Dean Rusk,
Robert McNamara and LBJ.

IR-A-44
YOUTH TO MATURITY   SCA
      UBV   C   1979
      SSSS   29 min
Discusses the evolution of a weak, isolated nation into a world power by the dawn
of World War I. Described are Admiral Perry's visit to Japan, strained relations
with Britain during the Civil War, the Spanish American War, the Philippines
expedition, the Boxer Rebellion, the "Open Door Policy" on China, "dollar
diplomacy" in the Caribbean, and the construction of the Panama Canal.

International Relations - Contemporary Foreign Policy

IR-B-1
AFRICAN-AMERICAN RELATIONS   SCA
      Audio-cassette   1981
      NPR   29 min
America imports about forty percent of its oil from Africa and our trade deficit
with that continent exceeds thirty billion dollars. This program examines American
business interests in Africa and some conflicts between those interests and
current U.S. policy there. Former U.S. Ambassador Andrew Young and Nigerian
Ambassador Akporode Clark discuss independence for Namibia and U.S. policy
towards South Africa.

IR-B-2
AMERICAN MILITARY PRESENCE IN THE MIDDLE EAST:
A DEBATE   C A
            Audio-Cassette   1981
            NPR   29 min
Producer Jeff Rosenberg highlights a debate between Robert Rucker of Johns
Hopkins University and Daniel Aaron, deputy director of the National Security
Council under President Carter. Aaron favors partnerships with countries in the
Middle East. Tucker advocates an interventionist policy, including seizure of oil
fields, if necessary.

IR-B-3
AND WHO SHALL FEED THIS WORLD?   C A
            16mm   Sd   C   1974
            Films, Inc.   54 min
An NBC White Paper which examines the nature and causes of the world food
problem. The problems are personalized by contrasting two farm families -- one in
India and one in North Dakota. Includes comments by Rep. William Poage,
Chairman, Agriculture Committee; Lester Brown, Overseas Development Council;
Earl Butz, Secretary of Agriculture; Daniel Moynihan, former Ambassador to India;
and Senator Hubert Humphrey. Points out the political, religious, economic, and
social complexities which make it so difficult to find a solution to the problem of
world hunger, and raises the question of America's responsibility in this area.

IR-B-4
BLOOD AND SAND -- WAR IN THE SAHARA   S C A
            16mm   Sd   C   1982
            First Run Features   58 min
A report on U.S. involvement in the Western Sahara War. Presents revealing
interviews with key policymakers in the Carter and Reagan administrations. In
addition, the filmmakers travelled hundreds of miles of barren desert on both sides
of the battlefront. Offers an analysis of U.S. foreign policy and a detailed
account of U.S. arms sales.

IR-B-5
BUILDING THE PEACE: U.S. FOREIGN POLICY
FOR THE NEXT DECADE   C A
            Audio-cassette   1982
            NPR   59 min
Former Secretary of State Cyrus Vance and professor Stanley Hoffman of Harvard
University discuss the future of U.S. foreign policy. Sometimes critical of the
Reagan Administration, they consider the American-Soviet conflict, global arms
control, human rights in the Third World, and U.S. diplomatic relations with China,
Japan, and the Mid-East.

IR-B-6
CAUSE I'VE ALREADY BEEN TO HELL   S C A
            16mm   Sd   C   1983
            MTPS   27min
Provides insight into the readjustment to civilian life of nine Vietnam veterans.
Their devastating experiences make a powerful anti-war statement.

IR-B-7
CENTRAL AMERICA: SPHERE OF INTEREST
OR INFLUENCE?   C A
     Audio-cassette   1981
     NPR   29 min
This program examines the U.S. role in Central America and the challenges facing
the Reagan Administration. Participants from a 1981 conference on the
international aspects of the crisis in Central America analyze events there and
discuss whether they pose a threat to U.S. interests. Guests include Soviet analyst
Jiri Valenta and Mario Ojeda of the Research Institute, El Colegio de Mexico.

IR-B-8
THE CHINA SCENE   SCA
     Audio-cassette   1982
     NPR   29 min
Looks at Chinese-American relations and their impact on U.S.-Soviet relations and
the Taiwan issue. Former Secretary of State Cyrus Vance, former Secretary of
State Alexander Haig, President Reagan, and former Assistant Secretary of State
for Asian Affairs Richard Holbrooke give interviews.

IR-B-9
THE COLD WAR: Then and Now   SCA
     Audio-cassette   1982
     NPR   29 min
After a decade of detente, the Soviet invasion of Afghanistan and the imposition
of martial law in Poland have brought the Cold War back to a point reminiscent
of the 50's and 60's. Host Peter Osnos interviews Ambassador Martin Hillenbrand
of the Atlantic Institute; Daniel Yergin, Harvard Historian; and Melor Sturva,
correspondent for -Izvestia-.

IR-B-10
THE DEEP COLD WAR   C A
     16mm   Sd   C   1980
     Films, Inc.   50 min
A new cold war is being fought deep under the oceans of the world, a dark and
shadowy conflict that continues day and night. This is a report on the secret and
silent struggle between NATO's antisubmarine forces and the Soviet submarine
fleet -- the biggest underwater armada in history. It asks: Could the Russians
exercise a stranglehold over vital oil and other supplies? In a coflict at sea what
would be the losses?

IR-B-11
FACING THE 80'S   C A
     Audio-cassette   1981
     NPR   29 min
Foreign policy experts discuss relations between the U.S. and the Soviet Union,
containment of Communism, and U.S. policy towards Japan, China and Pakistan.
Panelists include: Senator Richard Lugar (R-IN), member of the Foreign Relations
Committee; Representative Les Aspin (D-WI), member of the House Armed
Services Committee; Honorable Paul Nitze, chairman of the Committee for the
Present Danger; and Richard Holbrooke, former Assistant Secretary of State for
Asian Affairs.

IR-B-12
HANDS ACROSS THE WATER: The Special
Anglo-American Relationship   SCA
          Audio-cassette   1982
          NPR   29 min
Many Americans and Britons feel bound to one another by language, culture,
history and shared values. Experts from both sides of the Atlantic look at the
history and integrity of this special Anglo-American relationship — whether it can
survive changing political and economic conditions and if it can benefit either
country in the future.

IR-B-13
ISRAEL   SA
          16mm, UBV   Sd   C   1979
          Films, Inc.   13min
Israel is a microcosm of the Middle East conflict — a conflict about land, about
religion. In the past, Israel has depended on its military strength, but oil is a new
kind of weapon and one against which Israel has no defense. How the U.S.
reconciles our historical and moral ties to Israel with our need for Arab oil is a
delicate problem which must be solved.

IR-B-14
MEXICO AND CENTRAL AMERICA IN THE 80's   SCA
          Audio-cassette   1981
          NPR   29 min
This program combines contemporary Mexican poetry and music with commentaries
by Latin American experts to explore the Mexican political system, the
relationship of Mexico and Central America to the U.S., and the effects of U.S.
domestic and foreign policy on Mexico and Central America.

IR-B-15
THE PERSIAN GULF: PROTECTING U.S. INTERESTS   SCA
          FS, Cassette   C   1982
          SSSS
Why is the Persian Gulf of such vital interest to the U.S.? This filmstrip program
brings students up to date on recent events in the Near East — the Iran-Iraq war,
the continuing Arab-Israeli conflict, the potential legitimization of the PLO —
exploring how the U.S. can maintain an assertive yet diplomatically neutral
presence in the area. Investigating such alternatives as a Rapid Deployment
Force, the program considers possible economic, political, and military solutions to
the question. A concise survey of American policies under the Nixon and Carter
administrations is offered as well as a look at possible future directions of
American foreign policy.

IR-B-16
PRESSURE POINTS: Oman, South Yemen, North Yemen   SCA
          16 mm, UBV   Sd   C   1979
          Films, Inc.   21min
Oil has forced the U.S. into a new relationship with countries with which it has
no cultural ties and no long-standing political partnership. The entire Arabian
peninsula is the center of an important power struggle. The strategic positions of
Oman and North Yemen make them vulnerable, especially with South Yemen under
communist control with a Soviet naval and air base at Aden.

IR-B-17
PUERTO RICO: A COLONY THE AMERICAN WAY   SCA
      16mm   C   1981
      Terra Productions   27 min
A current investigative reportage on the political/economic/social crisis emerging
in Puerto Rico, centering on the unresolved question of status vis-a-vis the United
States and the impact of an 82-year-old link to U.S.

IR-B-18
TERRORISM: THE REAGAN VIEW   SCA
      Audio-cassette   1981
      NPR   29 min
Producer Jeff Rosenberg presents an examination of the Reagan Administration's
plans and policies for dealing with political terrorism. Host Morton Kondracke
talks with government and university experts about the role of the U.S.S.R. in
international terrorist activities, how to fight terrorism with U.S. foreign policy,
and the impact on domestic intelligence as anti-terrorist measures toughen.

IR-B-19
THE THIRD WORLD   SCA
      FS, cassette, guide   C   1983
      SSSS
The absence of a consistent American policy toward developing countries has
become a matter of national concern. This color filmstrip surveys U.S. foreign
policy after World War II and its evolving Third World focus, examines the Reagan
administration's recent economic initiatives, and explains possible courses of
action (from direct financial aid to private investment) which might help "have
not" nations to become economically self-reliant. The program also considers the
efforts of China and the Soviet Union as they compete with the U.S. to enhance
their images in the eyes of the Third World.

IR-B-20
U.S. HUMAN RIGHTS POLICY   SCA
      Audio-cassette   1981
      NPR   29 min
Some nations with close ties to the United States are human rights violators.
Torture, kidnapping, and inhumane treatment of prisoners have been reported from
Argentina, South Korea, Liberia, and South Africa. This program looks at the
importance of human rights in U.S. foreign policy and Reagan's controversial
restructuring of this policy. Author Jacob Timerman and columnist Philip Geyelin
discuss the issues.

IR-B-21
WORLD HUMAN RIGHTS: POLICY AND PRACTICE   SCA
      Filmstrip, cassette, guide   C   1980
      SSSS
President Carter called for worldwide implementation of universal human rights in
1976 as did the United Nations in 1948. This multimedia program explores why this
issue has suddenly gained attention, discusses the work such organizations as
Amnesty International do to publicize violations of human rights, and assesses the
role the U.S. plays -- and does not play -- in furthering human rights in countries
such as Chile, Argentina, and South Africa. The program contains a teacher's
guide with discussion questions and a student worksheet on a spirit duplicating
master.

IR-B-22
YANKEE GO HOME: DECLINING U.S. POWER?   SCA
        FS, Cassette   C   1980
        SSSS
Since America lost face in the Vietnam War, which ended in March, 1973, there
has been a seeming slide in U.S. prestige and clout abroad. America is more
dependent on foreign oil, the dollar has fallen on world markets, the economy
suffers from yearly trade deficits, and the Soviet Union has matched if not
surpassed U.S. military capability. Is the United States a second-rate power? Or is
the outlook not quite so serious?

                    International Relations - Defense

IR-C-1
THE ATOMIC CAFE   SCA
        16mm,UBV   Sd   C/B   1982
        SSSS, New Yorker Films   92 min
A telling and often ironic juxtaposition of clips from documentary footage,
training films, TV shows and newsreels, and more - all relating to "The Bomb" and
how Americans perceived and misperceived it in the forties and fifties. The
presentation begins with personal reminiscences and film on the early Manhattan
Project tests and the events surrounding Hiroshima and Nagasaki. Other highlights
interspersed with period songs include Nixon and the Alger Hiss tapes, the
Rosenberg executions, naive advice on civil defense shelters, and a musical "duck
and cover" education piece for kids. The program lets these chilling and humorous
clips speak for themselves without narrative commentary.

IR-C-2
THE BULL'S EYE WAR   SCA
        16 mm, UBV   Sd   C   1980
        Films, Inc.   50min
How are our tax dollars being spent? Preparations for electronic warfare account
for an increasing share of military budgets. Precision Guided Weapons -- "smart"
bombs -- make truly pinpoint accuracy possible for the first time in history.
Guided by laser, radar, infrared sensor, or TV camera, these weapons have
changed the face of conventional warfare with alarming implications for NATO's
defensive posture against the Warsaw Pact nations.

IR-C-3
DR. STRANGELOVE -- OR, HOW I LEARNED TO STOP
WORRYING AND LOVE THE BOMB   SCA
        UBV   1964
        SSSS   93 min
Stanley Kubrick's classic 1964 comedy offers a darkly humorous vision of the
dangers of nuclear warfare. Sterling Hayden plays a paranoid general who seals
his base and launches a full scale pre-emptive B-52 attack against the Russians to
"preserve our precious bodily fluids." Peter Sellers offers a triple performance as
an R.A.F. captain who frantically tries to stop the attack, the President of the
United States, and Dr. Strangelove -- the president's wheelchair-riding ex-Nazi
science advisor. Although some aspects of the movie are dated, this film is an
entertaining supplement to classroom discussion of the current issues of weapons
armament and the growing nuclear freeze movement. Also starring George C.
Scott and Slim Pickens.

IR-C-4
FACING UP TO THE BOMB   SCA
        UBV   C   1982
        Films, Inc.   52min
Experience the facts behind the world's current nuclear dilemma as both Soviet
and American experts tell the story of the nuclear arms race, and how the human
race reached the unbelievable position of creating enough fire power to drop what
amounts to 10 tons of TNT on every human being on this planet. The film
examines the nuclear freeze movement and discusses alternatives to nuclear
control, what could cause a nuclear exchange and whether it could be limited in
scope.

IR-C-5
A GUIDE TO ARMAGEDDON   SCA
        16mm, UBV
        Films, Inc.   25min
Depicts in alarming detail the projected outcome of a one megaton nuclear bomb
exploding a mile above the center of London. Through dramatic simulations, and
with the help of two volunteer couples, the program explains in scientific terms
the various effects of the bomb and assesses the effectiveness of measures
governments have proposed to protect their populations. Exactly what would be
the effect of the blast on houses? Or the supersonic wind that would follow?
Which, if any, of London's landmarks would survive? And what of the millions of
people who live in the capital? Using some ingenious camera techniques and some
startling demonstrations, the film shows what would happen to both places and
people caught in the vicinity of a nuclear explosion.

IR-C-6
A HIGHER FORM OF KILLING -- Chemical Warfare   SCA
        16mm, UBV   C   1981
        Films, Inc.   50min
While nuclear weapons remain man's main concern, they represent only one facet
of the dangers humanity faces. In 1915, the Germans launched the first gas attack
against the Allies at Ypres. It was, said its inventor, "a higher form of killing."
By 1918, it had claimed the lives of 100,000 men. Sixty years later, the world has
developed nerve gases many thousands of times more powerful, and the Russians
and Americans both have enormous stockpiles. The film investigates the continued
development of one of the most feared weapons.

IR-C-7
HOME ON THE RANGE -- U.S. Bases In Australia   SCA
        16mm   C   1980
        Australian Film Commission   40 min
Australia currently plays host to 20 U.S. bases vital to American strategic
capability. Three times in the last decade these bases have been placed on "Red
Alert." This is the last stage before nuclear exchange; bases such as Pine Gap are
priority targets for nuclear strike by the U.S.S.R. and involve Australia in the
global power struggle.

IR-C-8
NATIONAL DEFENSE   SCA
        FS, Cassettes (2)   C   1982
        SSSS
Our nation is once again engaged in a debate over national defense. Is America
strong enough? Are we ready to defend ourselves if it becomes necessary? How
much of the national budget should go to defense? This filmstrip program offers a

timely, in-depth look at the entire question of national defense. It examines the pros and cons of an all-volunteer army, increased defense spending, treaties limiting arms, and other relevant topics.

IR-C-9
NUCLEAR PROLIFERATION: Race to Extinction?   SCA
        FS, Cassette   C   1982
        SSSS
This filmstrip program paints a disturbing picture of our nuclear armed future. Chronicling the history of the arms race -- Hiroshima, the cold war, NATO agreements, SALT I -- the program describes how our nuclear arsenals are expanding in size and sophistication. Various weapons such as ICMBs, multiple warheads, antiballistic missiles, and B-1 bombers, are defined and pictured. The program also highlights recent developments, such as the European antiwar movement, the increasing number of nations developing nuclear weapons, and the Reagan administration's proposals to increase defense spending.

IR-C-10
THINKING TWICE ABOUT NUCLEAR WAR   CA
        UBV   SD   C   1983
        Public Interest Video Network   58 1/2min
Hosted by Mike Farrell of "MASH" fame, this film explains how Americans are dealing with the threat of nuclear war and documents efforts of individuals to prevent it.

IR-C-11
THE WAR GAME   A
        16 mm, UBV   Sd   B   1966
        Films, Inc.   49min
This classic film will open the eyes of audiences to the reality of a nuclear war. It shows what it would be like in detail, based on information supplied by experts in nuclear defense, economics and medicine. The use of cinema verite' -- man on the street interviews, on- location shooting with hand-held camera and amateur actors -- has such potency that it has kept the film off television.

IR-C-12
WAR WITHOUT WINNERS   SCA
        16 mm, UBV   Sd   C   1979
        Films, Inc.   28min
We are the most powerful nation on earth, but we can be destroyed with less than thirty minutes warning ... so can the Russians. This film explores the dangers of nuclear war both from the scientific, political and military points of view, and from the viewpoint of the people -- Americans and Russians -- who express their fears and hopes in this age where civilization can be incinerated in minutes.

International Relations - Economics

IR-D-1
CONTROLLING INTEREST: The World Of The
Multinational Corporation   CA
        16mm   Sd   C   1978
        California Newsreel   45 min
An account of the growing power of international conglomerates and their influence over global affairs. Central to the film are some remarkably candid

interviews with major corporate figures. Raises disturbing questions about the compatability of their pursuit of profit and pressing social needs.

IR-D-2
THE FOOD WEAPON   SCA
       Audio-cassette   1980
       NPR   29 min
Producer Jeff Rosenberg analyzes the economic, poltical, and moral aspect of a food embargo to retaliate against other countries, especially Russia. Earl Butz, former Secretary of Agriculture, James Callaghan, former British Prime Minister, former President Carter, President Reagan, and Senator Ted Kennedy (D-Mass) participate.

IR-D-3
THE LONG CHAIN   SCA
       16mm   B   1972
       Tricontinental Film Center   20 min
This Swedish production examines the economic and political role of U.S. corporations such as I.T.T. and First National City Bank in India. Focusing on the construction of two buildings for U.S. companies in Bombay, it reveals how women construction workers are brought from South India to Bombay where they work for starvation wages, then find themselves stranded in the city's slums when the construction is finished. Another cogent reminder that other countries do not always see U.S. foreign aid and overseas investments in the same light that we do.

IR-D-4
OIL AND AMERICAN POWER SERIES   A
       16 mm, UBV   Sd   C   1979
       Films, Inc.

       Egypt   16 min
       Iran   22 min
       Israel   13 min
       Pressure Points: Ornan, South Yemen,
       North Yemen   21 min
       Saudi Arabia   18 min
The unstable Middle East, its geography and internal politics, is detailed in this series. The fact that 57% of the world's oil lies under the sands of the Middle East again raises the question of how we can use our tremendous power to guarantee our access to that oil.

IR-D-5
OIL IN THE MIDDLE EAST   A
       16 mm, UBV   Sd   C   1973
       Films, Inc.   20 min
An NBC White Paper that examines the delicate position in which the U.S. finds itself vis-a-vis the Middle Eastern oil-producing nations. Saudi Arabia, Iran, and Kuwait own more than half of the world's known oil reserves, and the U.S. depends on these sources of oil. The U.S. also has an emotional if not a military commitment to Israel. The energy crisis has made oil a political tool to apply pressure on the U.S. to change policies concerning Israel. At the same time, the U.S. has a strategic interest in avoiding conflict with Russia in the Middle East. Our foreign policy must attempt to reconcile these elements.

IR-D-6
PESTICIDES & PILLS: For Export Only -
Part One: Pesticides   SCA
         16mm   Sd   C   1981
         Robert Richter Productions   56 min
A provocative look at the global problem of exporting to Third World countries
certain pesticides that have been prohibited or severely restricted for use in the
U.S. and/or western Europe, and the related issue of the residues of pesticides
appearing on food we import from the Third World. Filmed in Malaysia,
Bangladesh, Kenya, Ghana, Brazil, Colombia, Costa Rica, the U.S. and
Switzerland.

IR-D-7
THE RIGHT TO POLLUTE   SCA
         FS, Cassettes (2)   C   1976
         SSSS
Focusing on the global conflict between industrialized nations worried about
pollution and the Third-World concerned about economic development, this
two-part filmstrip discusses the problems of each and ways in which the dilemma
might be resolved. The program points out the dangers in industrial development,
with a special case study on the Mnamata disease and its origins in factory
pollutants. The plight of the Third World is discussed, and the program shows how
some aid efforts -- such as the Aswan Dam and the Green Revolution -- have
backfired ecologically.

IR-D-8
WORLD RESOURCES AND RESPONSIBILITIES   SCA
         FS, Cassettes (2)   C   1976
         SSSS
This two-part color sound filmstrip examines the problems of growing global
interdependence, where some nations have wealth and resources and others do not
have the food to feed their growing populations. Do nations with resources, such
as the oil-rich Arab states, have responsibilities to poorer nations, such as India?
Does the United States, as the largest food producing nation, have the right to
withhold aid from such countries as Bangladesh, whose population would starve
without it? Students are asked to analyze the world situation and discuss the
practical and moral positions of the United States and other wealthy nations.

                    International Relations - Decision-Making

IR-E-1
AMBASSADOR   SCA
         16mm   C   1978
         Screenscope, Inc.
People relate on many levels, and the work of an American ambassador -- in this
case, to El Salvador -- includes the interrelationship not only of himself with
other diplomats but that of his family and himself with the people of the country
to which he is appointed.

IR-E-2
AMERICAN FOREIGN POLICY: How It Works   SCA
         FS, Cassettes (2)   C   1973
         SSSS
Describes how foreign policy decisions emerge from a complex system of bureaus

and agencies, some created by the Constitution and others created by the Congress or the president. Discussions with scholars, members of Congress and State Department officials trace how the system developed, how it works, and how the federal system of checks and balances operates to control it. Includes an actual confrontation between the secretary of state and a congressional committee.

IR-E-3
THE C.I.A.
SSSS
FS, Cassettes (2)　　　　　　　　　　　C　　SCA
　　　　　　　　　　　　　　　　　　　　　　1976

This two-part filmstrip examines the evolution of the Central Intelligence Agency, providing students with the material to assess whether and to what extent it has overstepped its original purpose. Interviews with Senator Frank Church, former CIA director William Colby, and former CIA employees are utilized to question the nature and executions of CIA operations at home and abroad. The agency's development is viewed in the context of the World War II demand for improved intelligence gathering, the Cold War, and other jusifications for secretive activities which went largely unnoticed until Vietnam and Watergate.

IR-E-4
CONTROLLING THE C.I.A.
Audio-cassette
NPR
CA
1980
29 min

Events in Afghanistan, Iran, and Cuba have renewed interest in the activities of the C.I.A. and the intelligence community. This program examines the argument for greater leeway for the C.I.A., as well as the demands for even stricter oversight. Guests include Representative Les Aspin (D-WI), former Senator Birch Bayh (D-IN), and former C.I.A. director William Colby.

IR-E-5
THE DEPARTMENT OF STATE
FS, Cassettes (2)　　　　　　　　　　　C　　SCA
SSSS　　　　　　　　　　　　　　　　　　1978

Featuring exclusive interviews with former Secretaries of State, this program illustrates the intricate workings of the oldest executive department in the U.S. government. From the Secretary to ambassadors and policy planners, comments reveal the functions and organizational structure of what may be the most important of all federal agencies. The program also reviews the history of the agency and the influence of Secretaries from Jefferson to Cyrus Vance.

IR-E-6
THE MAKING OF AMERICAN FOREIGN POLICY　　　SCA
FS, Cassettes (4)　　　　　　　　　　　C
SSSS

A multimedia kit designed to promote a clearer understanding of the complex machinery of foreign policy decision-making. The filmstrips offer an in-depth examination of the individuals and institutions involved in making American foreign policy, focus on the ways in which other nations are governed, investigate how our national security interests are determined, and trace the impact of economic interests in shaping foreign policy. Coordinated follow-up materials include a teacher's guide, readings on spirit masters and masters for transparencies.

IR-E-7
MAKING FOREIGN POLICY: White House and
State Department   SCA
            Audio-cassette   1980
            NPR   29 min
How can the U.S. formulate and implement foreign policy when an unresolved
conflict between the Secretary of State and the National Security Advisor exists?
Dr. Joseph Sisco, former Undersecretary of State, General Brent Scowcroft,
former National Security Advisor, and former President Ford discuss the effects
of this conflict.

IR-E-8
THE QUIET BATTLE   A
            16mm   Sd   C   1964
            NAVC   28 min
This government-produced film portrays the U.S. foreign assistance program at
work. Focuses on how this "quiet battle" to help the people of developing nations
achieve a better life for themselves was won in Greece and Taiwan and still
continues in other countries. The commentary states that economic and social
development stimulate "a basic goal of U.S. foreign policy: the strengthening of
the free world."

IR-E-9
THE SENATE FOREIGN RELATIONS COMMITTEE   SCA
            Audio-cassette   1981
            NPR   29 min
The role of Congress in setting American foreign policy and the part played by
the Senate Foreign Relations Committee are examined in this program. Listeners
hear proceedings of the committee as it considers U.S. involvement in Vietnam,
the second treaty to limit strategic arms, and the confirmation of General
Alexander Haig as Secretary of State. Joe Biden (D-Del), Senator Charles Mathias
(R-Md), and Carl Marcy, former staff director of the committee are interviewed.

IR-E-10
SHOWROOM TO THE WORLD   A
            16mm   C   1978
            NAVC   6 min
Explains what a US Trade Center is, and what it does as a service of the
Departments of Commerce and State. These centers offer American business a
place to exhibit their products in coordinated marketing expositions. Gives a
viewer a look at these centers in New York, Paris and Stockholm. Describes how
one company has success in utilizing this marketing service.

IR-E-11
SO FAIR A LAND   A
            16mm   Sd   C   1977
            NAVC   15 min
Shows how the U.S. Foreign Aid Program works in the Dominican Republic. Also
demonstrates how aid assisted activities are making a difference in the lives of
the forest people.

International Relations - Concepts

IR-F-1
BALANCE OF POWER
     FS, Cassettes (2)
     SSSS
                                            C   SCA 1976

This two-part color sound filmstrip examines the nature of the balance of power that, for the present, suspends hostilities between the major world powers. The program examines the changing nature of the balance of power and how in recent years it has ceased to be a balance of total resources and alliances. Detente is analyzed, and several people in government give their views about its effectiveness, including Senators Henry Jackson and Edward Kennedy.

IR-F-2
DOOMSDAY: 21ST CENTURY?
     FS, Cassettes (2)
     SSSS
     C   SCA

Using expert testimony from such organizations as the Club of Rome, World-watch Institute, and the Overseas Development Council, this two-part filmstrip examines how modern society is overtaxing the resources of the planet and the possible consequences. The programs examines food shortages, resource scarcity and evironmental destruction, then considers some of the technological solutions and compromises in lifestyles which could prevent doomsday from occurring in the 21st century.

IR-F-3
EXPLORING POLITICAL TERRORISM
     FS, Cassettes (3)
     SSSS
     C   SCA 1982

An attempt to answer some fundamental questions on political terrorism: What is it? What gives terrorism its power? Why do people become terrorists? How do they operate? How can terrorism be controlled and eradicated? Using both historical and recent incidents as illustrations, this three-part filmstrip program gives a psychological profile of the "average" terrorist, discusses the role of such foreign governments as the USSR and Libya in supporting terrorism, explores antiterrorist tactics (refusal to negotiate, survival courses, formation of an international police force), and examines such disparate groups as anarchists, the PLO, the IRA, the Weather Underground, neo-Nazis, and the SLA.

    1. Tactics, Methods & Organization
    2. Terrorism, Past & Present
    3. Controlling Terrorism

IR-F-4
IMPERIALISM
     FS, Cassette
     SSSS
     C   SCA

The word imperialism has been used so frequently and in so many different contexts that its value as a descriptive term has been considerably eroded. Is there such a thing as imperialism today? If so, is it anything like the imperialism of the 19th century? The theories on imperialism of Hobson, Lenin, and Schumpeter are described and compared. They are then applied to such events as the Boer War and the Spanish-American War in order to examine how well they explain their causes and effects. The filmstrip demonstrates the inadequacy of these theories in explaining great power behavior today, and outlines the efforts of contemporary writers to develop new concepts and new explanations. The multinational corporation is examined as it relates to theories on imperialism.

IR-F-5
REVOLUTION   SCA
          FS, Cassettes (4)   C
          SSSS
What, exactly, is involved in a revolution? This four-part color sound filmstrip examines the elements of revolution by surveying the events of three revolutionary movements, then discussing generalization about revolutionary causes, justifications, and results. The program first examines the revolutions of France, Russia, and Cuba. The fourth filmstrip covers theories of revolution generated by such thinkers as Thomas Jefferson, Karl Marx, Albert Camus, and Milovan Djilas. A teacher's guide contains complete scripts and suggestions for discussions and projects.

IR-F-6
TERROR: To Confront or Concede   SCA
          16mm, UBV   C   1978
          Films, Inc.   50min
Political outrage is nothing new, but its latest manifestation in terrorist violence has made it schockingly clear that a small band of dedicated guerrillas can create havoc out of all proportion to its numbers. Uruguayan terrorists and members of the Quebec liberation front are interviewed about their political ambitions and terrorist tactics. A diplomat kidnapped and later released is interviewed. What can be done to meet terrorism?

IR-F-7
TERRORISM   SCA
          FS, Cassettes (2)   C   1979
          SSSS
A two-part sound filmstrip on the recent expansion of worldwide political terrorism. Focusing on the murders, bombings, and hijackings by the Japanese Red Army, the I.R.A., and the P.L.O., these filmstrips raise fundamental questions regarding the political motivation and effects of these actions, as well as the role of governments and counter intelligence agencies in protecting the innocent. The fine line between the need for security and the rights of personal freedom and privacy is examined. Eight spirit duplicating masters include scripts and suggestions for further activities.

IR-F-8
THE UNITED NATIONS: End of A Dream   CA
          FS, Cassette   C   1977
          SSSS
Has the United Nations outlived its usefulness as a force for world peace? This filmstrip outlines the hopes which the world held for the UN and discusses recent events which have brought the international organization into question. The program traces the ways in which the UN is being bypassed in major international questions, discusses its political and financial difficulties, and questions the purposes it serves.

IR-F-9
WAR CRIMES   SCA
          FS, Cassette   C
          SSSS
This sound filmstrip shows how war crimes, a violation of international law, can

become a very personal problem for a young man drafted into the Army. Explores the questions: Does international law really exist? Is it the same as domestic law? How can the killing which the soldier is ordered to do by his government be considered a crime? It traces the concept of war crimes from the Hague Conventions through the Nuremberg Trials to the war in Vietnam and the trial of Lt. Calley. It examines the responsibilities of soldiers in the field and their commanders.

IR-F-10
WORLD TERRORISM: What Can Be Done?   SCA
       FS, Cassette   C   1983
       SSSS
Terrorists worldwide aspire to widely disparate goals, from media manipulation to the topping of governments. Where should the line be drawn between organized resistance to totalitarian oppression and professionally orchestrated violence? Comparing and contrasting specific international incidents, this filmstrip program outlines suggested strategies for suppression. A timely treatment attempting to probe the terrorist psyche, the filmstrip investigates such motivational forces as religious grievance, economic oppression, and ideological conflict. Teacher's guide provided.

Language, Literature, and Journalism

Miles Orvell

The user may find it useful to know what is and what isn't in the listing that follows. The materials in this catalogue are in general not primary but secondary in nature; that is, they are <u>about</u> language, literature and journalism, rather than original sources. Nevertheless, in many cases examples of primary materials have been incorporated into the various commentaries and discussions. And in a few cases, where materials that are originally of a printed nature have been judged to be strongly oral in nature, primary sources have also been included. For example, Whitman's poetry, or Vachel Lindsay's exist as much as spoken words as they do as printed text, so recordings have been included in the listing; the same goes for recordings of historic speeches, which were of course originally designed to be heard, and so are included under "Language" as recordings.

Most of the materials are no earlier than 1970, though in a few cases, where recent productions are not available, earlier listings are included.

Finally, the user should be aware of some resources not included in this catalogue that may be of great interest to students of American language, literature, and journalism. Available primary materials are rich in these fields and include the following: the <u>Caedmon</u> catalogue of "Spoken-Word Classics" on audio-cassette, a rich library of American literature and theatre; the catalogue of <u>Spoken Recordings</u>, available on LP records and cassette tapes, produced by the Library of Congress; the <u>American Audio Prose Library</u>, a collection of interviews with, and readings by, contemporary authors, produced by KOPN in Columbia, Missouri; and, of course, students of the novel may be interested in viewing the many American films that have been produced over the course of the twentieth century based on novels. These are available from a variety of film distributors.

LANGUAGE, LITERATURE AND JOURNALISM (La,Li,Lj)

La-A	Structure and Function
La-B	Historic Speeches
Li-A	Fiction
Li-B	Poetry
Li-C	Drama
Li-D	History and Background
Li-E	Regional Cultures
Li-F	Women
Li-G	Black
Lj-A	History
Lj-B	Social Issues
Lj-C	Newspapers
Lj-D	Television

Language — Structure and Function

La-A-1
DEFINITION OF LANGUAGE, A   SC
     16mm   Sd   B   1957
     Net Film Service   30 min
Dr. Henry Lee Smith, Jr., continues the definition of language begun in the film
LANGUAGE AND WRITING and explains the relationship of language to culture.

La-A-2
EFFECTIVE COMMUNICATION: BETTER CHOICE OF WORDS   S
     16mm   Sd   C   1974
     Coronet   10 min
Lou finds his small vocabulary a real handicap when he tries to describe a lovely
girl and an exciting dragstrip race. As we watch Lou widen his word choice, we
see the value of the dictionary and thesaurus in making speaking and writing more
effective. The importance of context and connotations for better comunication is
entertainingly presented.

La-A-3
ENGLISH LANGUAGE, THE: ITS SPELLING PATTERNS   SC
     16mm   Sd   C   1972
     Coronet   14 min
When researchers programmed a computer to help improve the teaching of
spelling, the results showed that most English words follow predictable spelling
patterns and that the history of the language usually explains the exceptions.
Learning basic patterns plus using the dictionary can help us overcome spelling
problems.

La-A-4
GOOD OLD AMERICAN ENGLISH   S
     Audio-cassette   1979
     NPR   59 min
Is language deteriorating through chronic misuse and is technical jargon making it
harder to communicate? Participants discuss communication, double-talk, poor
grammar, and the present state of American language. Traditionalists debate with
proponents of a flexible colloquial language.

La-A-5
IMPROVE YOUR PRONUNCIATION   S
     16mm   Sd   C   1972
     Coronet   11 min
Four teen-agers and a narrator engage in a discussion of pronunciation problems.
They identify such common problems as sound smudging, word grunting, and
tranposing, changing, dropping and adding sounds. They learn that pronunciation
can be improved by using the dictionary, listening to yourself, and listening to
others.

La-A-6
THE LANGUAGE OF MAN: HOW WORDS CHANGE OUR LIVES   S
     35mm, Cassettes (2)   Sd   C   1974
     Center for Humanities   120 slides
Explores how we structure our world with words and how we derive general
conclusions from specific observations through the use of abstraction. Also
discusses the use of stereotypes, euphemisms and loaded words.

La-A-7
NOAM CHOMSKY   SC
        Audio-cassette   1980
        NPR   60 min
Linguist Noam Chomsky believes that the natural ability of people to learn
language is the essence of human nature. This program humorously explores the
structures of language and its varied uses.

La-A-8
THEORIES OF ENGLISH GRAMMAR   S
        16mm   1964
        MGHT   30 min
In this film, three theories of English grammar are discussed with the aim of
demonstrating how adequate each is as a theory. The theories discussed are the
traditional, the structural and the transformational.

La-A-9
WATCH YOUR LANGUAGE: USAGE (AND ABUSAGE)   S
        35mm, Cassette (2)   1977
        Center for Humanities   120 slides
Sharpens students' awareness of the language they speak, hear, read and write.
Demonstrates what happens when words are used carelessly, deceptively or
maliciously and helps students understand the distinction between standard and
non-standard English.

                    Language -- Historic Speeches

La-B-1
GREAT AMERICAN INDIAN SPEECHES   SC
        Audio Cassette (2)   1975
        Caedmon
In the field of oratory the American Indian can show clear mastery. The
eloquence of the speeches of Geronimo, Standing Bear, Cochise, Ten Bears and
many others are preserved here, for listening and contemplation. Speeches by:
Powhatan; Canassatego; Chief Logan; Chief Buckangahelas; Pontiac; Red Jacket;
Chief Tecumseh; Pushmataha; Red Eagle; Metoa; Chief Patalesharo; Senachwine;
Black Hawk; Arapooish; Chief John Ross; Chief Seattle; Little Crow; Cochise;
Lone Wolf; Chief Ten Bears; Chief Satanta; Chief Manuelito; Chief Red Cloud;
Little Raven; Chief Charlot; Chief Joseph; Geronimo; Black Elk; Standing Bear.

La-B-2
GREAT AMERICAN SPEECHES: 1775-1986   SC
        Audio Cassette (2)   1958
        Caedman
PATRICK HENRY: Liberty or Death; GEORGE WASHINGTON: First Inaugural
Address; THOMAS JEFFERSON: First Inaugural Address; JOSIAH QUINCY: On the
Admission of Louisiana; HENRY CLAY: On the War of 1812; ABRAHAM LINCOLN:
The "House Divided" Speech; The Cooper Union Speech; The Gettysburg Address;
CHARLES SUMNER: The Crime Against Kansas; ROBERT TOOMBS: On Secession;
ROBERT E. LEE: Farewell to His Troops; WILLIAM JENNINGS BRYAN: The
"Cross of Gold" Speech.

La-B-3
GREAT AMERICAN SPEECHES: 1898-1918   SC
    Audio Cassette (2)   1958
    Caedmon
WILLIAM JENNINGS BRYAN: Naboth's Vineyard; ALBERT JEREMIAH BEVERIDGE:
The March of the Flag; MARK TWAIN: Public Education; THEODORE
ROOSEVELT: The Man with the Muck Rake; CLARENCE SEWARD DARROW: To
the Jury: Self-defense ROBERT M. LAFOLLETTE: Soldier's Pay; WOODROW
WILSON: Fourteen Points.

La-B-4
GREAT AMERICAN SPEECHES: 1931-1947   SC
    Audio Cassette (2)   1958
    Caedmon
OLIVER WENDELL HOLMES, JR: On His Ninetieth Brithday; FRANKLIN D.
ROOSEVELT: First Inaugural Address; Declaration of War; WILL ROGERS:
Morgenthau's Plan; HERBERT HOOVER: War Comes to Europe; WENDELL
WILLKIE: Loyal Opposition; DWIGHT D. EISENHOWER: Order of the Day; HARRY
S. TRUMAN: The Truman Doctrine; GEORGE C. MARSHALL: The Marshall Plan.

La-B-5
GREAT AMERICAN SPEECHES: 1950-1963   SC
    Audio Cassette (2)   1958
    Caedmon
WILLIAM FAULKNER: Nobel Prize Speech; DOUGLAS MACARTHUR: Address
before Congress; ADLAI STEVENSON: Acceptance of Nomination; Eulogy for John
Kennedy; CARL SANDBURG: Abraham Lincoln; JOHN F KENNEDY: Opening
Statement, the Fourth Kennedy-Nixon Debate; Inaugural Address; RICHARD
NIXON: Opening Statement, the Fourth Kennedy-Nixon Debate.

La-B-6
GREAT AMERICAN WOMEN'S SPEECHES   SC
    Audio Cassette   1972
    Caedmon
Declaration of Sentiments and Resolutions: The First Woman's Rights Convention,
Seneca Falls, New York; LUCRETIA MOTT: A Demand for the Political Rights of
Women; SOJURNER TRUTH: The Women Want Their Rights!; Ain't I a Woman?;
ERNESTINE POTOWSKI ROSE: Remove the Legal Shackles from Women; LUCY
STONE: Disappointment is the Lot of Woman; ELIZABETH CADY STANTON:
Address to the New York State Legislature; Womanliness; Solitude of Self; "We
Who Like the Children of Israel"; Susan B. Anthony: Are Women Persons?;
CARRIE CHAPMAN CATT: Address to the National American Woman Suffrage
Association; FLORENCE KELLY: Working Women Need the Ballot; ANNA
HOWARD SHAW: Emotionalism in Politics.

La-B-7
GREAT BLACK SPEECHES   SC
    Audio Cassette (2)   1974
    Caedmon
This recording includes speeches by four famous black Americans, written and
delivered in the nineteenth century. Frederick Douglass appeals to the British
people to examine their feelings about slavery, and Booker T. Washington
discusses the problems after Emancipation.

FRANCES MARIA STEWART: O Ye Sons of Africa; HENRY HIGHLAND CARMET:
Rather Die Freemen Than Live to Be Slaves; FREDERICK DOUGLASS: An Appeal

to the British People; BOOKER T. WASHINGTON: Atlanta Exposition Address.

Literature -- Fiction

Li-A-1
AGEE, JAMES, EVANS, WALKER: LET US NOW PRAISE   SC
FAMOUS MEN
          Audio-cassette   1980
          Caedmon
This recording contains readings from the classic documentary study of a white
sharecroper family in the Depression South. It tells of the lives of three families,
the George Gudgers, the Bud Woods, and the Fred Ricketts, caught in the terrible
grinding poverty of tenant-farmers.

Li-A-2
AMERICAN SHORT STORY, THE: A SERIES   SCA
          16MM, UBV   SD   C   1977&80
          CORONET
The series consists of 18 films of varying length which dramatize short stories by
America's best short story writers.

Introduction to the Series	23 1/2min
Rappaccini's Daughter (Nathaniel Hawthorne)	57min
Parker Adderson, Philisopher (Ambrose Bierce)	38 1/2min
The Jolly Corner (Henry James)	43min
Barn Burning (William Faulkner)	41min
The Blue Hotel (Stephen Crane)	54 1/2min
The Man That Corrupted Hadleyburg (Mark Twain)	40min
Paul's Case (Willa Cather)	54 1/2min
I'm A Fool (Sherwood Anderson)	38min
Soldier's Home (Ernest Hemingway)	41 1/2min
The Golden Honeymoon (Ring Lardner)	52min
Bernice Bobs Her Hair (F. Scott Fitzgerald)	47 1/2min
The Greatest Man In The World (James Thurber)	51min
Almos' A Man (Richard Wright)	39min
The Jilting of Granny Weatherall (Katherine Anne Porter)	57min
The Sky Is Gray (Ernest Gaines)	46 1/2min
The Displaced Person (Flannery O'Connor)	57 1/2min
The Music School (John Updike)	30min

Li-A-3
ART OF HUCKLEBERRY FINN, THE   SC
          16mm   Sd   C   1965
          EBEC   25 min
Here, Clifton Fadiman deals with the novel as a work of literary art. He identifies
three unifying threads in the novel; the idea of a central point of view,
development of two major symbols -- the river and the shore.

Li-A-4
AUTHORITY AND REBELLION   SC
          16mm   Sd   C   1973
          LCA   31 min
This is a specially edited version of the feature film, "The Caine Mutiny," with

Humphrey Bogart. Focuses on the first half of Herman Wouk's novel. Discusses the theme of our acceptance of authority and the relationship between moral responsibility and rebellion.

Li-A-5
BARTLEBY, A DISCUSSION OF   SC
         16mm   Sd   C   1969
         EBEC   10 min
Dr. Charles Van Doren, author, Associate Director of the Institute for Philosophical Research, presents his insights and ideas on Herman Melville's Bartleby, using flashbacks from the original film footage to illustrate his points.

Li-A-6
DOROTHY PARKER: DOROTHY PARKER STORIES   SC
         Audio-cassette
         Caedmon
All the stories reveal Parker's wit, compassion, understatement and marvelous ear for straight talk. Four stories, performed by Shirley Booth.

Li-A-7
DR. HEIDEGGER'S EXPERIMENT, A Discussion Of Use   SC
         16mm   Sd   C   1969
         EBEC   11 min
Clifton Fadiman, author and General Editor of Encyclopedia Britannica's Humanities Film Series, presents his insights and ideas on Nathaniel Hawthorne's Dr. Heidegger's Experiment, using flashbacks from the original film footage to illustrate his points.

Li-A-8
EDGAR ALLAN POE: BACKGROUND FOR HIS WORKS   SC
         UBV   Sd   C   1979
         Coronet   13 min
Shows Poe as an innovator of horror stories, detective stories and science fiction. Includes excerpts from his poems "To Helen" and "The Raven" and his stories "The Fall of the House of Usher" and "The Murders in the Rue Morgue".

Li-A-9
ERNEST HEMINGWAY   SC
         Audio Cassette   1981
         NPR   40 min
This segment features actor Peter Weller reading from the 1924 short story "Big Two-Hearted River." Critic Leslie Fiedler discusses the relationship between the individual and the wilderness in Hemingway's work. Also, segments on Stephen Crane, James Jones, and Raymond Chandler.

Li-A-10
EUGENE O'NEILL   SC
         Audio-cassette   1981
         NPR   40 min
Tony award winning actor Len Cariou reads from O'Neill's works, and biographer Barbara Gelb shares her thoughts about the author's torturous yet successful life. Also, segments on James Agee, Delmore Schwartz, and Jack London.

Li-F-11
FALL OF THE HOUSE OF USHER, A DISCUSSION OF   SC
(Short Story Showcase from Humanities Series)
            16mm   Sd   C   1976
            EBEC   12 min
Science fiction writer Ray Bradbury comments on the story, compares this screen
play to the written work, and discusses the gothic tradition and Poe's influence
on contemporary science fiction.

Li-A-12
GREAT AMERICAN NOVEL, THE: BABBITT   SC
            16mm   Sd   C   1968
            BFA   26 min
Feel the test of timelessness of this great novel as you listen to Lion's Club
businessmen of Duluth, Minnesota, the "Zenith City" of the story. Many facets of
Babbitt are discussed. The viewer will see how well Sinclair Lewis captured the
picture of the typical businessman of forty years ago.

Li-A-13
GREAT AMERICAN NOVEL, THE: SC
THE GRAPES OF WRATH
            16mm   Sd   C   1968
            BFA   29 min
How different are the people in The Grapes of Wrath, uprooted by the great
depression from their farm, from similar people of today who are migrating from
rural areas? John Steinbeck gives an exceptionally vivid portrayal of people
uprooted through no fault of their own.

Li-A-14
GREAT AMERICAN NOVEL, THE: MOBY DICK   SC
            16mm   Sd   C   1969
            BFA   25 min
A modern-day fishing trawler, its captain and crew are used to illustrate the
universality of Herman Melville's monumental novel. We examine both the
temporal and philosophical aspects of this modern voyage. The effect is to create
an awareness of the timelessness of Melville's work and to suggest that similar
values lie in all great literature.

Li-A-15
HEMINGWAY   SC
            16mm   Sd   B   1961
            MGHT   51 min
The film emphasizes Hemingway's lifelong bravery, integrity, and devotion to sport
and to art. Using still photographs and motion pictures for insight into key
episodes of Hemingway's life and times, the film moves from a discussion of the
Hemingway code to material about his parents and his own children, to his
schooling at home, in the classroom and abroad on the field of battle.

Li-A-16
HENRY MILLER: An Interview   S
            Audio-cassette ·   1977
            NPR   59 min
In 1977, producer Connie Goldman interviewed Henry Miller. He candidly
articulates his reasons for being a writer, influences on his writing, and paradoxes
in his personality and his world.

Li-A-17
HERMAN MELVILLE   SC
            Audio-cassette   1981
            NPR   40 min
This program celebrates the publication of the monumental novel Moby Dick, one
of the greatest works in English. Critics Alfred Kazin and Leslie Fiedler discuss
Melville's literary career and the importance of Moby Dick to the literary canon.
Actor George Hearn reads from the famous opening and closing passages of the
novel, published in 1851. Also segments on Theodore Dreiser, Joyce Carol Oates,,
and Zane Grey.

Li-A-18
HUCKLEBERRY FINN AND THE AMERICAN EXPERIENCE, III   SC
            16mm   Sd   C   1965
            EBEC   27 min
Clifton Fadiman prompts us to see the story of "Huck" as a viable experience that
spans time.

Li-A-19
JACK KEROUAC   S
            Audio-cassette   1979
            NPR   59 min
Lawrence Lee, co-author of A Biography of Jack Kerouac, comments on his
subject, a novelist who shaped the "beat generation" of American writers. Mr.
Lee's lively analysis provides a good introduction to Kerouac. Produced by Glen
Mitchell of NPR member station KERA.

Li-A-20
JAMES MICHENER   S
            Audio-cassette   1979
            NPR   59 min
James Michener appears at a National Press Club meeting to discuss the state of
the novel. He talks extensively about many contemporary writers, including women
writers Oates, Plath, Didion, and Rossner. Produced by Rich Firestone.

Li-A-21
JAMES THURBER'S THE NIGHT THE GHOST GOT IN   SC
            16mm   Sd   C   1976
            NPR   15 min
This is an interpretation of Thurber's story designed to provide enjoyment.

Li-A-22
JOHN DOS PASSOS: U.S.A.   CA
            Audio-cassette   1979
            Caedmon
These are selections from 42nd Parallel, giving a panoramic picture of life and
events in the United States in the period just preceding World War One. This is
the work of a master storyteller.

Li-A-23
KURT VONNEGUT: A Self-Interview   S
            Audio-cassette   1977
            NPR   59 min
Vonnegut discusses western art and meditation, films and writing, the effects of
media on the imagination and the intellect, his family background, and his
experiences in World War II. The Program concludes with Vonnegut reading an
excerpt from an early draft of his most recent novel, Jailbird.

Li-A-24
KURT VONNEGUT: "DEADEYE DICK"   SCA
        16mm   Sd   C   1983
        Wombat Productions   60min
Vonnegut narrates excerpts from his books, revealing himself as a gentle and
life-loving man. Includes dramatized episodes enabling his main character and
acknowledged alter-ego, Kilgore Trout, to emerge from the printed page and
interact with Vonnegut himself.

Li-A-25
THE LEGEND OF MARK TWAIN   SC
        16mm   Sd   C
        Benchmark Films   32 min
THE LEGEND OF MARK TWAIN follows the life and influence of Samuel Clemens
on the American scene and dramatizes selections from two of his well-known
classics: The Celebrated Jumping Frog of Calaveras County and The Adventures
of Huckleberry Finn.

Li-A-26
LIFE ON THE MISSISSIPPI   SC
        16mm,UBV   Sd   C   1981
        NETCHE   120min
Life on the Mississippi is a dramatization of Mark Twain's epic chronicle of a
young man's coming of age on America's greatest river. The novel grew out of
Twain's own experiences when, as a young man, he fulfilled his boyhood ambition
to become a river pilot. After a difficult apprenticeship during which he braved
the hazards of the deceptive ever-changing river and a potentially disastrous
brush with an egomaniacal pilot, he earned his license, and with it, a new
maturity.

Li-A-27
LITERATURE IN AMERICA: THE SHORT STORY   SC
        16mm film   Sd   C   1962
        Grover Jennings Prod.   20 min
Presents examples of composition by Edgar Allan Poe, Washington Irving,
Nathaniel Hawthorne, Mark Twain, O. Henry, William Faulkner, John Steinbeck,
James Thurber, and others.

Li-A-28
LOTTERY, THE: A Discussion Of   SC
        16mm   Sd   C   1969
        EBEC   10 min
Dr. James Durbin, Associate Professor of English at the University of Southern
California, shares his insights and ideas about Shirley Jackson's "The Lottery,"
using flashbacks from the original film footage to illustrate his points.

Li-A-29
MARK TWAIN   SC
        Audio-cassette   1981
        NPR   40 min
This two-part program features actor Len Cariou reading from the lectures,
letters, diaries, and novels of this most American of authors. Alfred Kazin
comments. Also, segments on Henry Miller, Jack Kerouac, and John Dos Passos.

Li-A-30
MARK TWAIN   SC
    16mm   Sd   B   1963
    MGHT   26 min
We see here, through the use of a actual photographs, a comprehensive picture of
Twain's life -- its color and its excitement, its tragedies and its successes.

Li-A-31
MARK TWAIN: BACKGROUND FOR HIS WORK   S
    16mm   B,C   1957
    Coronet   14 min
Authentic backgrounds, quotations, and re-enactments enrich the study of Mark
Twain's works. The variety and color of his boyhood on the Mississippi are shown
to be a source of his major writings; his other works reflect his life as journalist,
yarn-spinner, and humorist.

Li-A-32
MARK TWAIN: BENEATH THE LAUGHTER   SCA
    16mm, UBV   1979
    Pyramid Films   58 min
Explores the nature of "the dark side of Twain" and the deep cynicism of his later
years. A dramatization.

Li-A-33
MARK TWAIN GIVES AN INTERVIEW   SC
    16mm   B   1961
    Coronet   13 min
Hal Holbrook's classic impersonation of Mark Twain is recreated.

Li-A-34
MARY HEMINGWAY: LIFE WITH ERNEST   S
    Audio-cassette   1977
    NPR   59 min
Mary Hemingway, wife of Ernest Hemingway, talks with Susan Stamberg, co-host
of NPR'S All Things Considered, providing a straightforward, self-effacing
account of her life with this famous American author.

Li-A-35
MR. CLEMENS AND MARK TWAIN:
THE WRITER AS AMERICAN   S
    FS, Cassettes(2)   C   1979
    Center for Humanities
Offers insight into Mark Twain's main themes and best-known works through
dramatically read excerpts from his fiction, essays and letters.

Li-A-36
MY OLD MAN, A Discussion Of   SC
    16mm   Sd   C   1969
    EBEC   11 min
Blake Nevius, Professor of English, University of California at Los Angeles,
presents his insights and ideas on Ernest Hemingway's "My Old Man," using
flashbacks from the original film footage to illustrate his points.

Li-A-37
PEARL S. BUCK (Wisdom Series)   SC
        16mm   B   1960
        EBEC   30 min
Miss Buck describes some of the happiest days of her childhood in China, points
out basic differences between the Western and Oriental approaches to living,
discusses the changes that have taken place under the Communist regime in
China, and considers ways in which America may recover the good will which has
been lost in Asia.

Li-A-38
SCIENCE-FICTION WRITER
BEN BOVA   CA
        Audio-cassette   1979
        NPR   59 min
Ben Bova talks about when and how he began to write science fiction, how and
where he gets his ideas, and the sometimes prophetic nature of science-fiction
writing.

Li-A-39
SINCLAIR LEWIS: IT CAN'T HAPPEN HERE   SC
        Audio-cassette   1973
        Caedmon
This condensation of the important and topical novel focuses on the steps by
which the United States might slip into totalitarianism through a series of
carefully manipulated conspiracies by a popular President, with the aid of "a few
men at the top." Read brilliantly by the author's son, who was also a gifted actor,
this recording offers a penetrating analysis of America's present and potential
future.

Li-A-40
STEPHEN CRANE (The Authors Series)   SC
        16mm   Sd   C   1978
        Journal Films   21 min
Crane is portrayed retelling the story of his life. He reviews the motivation,
critical acclaim and financial reward for his masterpiece The Red Badge of
Courage, as well as his other well-known works.

Li-A-41
THOMAS WOLFE   SC
        Audio-cassette   1981
        NPR   40 min
Critic James Atlas talks about Wolfe's lyric style and the relationship of his life
to his art. Actor Sam Waterston reads from novel, Wolfe's first: Look Homeward,
Angel. Also, segments on Edith Wharton, Carson McCullers, and Randall Jarrell.

Li-A-42
WHAT DOES HUCKLEBERRY FINN SAY?   SC
        16mm   Sd   C   1965
        EBEC   28 min
Clifton Fadiman takes the intellectual content of the novel as a whole. Points out
that Huckleberry Finn can be viewed from three angles: as an adventure story, as
the picture of a world, and as a drama of moral conflict.

Li-A-43
WILLIAM FAULKNER   SCA
     Audio-cassette   1980
     NPR   60 mins
This program features Tennessee Williams as William Faulkner in dramatized
excerpts from several of his novels and vivid recreations of his personal life.

Li-A-44
WILLIAM FAULKNER: A LIFE ON PAPER   SC
     16mm   Sd   C   1980
     Mississippi ETV
This is the definitive recollection of the life of the Nobel Prize winning author by
friends from his home town of Oxford, Mississippi including his daughter, Jill
Faulkner Summers, and his Hollywood friends Lauren Bacall, Howard Hawks, Anita
Loos, George Plimpton, and playwright Tennessee Williams.

Li-A-45
WILLIAM FAULKNER'S MISSISSIPPI   SC
     16mm   B
     Benchmark Films   49 min
Recreates this distinguished author's background to explain the subtle conflict
within, both black and white. The film includes readings from the following books
by Faulkner: Absolom, Absolom ... Intruder in the Dust ... Requiem for a Nun ...
The Hamlet ... The Mansion ... The Sound and the Fury ... The Town ... The
Unvanquished.

Li-A-46
WRITING: AN INTERVIEW WITH IRVING STONE   SCA
     UBV   1978
     Coronet   18 1/2min
In an informal interview at his home-studio, Irving Stone traces his writing career,
reveals his motivation, methodology and tips to novice writers.

                          Literature -- Poetry

Li-B-1
AUTUMN: FROST COUNTRY   SC
     16mm   Sd   C   1969
     Holt, Rhinehart, Winston   9 min
Around a framework of two of Robert Frost's poems the film captures the
hypnotic beauty of a New England autumn. Opening with "The Road Not Taken,"
visuals enhance the poem's mystique. The journey and the season end with Frost's
"Reluctance."

Li-B-2
BENET, STEPHEN VINCENT, BENET, ROSEMARY:
A BOOK OF AMERICANS   SC
     Audiocassette (2)   1974
     Caedmon
This delightful collection of light verse is recorded here in its entirety.

Li-B-3
BERRIGAN, DANIEL: BERRIGAN RAPS   SC
          Audio-cassette   1970
          Caedmon
Dan Berrigan reads his poetry and talks about the War, the System, the Church,
the Future and his arrest.

Li-B-4
CARL SANDBURG (Wisdom Series)   SC
          16mm   Sd   B   1958
          EBEC   28 min
The famous American poet plays his guitar and sings folk songs. He recalls some
of his adventures as a newspaper reporter, and speaks with gentle and
heart-warming eloquence of his life-long dedication to his writings on the life of
Lincoln.

Li-B-5
CARL SANDBURG   SC
          Audio-cassette   1980
          NPR   29 min
This program is taken from his last book, Breathing Tokens, published
posthumously in 1978 in which 118 previously unpublished poems appear. The
selections presented here demonstrate his ability both to articulate his traditional
themes as well as express more contemporary, experimental subject matter.

Li-B-6
CARL SANDBURG DISCUSSES HIS WORKS   SC
          16mm   1961
          Coronet   13 min
We gain a fascinating insight into the character of this great American as he
speaks of his early years, his struggle to gain fame, and his philosophy.

Li-B-7
CARL SANDBURG DISCUSSES LINCOLN   SC
          16mm   Sd   1961
          Coronet   11 min
Carl Sandburg speaks of the Abraham Lincoln he knows so intimately.

Li-B-8
E.E. CUMMINGS   SC
          Audio-cassette   1981
          NPR   29 min
This program presents a selection of his work taken from Complete Poems
1913-1962.

Li-B-9
EMILY DICKINSON AND MARIANNE MOORE   SC
          Audio-cassette   1980
          NPR   29 min
Through dramatic readings, this program presents the work of two of America's
most distinguished poets, Emily Dickinson and Marianne Moore. Both poets share a
gift for judicious idiosyncracy, precise imagery and the unexpected but persuasive
turn of phrase.

Li-B-10
ROBERT FROST (Wisdom Series)   SC
        16mm   Sd   B   1958
        EBEC   28 min
Discusses his life and work with Bela Kornitzer, Hungarian-born author, at his
farm home in Vermont. Frost recalls the wide range of personal experiences — as
a mill worker, country school teacher, cobbler, small-town editor, and farmer —
that furnished the background for his achievements in poetry.

Li-B-11
ROBERT FROST   SC
        Audio-cassette   1980
        NPR   60 min
Robert Frost is featured reading some of his own poems and in conversation with
fellow poet John Ciardi. Russell Horton portrays Frost.

Li-B-12
GARY SNYDER   SC
        Audio-cassette   1981
        NPR   29 min
This program features readings from Gary Snyder's Turtle Island, which was
awarded the Pulitzer Prize for Poetry in 1975. Snyder's poetry reflects both
Eastern and Western influences, but it is always grounded in the natural world.

Li-B-13
GREAT AMERICAN POETRY   SC
        Audio-cassette (2)   1962
        Caedmon
Performance by Vincent Price, Julie Harris, Eddie Albert, Helen Gahagan Douglas,
Ed Begley. Selections from outstanding American poets perfomed by outstanding
actors.

Li-B-14
HENRY WADSWORTH LONGFELLOW   S
        16mm   B   1949
        EBEC   17 min
Dramatizes events which reveal Longfellow's dedication to create a native
American poetry, and to encourage a taste for the poetry of other countries.

Li-B-15
LINDSAY, VACHEL: THE POETRY OF VACHEL LINDSAY   SC
        Audio-cassette   1967
        Caedmon
On this recording Vachel Lindsay's son, Nicholas Cave Lindsay, reads a selection
of the poet's most representative poems.

Li-B-16
LINDSAY, VACHEL: VACHEL LINDSAY READING THE CONGO,
CHINESE NIGHTINGALE AND OTHER POEMS   SC
        Audio-cassette   1956
        Caedmon
Lindsay became a phenomenon of the American Scene as he toured the country
reading and singing in the period that accompanied the First World War and its
aftermath.

Li-B-17
MODERN AMERICAN POETS   SC
          Audio-cassette   1980
          NPR   50min
This two-part section includes a generous sampling of modern American poetry,
from its beginnings to the present day.

Part A - 50 min

1. EMILY DICKINSON -- See: EMILY DICKINSON and MARIANNE MOORE

2. ADRIENNE RICH -- One of America's most recognized contemporary poets.
Adrienne Rich has dedicated her life to social and political change, particularly
the Women's Movement. This segment features Adrienne Rich reading works from
her most recent book of poetry, A Wild Patience Has Taken Me This Far,
including the title poem. Rich discusses the role of the woman writer and the
relationship between her life, her art, and society.

3. JAMES RUSSELL LOWELL -- James Russell was expelled from Harvard for
cutting classes, became famous as a writer of poetic satire, and moved from being
a left-winger in his youth to an arch conservative in his later years. He founded
the Atlantic Monthly magazine, taught at Harvard University and became U.S.
Ambassador to Great Britain as an elderly man. His early verse remains full of
zest and humor to readers today. Readings are performed by actor Ed Herrmann.

4. AMY LOWELL -- Amy Lowell wrote free verse, was an imagist after Ezra
Pound, and never married but lived with her female lover on her huge estate near
Boston. She liked to shock people, made public appearances across the U.S. as a
kind of "saleswoman" of modern poetry, was hugely obese, and smoked cigars. Her
poetry, which always sold well, is read by actress Maureen Anderman.

5. WALLACE STEVENS -- This program profiles one of modern poetry's most
original and influential writers. Actor Sam Waterston reads from the poetry of
Wallace Stevens, and critic Peter Brazeau provides commentary.

6. WALT WHITMAN -- Broadcast in November 1980, this program examines the
distinctly American poetry of Walt Whitman, Actor Mark Hammer reads from
Whitman's poetry. Critic Alfred Kazin and biographer Justin Kaplan discuss the
unique style of this most American of poets.

Part B - 60 min

7. STEPHEN CRANE -- Novelist, poet, and war correspondent, Stephen Crane
published his most famous work, The Red Badge of Courage, in 1895. Actor
William Atherton reads from Crane's poetry and prose, which brought him
worldwide fame until his early death at the age of twenty-eight. Professor James
Culvert talks about Crane's short but exciting life.

8. LANGSTON HUGHES -- see: LANGSTON HUGHES -- LITERATURE OF THE
BLACK EXPERIENCE. (See Li-G-2 below)

9. MARIANNE MOORE -- see: EMILY DICKINSON AND MARIANNE MOORE

10. ARCHIBALD MacLEISH -- Archibald MacLeish is one of America's foremost
men of letters. This segment, broadcast on MacLeish's 89th brithday, features
reading of his works by the poet himself and by actor Michael Moriarity. Also

included is a discussion by MacLeish of the importance of poetry to the awareness and enlightenment of mankind.

11. WILLIAM CARLOS WILLIAMS -- William Carlos Williams practiced medicine in Rutherford, New Jersey, all his life. He was also a prolific poet who exerted a powerful influence on American poetry in the twentieth century. He was posthumously awarded the Pulitzer Prize for poetry in 1963. Readings are performed by actor Michael Tolan. Critical comments are suppled by Reed Whittemore, Williams' biographer.

Li-B-18
PATTERNS AND OTHER POEMS BY AMERICAN WRITERS   SC
          FS, Cassette   C   1970
          Educational Filmstrips
A visual anthology of poetry.

Li-B-19
POETRY AND THE LIFE OF MAN: A Tribute To
Archibald MacLeish   SC
          Audio-cassette   1981
          NPR   29 min
Archibald MacLeish is one of America's leading poets. Born in 1892, he has won two Pulitzer Prizes for his poetry and poetic drama. In this program MacLeish discusses the public and private sides of the poet's craft with friend and fellow poet John Ciardi. Poetry to MacLeish is the comprehension of what it is to be human. He says, "No one can practice the art of poetry who doesn't believe in man." MacLeish reads selections from some of his own poetry, including the poem "You Andrew Marvell" and others. Actor Michael Moriarty recites "The End of the World," "In the 30th Year of My Life," and an excerpt from the radio play The Fall of the City.

Li-B-20
POETRY: IN SEARCH FOR HART CRANE   SC
          16 mm   B   1966
          NET Film Service   90 min
One of the salient figures of 20th Century American Poetry, Hart Crane, is portrayed through the recollections of living friends who are interviewed by his biographer, John Unterecker; through his letters, manuscripts, notebooks, portraits, drawings; and through family photographs.

Li-B-21
THE POETRY OF WALLACE STEVENS   A
          Audio-cassette   1980
          NPR   29 min
The poems of Wallace Stevens are impressionistic, full of vivid sensory experience. The readings in this program are taken from The Collected Poems of Wallace Stevens, which won the National Book Award and the Pulitzer Prize for Poetry in 1955.

Li-B-22
SPOON RIVER ANTHOLOGY (Based on the Poetry of
Edgar Lee Masters)   SC
          16mm   C   1976
          BFA   21 min
Who were the people who lived and died in the supposedly idyllic days of rural America? SPOON RIVER ANTHOLOGY probes beneath the surface to reveal their

very human strength and weaknesses. Reveals the public reaction to the poem when it was published and gives a sense of the complexity of American life as it entered the twentieth century.

Li-B-23
WALT WHITMAN: BACKGROUND FOR HIS WORKS   SC
    16mm   Sd   B   1957
    Coronet   13 min
Whitman's works were strongly influenced by significant facets of changing nineteenth-century America. Scenes of the poet's life and of his America give meaning to selections from his poetry.

Li-B-24
WALT WHITMAN: POET FOR A NEW AGE   SC
    16mm   C   1972
    EBEC   29 min
This sensitive study of poet Walt Whitman -- reveals the "cosmic consciousness of Whitman: his strong belief in democracy; the oneness and sacredness of all living things, and the mystical truths of life and death; his distaste for war; and his concern for the primacy of personality and love.

Li-B-25
WHITMAN, WALT: CROSSING BROOKLYN FERRY   SC
AND OTHER POEMS   1972
        Audio-cassette
        Caedman
Whitman celebrated above all the grandness of the human condition, the vitality of mankind. Rhetorical devices, recitative, techniques of declamation -- all make his poetry especially appropriate for recorded interpretation. Performance by Ed Begley.

Li-B-26
WILLIAM CARLOS WILLIAMS   A
        Audio-cassette   1980
        NPR   29 min
Poet and critic Randall Jarrell once wrote of Williams, "He is the America of poets." Born in 1883, Williams practiced medicine all his life in his native New Jersey, and this fact is reflected in Williams' writing. His poetry is fiercely organic, firmly rooted in the facts of reality. This program features readings from his collected poems from 1950-1962, Pictures from Brueghel, which was awarded the Pulitzer Prize for poetry in 1963.

Literature -- Drama

Li-C-1
LEARNING TO WRITE PLAYS   A
        Audio-cassette   1978
        NPR   59 min
Ronald Ribman, Corinne Jacker, Bernard Slade, Barbara Field, and Robert Patrick discuss the writing process, how they are moved to write, and reactions to their work.

Li-C-2
OUR TOWN AND OURSELVES (Humanities Series)   SC
        16mm   Sd   C   1959
        EBEC   30 min
This film discusses Our Town and the playwright's use of music, of light motif and
variations, and of the condensed line or word. Clifton Fadiman comments on the
significance of the play to the individual member of the audience.

Li-C-3
OUR TOWN AND THE UNIVERSE (Humanities Series)   SC
        16mm   Sd   C   1959
        EBEC   30 min
The basic story of Our Town and its unusual conventions are introduced. Mr.
Fadiman also analyzes the play as commentary on "the contrast between each tiny
moment of our lives and the vast stretches of time and place in which each
individual plays his role."

Li-C-4
SALUTE TO THE AMERICAN THEATRE, A   SC
        16mm   Sd   B
        Anti-Defamation League   44 min
Plays divert, entertain and, sometimes, unsettle the audience. Others bring
people's attention to the human dilemma. The ideal is a drama and makes us
aware of defects in society. Those plays included in this salute have largely
succeeded in this combination.

Li-C-5
TENNESSEE WILLIAMS: Theater in Progress
(Short Story Showcase from Humanities Series)   SC
        16mm   Sd   C   1976
        EBEC   29min
Takes the viewer behind the scenes for a glimpse of the theater playgoers seldom
see: the creation of the play itself -- from first rehearsals through opening
performances. The play in process is Tennessee Williams's The Red Devil Battery
Sign.

Literature -- History and Background

Li-D-1
THE AMERICAN EXPERIENCE IN LITERATURE --
    The Romantic Age   SC
        FS   1977
        EBEC
Spotlights the literary renaissance. Uses portraits and photos of Poe, Thoreau,
Melville, Hawthorne and Emerson.

Li-D-2
AMERICAN LITERATURE: COLONIAL TIMES   S
        UBV   1954
        Coronet   10 min
The beginnings of literature in this country took the form of practical, useful
documents, reflecting the natural wonders of the new world to which the settlers
had come and their hard pioneer life and deep religious faith. We see how colonial
literature has inspired later American writers.

Li-D-3
AMERICAN LITERATURE: EARLY NATIONAL PERIOD   S
            UBV   1954
            Coronet   9 1/2min
The first real literature of America is presented here in the writings of Freneau,
Bryant, Irving and Cooper, who found their subjects in the natural beauty, folk
legends, humor and traditions which were characteristically American.

Li-D-4
AMERICAN LITERATURE: THE REALISTS   S
            UBV   1954
            Coronet   10 1/2min
Discusses the writings of Sinclair, Dreiser, Garland, Crane, London, Tarkington,
Lewis, and associates the theme of realism with many of our present-day
novelists, poets, essayists and dramatists.

Li-D-5
AMERICAN LITERATURE: REVOLUTIONARY TIMES   S
            UBV   1975
            Coronet   9min
The literature of defiance spread throughout the colonies linking a network of
patriots from Savannah to Boston. Writings that reflect the beginnings of a
national consciousness are selected from Franklin, Henry, Paine, Hopkinson,
Wheatley, Freneau and deCrevecoeur.

Li-D-6
AMERICANS ON AMERICA: Our Identity and Self-Image   SC
            35mm, Cassette (2)   1976
            Center for Humanities   120 slides
Traces the twin concepts of freedom and equality as they appear time and again
in American history and literature. Describes the forging of these ideals by the
American colonists and later immigrants.

Li-D-7
THE COMIC IMAGINATION IN AMERICAN LITERATURE:
Washington Irving to Woody Allen   SC
            35mm, Cassette (2)   1977
            Center for Humanities   120 slides
Discusses the purpose of comedy and its relationship to human nature and values.
Illustrates a wide range of comedic genres, including satire, parody, put downs
and black humor. Enhances students' appreciation and enjoyment of comedy.

Li-D-8
COMING OF AGE IN AMERICA: The Adolescent in Literature   SC
            35mm, Cassette (2)   1976
            Center for Humanities   120 slides
Focuses on three basic elements of coming of age -- the changes adolescents feel
within themselves, their changing relationships with their parents and their search
for identity. It then concentrates on peer-group interactions.

Li-D-9
CONFLICT IN AMERICAN VALUES: Life-Style vs.
Standard of Living   S
            35mm, Cassette (2)   1973
            Center for Humanities   120 slides
Traces the evolution of the American value system, giving particular attention to

controversies over life-styles that differ from the American norm. Explores the resurgence of American Indian values, changing aims of the black community and efforts at developing alternative life-styles.

Li-D-10
CROSS-CURRENTS IN AMERICAN LIFE   SC
        Audio-cassette   1981
        NPR   50 min
One of the greatest assets to American literature is the diversity of its people and their experience, as American literature has become an increasingly vital part of writing. These selections include writings on Jewish, American Indian, and Chicano experience, and a special two-part program on the experiences of the American immigrant. The audio sketches included are:

1. LITERATURE OF THE IMMIGRANT EXPERIENCE — This two-part program features profiles of Pietro Di Donato and Henry Roth, two authors who have written novels about their immigrant experience. Part One features interviews with Pietro Di Donato and a rare, commercially unavailable recording of a dramatization of Di Donato's 1938 novel Christ In Concrete, read by actor Eli Wallach. Part Two focuses upon Henry Roth's Call It Sleep, published in 1934. Actor Richard Bower reads from the novel, and critic and historian Irving Howell provides commentary.

2. ALFRED KAZIN — Broadcast on the first day of Hanukkah, 1980, this segment focuses on Kazin's prose poem "A Walker in the City," a recollection of growing up in a Jewish-neighborhood in Brooklyn in the 1930's. Actress Laura Esterman reads from the poem, and Kazin, a respected critic as well as poet, talks about the Jewish tradition and what it means to his writing.

3. RALPH ELLISON — see: RALPH ELLISON — Literature of the Black Experience. Readings from Invisible Man, Ellison's only novel.

4. JAMES WELCH — This segment focuses upon Welch's first novel, Winter in the Blood. Welch, an American Indian novelist and poet from Montana, talks about the influence of Indian heritage and the landscape of the West upon his writing.

5. GARY SOTO — This profile features an interview with Gary Soto who now teaches Chicano Studies at the University of California at Berkeley. Soto's poetry revolves around scenes from childhood and the plight of the poor and poverty-stricken. Actress June Gable reads from Soto's first volume of poetry, The Elements of San Joaquin.

Li-D-11
THE EXPATRIATE WRITERS   A
        FS, Cassette   C   1972
        Guidance Associates
Explores literary reactions to WWI and post-war conditions through the writings of Hemingway, Pound, Dos Passos, Cummings, Fitzgerald and the influence of Gertrude Stein.

Li-D-12
MENCKEN, H.L.: HENRY MENCKEN CONVERSING   SC
        Audio-cassette   1958
        Caedmon
A rare self-portrait of the "enfant terrible" of American literature, speaking of his triumphs, defeats and rambunctious contentions. Mencken, who was reluctant

to speak on radio or television, consented to this conversation with an old friend, Donald Howe Kirkley, Jr., of the Baltimore Sun.

Li-D-13
THE ORIGINS OF AMERICAN VALUES:
The Puritan Ethic to the Jesus Freaks   S
        35mm, Cassette (2)   1973
        Center for Humanities   120 slides
Explores the wide range of life-styles pursued in America, the nature of subcultures and focuses on individuals who have established distinctive life-styles for themselves.

Li-D-14
SOCIO-POLITICAL LITERATURE   SC
        Audio-cassette   1981
        NPR   60 min
This selection of programs gives the listener a sense of the range of socio-political literature in America, including writings by a powerful anarchist as well as a past President. This selection includes addresses, autobiographies, memoirs, theses, fiction, and poetry. The audio sketches included are:

1. MARGARET FULLER -- A writer and teacher in her native New England, a Transcendentalist and colleague of Emerson, Margaret Fuller was a fine literary critic and is cited as America's first woman political journalist. Actress Frances Sternhagen reads from the diverse writings of Margaret Fuller, and Ann Douglas, author of The Feminization of American Culture, offers her thoughts about Fuller's life and work.

2. THOMAS JEFFERSON -- This segment looks at Thomas Jefferson, the man. Historical anecdotes and well-known writings show the changes Jefferson brought to the Presidency and his feelings in favor of democracy and against republicanism. Actor Jason Robards, Jr., reads from Jefferson's First Inaugural Address, and historians offer comment.

3. HENRY ADAMS -- Henry Adams, journalist, novelist, essayist, diplomat, and historian, was the first great pessimist of American letters. He wrote of the menace of science and technology at the turn of the century, a time of great confidence and prosperity. Actor William Hurt reads from Adams' life and vision of this enigmatic and profound thinker.

4. EMMA GOLDMAN -- An anarchist in the tradition of Trotsky and Thoreau, Emma Goldman was one of America's most moving public speakers. Actress Marsha Jean Kurtz reads from Goldman's book Living My Life, published in 1931.

5. W.E.B. DUBOIS -- See: W.E.B. DuBois -- Literature of the Black Experience. Readings from his essays and thoughts on black activists.

6. THEODORE DREISER -- The discovery of the original, uncensored manuscript of Dreiser's novel Sister Carrie -- containing language previously considered too graphic for post-Victorian readers -- has spurred renewed interest in Dreiser's work. Actor Harris Yulin reads from Sister Carrie, and critics Alfred Kazin and James West discuss the novel's impact when first published.

7. LITERATURE OF THE VIETNAM WAR -- Broadcast on Veteran's Day, 1980, this segment provides an introduction to the literature of the Vietnam War. Two Vietnam veterans talk about their experiences in S.E. Asia and their feelings

about the war upon returning to the United States. Critic Peter Marin discusses the cultural importance of literature about the war in shaping and reflecting social perceptions. Vietnam veteran Tim O'Brien reads from his novel Going After Cacciato, which won the National Book Award of 1978.

Li-D-15
TOWARD A NATIONAL LITERATURE   SC
          FS, Cassette   C   1978
          Films for the Humanities   30 min
Criticism and interpretation on American literature of the 19th century and Romanticism.

Li-D-16
THE TRANSCENDENTALISTS   SC
          FS, Cassette   C   1978
          Films for the Humanities   30 min
Criticism and interpretation on Thoreau, American literature -- 19th century, and Transcendentalism (New England).

Li-D-17
THE WRITER AND THE CITY (Great Minds
   of Our Times Series)   SCA
          16mm   1973
          ASTF   28 min
The work and philosophy of renowned artists.

Li-D-18
THE WRITER IN AMERICA: JANET FLANNER   A
          FS, Cassette   1978
          Perspective Films   29 min
In her usual spirited manner, Ms. Flanner, who wrote for five decades as Genet, the chronicler of an era, discusses her world. Through her eyes and sensibilities, we again see Hemingway, Picasso, Braque, Stein; we share her friendships and come to know her as friend, journalist, artist and certainly, constantly, as woman.

Literature -- Regional Cultures

LI-E-1
AMERICAN LITERATURE: WESTWARD MOVEMENT   SC
          16mm   1957
          Coronet   10 1/2min
Shows how the people and themes of the westward movement have served as a source of material for writers from the early nineteenth-century to the present. Characteristic scenes of the movement are combined with quotations from the works of poets, historians and novelists.

Li-E-2
APPALACHIAN WRITERS   A
          Audio-cassette   1980
          NPR   59 min
The region of eastern Kentucky has yielded up much more than simply its coal. James Still, Verna Mae Slone, and Gurney Norman, each a successful author, share that common setting for their stories, but differ in writing style and viewpoint. Reading and discussing their own work, each explains how modern America has

affected traditional Appalachian values and culture. Produced by Bob Edwards.

Li-E-3
CONCORD, A NATION'S CONSCIENCE: THE VOICES OF
EMERSON AND THOREAU   S
          35mm, Cassette (2)   1968
          Center for Humanities   120 slides
The calm beauty of New England inspired both Ralph Waldo Emerson and Henry
David Thoreau. In their writings, students hear expressions of social protest, moral
outrage and personal integrity. This program uses biographical notes and extensive
excerpts to demonstrate the eloquence and passion of these authors' protests
against materialism, commercialism, social neglect, religious hyprocrisy, slavery
and the Mexican War.

Li-E-4
MIDWEST LITERATURE: THE FARM BACKGROUND   SC
          UBV   C   1970
          Coronet   12 1/2min
Reflects the vigorous styles of writers influenced by the Midwest's largest city,
Chicago: Theodore Dreiser, Carl Sandburg and Ben Hecht; Upton Sinclair, Frank
Norris and James T. Farrell; Richard Wright, Nelson Algren, Lorraine Hansberry
and Gwendolyn Brooks. Relates each author's work to the history of the city and
the nation.

Li-E-5
MIDWEST LITERATURE: THE FARM BACKGROUND   SC
          UBV   C   1970
          Coronet   10 min
Dramatizes works by James Whitcomb Riley, Hamlin Garland, Ole Rolvaag and
Willa Cather, analyzing literature in terms of the Midwestern farmland where the
writers were raised.

Li-E-6
MIDWEST LITERATURE: THE TOWN BACKGROUND   SC
          UBV   C   1970
          Coronet   12 1/2min
Explores the writing of Samuel Clemens, William Dean Howells, Sherwood
Anderson, Edgar Lee Masters, Booth Tarkington, Sinclair Lewis, Vachel Lindsay
and Conrad Richter. Dramatizes selections from the authors' works.

Li-E-7
NEW ENGLAND: BACKGROUND OF LITERATURE   S
          UBV   C   1977
          Coronet   12 min
The ruggedness of the New England landscape and climate, the sea, New England's
role in American history -- all have shaped its literature. Selections from Bryant,
Longfellow, Whittier, Emerson, Hawthorne, Holmes, Lowell, Thoreau, Dickinson and
Frost illustrate the varied literature and philosophy of New England.

Li-E-8
TALKING WITH THOREAU   SC
          16mm   Sd   C   1975
          EBEC   29 min
What can Henry David Thoreau, a gentle 19-century philosopher, possibly say to a
modern urban-oriented society? Plenty, according to this film. Using the
"time-travel" technique, four contemporary Americans drop in at Walden Pond for

a chat. Conservationist, David Brower; psychologist, B.F. Skinner; civil rights activist Rosa Parks and former U.S. Attorney General, Elliot Richardson question Thoreau. His ideas are both attacked and defended, but always found relevant.

Li-E-9
THOREAU'S MAINE WOODS   SC
        16mm   Sd   C   1978
        Fenwick Productions   21 min
In a literary as well as a wilderness adventure, two canoeists retrace the trips through the Maine Woods made by Henry David Thoreau in the mid-nineteenth century. The film captures the essence of Thoreau's philosophy, his reverence for nature and his commitment to conservation.

                        Literature -- Women

Li-F-1
FOUR GENERATIONS OF WOMEN POETS   SC
        Audiocassette   1980
        NPR   60 min
This sampler of women poets spans nearly three hundred years of American literature, from Anne Bradstreet to Denise Levertov. The audio sketches included are:

1. ANNE BRADSTREET -- Anne Bradstreet has the distinction of being the first important colonial poet. Her poetry is not sentimental, yet it is more personal than other poetry written by the Puritans, a fact which contributes to its lasting value. Actress Charlotte Moore reads from the poetry of Anne Bradstreet, and critic Ann Stanford discusses Bradstreet's importance in the American literary tradition.

2. EMILY DICKINSON -- This special two-part program features actress Frances Sternhagen reading the poetry of Emily Dickinson, most notable for the famous poem "Because I Could Not Stop for Death, He kindly Stopped for Me." Critic Alfred Kazin offers commentary, and a recent Dickinson conference in Amherst, Massachusetts, is visited.

3. MARIANNE MOORE -- In 1952 she was awarded the National Book Award and Pulitzer and Bollingen Prizes for poetry, and is now regarded as a major figure in the modern movement. Acress Diane Wiest reads the work of Marianne Moore, and friend Jeffrey Kindley talks about her life and work.

4. MURIEL RUKEYSER -- Muriel Rukeyser is one of the most distinguished contemporary female poets. Fellow poet Carolyn Kizer, discusses the diversity and intensity of Rukeyser's renowned work. Rukeyser herself reads her poems "Waiting for Icarus" and "What Do We See?"

5. LOUISE BOGAN -- Louise Bogan was the first woman poet to be honored as Poetry Consultant to the Library of Congress, in 1945. The master of finely-crafted lyric poems, Bogan is now becoming known for her journal and letters, published in two volumes since her death in 1972. Readings of Bogan's work are given by actress Marian Seldes.

6. DENISE LEVERTOV -- Born in England in 1923, Denise Levertov has become one of our most prolific poets. Levertov expresses her views on the responsibility of writers to speak out on political issues and discusses the writing of poetry.

Li-F-2
I STAND HERE IRONING   SCA
    16mm   Sd   C,B   1978
    Film Boston   20 min
A thoughtful reverie of a mother performing the ritual chore of ironing, as she
re-evaluates her relationship with her nineteen-year-old daughter. The memories
of mother and daughter, photographed in black and white, as a montage, interrupt
the color images of ironing.

Li-F-3
KATE CHOPIN'S "THE STORY OF AN HOUR"   SC
    16mm   Sd   C   1981
    ISHTAR   24 min
This dramatization based on Kate Chopin's celebrated and daring short story of
the 1890's is narrated by Elizabeth Ashley. Upon hearing of the death of her dear
husband, Mrs. Mallard is shocked to discover that for the first time in her life,
she is free to live for herself -- a discovery which leads to tragedy. A glimpse
into the thoughts and milieu of Kate Chopin precedes the story.

Li-F-4
WOMEN WRITERS: VOICE OF DISSENT   S
    FS, Cassette   C   1975
    Educl Enrichment Materials
Discusses the work of Edith Wharton, Ellen Glasgow and Willa Cather.

Li-F-5
WOMEN'S FICTION   SC
    Audio-cassette   1981
    NPR   60 min
Selections from five diverse writers. The audio sketches included are:

EDITH WHARTON -- Part One of this two-part program focuses on an important
but often ignored aspect of her work: sexuality. Actress Ann Stone reads from a
recently-discovered erotic fragment, "Beatrice Palmatto," and biographer Cynthia
Wolfe discusses Wharton's feelings about sex. Part two features Stone reading
from The Age of Innocence, and Cynthia Wolfe offers analysis of the novel and
its structure.

GERTRUDE STEIN -- This program features actor William Hurt portraying
Hemingway and actress Frances Sternhagen portraying Stein. Critic Alfred Kazin
provides commentary.

ELLEN GLASGOW -- Wrote about a world of which few remnants remain: the
American South at the turn of the century. Actress Frances Sternhagen reads
from Glasgow's The Woman Within and The Sheltered Life, and Alfred Kazin
offers critical comment.

CARSON McCULLERS -- Carson McCullers' one great theme was the wonder of
love. Her novels include The Heart Is a Lonely Hunter and Ballad of the Sad Cafe.
Actress Frances Sternhagen reads from McCullers' works, and biographer Virginia
Spencer Carr, author of The Lonely Hunter, talks about McCullers' life and how it
influenced her work.

JOYCE CAROL OATES -- This novelist, one of our younger and most
accomplished, is interviewed about her distinctly gothic novels and stories. Actor
James Cunningham reads from her novels and professor Ellen Friedman, author of

the critical biography <u>Joyce Carol Oates</u>, talks about the unique quality of Oates' work.

KATHERINE ANNE PORTER -- Katherine Anne Porter's fiction of the 1920's and 30's shows women in conflict over love, independence, and loneliness. Susan Sarandon reads from Porter's work, and critic Jane de Mouy offers an analysis of the women characters.

Literature -- Black

Li-G-1
A CELEBRATION OF BLACK WOMEN IN LITERATURE:
ALICE WALKER   SC
      Audio-cassette   1980
      NPR   29 min
Author Alice Walker talks about her novel, Meridian, the story of a woman's pilgrimage to free herself from the guilt of the past by working with the poor of the South during the Civil Rights Movement of the 60's. Actors and actresses dramatize the novel, and the author discusses its symbolism.

Li-G-2
LITERATURE OF THE BLACK EXPERIENCE   SC
      Audio-Cassette   1981
      NPR   60 min
These programs deal with the challenges of the black experience in America, from the Deep South to New York City, from the years of the Harlem Renaissance to yesterday. The audio sketches included are:

W.E.B. DUBOIS -- This segment celebrates the birthday of this great American sociologist and black activist. Actor Christopher Moore reads from the essays of W.E.B. DuBois, and Georgia State Senator Julian Bond offers his thoughts on the courage and wisdom of DuBois' life and vision.

LANGSTON HUGHES -- Langston Hughes, "the most loved voice in Harlem," died there in 1967 -- but not before he captured, more than any other writer, the spirit of the Harlem Renaissance. Owen Dodson, playwright, novelist, and poet, talks about the Harlem that Hughes knew so well and the poet's dedication to it until his death. Music from the period provides the settings for readings of Hughes's work by actor Al Freeman.

RALPH ELLISON -- <u>Invisible Man</u>, Ralph Ellison's only novel, was immediately recognized as a great work upon its publication in 1953, receiving both the National Book Award and the Medal of Freedom. This segment features readings from the novel and discussion of the main character's search for identity and self-realization in mid-20th century New York.

ALICE WALKER -- Alice Walker is one of the most prolific and respected writers in America today. In this segment broadcast in 1981 on Walker's 37th birthday, actor Christopher Moore reads from her first novel, <u>The Third Life of Grange Copeland</u>. Walker discusses the need to write and the role of the black writer in modern society.

AMIRI BARAKA -- This segment, broadcast in 1980, features an interview with Imamu Amiri Baraka, known until 1966 as Leroi Jones, one of America's most prominent contemporary black poets and playwrights. Baraka talks about his role as a black poet, and reads "Dope" and "Prez Spoke in a Language."

RICHARD WRIGHT -- Born in poverty in rural Mississippi in 1908, Wright published his first novel, the shocking Native Son, in 1940. Readings from Native Son and Wright's autobiography, Black Boy, are given by actor Carl Lumbly.

Li-G-3
TAPESTRY: A BLACK THEATER CULTURAL REVIVAL   S
                         Audio-cassette   1979
                         NPR   29 min
This program explores black theater and its various elements and how this art from has been a vital part of the black cultural scene. Among those interviewed during the Black Arts Festival at New York's Lincoln Center in 1979 are Marcus Hemphill, author of Inacent Black; Hazel Bryant, producer of Black Theater Festival, U.S.A.; three designers from the Billie Holliday Theater; and four black actors.

Li-G-4
W.E.B. DuBOIS   A
                         Audio-cassette   1980
                         NPR   60 min
Sociologist W.E.B. DuBois was the first black scholar to consider seriously the plight of black Americans. In this program Douglas Turner Ward's renowned Negro Ensemble Company recreates the life and times of W.E.B. DuBois using excerpts from his writings.

Journalism -- History

Lj-A-1
ALISTAIRE COOKE ON H.L. MENCKEN   S
                         Audio-cassette   1980
                         NPR   59min
Essayist and journalist Alistaire Cooke addresses the National Press Club to pay tribute to his friend H.L. Mencken on the anniversary of his 100th birthday. Cooke calls Mencken "an outrageous rebel" who championed a public outcry against the critics and a "literary dictator" who single-handedly destroyed the marshmallow gentility of American letters in the late 1910's-1920's

Lj-A-2
ALL THINGS CONSIDERED: 10TH ANNIVERSARY   S
                         Audio-cassette   1981
                         NPR   30 min
On May 3, 1981, NPR's Peabody Award-winning news magazine All Things Considered, celebrated its 10th anniversary. This 30-minute retrospective celebrates the event by combining excerpts from some of ATC's best programs with reminiscences and observations from present and former staff members.

The special includes portions of ATC's first broadcast, coverage of the 1971 May Day anti-war demonstration in Washington, D.C., a sky diver's spontaneous reaction to his first jump, a whimsical scientific experiment with a wintergreen lifesaver, host Susan Stamberg's famous cranberry relish recipe, a dress rehearsal of a sunset, and the sounds of natural childbirth.

In addition to providing a retrospective of ATC's best work, the special also offers a glimpse behind the scenes at how a daily 90-minute radio news and information program is put together. Produced by Jim Anderson and M'lou Ollswang.

Lj-A-3
THE BLACK PRESS: VIABLE, RELIABLE OR DEAD?   S
            Audio-cassette   1980
            NPR   29 min
This program examines the history of the black press in America, from its origins in 1827, when it first challenged the hegemony of the wealthy black church to the present. Interviews with black publishers, editors, writers, and historians reveal the ever-changing role of the black press in the U.S.

Lj-A-4
EDWARD R. MURROW   S
            Audio-cassette   1980
            NPR   59 min
In 1938, when Hitler drove triumphantly into Vienna, Edward R. Murrow made his first official radio broadcast. His eyewitness accounts and graphic reporting brought the war into American living rooms for the first time and established broadcasting as an increasingly powerful tool for journalists. This program pays tribute to Mr. Murrow, the thin, shy, serious young man from Pole Cat Creek, North Carolina. Interviews with Eric Sevareid, Carl Sandburg, and other friends and colleagues, along with excerpts from his broadcasts, document the significant contributions Edward R. Murrow made to radio and television journalism and the American people.

Lj-A-5
EXHIBITION OF RADIO ART, AN   S
            Audio-cassette   1978
            NPR   59 min
These selections represent the best of public radio. After traveling to a beach in Massachusetts, a school in California, a Civil War battlefield in Virginia, and the Bureau of Engraving in Washington, D.C., one hears the birth of a baby and then takes a space voyage around the whole planet. Following each segment, the producer discusses the technical aspects of the recording.

Lj-A-6
HENRY BEETLE HOUGH: A COUNTRY EDITOR   S
            Audio-cassette   1980
            NPR   29 min
The biology of a salt marsh, the sparkle of the air, the clapboard houses of the island -- these and other ordinary aspects of coastal life have been made extraordinary by the rich perceptions of author and fabled editor Henry Beetle Hough. His life is inextricably entwined with his home, Martha's Vineyard. As owner of the weekly newspaper Vineyard Gazette since 1920, Hough's work and writings have addressed the enduring values of small town life and the trends of modern life. Here, with producer Noah Adams, Hough offers vintage reflections of his eighty-plus years and provides listeners with insightful glimpses of island life.

Lj-A-7
MURROW VS MCCARTHY - Two Parts   A
        16mm   B   1954
        CBS News   27 min ea
American journalism achieved one of its finest moments on March 9, 1954 when
Edward R. Murrow challenged Senator Joseph McCarthy. In one of his CBS See It
Now broadcasts, Murrow delivered a devastating attack on the Senator from
Wisconsin whose witch-hunting for alleged Communists in government and all
areas of American life had made a mockery of Constitutional rights and ruined
countless lives and careers. McCarthy was given equal time to respond, but he
never again recovered the fearful power he had wielded before Murrow exposed
him and his methods to public scrutiny. An outstanding example of freedom of the
press (and the power of the press) in action, and a vivid reminder of why this is
such a vital right in a free society. Both the original Murrow broadcast and
McCarthy's response are available.

Lj-A-8
STRINGER -- PORTRAIT OF A NEWSREEL CAMERMAN   SCA
        16 mm   1979
        Films, Inc.   28min
From 1928 until 1940 Mike Gittinger was a "Stringer," a freelance cameraman for
the major newsreels. Since he was only paid for film that was used, when no news
was happening he would search for the absurd or stage fictional events. He gave
the world the cat that nursed a litter of chicks, and the skater who tied rockets
to his back and caught fire. Mike talks about his exploits.

Lj-A-9
THIS IS EDWARD R. MURROW   A
        16mm   Sd   B   1976
        Carousel Films   44 min
Highlights Murrow's career.

Lj-A-10
TIGER'S TAIL, THE: THOMAS NAST vs.
BOSS TWEED   SC
        16mm   Sd   B   1962
        INUAVC   19 min
Significant emphasis is placed upon the editorial cartoon in American journalism
and life. The power of the press is demonstrated in remedying social abuses.
Thomas Nast is characterized as a man of integrity. An interesting sense of
documentary immediacy is introduced through the intercutting of reproductions of
Nast's original cartoons into the film continuity.

Lj-A-11
WE TAKE YOU NOW, BY RADIO, TO THE 1960'S   SC
        Audio-cassette   1979
        NPR   59 min
Listeners return to the 60's to think about how they as individuals have changed
over the years. They first hear a radio program produced by WBAI-FM in New
York with Larry Josephson, then move on to tapes made by Calos Hagen during
the 1967 "summer of love" in Golden Gate Park, and round off their nostalgic
journey with an extended essay, also by Carlos Hagen, on "Whatever Happened to
the 60's?"

Lj-A-12
YESTERDAY'S WITNESS: A TRIBUTE TO THE
AMERICAN NEWSREEL   A
      16mm   Sd   C   1976
      Blackwood Productions   52 min
The history of the newsreel.

Journalism -- Social Issues

Lj-B-1
FASHION IN THE MAKING   A
      UBV   Sd   C   1978
      Coronet Films   10 min
A real live magazine crew on location down in the Bahamas. Assignment: bring
back the most incredible, eye-catching, attention-riveting fashion photos ever for
the upcoming pages of Gentlemen's Quarterly.

Lj-B-2
INVESTIGATIVE REPORTING   S
      16mm, UBV   C   1979
      USIA   25 min
A broad look at investigative reporting and the legal questions relating to this
form of journalism, and its roots in American society.

Lj-B-3
THE NEWSMEDIA: REPORTING OR DISTORTING?   SA
      FS, Cassette   B   1977
      Educl Enrichment Materials
Considers many questions about the role of the media today.

Lj-B-4
THE PEOPLE'S RIGHT TO KNOW: POLICE VS. REPORTER   A
      16mm   B   1979
      Vision Quest   12 min
Chicago newspaper photographer Paul Sequiera relates his experiences with the
police while attempting to cover the 1968 Democratic convention in Chicago.

Lj-B-5
ROBERT MACNEIL AND DAN RATHER ON THE MEDIA   S
      Audio-cassette   1977
      NPR   59 min
Part one features (PBS) commentator Robert MacNeil on "What the People Have a
Right to Know, and What They Don't." The second half of the program is an
interview with Dan Rather.

Lj-B-6
SEXUALITY ON TELEVISION   S
      Audio-cassette   1979
      NPR   59 min
David Frost moderates a forum on sex and sexuality on television. Panelists
consider whether there is too much sexual behavior on the screen, the degree of
sexploitation, the portrayal of women, and how commercials affect the roles of
males and females in this country.

Lj–B–7
TV AND VIOLENCE   S
            Audio–cassette   1978
            NPR   59 min
Dr. George Gerbner, Dean of the Annenberg School of Communications, University
of Pennsylvania, explores the relationship of television to violence.

Lj–B–8
WOMEN IN ADVERTISING   S
            Audio–cassette   1979
            NPR   59 min
Jane Trahey, president of Trahey Advertising, Inc., and Barbara Proctor, president
and creative director of the Proctor and Gardner Advertising Agency in Chicago,
discuss the portrayal of women in commercials.

                    Journalism — Newspapers

Lj–C–1
FIRST EDITION   SC
            16mm   Sd   C   1977
            Films, Inc.   31 min
One intense day in the life of a major newspaper.

Lj–C–2
NEWSPAPER ... BEHIND THE SCENES   SC
            16mm   Sd   C   1970
            AIMS   16 min
This film deals with all the important aspects of a modern metropolitan
newspaper, from the copy desk to the editorial room to "topping" the bundles for
delivery.

Lj–C–3
NEWSPAPER STORY (2nd Edition)   SC
            16mm   Sd   C   1973
            EBEC   27 min
Traces a 24 hour period in the life of the Los Angeles Times. Shows how news is
gathered, written and edited, and how newspapers are printed. The people being
photographed describe what they do.

Lj–C–4
WHAT IS JOURNALISM?   S
            35mm, Cassettes (2)   1976
            Center for Humanities   120 slides
Shows students what news is and how to identify and interpret various types of
stories, including hard-news, feature, editorial, sports, political and satirical
pieces. Incorporates extensive commentary by Edwin Newman and uses examples of
distinguished photo journalism to illustrate the concepts being taught.

Journalism — Newspapers

Lj-C-1
FIRST EDITION   SC
     16mm   Sd   C   1977
     Films, Inc.   31 min
One intense day in the life of a major newspaper.

Lj-C-2
NEWSPAPER ... BEHIND THE SCENES   SC
     16mm   Sd   C   1970
     AIMS   16 min
This film deals with all the important aspects of a modern metropolitan
newspaper, from the copy desk to the editorial room to "topping" the bundles for
delivery.

Lj-C-3
NEWSPAPER STORY (2nd Edition)   SC
     16mm   Sd   C   1973
     EBEC   27 min
Traces a 24 hour period in the life of the Los Angeles Times. Shows how news is
gathered, written and edited, and how newspapers are printed. The people being
photographed describe what they do.

Lj-C-4
WHAT IS JOURNALISM?   S
     35mm, Cassettes (2)   1976
     Center for Humanities   120 slides
Shows students what news is and how to identify and interpret various types of
stories, including hard-news, feature, editorial, sports, political and satirical
pieces. Incorporates extensive commentary by Edwin Newman and uses examples of
distinguished photo journalism to illustrate the concepts being taught.

Journalism — Television

Lj-D-1
LIFE IN THE GARDEN OF MEDIA   S
     Audio-cassette   1977
     NPR   59 min
American television not only affects but also creates political, social, and ethical
issues. In this program, critics and television professionals examine some of these
issues, including violence, mass taste, and television's influence on children.
Produced by Keith Talbot.

Lj-D-2
SHAPING NEWS FOR THE CONSUMER   SC
     16mm   1976
     BFA   17 min
Although more people believe in the truth of TV news than in other forms of
news, its function is rather limited. We watch the process of preparing one TV
story as the basis of the idea that TV is primarily a headline service. We conclude
that each of the other sources has advantages and disadvantages.

Lj–D–3
TELEVISION JOURNALISM: AN ALTERNATIVE   A
         16mm   1981
         USIA   30 min
Contrasts the format of the MacNeil/Lehrer Report on public television with the
three commercial network news programs. Shows the staff of this program in
action and explains the philosophy behind their format.

Lj–D–4
TV NEWS: BEHIND THE SCENES   SC
         16mm   1973
         EBEC   27 min
A documentary on New York's ABC Eyewitness News reveals the tight editorial
and technical teamwork responsible for a local TV news program.

Lj–D–5
TV NEWS: INFORMATION OR ENTERTAINMENT?   S
              35mm, Cassette (2)   1978
              Center for Humanities   120 slides
Designed to help students understand the political, economic and social forces
that shape television news.

Lj–D–6
THE TV SHOW   S
              Audio–cassette   1980
              NPR   59 min
Broadcasters, advertisers, scientists, sociologists, psychologists, government
officials, children, and parents air their views about television's social influence.

Performing Arts

Vidge Hitchens

Frequently, the performing arts have been included in the study of Arts, Popular Culture, or Literature. The editors of this catalogue and their advisors felt that the American "lively arts" deserve to be studied independently, for at least two reasons. First, their growth and contribution to current American culture make theatre, dance, music and film very important parts of this society. Second, these arts, like the graphic arts, are extending their traditions in America — are in fact leading artists in other milieu to new forms and techniques of human expression.

The audiovisual materials selected for inclusion here are grouped into four categories:

PERFORMING ARTS (PA)

PA-A	Dance
PA-B	Film
PA-C	Music
PA-D	Theatre

Performing Arts - Dance

PA-A-1
AMERICAN BALLET THEATRE: DANCING FOR LOVE   SCA
        16mm   Sd   C   1978
        WDVM-TV   28min
Profiles Baryshnikov and ABT during his performance in Don Quixote.

PA-A-2
ARTS AMERICA II   SCA
        16mm   Sd   C
        USIA   28min
Presents three American artists, Conductor Calvin Simmons, Choreographer
Patricia Birch, Film Director Sidney Lumet.

PA-A-3
BEGINNINGS   SCA
        16mm   Sd   C   1977
        LightWorks   25min
A fast-paced visual narrative of sweat and spirit at the School of American
Ballet, a magnet for the most talented young ballet students in the country.

PA-A-4
CHOREOGRAPHY BY BALANCHINE, PART ONE   SCA
        UBV   Sd   C   1980
        Films, Inc.   60min
Members of the New York City Ballet join in a one-hour performance of three
pieces: "Tzigane," with music by Ravel, featuring Suzanne Farrell and Peter
Martins, the "Andante Movement" from Divertimento No. 15, music by Mozart,
including dancers Merrill Ashley and Robert Weiss; and concluding with "The Four
Temperaments," with music by Hindmith.

PA-A-5
CHOREOGRAPHY BY BALANCHINE, PART TWO   SCA
        VC   Sd   C   1980
        Films, Inc.   90min
This consists of two works--Three pieces from "Jewels", excerpts from "Emeralds,"
music by Faure, dancers including Karin von Aroldigen and Sean Lavery; the pas
de deux from "Rubies," music by Stravinsky, danced by Patricia McBride and
Robert Weiss; and the same from "Diamonds," music by Tchaikovsky, danced by
Suzanne Farrell and Peter Martins. The program concludes with "Stravinsky Violin
Concerto."

PA-A-6
THE CHUCK DAVIS DANCE COMPANY   SCA
        16mm   Sd   C
        USIA   10min
The Company rehearses and performs selections from two of their full-length
dances: Buffalo Soldier, and the Sea Ritual.

PA-A-7
DANCE IN MUSICAL COMEDY   SCA
        35mm   C   1978
        Pictura Films   10 frs
Examines dance in musical comedy from 1930s to 1970s.

PA-A-8
DANCE ON A MAY DAY   SCA
    16mm   C   1978
    LCA   11min
Ballet star Jacques d'Amboise founded the National Dance Institute in 1976 to
introduce boys to dance. On an afternoon in May, 1977, the boys gave an exciting
performance at New York's Lincoln Center.

PA-A-9
DANCE SPACE   SCA
    16mm,UBV   Sd   C   1980
    Films, Inc.   14min
Jacques d'Amboise, longtime principal dancer with the New York City Ballet, now
concentrates on introducing children to the joy of dance. His pupils now number
hundreds of boys and girls. Lessons culminate in a year-end performance at
Lincoln Center, with a grand finale led by Mihkail Baryshnikov.

PA-A-10
A DIVINE MADNESS   SCA
    16mm   Sd   C   1979
    Oak Creek Films   28min
Charlotte Perry and Portia Mansfield travelled to Steamboat Springs, Colorado in
1914 and founded a camp dedicated to the study of theatre and dance. They story
of this unique school and its contribution to the arts is narrated by Julie Harris.

PA-A-11
FEET FIRST   SCA
    16mm   Sd   C   1981
    Temple University   22min
A nostalgic yet ironic look at partner dancing. We witness the frustrations of
dance students and the joys of the competition winner.

PA-A-12
FULL OF LIFE A-DANCIN'   CA
    16mm   Sd   C   1978
    Phoenix Films   29min
Features the champion clog dance team of the Southern Appalachian mountains.

PA-A-13
JAZZ HOOFER   SCA
    16mm   Sd   C   1981
    Bruce Ricker   30min
Traces the development and decline of a unique American art form—tap
dancing—through the words and movements of one of its major practitioners, Baby
Laurence.

PA-A-14
JENNIFER MULLER & THE WORKS   SCA
    16mm   Sd   C
    USIA   28min
The New York Based modern dance company performs three of their major works
choreographed by Muller.

PA-A-15
KATHY'S DANCE   SCA
        16mm   Sd   C   1978
        Sears Roebuck Foundation   28min
Several months in the life of dancer Kathy Posin as she choreographs a new dance
for her troupe, gives solo performances as an Affiliate Artist in several
communities to support her work, and finally premieres the new dance in New
York.

PA-A-16
KENNEDY CENTER TONIGHT: STRAVINSKY'S
    FIREBIRD BY THE DANCE THEATRE OF HARLEM   SCA
        16mm   Sd   C   1983
        WQED/Pittsburgh   60min
A behind-the-scenes look at the seemingly endless hours of preparation for a
dance performance. Choreographer John Taras creates a new Firebird and
Geoffrey Holder fashions the costumes and sets, all culminating in the
performance at the Kennedy Center.

PA-A-17
IN A REHEARSAL ROOM   SCA
        16mm   Sd   C   1976
        Films, Inc.   11min
In the warm, diffused light of a rehearsal room, two young dancers (Cynthia
Gregory and Ivan Nagy of the American Ballet Theatre) limber at the barre. They
come together and dance a sensual pas de deux to the pulsing melody of
Pachelbel's Canon in D.

PA-A-18
LAR LUBOVITCH AT JACOB'S PILLOW   SCA
        16mm   Sd   C
        USIA   25min
Lar Lubovitch, artistic director, rehearses his company in the Berkshires in
Massachusetts, and prepares for a world premier of his dance American Gesture.

PA-A-19
LIVING AMERICAN THEATRE DANCE   SCA
        16mm   Sd   C   1981
        Phoenix Films   11min
The American Dance Machine is a company specifically devoted to preserving
Broadway theatre dances and choreography. The troupe practices and performs
numbers from plays such as West Side Story, as well as lesser known plays from
the thirties and forties.

PA-A-20
MAKING DANCES   SCA
        16mm   Sd   C   1980
        Blackwood Productions   90min
Explores the post-modern dance scene through the work of seven New York-based
choreographers: Trisha Brown, Lucinda Childs, David Gordon, Douglas Dunn,
Kenneth King, Meredith Monk and Sara Rudner.

PA-A-21
THE MARTHA GRAHAM DANCE COMPANY   SCA
         16mm   Sd   C   1977
         INUAVC   90min
Martha Graham appears in conversation, and her company performs six dance
creations: "Diversion of Angels", "Lamentation", "Frontier", "Adorations", "Cave of
the Heart", and "Appalachian Spring". Introduction by Gregory Peck.

PA-A-22
MARTHA CLARKE: LIGHT AND DARK   SCA
         16mm   Sd   C   1980
         Phoenix Films   54min
Portrays an artist's imaginative sources and the process through which she creates
an original evening of theatrical dance.

PA-A-23
PAUL TAYLOR   SCA
         UBV   Sd   C   1978
         Films, Inc.   60min
Critic Clive Barnes called the Paul Taylor Dance Company "one of the most
exciting, innovative, and delightful dance companies in the entire world." They
perform two works: "Esplanada," and "Runes."

PA-A-24
PILOBOLUS   SCA
         UBV   Sd   C   1977
         Films, Inc.   60min
Pilobolus Dance Theatre is an eclectic group of dancers with an eclectic style.
This program features four dances which span the company's nine year history:
"Walklyndon", "Momix", "Alraune", and "Molly's Not Dead".

PA-A-25
ROSIE RADIATOR   SCA
         16mm   Sd   C   1981
         Ron Taylor   8:30min
Rosie Radiator is one of San Francisco's most famous street artists. Rosie
demonstrates her unique style of tap dancing: the super shuffle.

PA-A-26
RUTH PAGE: AN AMERICAN ORIGINAL   SCA
         16mm   Sd   C   1978
         Films, Inc.   59min
The film traces the life of a warm, vital woman whose influence on dance spans
three continents and more than fifty years. Page reminisces about Pavlova,
Diaghilev, Adolph Bohm and others.

PA-A-27
SUE'S LEG   SCA
         16mm   Sd   C   1977
         INUAVC   30min
Twyla Tharp and her dance company performing, "Sue's Legs".

PA-A-28
TAPDANCIN'   SCA
    16mm   Sd   C
    Blackwood Productions   58min
Explores the art of tap dance through stage performances, film clips and
interviews.

Performing Arts - Film

PA-B-1
AMERICAN FILM, THE   A
    16mm   Sd   C   1966
    INUAVC   16min
Charlton Heston introduces excerpts from Fred Zinneman's High Noon, Alfred
Hitchcock's North By Northwest, Elia Kazan's On The Waterfront, George Steven's
Shane, and William Wyler's Friendly Persuasion to illustrate the work of these
five American directors.

PA-B-2
D.W. GRIFFITH: AN AMERICAN GENIUS   CA
    UBV   Sd   C   1975
    Blackhawk Films   58min
A penetrating documentary of a legendary filmmaker, narrated by film critic
Richard Schickel. Excerpted works include early Biographs, Birth of a Nation, Way
Down East and Intolerance.

PA-B-3
FILMMAKER: A DIARY OF GEORGE LUCAS   SCA
    16mm   Sd   C   68
    Direct Cinema, Ltd.   33min
Filmed in 1968 and revised in 1982 by George Lucas, this is an on-the-spot record
of director Francis Coppola making The Rain People . Lucas captures the passion,
intensity, and humor of Coppola at work.

PA-B-4
THE MAKING OF RAIDERS OF THE LOST ARK   SCA
    16mm   Sd   C   1982
    Direct Cinema, Ltd.   58min
The excitement of moviemaking comes alive in the only film to document the
personalities (including Steven Spielberg and George Lucas) and the places which
make Raiders one of the most exciting films of the decade. The processes needed
to create a film—story boards, set building, Spielberg working with actors and
crew, stunts, and special technical effects— are shown.

PA-B-5
MOVIES TODAY   SCA
    16mm, UBV   Sd   C   1976
    Time-Life Multimedia   37min
Examines the morality of the 60s and takes a look at the life of Marilyn Monroe.

PA-B-6
OSCAR MICHEAUX, FILM PIONEER   CA
    16mm   sd   C   1982
    Beacon Films   28min
Oscar Micheaux is remembered for his work as a pioneer producer-director whose
films offered a positive image and alternative for Black people in the 1920s and
1930s.

PA-B-7
SLAPSTICK   SCA
    16mm   Sd   B   1960
    STERLED   35min
This film covers the slapstick era of visual comedy. Includes some of the top
comics of America in the 1920's.

PA-B-8
STORYVILLE STORY   SCA
    16mm   Sd   C   1982
    Arthur Cantor, Inc.   25min
Behind-the-scenes look at the making of "Pretty Baby", interviewing director
Louis Malle, screenwriter Polly Platt, and the cast. Also includes a brief history
of Storyville, with excerpts from the diary of a woman who lived and worked
there.

PA-B-9
UNKNOWN CHAPLIN - MY HAPPIEST YEARS (1916-1917)   SCA
    16mm   Sd   C   1983
    The Media Guild   52min
First part of a three-part documentary that covers the period Chaplin spent with
the Mutual Film Company, for whom he made twelve two-reel comedies. We
follow Chaplin through the hard work of improvising a film, only to watch him
throw it all away and start again. Uses some previously unseen, uncut rushes.

PA-B-10
WHEN COMEDY WAS KING   SCA
    16mm   Sd   C   1960
    Carousel Films   81min
Excerpts from silent comedies ranging from early Mack Sennett films of 1914 to
the sophisticated Hal Roach efforts of 1928. Entire sequences from Keaton's Cops
and Laurel and Hardy's Big Business.

Performing Arts - Music

PA-C-1
AHORA NO. 94: THESE FESTIVALS OF SUMMER   SCA
    16mm   Sd   C
    USIA   28min
Sights and sound of summer music festivals in the United States.

PA-C-2
AMAZING GRACE   SCA
        16mm   Sd   C   1979
        NAVC   10min
An enchanting look at the giant Sequoia in all seasons. This lyrical program
communicates through images alone.

PA-C-3
ANITA ELLIS: FOR THE RECORD   SCA
        16mm   Sd   C
        Tony Silver Films, Inc.   30min
Documentary of a recording session by Anita Ellis, the classic jazz vocalist and
song stylist. The singer talks about her life and art and we glimpse the hard work
that underlies them both.

PA-C-4
AND ALL THAT JAZZ   SCA
        FS (6)   Sd   1974
        Prentice-Hall Media   116 frs ea
Six part series. Surveys the social and political forces which led to jazz's
development and elements that distinguish it from other music.

PA-C-5
ARE MY EARS ON WRONG?   SCA
        16mm   Sd   C   1981
        The Media Guild   25min
Performances by pianist John Kirkpatrick, the Chilingirian String Quartet and the
BBC Symphony Orchestra, this film documents the influences that affected Ive's
patchwork music with its dissonance, sounds from life, ideas from jazz and
rollicking humor.

PA-C-6
BILLY JOEL   SCA
        UB   Sd   C   1976
        Time-Life Multimedia   20min
Features his most popular songs in a live performance.

PA-C-7
BLACK MUSIC IN AMERICA: FROM THEN TILL NOW   SCA
        16mm   Sd   1971
        LCA   28min
The history of the black people's contribution to American music is traced in
unforgettable performances by such great black musicians as Louis Armstrong,
Mahalia Jackson, Duke Ellington, Count Basie, Nina Simone, and the only film ever
recorded of the great Bessie Smith--to name only a few. Interspersed with the
performances are woodcuts showing the history of the music which is in effect
the history of the black people in America.

PA-C-8
BLACK MUSIC IN AMERICA: THE SEVENTIES   SCA
        16mm   Sd   1979
        LCA   32min
A musical excursion through the world of black music in the 1970s from the
Motown sound of Diana Ross to the disco beat of Donna Summer.

PA-C-9
BUFFY SAINTE-MARIE   SCA
     16mm   Sd   C   1976
     CAPCBC   51min
Presents a candid portrait of the songwriter, performer, activist.

PA-C-10
DAVE BRUBECK   SCA
     16mm   Sd   C   1977
     Time-Life Multimedia   52min
The original Dave Brubeck Quartet made Brubeck's cool jazz famous in the 50s
and early 60s. Recently, the members reassembled for a 25-city Silver Jubilee
tour.

PA-C-11
DEVO (MUSICAL GROUP)   SCA
     UBV   Sd   C   1980
     Time-Life Video   50min
New Wave rock group Devo perform robot-like interpretations of songs from their
first album.

PA-C-12
DIZZY   SCA
     UBV   Sd   B   1979
     Flower Films   22min
Features Dizzy Gillespie, his beginnings and his music.

PA-C-13
GYPSY YODELER   SCA
     16mm   Sd   C   1978
     Canyon Cinema Co-op   10min
A man from the hills of Tennessee explains why and how he yodels, from field to
love yodels. We see his family and lifestyle, ending with an expressive cinematic
dog yodel!

PA-C-14
HOMEMADE AMERICAN MUSIC   SCA
     16mm   Sd   C
     Lawren Productions, Inc.   41.75min
A story about America's rich heritage of do-it-yourself music, once in danger of
dying but now finding a new life.

PA-C-15
JAZZ ON A SUMMER'S DAY   SCA
     16mm   Sd   C   1958
     New Yorker Films   85min
Takes a look at the music, musicians, people at Newport Jazz Festival, 1958.

PA-C-16
LOVE IT LIKE A FOOL: A FILM
 ABOUT MALVINA REYNOLDS   SCA
     16mm   C   1977
     Red Hen Films   28min
Follows Malvina Reynolds, a 76-year-old songwriter, folksinger, activist, as she
writes her songs, records an album, performs in concert. She talks about her
attitudes towards aging and dying.

PA-C-17
MAKING MUSIC: THE EMERSON STRING QUARTET   SCA
     16mm   Sd   C   1982
     Vineyard Video Productions   27min
A close look, through conversation and performance, at the personal and musical
qualities that must combine to make an ensemble of excellence.

PA-C-18
MAHALIA JACKSON   SCA
     16mm, UBV   Sd   C   1974
     Phoenix Films   34min
A portrait of gospel singer Mahalia Jackson and footage of her performing eleven
songs.

PA-C-19
MANHATTAN TRANSFER   SCA
     UBV   Sd   C   1979
     Time-Life Multimedia   40min
A live performance featuring selections from 1940s and 50s.

PA-C-20
MAXWELL STREET BLUES   SCA
     16mm   Sd   C   1980
     Linda Williams   56min
Explores the tradition of blues and gospel music as it is still played on the streets
of Chicago's Maxwell Street open-air market.

PA-C-21
OPENING NIGHT: THE MAKING OF AN OPERA   SCA
     16mm   Sd   C   1980
     KCET-TV   58:20min
A look backstage at the tempers and talents which go into the making of a
gigantic operatic production. The film features Luciano Pavarotti, Renata Scotto
and a cast of hundreds responsible for bringing grand opera (in this case, La
Gioconda), to the stage.

PA-C-22
OUTLINE FOR THE NEXT WAVE:
  THE NEW PERFORMING ARTIST   SCA
     Audio Cassette   1982
     NPR   29min
The first generation of Americans brought up on television has created a new
performing art form using sophisticated sound and video techniques. Bob Wisdom
speaks with four of these new peformers. They discuss their ideas on culture,
perception, and art.

PA-C-23
RALPH STANLEY'S BLUEGRASS FESTIVAL   SCA
     16mm   Sd   C   1982
     Amberola Productions   15min
A portrait of Ralph Stanley with the Clinch Mountain Boys at his annual Memorial
Day music festival. The film traces his early years in The Stanley Brothers, and
his decision to continue the act after the death of his brother.

PA-C-24
ROCK N' ROLL, VOICES IN THE WIND SERIES   SCA
          Audio Cassette   1982
          NPR   59min
Thi program takes an informative and entertaining look at the world of Rock n'
Roll. It features music by Chuck Berry, Buddy Holly, The Beatles, The Band, Patti
Smith, Marshall Chapman, Bob Seger, and Bruce Springsteen.

PA-C-25
SONNY TERRY   SCA
          16mm, UBV   Sd   C   1976
          Lawren Productions   6min
A great performance by the blind master of the blues harmonica.

PA-C-26
TO HOPE: A CELEBRATION WITH DAVE BRUBECK   SCA
          16mm,UBV   Sd   C
          Frost Media Associates, Inc.   58min
Features three performances of a new composition by jazz "great" Dave Brubeck
and a behind-the-scenes look at concert preparations.

PA-C-27
VIRGIL THOMSON, COMPOSER   SCA
          16mm   Sd   C
          Film America, Inc.   58:30min
A portrait of the witty and outspoken American composer.

PA-C-28
THE WEAVERS: WASN'T THAT A TIME   SCA
          16mm   Sd   C   1982
          Films, Inc.   75min
The Weavers--Pete Seeger, Ronnie Gilbert, Fred Hellerman, Lee Hays--were one
of the most popular folksinging groups in the early 1950s. Filled with the
Weavers' music, the film culminates in a historic reunion concert at Carnegie Hall
in 1980.

PA-C-29
THE WIZARD OF WAUKESHA: A FILM ABOUT LES PAUL   SCA
          16mm   Sd   C
          Stray Cat Productions   58min
Portrait of Les Paul's career as musician, inventor and performer.

PA-C-30
ZUBIN MEHTA: COMMITMENT AND FULFILLMENT
   AS A WAY OF LIFE   SCA
          16mm   C   1978
          Esmeralda Films   22min
A study of Zubin Mehta and his approach to life. The renowned conductor
discusses his constant search for fulfillment, both personally and professionally.

Performing Arts - Theatre

PA-D-1
AMERICAN THEATRE: A SERIES   SCA
         FS, Cassette (4)   C   1977
         ACCOD   64 frs ea
This four part series covers the history and evolution of the American theatre
from early American plays to 1970s musicals. Includes a discussion of American
playwrights and the acting profession.

PA-D-2
BLACK THEATRE IN AMERICA   SCA
         FS, Cassettes (4)   1975
         Olesen Films
Introduces Black theatre in the United States - in four parts.

         African Grove to Uncle Tom's Cabin   42 frs
         African Heritage to Minstrel Shows   49 frs
         Musical comedy to Porgy and Bess   55 frs
         Nineteen Hundred Through the Thirties   53 frs

PA-D-3
THE BOOTHS: PREMIER FAMILY OF
   THE AMERICAN THEATRE   A
         FS, Cassette   C   1975
         Olesen Films   63 frs
Surveys the contributions of the Booth family to the American Theatre in the
19th century.

PA-D-4
COMMEDIENNE   SCA
         16mm   Sd   C   1983
         Straight Face Films   82min
Covers three years in the lives of two women in New York who are struggling to
express themselves through the art of stand-up comedy.

PA-D-5
DARK AT THE TOP OF THE STAIRS   SCA
         16mm   Sd   B
         IDEAL   124min
This brilliant play by William Inge dramatizes the lives of a couple married 17
years.

PA-D-6
EXITS AND ENTRANCES   SCA
         16mm, BV   Sd   1974
         Time-Life Multimedia
Film clips of "show biz" personalities from the post-vaudeville era, including radio
stars.

PA-D-7
GOODSPEED OPERA HOUSE   SCA
    16mm   Sd   C
    IBM Corporation, Data Processing Division   10:30min
Demonstrates the interdependence, plus individual contributions, required to
produce musical productions successfully, season after season, at the Goodspeed
Opera House, East Haddam, Connecticut.

PA-D-8
LA, LA, MAKING IT IN L.A.   SCA
    16mm   Sd   C
    Phoenix Films, Inc.   58min
An entertaining, enlightening look at young hopefuls who come to Los Angeles,
trying to make their names in show business.

PA-D-9
LITTLE PLAYERS   SCA
    16mm   Sd   C
    Contemporary Films, Inc.   58:30min
A fascinating glimpse at the creative process behind the scenes at the Little
Theatre.

PA-D-10
THE LONG CHRISTMAS DINNER BY THORNTON WILDER   SCA
    16mm   Sd   C   1976
    EBEC   37min
An example of the modern trend toward non-representational, symbolic theater,
this play represents ninety Christmas dinners (and ninety years of life) in the
Bayard Household.

PA-D-11
OUR TOWN AND OUR UNIVERSE, I   SCA
    16mm   Sd   C   1959
    EBEC   29min
Clifton Fadiman analyzes the play as a commentary on "the contrast between
each tiny moment of our lives and the vast stretches of time and place in which
each individial plays his role."

PA-D-12
OUR TOWN AND OUR UNIVERSE, II   SCA
    16mm   Sd   C   1959
    EBEC   30min
This film opens with a discussion of the playwright's use of music, of light motif
and variations, and of the condensed line or word.

PA-D-13
THE PALACE OF DELIGHT   SCA
    16mm   Sd   C   1982
    Time-Life Video   57min
The Exploration of San Francisco, which has been called "the best science museum
in the world," operates on the principle that people learn by doing, not just
seeing.

PA-D-14
PAUL ROBESON: TRIBUTE TO AN ARTIST   SCA
            16mm   Sd   C   1980
            Films, Inc.   29min
Foremost concert artist, renowned motion-picture and Shakespearean actor,
All-American athlete, scholar, champion of human rights--Paul Robeson was a true
Renaissance figure of the 20th century. Sidney Poiter's narration underscores
footage of Robeson throughout his career.

PA-D-15
THE PERFORMING ARTS   SCA
            16mm   Sd   B
            USIA   30min
Examines the role of the performing artist in America.

PA-D-16
PUTTING UP THE PICKLES   SCA
            16mm   Sd   C   1981
            Direct Cinema   29min
Allows a peek behind the scenes at the Pickle Family Circus. This circus is a way
of life.

PA-D-17
SOME OF OUR VOICES   SCA
            16mm   Sd   B
            USIA   30min
Shows the cultural heritage of the U.S. and the present state of the arts.

PA-D-18
UNDERSTANDING AMERICAN DRAMA   SCA
            FS, Cassette (4)   C   1972
            EDDIM   80 frs ea
A 4-part study of the American playwrights and the plays that shaped the
theatre. Uses as examples Elmer Rice, Thornton Wilder, Eugene O'Neill, Arthur
Miller, William Inge and Edward Albee.

PA-D-19
YOUNG PEOPLE CAN DO ANYTHING!   SC
            16mm   Sd   C   1973
            AMEDFL   16min
Two young people help raise money for a center for the performing arts for black
students as well as white students.

Political Science

Patrick O'Meara

The films in this section range from documentaries to feature-length films and video tapes. All documentaries included may be seen as primary items or sources. They involve interviews with political leaders, or descriptions of particular political events, phenomena or situations. Feature-length films, on the other hand, are dramatized interpretations of the political process. Both provide an excellent and complimentary view of the American political system. Films about the American political system are an immediate and ideal means of conveying first hand awareness of the political process.

The presidency as presented here is the modern presidency and essentially focuses on the period from Dwight Eisenhower to Ronald Reagan. The history section covers earlier presidencies. Also included is a general category in which social issues are dealt with; for example, films on race, immigration, etc.

Because of the increasing importance of the media in American politics, there is a separate category for it. This includes both documentaries and feature-length films (e.g. The Candidate) and the topics within this cateogry range from the use of the media in specific political campaigns to the role of the media in contemporary US political culture.

Documentary and feature-length films predominate in this selection, and there are only passing references to audio tapes, for example, in part because of my ongoing interest in these areas, and in part because of availability. There has thus been a subjective quality to the selection process.

In some areas, a wide number of films are available; for example, the Presidency, Congress and political parties. While for others, there is only limited availability; for example, on the bureaucracy. In all cases, easy purchasing or rental has been one of the guiding principles for selection. Less readily available sources of interesting material abound. Forexample the following give some indication of the nature of these resources:

The Vanderbilt Television News Archives Joint University Libraries, Vanderbilt University, Nashville, TN 37207 (615) 332-2927, tape Nightly News Broadcasts of ABC, CBS, NBC; Special News Reports of ABC, CBS, NBC and PBS; Face the Nation, Issues and Answers, Meet the Press. These are available in audio-cassette, and video.

Julian Kanter Archives of Presidential Campaign Spots, 1821 Rosemary Road, Highland Park, ILL 60035. This valuable resource includes presidential political campaign commercials from 1960 onwards as well as excellent examples of TV commercials used in congressional and gubernatorial races.

The Poynter Center, Indiana University, 410 North Park Avenue, Bloomington, Indiana 47405 has a wide collection of video-tapes which may be borrowed or copied. The material ranges from Senator Sam Ervin discussing Watergate to Gloria Steinem and Paula Gordon discussing the women's movement.

POLITICAL SCIENCE (PolS)

PolS-A General Government Background
PolS-B Political Parties
PolS-C Elections
PolS-D Interest Groups
PolS-E The Media
PolS-F The Constitution
PolS-G The Supreme Court
PolS-H Judiciary/Court System
PolS-I Congress
PolS-J Modern Presidency
PolS-K Presidents
PolS-L Executive Departments
PolS-M Civil Rights
PolS-N Unions
PolS-O Domestic Unrest/Civil Disobedience
PolS-P Other Social Problems
PolS-Q ForeignPolicy
PolS-R State Government
PolS-S Local Government

Political Science - General Government Background

PolS-A-1
CITY OUT OF WILDERNESS: WASHINGTON   SCA
        16mm, UBV   Sd   C   1975
        Films, Inc.   30min
This is the definitive history of our nation's capital, utilizing old prints,
documents, daguerrotypes and photos by Matthew Brady.

PolS-A-2
THE FEDERAL SYSTEM: CHECKS AND BALANCES   A
        FS (2)   Sd   C   1980
        SSSS
The checks and balances that make up the mosaic of the federal government are
the subject. The roots of our constitutional separation of powers into executive,
legislative, and judicial branches are examined.

PolS-A-3
GOVERNMENT   CA
        16mm   Sd   C   1964
        MGHT   11min
This film incorporates the appeal of animation and music to provide a sprightly
view of how governments operate on the national, state, and local levels, and
explains how governments provide protection, collect and distribute tax monies,
and make the laws.

PolS-A-4
GOVERNMENT: HOW MUCH IS ENOUGH?   SCA
        FS Cassettes (4)   C
        SSSS
The question of the government's presence in American life is investigated in four
areas: welfare, the economy, regulation, and personal freedom.

PolS-A-5
GOVERNMENT IN THE UNITED STATES   S
        FS, Cassettes (5)   Sd   1976
        NGS   14-17min
1. Federal Government: The Legislative Branch
2. Federal Government: The Judicial Branch
3. Federal Government: The Executive Branch
4. Local and County Government
5. State Government

PolS-A-6
OUR CHANGING CONSTITUTION   CA
        FS, Cassettes (2)   C   1981
        SSSS
This program focuses on the flexibility that was built into the Constitution
through the amendment process, by vote of Congress and judicial interpretation.

PolS-A-7
OUR FEDERAL GOVERNMENT   SCA
          FS, Cassettes (5)   C   1980
          SSSS
This program provides an in-depth examination of each of the three branches of
government and explains the system of checks and balances that maintain a
balance of power.

PolS-A-8
A POLITICAL PRIMER   A
          FS, Cassette   1972
          RMI Film Productions   53 frs
Examines the meanings of the terms liberal, conservative, reactionary and radical;
and describes the characteristic political attitude and behavior of those who
support these views.

PolS-A-9
THE REGULATORS: OUR INVISIBLE GOVERNMENT   CA
          16mm   Sd   1982
          LCA   50min
Focuses on federal regulations and how effective they are. Especially spotlights
the EPA's drafting of the Clean Air Act.

PolS-A-10
U.S. GOVERNMENT IN ACTION   SCA
          FS (2), Cassettes (6)   C
          SSSS
Explains the complex workings of our federal government in clear, graphic terms.
          1. The House of Representatives   4. The Senate
          2. The Supreme Court   5. Reg. Agencies
          3. The Cabinet   6. The Presidency

PolS-A-11
U.S. GOVERNMENT: 200 YEARS OF CHANGE   A
          FS (6), Cassettes   C   1978
          SSSS
Tracing the changes in government from the Articles of Confederaton to today.

PolS-A-12
VALUES IN A DEMOCRACY--
NATIONAL ISSUES, WHAT'S RIGHT?   S
          FS, Cassette   Sd   1976
          Guidance Associates   133 frs
Focuses on moral issues dealing with local and national politics.

PolS-A-13
WASHINGTON, D.C.   S
          FS (2), Cassettes   1980
          NGS   14min ea
          1. Visiting Our Government Buildings
          2. Monuments and Museums
Tour government buildings, monuments, and museums.

PolS-A-14
WASHINGTON, D.C.: STORY OF OUR CAPITAL   SC
         UBV   Sd   C   1956
         Coronet   10.5min
Through the words of the designer of the master plan of our nation's capital,
students are given the early history of Washington, D.C.

PolS-A-15
THE WHITE HOUSE, PAST AND PRESENT   SC
         UBV   Sd
         Coronet   13min
This film captures the drama and history of America's past embodied in our
nation's Executive Mansion by taking us into famous rooms and offices seldom
seen by the public.

Political Science - Political Parties

PolS-B-1
AMERICAN POLITICAL PARTIES TODAY   A
         FS (2), Cassettes   C   1976
         SSSS
Examining the origins, development, functions, and workings of the two party
system.

PolS-B-2
OUR POLITICAL SYSTEM   S
         FS (2), Cassette   1981
         NGS   15-16min
Discover important aspects of politics in the United States.   Encounter party
leaders, workers, and political rivals.
Parties: The goals, functions, and history of political parties.
Elections: Follow candidates in contests for the support of the voters.

PolS-B-3
POLITICAL PARTIES IN AMERICA:
  GETTING THE PEOPLE TOGETHER   A
         16mm   Sd   C   1976
         EBEC   19min
Defines and explores the changing roles of American political parties from their
beginnings to the 1976 election.

PolS-B-4
POLITICAL PROTEST WITHIN A PARTY   A
         16mm   Sd   C   1973
         Pictura Films   15min
The power of protest resulted in 1968 Democratic Presidential primary battle
among McCarthy, Kennedy, and Humphrey. Excerpts from their speeches show the
strategy each pursued in attempting to win the elections.

Political Science - Elections

PolS-C-1
AL STACEY HAYES   SCA
        16mm   Sd   C   1969
        Jason Films   28min
Portrait of a high school student who worked to help elect a black Alderman to
the city council of Shelby, Mississippi. Reflects the various attitudes held by
blacks about the effect politics has on their lives.

PolS-C-2
CAMPAIGN   A
        16mm   Sd   C   1973
        Churchill Films   20min
A documentary account of Cathy O'Neill's campaign for state Senator in
California. Ms. O'Neill, a housewife and mother, came within one percent of
defeating her opponent.

PolS-C-3
CAMPAIGN AMERICAN STYLE   SCA
        16mm   Sd   C   1968
        BFA   49min
Shows how advertising and marketing are used by political candidates. The
election of a county official in Nassau County, N.Y. is detailed.

PolS-C-4
CANDIDATE, THE   A
        16mm   Sd   C   1972
        Warner Home Video   110min
Robert Redford gives perhaps the finest performance of his career as an idealistic
lawyer whose values are steadily eroded when he runs for the U.S. Senate.

PolS-C-5
CHISHOLM: PURSUING THE DREAM   SCA
        16mm   C   1974
        New Line Cinema   42min
A record of Congresswoman Shirley Chisholm's race in the Florida Presidential
primary in 1972.

PolS-C-6
THE CONVENTIONS--THE PROCESS IN CRISIS   SCA
        16mm   Sd   B   1970
        Films, Inc.   22min
Shows the Republican convention in Miami, Florida, Nixon's first-ballot
nomination. Depicts the Democratic convention in Chicago, and the riots. Portrays
a badly crippled Democratic party nominating Humphrey and Humphrey's
acceptance.

PolS-C-7
THE ELECTION--HOW VOTES ARE PACKAGED   SCA
        16mm   Sd   B   1970
        Films, Inc.   16min
Explains how a president would be chosen should three candidates run and none
receive a majority of electoral votes.

PolS-C-8
ELECTION OF 1932   SC
          16mm   Sd   C   1966
          Films, Inc.   20min
The background of the 1932 presidential election in the United States.

PolS-C-9
THE ELECTION PROCESS   SC
          FS (2), Cassettes   C   1979
          SSSS
Should the President be elected by popular vote or by the Electoral College? This question and many others are discussed in this multimedia kit on the process of electing the President and Vice President of the United States.

PolS-C-10
HOW WE ELECT OUR REPRESENTATIVES   SCA
          UBV   Sd   1972
          Coronet   10 1/2min
Presents the full story of a typical election from registration to the counting of ballots, including the use of voting machines and the impact of television.

PolS-C-11
LET'S VOTE   SC
          FS (5), Cassettes (3)   C
          SSSS
This series of 5 sound filmstrips is designed to educate and motivate the teen-age voter. The program explores the economic significance of the vote, voter registration, the nature and realities of political parties and campaigns, effective communication with elected officials, and the importance of minority groups in American politics.

PolS-C-12
MAKING OF THE PRESIDENT, THE   A
          16mm   Sd   C   1972
          Time Life Films   69min
Traces the 1972 Democratic and Republican presidential campaigns from the New Hampshire primary to the November election of Richard Nixon.

PolS-C-13
THE MAKING OF THE PRESIDENT 1960:
    THE BATTLE FOR THE NOMINATION   A
          16mm   Sd   B   1961
          Films, Inc.   40min
Depicts the struggles of the various candidates of both parties for the nomination. Shows the nomination of Kennedy at the Democratic convention and Nixon at the Republican convention.

PolS-C-14
THE MAKING OF THE PRESIDENT 1960:
    THE BATTLE FOR THE PRESIDENCY   A
          16mm   Sd   B   1961
          Films, Inc.   40min
Follows the campaigns of Nixon and Kennedy from their beginnings in August and September, through the Inauguration of Kennedy.

PolS-C-15
THE MAKING OF THE PRESIDENT 1964   A
            16mm   Sd   B   1965
            Films, Inc.·   40min
Shows the 1964 political conventions and campaigns for the Presidency, from John
F. Kennedy's assassination through Lyndon Johnson's election.

PolS-C-16
PERSUASION AND POWER   SC
            FS   Sd   1976
            EAV
Electioneering and political participation in the United States.

PolS-C-17
POLITICAL PROMISES   SCA
            FS, Cassettes (2)   C   1980
            SSSS
Should the electorate believe the politician's promises? This filmstrip investigates
this phenomenon and which presidents have kept their word.

PolS-C-18
PRESIDENCY, THE   SC
            16mm   Sd   B   1969
            EBEC   29min
A case study of the variety of strategies a contestant can employ to become his
party's candidate for president.

PolS-C-19
PRIMARY   A
            16mm   Sd   B   1965
            Time-Life Films   54min
A candid look at the primary campaigns of Hubert Humphrey and John F. Kennedy
in the state of Wisconsin.

PolS-C-20
THE PRIMARY SYSTEM   SCA
            FS, Cassettes (2)   C   1982
            SSSS
Why does the United States use statewide primaries to nominate national
cadidates? How do they work? And what effect have they had on the political
process?

PolS-C-21
THE RIGHT TO VOTE   SCA
            FS, Cassettes (4)   C   1980
            SSSS
Why do so few citizens vote and what are the implications of this widespread
apathy?

PolS-C-22
STATE OF THE UNION   SCA
            UBV   Sd   1948
            SSSS   122min
Based on the Pulitzer Prize-winning play by Howard Lindsay and Russel Crouse,
this movie is about the conflict between political power and personal ethics.

PolS-C-23
TIPPECANOE AND LYNDON, TOO   SCA
    16mm   Sd   C   1967
    MGHT   24min
The hoopla of national political conventions replete with balloons, bands, and buttons.

PolS-C-24
VOTE POWER   SCA
    16mm   Sd   C   1973
    American Educ'l Films   15min
A film encouraging young people to vote.

PolS-C-25
VOTING AT 18   SCA
    UBV   Sd   1972
    Coronet   12min
The 26th Amendment gave millions of young people the right to vote. By registering, finding out about the candidates and then voting, they can make their voices heard.

PolS-C-26
VOTING RIGHTS ACT   SC
    Audio-cassete   1981
    NPR   42min
The passage of the Voting Rights Act in 1965 has had a profound effect on the black voter registration in the South. When key provisions of the law expired in early 1982, Congress passed the new act intact.

PolS-C-27
THE WHOLE WORLD IS WATCHING   A
    16mm   Sd   B   1969
    INUAVC   55min
David Brinkley, Walter Cronkite, John Fisher, and Senator John O. Pastore discuss bias on television. Their conversation covers topics ranging from coverge of the 1968 Democratic national convention to proposed restraints on television.

PolS-C-28
THE YOUNG VOTE: POWER, POLITICS
  AND PARTICIPATION   SCA
    16mm   Sd   C   1972
    BFA   15min
The importance of the young vote is emphasized and the campaign of a 20-year-old is highlighted.

Political Science – Interest Groups

PolS-D-1
LOBBYING: A CASE HISTORY   SCA
    16mm   Sd   C   1977
    EBEC   17min
Demonstrates how the lobbying system can influence national government policy by focusing on a controversy in Alton, Illinois, over the replacement of a lock and dam.

PolS-D-2
LOBBYING: HOW DOES IT WORK?
  WHOM DOES IT WORK FOR?   SC
       FS   Sd   C   1977
       SSSS
Sound color filmstrip examines the recent scandals which have brought demands
for reform of the lobbying system and analyzes the ways in which lobbyists work.

PolS-D-3
PEOPLE POWER   SC
       FS, Cassettes (2)   C
       SSSS
This two-part filmstrip attempts to answer the question: Can individuals make a
difference in public life and government?

PolS-D-4
PRESSURE GROUPS IN ACTION   SCA
       16mm   B   1960
       Republic Steel Corp.   16min
Presents both the useful functions served by pressure groups and the dangers
which are inherent in their operation.

PolS-D-5
ROLE OF THE INTEREST GROUP LEADER, THE   SCA
       16mm   Sd   C   1973
       Xerox Films   23min
The Sierra Club employs a lobbyist to fight against strip mining. The film not only
examines his duties but also the issue.

                    Political Science - The Media

PolS-E-1
MEDIA PROBES: POLITICAL SPOTS   SCA
       16mm   Sd   C   1981
       Time-Life Video   30min
A primer on the techniques used by today's political media makers. Media
consultants Bob Squier and Bob Goodman explain the process involved in making
vote-winning TV commercials.

PolS-E-2
NETWORK   A
       16mm   Sd   C   1976
       MGM/UA   121min
A satire of television and the men behind the network.

PolS-E-3
THE PEOPLE'S RIGHT TO KNOW: POLICE VS. REPORTER   A
       16mm   Sd   B   1969
       Vision Quest   17min
A Chicago newspaper photographer relates his experiences with the police while
attempting to cover the 1968 Democratic Convention in Chicago.

PolS-E-4
RIGHT TO KNOW   A
    16mm   Sd   C   1973
    Journal Films   17min
Studs Terkel discusses the public's right to know and the importance of freedom
of information in a democratic society.

Political Science – The Constitution

PolS-F-1
THE CONSTITUTION AND CENSORSHIP   SCA
    16mm   Sd   B   1959
    INUAVC   29min
Deals with two court cases involving censorship, on religious grounds, by
governmental agencies--one involving The Miracle sequence from the film Ways of
Love and the other concerning religious soliciting in Connecticut by a minister of
the Jehovah's Witnesses. The origins of censorship in England are reviewed and
related to their influences on American law. Traces the legal proceedings and
precedents involved in the banning of The Miracle and the eventual reversal of
the ban. Through the case of Cantwell et. al vs. Connecticut the courts' decision
stated that governments do not have the power to censor materials on religious
grounds. Presents opposing views on censorship at close of the films.

PolS-F-2
THE CONSTITUTION AND EMPLOYMENT STANDARDS   SCA
    16mm   Sd   B   1959
    INUAVC   28min
Shows the relationship of the Constitution to wage-and-hour legislation by
recreating the case of United States vs. Darby Lumber Company. Rev
e   w   s   t   h   e
legal, social, and economic background, and aftermath of the Fair Labor Standards
Act of 1938. Emphasizes the constitutional standards and their shifting
interpretation used by the Supreme Court in judging the constitutionality of
federal regulation of labor standards. Illustrates the role of Supreme Court
decision-making in the American governmental system.

PolS-F-3
THE CONSTITUTION AND FAIR PROCEDURE   SCA
    16mm   Sd   B   1959
    INUAVC   29min
Presents the famous Leyra vs. Denno Case. Deals with the right to jury trial, the
right to be represented by counsel, and protection against unreasonable search
and seizure. Shows how the above principles apply to the average man.

PolS-F-4
THE CONSTITUTION AND MILITARY POWER   A
    16mm   Sd   B   1959
    INUAVC   29min
Deals with the exclusion and relocation of persons of Japanese ancestry from the
West Coast during World War II. Dramatizes the story of Fred Korematsu, a U.S.
citizen of Japanese ancestry, who fled to avoid detention and relocation. His suit
for freedom is followed through the courts. Summarizes a previous court decision
in 1866, Milligan Ex Parte, and compares the decisions of the court in cases of
Korematsu and Mitsuye Endo, also a Japanese-American. Raises the question of

the rights of the military to detain citizens without charges and represents an opinion dissenting with the Korematsu vs. U.S. case which states that relocation and exclusion of Japanese gave evidence of racialism under the excuse of military necessity.

PolS-F-5
THE CONSTITUTION AND THE LABOR UNION   SCA
    16mm   Sd   B   1959
    INUAVC   29min
Follows the dramatization of the trial of a test case to overthrow the Right-to-Work Law in North Carolina, Whittaker et al vs. North Carolina, in which the case was appealed through state courts to the Supreme Court where the validity of the law was upheld. Traces the previous decisions affecting labor in the Supreme Court and deals specifically with defeats involving the 14th Amendment and the right to contract. Touches upon decisions which held for labor; reviews labor's rise to political power; indicates that abuses of power have caused labor to be denied the privileges of judicial protection; and that labor must now seek to influence legislative bodies.

PolS-F-6
THE CONSTITUTION AND THE RIGHT TO VOTE   SCA
    16mm   Sd   B   1959
    INUAVC   29min
Follows the efforts to gain the right to vote for Negroes through a succession of legal decisions and social changes. Dramatizes the case of Smith vs. Allwright et al. Reviews the long conflict to extend voting rights to a large electorate beginning with the Constitutional Convention's compromise over dropping property requirements through and including the enactment of the 15th and 19th Amendments to the Constitution. Cites legal precedents established by the U.S. Supreme Court through their decisions concerning the control of state primaries in 1918 and 1935 and the later reversals in 1914 and 1944. Points to the issues involved in Federal encroachment upon state's rights.

PolS-F-7
CONSTITUTION OF THE UNITED STATES   SCA
    16mm   Sd   B   1956
    EBEC   22min
Pictures some of the historical background of the struggle by the colonies for independence and of the signing of the Constitution. Includes Shay's rebelling against the tariff, the weaknesses of the Articles of Confederation, and the disagreements among states. Shows how the misunderstanding between large and small states led to the establishment of a House and a Senate.

PolS-F-8
JUSTICE ON TRIAL   A
    16mm   Sd   C   1977
    MGHT   52min
Provides an overview of the U.S. criminal justice system and its inequities through interviews and discussions with those involved --victims, criminals, prosecutors, and judges.

Political Science - The Supreme Court

PolS-G-1
OUR LIVING BILL OF RIGHTS SERIES (6 Films)   SCA
        16mm   Sd   C   1969
        EBEC
A series dealing with law cases that were concerned with basic constitutional precepts.
1. The Schempp Case: Bible Reading in Public Schools   35min
2. Free Press vs. Fair Trial by Jury: The Sheppard Case   27min
3. Equality Under Law: The California Fair Housing Cases   25min
4. Freedom to Speak: People of New York vs. Irving Feiner   23min
5. Equality Under Law: The Lost Generation of
                         Prince Edward County   20min
6. Justice Under Law: The Gideon Case   23min

PolS-G-2
THE UNITED STATES SUPREME COURT:
   GUARDIAN OF THE CONSTITUTION   SCA
        16mm UBV   Sd   C   1973
        EBEC   24min
The film highlights the history and landmark cases of the Supreme Court, from its beginnings in 1789 to the present.

Political Science - Judiciary/Court System

PolS-H-1
ALTERNATIVES FOR A SAFER SOCIETY:
   NEW RESPONSES TO CRIMES AND VICTIMS   SCA
        FS, Cassette   C   1979
        SSSS
This program takes a long and penetrating look at the causes and possible remedies for our nation's high rate of violence.

PolS-H-2
AT ISSUE: CRIME AND PUNISHMENT   SCA
        FS, Cassettes (4)   C
        SSSS
This four-part sound color filmstrip examines the American system of punishment by imprisonment and what it does to and for criminals.

PolS-H-3
THE BILL OF RIGHTS   SCA
        35mm, Cassette   C   1980
        SSSS   80 slides
This program traces the document's tenets back to the philosophies of Englishmen John Locke and Thomas Hobbes. Each article is explained, the reason for its inclusion is presented, and its most important applications are described.

PolS-H-4
THE BILL OF RIGHTS IN ACTION   A
     16mm   Sd   C   1970
     BFA   23min
Can a reporter plead a special privilege not to answer questions before a court or
a Grand Jury, in order to protect his sources? An open-ended film for discussion.

PolS-H-5
BRANCHES OF GOVERNMENT: THE JUDICAL BRANCH   SCA
     16mm   Sd   C   1981
     NGS   23min
Based on the case of Zobel vs. the State of Alaska, in which Mr. and Mrs. Zobel
take the state of Alaska to the Supreme Court for a decision regarding dividends
given to all residents of Alaska, the amount of which is based solely on length of
residence.

PolS-H-6
THE CASE AGAINST SACCO AND VANZETTI   SCA
     FS, Cassette   C   1980
     SSSS
One of the most sensational trials of this century involved two Italian anarchists
who were tried for murder, found guilty, and executed. The filmstrip leaves the
question of their guilt open-ended.

PolS-H-7
THE CHICAGO CONSPIRACY TRIAL   A
     16mm   Sd   B   1971
     Time-Life Films   2 1/2Hrs
This BBC-TV production is a carefully researched reenactment based on actual
court records of the trial of the Chicago 7. At times the language is rough and
the emotional impact is overwhelming.

PolS-H-8
THE CONSTITUTION AND CENSORSHIP   A
     16mm   Sd   B   1957
     INUAVC   28min
This film covers First Amendment freedoms, focusing on the censorship of Roberto
Rosellini's film The Miracle by a New York State Board of review.

PolS-H-9
CONSTITUTIONAL LAW IN ACTION   SCA
     FS, Cassettes (4)   C
     SSSS
Four sound color filmstrips dramatize actual cases invoving rights granted by the
Constitution:
1. Search and Siezure
2. Due Process
3. Right to Counsel
4. State Action

PolS-H-10
FREE PRESS VS. FAIR TRIAL BY JURY   A
     16mm   Sd   C   1969
     EBEC   26min
Traces the history of the case of Dr. Sam Shepard, tried in 1954 for the murder
of his wife. Includes excerpts from the 1961 Supreme Court decision which

reversed the guilty verdict.

PolS-H-11
FREEDOM AND SECURITY: THE UNCERTAIN BALANCE   A
            16mm   Sd   C   1973
            Westinghouse Learning Corp.   50min
An investigative report on government practices of intelligence gathering, use of
informers, and use of the grand jury.

PolS-H-12
THE FIFTH AMENDMENT   SCA
            FS, Cassettes (2)   C
            SSSS
Both filmstrips look at the amendment legally and historically, including its
provision for grand jury indictments, protection against double jeopardy, and
guarantees of due process.

PolS-H-13
GREAT AMERICAN TRIALS   SCA
            FS, Cassettes (6)   C   1982
            SSSS
In this presentation, six landmark American trials are reenacted. From the 1692
Salem witchcraft trials to the 1968 trial of the Chicago Seven, the cases trace
the development of the American legal system.
1. The Salem Witch Trials
2. Peter Zenger
3. The Scopes Trial
4. Sacco and Vanzetti
5. The Case of Alger Hiss
6. The Chicago Seven

PolS-H-14
GREAT COURT TRIALS IN U.S. HISTORY   CA
            FS, Cassettes (4)   C
            SSSS
Recreates four court trials whose decisions established lasting precedents and
which reflect significant trends in American history.

PolS-H-15
GREAT TRIALS   A
            FS (6), Cassettes (12)   1982
            SSSS
These color sound filmstrips explore six famous American trials that have raised
important questions in American history or have reflected the prejudices of
certain periods.
1. The John Peter Zenger Trial
2. Benedict Arnold: Traitor or Patriot?
3. Dred Scott: Black Man in a White Court
4. Andrew Johnson Comes to Trial
5. Sacco and Vanzetti: Guilty as Charged?
6. The Rosenbergs: The Crime Worse Than Murder

PolS-H-16
GUILTY BY REASON OF RACE   A
            16mm   Sd   C   1972
            Films, Inc.   52min
Examination of the consequences of a Supreme Court ruling which sent 110,000
Japanese-Americans to concentration camps, following the bombing of Pearl
Harbor.

PolS-H-17
INHERIT THE WIND   CA
            FS, Cassettes (3)   1979
            SSSS
A lightly fictionalized re-creation of the Scopes "Monkey Trial" of 1925, starring
Spencer Tracy, Frederic March, and Gene Kelly.

PolS-H-18
INSIDE/OUT   SCA
            16mm   Sd   C   1980
            Centaur Productions   51 min
About the inmate theatre in Matsqui Institution.

PolS-H-19
THE JUDICIAL BRANCH: GOVERNMENT AS IT IS   SCA
            16mm   Sd   C   1980
            Pyramid Films   26min
The veteran Washington news man Jack Anderson takes us on a historical review
of the role of the Supreme Court has played in American history.

PolS-H-20
THE JUDICIAL SYSTEM OF THE UNITED STATES   S
            FS (2)   Sd   1983
            SSSS   15-17min
Law as the framework of government, imposing limits and protecting freedoms.

PolS-H-21
JUSTICE: CRIME, CRIMINALS AND THE SYSTEM   SCA
            16mm, UBV   Sd   1977
            Coronet   26.5min
Takes a hard look at our criminal justice system.

PolS-H-22
JUSTICE: FEAR, CRIME AND PREVENTION   SCA
            16mm, UBV   Sd   1977
            Coronet   23min
This film shows positive ways people are trying to control fear of crime.

PolS-H-23
JUSTICE: JUSTICE AND THE CRIMINAL COURT   SCA
            16mm, UBV   Sd   1977
            Coronet   28min
Some of the reasons behind the loss of respect and confidence in the judical
branch of our government.

PolS-H-24
JUSTICE: THE ROLE OF THE COMMUNITY   SCA
          16mm, UBV   Sd   1977
          Coronet   27 1/2min
This film examines organizations providing an essential human service.

PolS-H-25
KILLING TIME   SCA
          16mm   Sd   C   1980
          Sam Kauffman, Ellen Boyce   60min
Takes the viewer behind the walls of four Massachusetts' prisons (maximum,
medium, minumum and pre-release) for an in-depth look at the problems and
conditions.

PolS-H-26
LAW AND YOUTH   SCA
          FS, Cassettes (2)   C   1981
          SSSS
This filmstrip outlines the basic legal rights and responsibilities of young people.

PolS-H-27
MR. JUSTICE DOUGLAS   A
          16mm   C   1972
          Carousel Films   52min
Veteran reporter Eric Sevareid interviews Justice William O. Douglas, who at age
73 has served for 33 years on the Supreme Court.

PolS-H-28
MOM, I WANT TO COME HOME NOW   SCA
          16mm   Sd   C   1979
          Chronicle Prod.   56.5min
The story of juvenile prostitution in America today.

PolS-H-29
THE PAPER PRISON: YOUR GOVERNMENT RECORDS   A
          16mm   C   1974
          Macmillan Films   56min
An investigation of the use and abuse of information amassed by government
agencies on U.S. citizens, often without their knowledge.

PolS-H-30
PLEA BARGAINING: AN AMERICAN WAY OF JUSTICE   SCA
          16mm   Sd   C   1980
          Thurber Prod., Inc.   60min
Documents the daily activities of judges, prosecutors, and defense attorneys in a
large, overcrowded, urban criminal court system as they bargain--both in and out
of court--over guilty pleas.

PolS-H-31
PRISONS AND PRISON REFORM   SCA
          FS, Cassette (2)   C
          SSSS
This sound filmstrip program looks at prisons today, what they were designed to
accomplish, and what their achievements actually are.

PolS-H-32
RED SQUAD   A
        16mm   C   1972
        Impact Films   45min
An expose' of police political surveillance activities, focusing on the New York
City police department's Security Investigation Squad, better known as the "Red
Squad," and on similar FBI operations.

PolS-H-33
RIGHT OF PRIVACY   A
        16mm   Sd   B   1967
        INUAVC   59min
An expose of the many ways in which the privacy of citizens is violated.

PolS-H-34
THE SCALES OF JUSTICE: OUR COURT SYSTEM   SCA
        FS, Cassettes (2)   C
        SSSS
This two-part filmstrip program focuses first on the Supreme Court and shows how
through "judicial review" it has broadened its powers to influence every area of
American life and serve as an important "check" on the powers of the President
and Congress. The second part describes the salient features of both civil and
criminal trials and the functions of municipal, county, and state courts.

PolS-H-35
THE SHATTERED BADGE   A
        16mm, UBV   Sd   1982
        LCA   30min
In The Shattered Badge, police officers and psychologists examine the stress
problem and its effects upon the cop, his or her family, and the community.

PolS-H-36
THE U.S. SUPREME COURT:
    GUARDIAN OF THE CONSTITUTION   A
        16mm   Sd   C   1973
        EBEC   24min
The landmark cases which shaped the Constitution and the fabric of American life
are examined.

                        Political Science - Congress

PolS-I-1
AN ACT OF CONGRESS   SCA
        16mm   Sd   C   1979
        LCA   58min
The first documentary film to capture the people and the issues in the many-sided
struggle in the House of Representatives over legislation to amend the nation's
clean air laws.

PolS-I-2
BRANCHES OF GOVERNMENT: THE LEGISLATIVE BRANCH   SCA
        16mm, UBV   Sd   C   1982
        NGS   22min
This film follows a congressman through several hectic weeks of work. It

introduces the student to the intricate workings of the legislative branch.

PolS-I-3
CONGRESS: HOW IT WORKS--AND SOMETIMES DOESN'T   SCA
            FS, Cassettes (3)   C
            SSSS
This three-part filmstrip program traces the historic struggle of power between
Congress and the president.

PolS-I-4
THE HOUSE: A CONTEMPORARY LOOK   SCA
            FS, Cassette   C
            SSSS
A report on the changes that have taken place in the House of Representatives
during the past decade.

PolS-I-5
MR. SMITH GOES TO WASHINGTON   SCA
            16mm,UBV   Sd   B   1939
            SSSS   125min
James Stewart plays a Boy Scout leader from Montana who accidentally becomes
a U.S. Senator. He sees corruption in the government, but justice and truth
prevail.

PolS-I-6
MR. SPEAKER: TIP O'NEILL   SCA
            16mm   Sd   C   1978
            Films, Inc.   58min
This documentary offers an inside look at the day-to-day life and work of House
Speaker Thomas P. (Tip) O'Neill as he meets with the congressional elite,
glad-hands voters back home, relaxes with his family, and confers with President
Carter in the Oval Office.

PolS-I-7
THE ROLE OF THE CONGRESSMAN   S
            16mm   Sd   C   1972
            Xerox Films   23min
By contrasting liberal Congressman Richard Bolling with conservative
Congressman Chester Mize, the lobbying manipulations, and compromises necessary
for passage of a bill are shown.

PolS-I-8
THE SENATE: A CONTEMPORARY LOOK   SCA
            FS, Cassette   C
            SSSS
A filmstrip program examining the changes that have taken place in the Senate
since the Nixon presidency and the Senate's role in today's world.

PolS-I-9
THE UNITED STATES CONGRESS:
   OF, BY, AND FOR THE PEOPLE   SCA
            16mm   Sd   C   1972
            EBEC   26min
The development of the U.S. congressional system is surveyed from earliest times
to the present. The film examines the day-to-day work of a Congressman and a
Senator.

Political Science - Modern Presidency

PolS-J-1
BRANCHES OF GOVERNMENT: THE EXECUTIVE BRANCH   SCA
          16mm, UBV   Sd   C   1982
          NGS   22min
This film will show students how the actions of the executive branch affect
people's lives.

PolS-J-2
CONTROL OF A CRISIS   SCA
          16mm   Sd   B   1966
          INUAVC   30min
Presents an analysis of the Berlin crisis of 1961 and the Cuban missile crisis of
1962. Includes people such as Sen. Robert Kennedy, Gen. Louis Norstad, Senior
Russian Diplomat Vladillen Vassev and newsreel footage of Pres. John F. Kennedy.

PolS-J-3
HAIL TO THE CHIEF   SCA
          UBV   Sd   C   1977
          King Features Entertainment   30min
This program argues that the presidency is anything but isolated and imperial.

PolS-J-4
HOW TO BE PRESIDENT   SC
          Audio-Cassette   1981
          NPR   29min
Beginning with the inauguration of Ronald Reagan, producer Keith Talbot sets out
to discover how one becomes president, how chief executives go about their jobs,
and what powers the president has today. A ficticious journalist/private-eye gets
the story from various "students" of the presidency, who share their perceptions
of the office.

PolS-J-5
LEADERSHIP IN AMERICA   A
          FS, Cassette   C
          SSSS
Explores whether there is a universal definition of leadership or whether it varies
according to the circumstances. Examines American presidents' leadership
qualities from Theodore Roosevelt to Ford.

PolS-J-6
MORAL DILEMMAS OF AMERICAN PRESIDENTS:
   THE AGONY OF DECISION   A
          FS, Cassettes (5)   C
          SSSS
Crises faced by five Presidents are brought to life. Lincoln and the issues of
slavery and civil war, McKinley and the question of imperialism raised by the
annexation of the Philippine Islands, Wilson and the controversial League of
Nations, Truman and the issue of Communist aggression in Korea, and Kennedy
and the Cuban missile crises.

PolS-J-7
ORDEAL OF POWER: THE PRESIDENT AND THE
    PRESIDENCY   SCA
        FS, Cassettes (3)   C
        SSSS
The dramatic evolution of the office of president from Washington to Carter, the
built-in limits of power placed on the president by Congress and the Supreme
Court, and examples of presidential decision-making.

PolS-J-8
POWER AND THE PRESIDENCY   SCA
        16mm   Sd   C   1975
        BFA   24min
Traces the Office of the President of the United States from its
constitutionally-guided beginnings on through the many presidents who have
shaped that office with their individual personalities. Dramatizes how Washington
developed precedent-setting policies which would affect the Office, the people,
and the future presidencies for years to come. Outlines the Presidencies of
Jackson, Polk, McKinley, and Roosevelt, showing how each added to the power of
the Office of the Chief Executive.

PolS-J-9
THE PRESIDENCY: HOW MUCH ALONE?   SCA
        16mm   Sd   C   1978
        WGBH   29min
An analysis of how the office of President of the United States is affected by its
own limitations and by the strength of other political forces. The program
examines former President Jimmy Carter's difficulties with Congress (specifically,
his inability to pass two key social security reform measures and major energy
legislation) and demonstrates similar limitations of power encountered by former
Presidents Roosevelt, Truman, Eisenhower, Kennedy, and Nixon. Guests include
Sen. Jacob Javits (R-NY), Ambassador Elliot Richardson, House Speaker Thomas
O'Neill, syndicated columnists Joseph Kraft and David Broder.

PolS-J-10
THE PRESIDENT OF THE U.S.: TOO MUCH POWER?   SCA
        16mm   Sd   C   1971
        EBEC   25min
Examines and explains presidential power and the checkpoints on his power.

PolS-J-11
A QUESTION OF IMPEACHMENT   A
        16mm   Sd   C   1974
        Arthur Mokin Productions   39min
Bill Moyer's Journal presented an essay on the history and meaning of
impeachment. The controversial interpretations of "high crimes and misdemeanors"
are examined.

PolS-J-12
THE VICE-PRESIDENCY: A DECADE OF CHANGE   SCA
        FS, Cassette   C   1983
        SSSS
This color filmstrip shows how the vice president's role has increased during the
past decade and explores the position during the Ford, Carter, and Reagan
administrations.

PolS-J-13
WALTER MONDALE AT THE NATIONAL PRESS CLUB   SCA
        Audio Cassette   1982
        NPR   29min
Former Vice-President Walter Mondale outlines a five-fold plan for the nation's
economic recovery from a recession which he claims did not need to happen.

Political Science - Presidents

PolS-K-1
ALL THE PRESIDENT'S MEN   A
        FS, Cassettes (3), BV   C
        SSSS   50min
This extended-play filmstrip version traces key events in the unraveling of the
story from the break-in of June 1972 to Nixon's resignation in August 1974. Over
450 original frames from the motion picture. Based on Woodward and Bernstein's
book. Videocassette runs 135 mins.

PolS-K-2
THE EISENHOWER YEARS   SCA
        16mm   Sd   B   1963
        INUAVC   22min
Reviews significant events in Eisenhower's career as a soldier, his years as
President, and his retirement. Pictures the inaugural ceremony in 1953 and depicts
such events as the Supreme Court decision on integration, the McCarthy
investigations, and various international crises. Stresses social and scientific
changes, research, and the high levels of production and consumption.

PolS-K-3
ESSAY ON WATERGATE   SCA
        16mm   Sd   C   1973
        INUAVC   59min
Reflects Bill Moyer's personal attempt to understand how a political scandal the
proportion of Watergate could have occured. Reviews the taped testimony of
Mitchell, Ehrlichman, Magruder, and other Senate witnesses. Discusses with
journalists William White and Richard Strout, historian Henry Steele Commager
and several others, various other scandals in U.S. history, the expanding role of
the presidency, and aspects of American history that help to explain the
Watergate morality.

PolS-K-4
FIVE PRESIDENTS ON THE PRESIDENCY   SCA
        16mm   Sd   C   1973
        BFA   24min
Truman, Eisenhower, Nixon, Kennedy and Johnson speak about the power,
responsibilities, struggles, and successes of the Presidency.

PolS-K-5
HARRY S. TRUMAN:
  PORTRAIT OF POWER   SCA
        FS, Cassette   C   1979
        SSSS
This filmstrip and cassette show us who he was, where he came from, and events
as he saw them.

PolS-K-6
JOHN FITZGERALD KENNEDY:
  A HISTORY OF OUR TIMES   SCA
        16mm   Sd   B   1967
        LCA   50min
This warm and intimate documentary explores the Kennedy wit, courage and
humanity. We glimpse Kennedy's administration through footage of the Cuban
missile crisis, meetings with De Gaulle and Khruschev, and the horrifying
assassination in Dallas in this honest and affecting history that goes back to the
time of JFK's grandfather.

PolS-K-7
JOHN F. KENNEDY: GREAT FIGURES IN HISTORY   SCA
        BV   Sd   C,B   1981
        SSSS   104 min
A three-part portrait of Kennedy using candid footage, excerpts from televised
speeches, interviews, and clips from news programs. First:The Presidential Years.
Four Dark Days recounts the assassination. The third section consists of an
informal conversation between Rose Kennedy and Harry Reasoner.

PolS-K-8
JOHN F. KENNEDY: THE INAUGURATION SPEECH   SCA
        UBV   Sd   C   1976
        American Educ'l Films   17min
JFK's complete 1961 speech is chronicled here. Includes the "Ask not what your
country can do for you ..." phrase.

PolS-K-9
JOHN F. KENNEDY: PORTRAIT OF
  POWER   SCA
        FS, Cassette   C   1982
        SSSS
The hopeful excitement of John F. Kennedy's ascendence to the presidency and
the terrible shock of his assassination are recreated in this filmstrip program.

PolS-K-10
KENNEDY--YEARS OF CHARISMA   SCA
        16mm   Sd   B   1980
        LCA   23min
A tribute to Kennedy from those who knew him. Upon his death, he became a
hero.

PolS-K-11
LYNDON B. JOHNSON:
  PORTRAIT OF POWER   SCA
        FS, Cassette   C   1979
        SSSS
This filmstrip presentation focuses on his five years as President. Assassinations,
student uprisings, Black militancy, urban riots, and the Vietnam War.

PolS-K-12
NIXON'S CHECKERS SPEECH   SCA
        16mm   B   1971
        New Yorker Films   30min
During the 1952 Presidential campaign, Richard Nixon, Eisenhower's running mate, was accused of unethically using special campaign funds. He then went on nationwide television to tell the details of his financial life, including the story of his dog Checkers, given to him by an admirer. It is an indication of the power of the television medium.

PolS-K-13
THE PRESIDENCY: A DECADE OF
    CHANGE   SCA
        FS, Cassette   C   1983
        SSSS
A look at the position of the presidency under its last three incumbents: Ford, Carter, and Reagan.

PolS-K-14
THE PRESIDENCY RESTORED   SCA
        16mm   Sd   C   1982
        Gerald Ford Presidential Museum   28.5min
Reveals those qualities and experiences of Mr. Ford's life which contributed to making his term as President a time of national healing.

PolS-K-15
PRESIDENTS OF THE UNITED STATES SERIES   S
        FS, Cassette   1980
        NGS
A series on major American Presidents: their personalities, early lives, families, careers.
Part VII: Harry S. Truman, Dwight D. Eisenhower
Part VIII: John F. Kennedy, Lyndon B. Johnson

PolS-K-16
REPORT   SCA
        16mm   Sd   B   1965
        LCA   13min
The initial subject matter of Report is the John Kennedy assassination. Endless repetitions of part of a film of Kennedy passing in his car seem to suspend him at the moment just before the shooting; once he is shot, the imagery shifts to rapid black-and-white flicker, suggesting the incomprehensible shock many felt at the time, shock for which no image could be found.

PolS-K-17
RICHARD NIXON--CHECKERS, OLD GLORY, RESIGNATION   SCA
        UBV   Sd
        SSSS   45min
Presents a classic look at the only American president to be forced from office.

PolS-K-18
RONALD REAGAN: FORTIETH PRESIDENT
    OF THE UNITED STATES   A
        16mm   Sd   C
        USIA   13min
This biography traces Ronald Reagan's life from his early youth, through college,

his broadcasting days, early screen career, war years, Presidency of the Screen Actors Guild, development of his political career, Governorship of California, the 1980 campaign for the Presidency of the United States.

PolS-K-19
THE UN-MAKING OF A PRESIDENT   A
        FS, Cassettes (2)   C
        SSSS
Studies the removal of Richard Nixon from office as a case study of American government in action. Part I traces the political biography of Nixon. In Part II editorial columnist Jack Anderson and historian James MacGregor Burns explore the significance and impact of the constitutional "surgery" that led to the first removal of a President and the smooth transition to a successor.

PolS-K-20
WATERGATE: TEN YEARS AFTER   CA
        Audio-Cassette   1982
        NPR   29min
This program presents three reports of the Watergate conspiracy ten years after initial break-in.

Political Science - Executive Departments

PolS-L-1
AMERICA IN SEARCH OF ITSELF   A
        UBV   Sd   C   1982
        LCA   43min
How Ronald Reagan won the 1980 Presidential election--based on the social and political trends of the past 25 years which have changed the face of the nation--is examined in this NBC Report. John Chancellor and Theodore H. White ("The Making of the President") explore the crises that prompted millions of Americans to question the liberal traditions which had dominated American politics for 25 years.

PolS-L-2
THE CABINET   SCA
        FS, Cassettes (2)   C   1982
        SSSS
Describes the origin of the cabinet with the establishment by Congress of the departments of State, War, and Treasury in 1789.

Political Science - Civil Rights

PolS-M-1
THE AUTOBIOGRAPHY OF MISS JANE PITTMAN   SCA
        16mm   Sd   C   1974
        LCA   110min
The moving story of a 110-year-old woman who was born into slavery. Her strong will and undying faith in her people allowed her to survive adversity and take part in the Civil Rights demonstrations of the 60s.

PolS-M-2
THE BIRTH OF A NATION   SCA
         UBV   Sd   C   1915
         Thunderbird Films   129min
A special silent film about events leading up to the Civil War.

PolS-M-3
BLACK PEOPLE IN THE SLAVE SOUTH   SCA
         16mm   Sd   C   1972
         EBEC   11min
In 1850 black slaves were imported to provide cheap labor for the cotton kings in
Mississippi. They faced harsh treatment from white planters and politicians who
subjugated blacks for profit and claimed them mentally inferior to their white
brothers.

PolS-M-4
FREDERICK DOUGLASS   SCA
         16mm   Sd   C   1972
         EBEC   9min
Depicts the contributions of runaway slave, Frederick Douglass, who fathered the
black protest movement.

PolS-M-5
GOD ON THE RIGHT   SCA
         16mm   Sd   C   1980
         William Darnell   57min
The effect of the New Right and the TV "preachers-into-politics" on the 1980
elections. This documentary traces the growth of this powerful new movement
primarily through the eyes of the men who have made it all possible.

PolS-M-6
HARLEM IN THE TWENTIES   SCA
         16mm   Sd   C   1971
         EBEC   10min
This once fashionable, white suburb became a black ghetto during the early
twenties. From the squalor and poverty came such greats as Bill Robinson, Ethel
Waters, Josephine Baker, Paul Robeson, Duke Ellington, and other fine black
artists.

PolS-M-7
"I HAVE A DREAM..." THE LIFE
  OF MARTIN LUTHER KING   SCA
         16mm   Sd   C   1968
         BFA   33min
Uses news film footage to study the life of Martin Luther King. Discusses King's
philosophy of non-violence, his relationship with NAACP leader Rev. Wilkins, and
his dream of equal rights for all blacks.

PolS-M-8
KU KLUX KLAN--THE INVISIBLE EMPIRE   SCA
         16mm   Sd   B   1965
         Carousel Films   46min
Examines the aims and mentality of the Knights of the Ku Klux Klan from their
beginnings in Tennessee over a hundred years ago to their still active, prejudicial
treatment of Black, Jewish, and Catholic communities. Explores the rituals,
meetings, and Klan rallies that have spurred hatred and a reign of terror through

the South for the past century. Employs rare film footage of a 1915 Klan ritual
and shows many excerpts from actual meetings and secret ceremonies.

PolS-M-9
THE LAST HURRAH   A
    16mm   Sd   B   1958
    MGHT   121min
Mayor Frank Skeffington's final re-election campaign pits him against all his old
enemies.

PolS-M-10
THE LEARNING TREE   SCA
    16mm   Sd   C   1969
    LCA   107min
Set in Kansas during the 1920s, this powerful autobiographical story documents a
year in the life of a black teen-ager and records the deluge of events that force
him into sudden manhood.

PolS-M-11
MARTIN LUTHER KING, JR.   SC
    16mm   Sd   C   1971
    BFA   9min
Presents the life of Martin Luther King, Jr. Emphasizes the move away from
King's philosophy of nonviolence during the middle 60s.

PolS-M-12
MARTIN LUTHER KING, JR.   SCA
    UBV   Sd   C   1981
    EBEC   24min
Presents the biography of one of the greatest civil rights leaders.

PolS-M-13
ORGANIZED BIGOTRY: WHITE SHEETS AND
  SWASTIKAS   SCA
    FS, Cassette   C   1981
    SSSS
An investigation of the resurgence of the KKK and the Nazis.

PolS-M-14
PORTRAIT IN BLACK: A. PHILIP RANDOLPH   SCA
    16mm   Sd   C
    Sterled   11min
Shows the civil rights march on Washington, D.C. during Kennedy's administration.

PolS-M-15
RESURGENCE, THE MOVEMENT FOR
  EQUALITY VS. THE KKK   SCA
    16mm   Sd   C   1981
    First-Run Features   54min
Deals with the violent murders of five people at a peaceful anti-Klan rally. The
American Nazi Party and other white supremecist groups are shown. Resurgence
offers significant insight into a raging battle: at issue are jobs.

PolS-M-16
ROOTS   SCA
          16mm   Sd   C   1977
          Films, Inc.   9hr/39min
This multiple Emmy-winning production ranks as the biggest event in the history
of television, gaining the largest audience and following ever on record. Based on
Alex Haley's bestseller, Roots is the saga of an American family from the birth of
Kunta Kinte in the Mandinka village of Juffere, West Africa in 1750. Abducted to
America as a slave, his fight for freedom of body and soul continues throughout
his own life into the generations that follow on pre-Civil War America
plantations. Roots has a profound emotional impact in relating this rich cultural
heritage, relevant to everyone.

PolS-M-17
"SEPARATE BUT EQUAL"   SCA
          16mm   Sd   C   1972
          EBEC   8min
Examination of post-Civil War events. Shows how vote fraud, violence, "Jim
Crow" laws, and the KKK maintained segregation.

PolS-M-18
STRANGE FRUIT   SCA
          UBV   Sd   C   1979
          LCA   33min
Tells the story of a black painter in Georgia, in 1948, who faces racism.

PolS-M-19
TO KILL A MOCKINGBIRD   SCA
          FS, Cassettes (2)
          SSSS
Gregory Peck stars as Atticus, a small town Southern lawyer, in this sound
filmstrip version of the Universal film based on Harper Lee's acclaimed novel. The
filmstrips show the life of this rural town during the Depression through the eyes
of Atticus's two small children. Their carefree existence comes to an abrupt halt
when Atticus chooses to defend a Black man charged with raping a White girl.
This adult world of racial bigotry and hatred nearly ends in tragedy.

PolS-M-20
WE SHALL OVERCOME   SCA
          16mm   Sd   C   1965
          Current Affairs Films   10min
Uses the song to show the struggle for human rights and hope. A KKK meeting,
interviews with King and Wallace and mass demonstrations are recorded.

                         Political Science - Unions

PolS-N-1
JOE HILL   SCA
          16mm   Sd   C   1971
          Films, Inc.   114min
An intensely honest tribute to the legendary hero of unskilled immigrant laborers.
Joe Hill fought for decent pay, basic rights and a sense of human worth.

PolS-N-2
NORMA RAE   A
    16mm BV   Sd   C   1979
    Twentieth Century Fox   115min
A film about a courageous textile worker who fights for the right to better
conditions and unionize the mill in which she works.

PolS-N-3
ON THE WATERFRONT   A
    16mm   B   1954
    LCA   108min
About a man who stands up to corruption in the Longshoreman's Union.

PolS-N-4
SALT OF THE EARTH   A
    16mm   Sd   B   1954
    Fleetwood Films   94min
This semidocumentary of the actual year-long strike by Mexican- American zinc
miners in New Mexico focuses on the role of women in the events.

PolS-N-5
UNION MAIDS   SCA
    16mm   Sd   B   1977
    New Day Films   48min
Three women in their 60s--Sylvia, Kate and Stella--tell the way things really were
back in the days when people risked their jobs and lives to organize trade unions.

Political Science - Domestic Unrest/Civil Disobedience

PolS-O-1
AMERICA AFTER VIETNAM SERIES   SCA
    UBV   Sd   C   1979
    PBS Video
Broadcast journalist Daniel Shorr hosts this four-part series examining the ongoing
impact of the Vietnam war on American society. Each program explores a
different aspect of the war.
1. America and its Political Institutions   29min
2. America's Face to the World   29min
3. America Talks to Itself   29min
4. America's Disrupted Lives   29min

PolS-O-2
AMERICAN ATTITUDES: THEN AND NOW   SCA
    UBV
    PBS Video   29min
Host Ben Wattenberg is joined by a troupe of improvisational actors whose
humorous and incisive skits demonstrate changing attitudes in America from the
1960s to today.

PolS-O-3
THE BATTLE OF NEWBURGH   SCA
      16mm   Sd   C   1962
      NBC   54min
A probing look at the demoguery and emotionalism surrounding the welfare issue.
Examines the effect of a strict welfare code proposed for Newburgh, N.Y. by its
city manager.

PolS-O-4
THE DEHUMANIZING CITY...AND HYMIE SCHULTZ   SCA
      16mm   Sd   1972
      LCA   14min
The modern individual in conflict with complex bureaucratic systems.

PolS-O-5
DEMOCRACY: THE ROLE OF DISSENT   SCA
      16mm,UBV   1970
      Coronet   13min
A group of tenants demonstrate and consider a rent strike in protest against
living conditions in their apartment building.

PolS-O-6
DEMOCRACY: YOUR VOICE CAN BE HEARD   SCA
      16mm,UBV   Sd   1970
      Coronet   19.5min
Recreates the true story of a campaign by a group of Detroit high school students
for improvements at a public hospital.

PolS-O-7
HEARTS AND MINDS   SCA
      16mm   Sd   C   1974
      Paramount Home Video   112min
This study of the Vietnam War is an exploration of cherished ideals in conflict
with reality. U.S. policy-makers are interviewed, as are Vietnamese veterans.

PolS-O-8
KENT STATE: MAY 1970   SCA
      16mm   Sd   C   1972
      MGHT   23min
Right to assemble. This film reviews the events at Kent State University (Ohio)
which culminated in the killing of four students by the National Guard.

PolS-O-9
MY NAME IS ABBIE, ORPHAN OF AMERICA   SCA
      16mm   Sd   C   1981
      Icarus   28min
Abbie Hoffman's career sums up the currents and cause of the "Movement" of the
last two decades. My Name Is Abbie, Orphan of America is a humorous,
enlightening and perceptive oral history of the 1960s and 1970s. The film captures
the spirit of a dynamic period in America's cultural and political history; and it
provides valuable insight into a little understood, but crucial turning point in the
nation's life.

PolS-O-10
PENDULUM   SCA
        UBV   Sd   C   1978
        Coronet   26min
Award winning film made by Vermont high school students examines the events
and emotions that threaten to tear apart school and community over the
principal's resignation.

PolS-O-11
THE PENTAGON PAPERS: CONVERSATIONS
    WITH DANIEL ELSBERG   SCA
        16mm   B   1973
        Icarus Films   30min
Based upon the experiences of the man who released the famous "Pentagon
Papers" to the press, this film examines examples of government deception and
misinformation and discusses the right of the public to receive full information on
government policy.

PolS-O-12
THE SELLING OF THE PENTAGON   SCA
        16mm   Sd   B   1971
        Carousel Films   54min
The film presents the Pentagon as a public relations machine which "sells" itself
to the public.

PolS-O-13
SELLING OF THE PENTAGON: REBUTTAL   SCA
        16mm   Sd   B   1971
        Carousel Films   22min
Richard Salant, president of CBS News, defends Selling of the Pentagon against
charges of bias made by the chairman of the House Armed Services Committee,
Secretary of Defense Melvin Laird, and Vice President Agnew.

PolS-O-14
60 MINUTES   SCA
        16mm   Sd   C
        Columbia Broadcasting System
These films present dramatic, illuminating explorations from "60 MINUTES", the
award-winning CBS News series. Incisive journalists Mike Wallace and Morley
Safer define and clarify the central issues and provide a balanced and impartial
account. None of the controversy has been removed.

1. Enemy of the People   20min

Henry Durham, a manager in a Lockheed's Georgia plant, discovered his company
was falsifying its records to the government. His superiors told him to keep his
mouth shut, and the Senate Armed Services Committee ignored him. When the
story broke in the papers, he was ostracised by his friends and neighbors, who
feared the potential loss of their jobs. Durham told the truth, but nobody wanted
to hear it.

2. The Pomeroy File   17min

After Bob Pomeroy spoke against a proposed nuclear power plant at an open
meeting, the Texas Department of Public Safety began a file on him and started
investigations. Pomeroy found out and revealed a nasty web of private, state and

corporate security forces who could open a file on anyone merely by picking up a phone. Morley Safer's interviews with all concerned pose important questions about intelligence gathering and the delicate nature of freedom.

PolS-O-15
TROUBLEMAKERS   SCA
         16mm   Sd   B   1966
         Films, Inc.   54min
Troublemakers is a film about community organizing in the Newark, New Jersey ghetto where Tom Hayden had been active. The film covers three months in the history of the Newark Community Project. Having spent over a year in the ghetto becoming acquainted with the neighborhood, familiarizing themselves with participants, and becoming involved with the inhabitants of the area, Machover and Fruchter were able to shoot the film naturally without the objection or discomfort of the subjects. The result is a spontaneous, unrehearsed drama—a portrayal of the ordinary realities of community organizing.

Political Science - Other Social Problems

PolS-P-1
AN AMERICANISM: JOE MCCARTHY   SCA
         16mm   Sd   C   1965
         Films, Inc.   82min
The story of his life and rise to power is told by friends, business associates, and fellow politicians.

PolS-P-2
THE ARMY-MCCARTHY HEARINGS   SCA
         FS, Cassette   C   1981
         SSSS
This filmstrip program uses news photos to depict the atmosphere of fear in which McCarthy rose to power. The hearings illustrate the differences between investigation and persecution, dissent and disloyalty, and accusation and proof.

PolS-P-3
AS LONG AS THE RIVER RUNS   SCA
         16mm   Sd   C   1971
         AMDOC   60min
The struggle of the American Indians of the Northwest to maintain their fishing rights and way of life.

PolS-P-4
BOOKS UNDER FIRE   SCA
         16mm   Sd   C   1982
         Films Inc.   55min
A report on the epidemic of book censorship in the nation's public schools.

PolS-P-5
CHARGE AND COUNTERCHARGE: A FILM OF
   THE ERA OF SENATOR JOSEPH MCCARTHY   SCA
         16mm   Sd   B   1968
         Appleton-Century-Crofts   43min
Television footage from the Army-McCarthy hearings. Recreates the climate of anti-Communist hysteria in the 1950s.

PolS-P-6
CHILDREN OF VIOLENCE   SCA
    16mm   Sd   C   1982
    Quest Productions   58min
A Chicano family's life is penetrated by adolescent violence. Depicts the psychological and social entrapment/dilemma of the well-meaning mother, the frustration of the adolescents and the overwhelmed juvenile justice systems.

PolS-P-7
CITIZEN: THE POLITICAL LIFE OF ALLARD K. LOWENSTEIN   SCA
    16mm   Sd   C   1983
    The Cinema Guild   72min
Describes the career of Allard K. Lowenstein, political activist and former N.Y. Congressman, who was assassinated in March 1980. Combines interviews with archival footageand traces Lowenstein's involvement in the civil rights and antiwar struggles in the last three decades, from voter registration campaigns in the South to Mccarthy's presidential campaign to the United Nations Human Rights Committee.

PolS-P-8
THE CONVERSATION   SCA
    16mm   Sd   C   1974
    Paramount Home Video   113min
Using the theme of eavesdropping and wire-tapping, but focusing on the personal life of an "electronic surveillance technician" rather than on his victims, Coppola offers a complex thriller, a psychological study, a social analysis and a political comment.

PolS-P-9
EASY RIDER   A
    16mm   Sd   C   1969
    LCA   94min
The film that began the New Hollywood revolution. Produced on a small budget, and shot entirely on location, Easy Rider created a sensation and became a permanent part of the American consciousness. It is an American Odyssey—the story of two men who set out to discover the country and their place in it.

PolS-P-10
THE EMERGING WOMAN   A
    16mm   Sd   B   1974
    Film Images   40min
Through engravings, photographs and newsreels the role of women in American Society from colonial times to the present is carefully traced.

PolS-P-11
THE EXILES   SCA
    16mm   Sd   B   1961
    MGHT   72min
Portrays 12 hours in the lives of an American Indian couple, transplanted from the reservation to downtown Los Angeles.

PolS-P-12
THE GODFATHER   A
    16mm   Sd   C   1972
    Paramount Home Video   171min
A serious, epic vision of an Italian-American family features Marlon Brando as the utterly amazing Corleone patriarch.

PolS-P-13
THE GODFATHER, PART II   A
            16mm   Sd   C   1974
            Paramount Home Video   200min
Continuing the saga of the Corleones, this winner of six Academy Awards
interweaves the story of Don Vito's rise to power with the story of what son
Michael does with that power.

PolS-P-14
THE GRAPES OF WRATH   SCA
            16mm   Sd   B   1940
            Twentieth Century Fox   129min
The story of the Joads, tenant farmers forced from their land by the Dust Bowl
drought and mechanized agriculture.   The Grapes of Wrath depicts poverty,
injustice, despair and hardship.

PolS-P-15
JEWS IN AMERICA – Two Part Series   SCA
            FS, Cassette   1974
            Anti-Defamation League   201 frs
Surveys American Jewry and its contributions to the nation.

PolS-P-16
LETTER FROM AN APACHE   SCA
            16mm   Sd   C   1982
            Barbara Wilk   11 1/2min
An animated dramatization of the true story of an Apache who was born in 1866,
captured in 1871, sold and brought to Chicago where he became a doctor and
returned to help his people.

PolS-P-17
MCCARTHYISM: ERA OF FEAR   SCA
            FS, Cassettes (2)   C   1981
            SSSS
The first program shows McCarthy at the pinnacle of his success.   The
Army-McCarthy hearings are examined in detail in Part II, climaxing in the
famous confrontation with Joseph Welch.

PolS-P-18
MURROW VS. MCCARTHY – Two Parts   SCA
            16mm   B   1954
            CBS News   27min ea
In one of his CBS See It Now broadcasts, Murrow delivered a devastating attack
on the Senator from Wisonsin, whose witch-hunting for alleged Communists in
government and all areas of American life had made a mockery of Constitutional
rights and ruined countless lives and careers.   McCarthy was given equal time to
respond, but he never again recovered the fearful power he had wielded before
Murrow exposed him and his methods to public scrutiny.

PolS-P-19
MY COUNTRY RIGHT OR WRONG   SCA
            16mm   Sd   C   1972
            LCA   15min
Patriotism and personal values.   A young college student and his father disagree
over the obligations of patriotism during the Vietnam war.

PolS-P-20
NAVAJO: THE LAST RED INDIANS   SCA
    16mm   Sd   C   1972
    Time-Life Films   35min
The Navajo have kept their native language. Forty thousand of them still speak no
English as they fight to preserve their way of life against the inroads of white
culture.

PolS-P-21
THE NEW DEAL FOR ARTISTS   SCA
    16mm   Sd   C,B   1979
    Icarus Films   92min
From 1935 to 1942 the United States government supported the most ambitious
arts program since Italian Renaissance. The WPA Arts Project supported
thousands of writers, theater people, painters, sculptors and photographers. This
fascinating documentary explores the profound artistic and political impact of the
WPA project, both in its time and today.

PolS-P-22
NOTHING TO FEAR--
  THE LEGACY OF FDR   SCA
    16mm   Sd   C   1982
    Films Inc.   52min
Explores the legacy of Franklin Delano Roosevelt. Examines his response to the
Great Depression and the radical changes in the role of the Federal government
under his leadership. The Roosevelt legacy includes Social Security, collective
bargaining, unemployment compensation and control of financial institutions.

PolS-P-23
NUCLEAR NIGHTMARES   A
    16mm   Sd   C   1980
    Icarus Films   90min
A frightening and visually explicit examination of four possible senarios for
nuclear holocaust.

PolS-P-24
OUR DAILY BREAD   SCA
    16mm   Sd   B   1934
    MCC   80min
This film about Mr. and Mrs. Anybody in the Depression follows their escape from
the hopelessness of their urban environment back to the land.

PolS-P-25
POINT OF ORDER   SCA
    16mm   Sd   B   1964
    New Yorker Films   97min
A documentary of the Army-McCarthy Hearings.

PolS-P-26
A SHOOTING GALLERY CALLED AMERICA?   SCA
    16mm   Sd   C   1975
    Films, Inc.   52min
Documents the wide range of social problems caused by the private ownership of
handguns and interviews homeowners, businessmen, and criminals to gain insight
into why people carry handguns.

PolS-P-27
SOLDIER BLUE   A
        BV   Sd   C   1970
        CBS Fox Video   112min
This landmark Western tells the tragic story of a white woman who has lived for
two years as the captive wife of a Cheyenne chief, and the disillusioned cavalry
officer who falls in love with her.

PolS-P-28
STREET SCENE   SCA
        16mm   Sd   B   1931
        MCC   82min
The cross-section of humanity that lives and dies in the film's "street scene" is
the subject of many dramatic vignettes which provide insight into the social
conditions of the 30s.

PolS-P-29
THE STRUGGLE   SCA
        16mm   Sd   B   1931
        MCC   90min
The tragedy of a very ordinary city family struggling to survive the Great
Depression.

PolS-P-30
UNCLE SAM ON TOUR   CA
        Audio-cassette   1982
        NPR   29min
The Radio Experience series. In this rediscovery of America, "Uncle Sam" travels
across the country commenting on changes in both government services and public
attitudes since Revolutionary times.

PolS-P-31
THE UNQUIET DEATH OF JULIUS AND ETHEL ROSENBERG   SCA
        16mm   Sd   C   1974
        Icarus Films   90min
This film examines the case of Julius and Ethel Rosenberg who were executed for
espionage during peacetime.

                        Political Science - Foreign Policy

PolS-Q-1
THE ANDERSON PLATOON   SCA
        16mm   Sd   B   1967
        Films, Inc.   65min
Producer Pierre Schoendorffer and his cameramen spent six weeks living with and
filming the days of an integrated combat unit in Vietnam. The film takes no sides
politically except, in the words of the producer, "the side of the soldier." This
film is not so much about the Vietnam War as it is a confrontation with the
quality of war—any war.

PolS-Q-2
INTERVIEWS WITH MYLAI VETERANS   A
    16mm   Sd   C   1970
    Texture Films   22min
The mass killings of Vietnamese civilians by U.S. troops in 1968 and the veterans
of that episode. We hear of executions of old men and women, and of the full
catalog of horror that was the Vietnam war.

PolS-Q-3
IN THE YEAR OF THE PIG   SCA
    16mm   Sd   B   1969
    MGHT   101min
An assemblage of news footage and interviews that presents an overview of the
Vietnam War.

PolS-Q-4
KISSINGER IN RETROSPECT   SCA
    UBV   Sd   C   1977
    PBS Video   89min
A critical analysis of former Secretary of State Henry Kissinger's diplomatic
approach and the mark he has left on the course of world affairs. A vast range of
opinions and sentiments are offered by a variety of guests.

PolS-Q-5
THE MISSILES OF OCTOBER   SCA
    16mm   Sd   C   1975
    LCA   155min
In October of 1962, Soviet missile bases were discovered in Cuba--just 90 miles
off U.S. shores. The Missiles of October is a superb recreation of that terrifying
time, filmed as "theater of fact," in which the viewer is an eyewitness to the
intricate workings of diplomacy and glimpses the agonizing burdens of power.

PolS-Q-6
THE PENTAGON PAPERS   SCA
    16mm   Sd   B   1972
    MacMillan Films   40min
This documentary chronicless Daniel Ellsberg's involvement with the American
military-industrial complex, as an employee of the Rand Corporation, as a
governmental consultant and as an observer on the Vietnamese battlefront. It
traces the growing disillusionment with United States foreign policy that led
Ellsberg to disclose the top secret military reports known as the Pentagon Papers.

PolS-Q-7
TIME OF THE LOCUST   SCA
    16mm   Sd   B   1966
    MacMillan Films   12min
This graphic, disturbing anti-war film reveals aspects of the war in South Vietnam
with devastating documentary candor, and with much sympathy for the victims.

Political Science - State Government

PolS-R-1
ALL THE KING'S MEN   SCA
        16mm   Sd   B   1949
        MGHT   109min
Robert Penn Warren's Pulitzer Prize-winning novel about Southern politics and
power-grabbing.

PolS-R-2
GOVERNMENT IN THE UNITED STATES   SCA
        FS   Sd   1976
        NGS
Examines roles and responsibilities of local, state and federal governments.

PolS-R-3
LEGISLATOR   SCA
        16mm   Sd   C   1975
        Churchill Films   26min
Examines the workings of a state government by focusing on the efforts of one
State legislator to get a controversial bill regarding jury duty passed.

PolS-R-4
MAKING DEMOCRACY WORK   SCA
        FS, Cassettes (4)   C
        SSSS
How are decisons made in city, state, and federal governments? This series of
four open-ended filmstrips investigates the decision-making process at a town
meeting, in a city council of a large urban area, in a state legislative
subcomittee, and in a panel of presidential advisors.

PolS-R-5
POLITICS, POWER AND THE PUBLIC GOOD   SCA
        16mm   Sd   B   1972
        LCA   19min
From the novel by Robert Penn Warren. Theme: Abuses of power; does the end
justify the means?

PolS-R-6
STATE GOVERNMENT   SCA
        16mm   Sd   C   1976
        EBEC   21min
State governments are getting a new look. All over the country they are taking
new initiatives. Governors from California to Maine discuss this change and the
need for even more.

PolS-R-7
STATE AND LOCAL GOVERNMENT IN ACTION   SCA
        FS, Cassettes (6)   C   1978
        SSSS
A program of sound filmstrips, spirit masters, and 23# x 27" wall charts that
teaches the nature, function, and operation of state and local governments.
1. The State, Part I   4. The City
2. The State, Part II   5. Towns and Villages
3. The County   6. The Citizens

PolS-R-8
YOUR VOTE COUNTS:
  STATE AND LOCAL GOVERNMENTS   SCA
      FS, Cassettes (2)   C
      SSSS
This two-part filmstrip program explores the organization and powers of three
different levels of government—state, county, and local

Political Science - Local Government

PolS-S-1
BEAU JAMES   SCA
      16mm   Sd   C   1957
      MGHT   105min
Bob Hope gives a fine dramatic performance as the legendary Jimmy Walker, the
playboy-politician mayor of New York in the 1920s.

PolS-S-2
THE BIG LEVER: PARTY POLITICS
  IN LESLIE COUNTY, KENTUCKY   SCA
      16mm   Sd   C   1982
      Appalshop Films   53min
In 1978, Nixon chose Leslie County, Kentucky for his first public appearance after
his resignation. The film gives insight into party loyalty and partisanship.

PolS-S-3
CITY GOVERNMENT: CLOSEST TO THE PEOPLE   SCA
      16mm   Sd   C   1975
      EBEC   20min
Examines local governments of five American cities from teeming Los Angeles to
placid Alexandria, Virginia, in an effort to isolate common problems and uncover
uncommon solutions.

PolS-S-4
THE CORRUPT CITY   SCA
      16mm   Sd   C   1969
      Westinghouse Learning Corp.   50min
Illustrates the results of citizen apathy toward government by depicting the
history of corruption and criminal influence in Reading, Pa.

PolS-S-5
A LOCAL CONFLICT   SCA
      16mm   Sd   C   1975
      Churchill Films   24min
Examines the workings of local government by focusing on one city council
member's efforts to get a building project bill through the city council.

PolS-S-6
LOCAL GOVERNMENT AND THE
  INDIVIDUAL   SCA
      FS, Cassettes (2)   C
      SSSS
This two-part sound color filmstrip examines the forms and functions of the many
levels of government below the national level. It shows how people can influence
legislation.

PolS-S-7
A LOOK AT LOCAL GOVERNMENT   SCA
        16mm   Sd   B   1960
        Modern Learning Aids   18min
Discusses the problems of local government from the standpoint of conflicts of
value and interest among union and non-union, commercial and non-commercial,
city dwellers and suburbanites, racial and ethnic groups.

PolS-S-8
MAYOR DALEY: A STUDY IN POWER   A
        16mm   Sd   B   1972
        Columbia Broadcasting System   49min
Surveys the operations of the political machine in Chicago and Cook County,
Illinois through the activities of Mayor Richard Daley.

PolS-S-9
OUR TOWN   SCA
        16mm,UBV   Sd   B   1940
        Thunderbird Films   90min
Typifies small-town America, particularly of the Yankee brand.

PolS-S-10
THE PHANS OF JERSEY CITY   SCA
        16mm   Sd   C   1979
        Howard Street Productions   49min
An intimate documentary portrait of a 20-member Vietnamese refugee family now
living in the United States. Tells the story of how they survive and at what price.

PolS-S-11
POLETOWN LIVES!   SCA
        UBV   Sd   C   1982
        Information Factory   56min
The story of life in a small town and the relationship of two young people.

PolS-S-12
THE POOR PAY MORE   SCA
        16mm   Sd   B   1967
        INUAVC   60min
Provides a close look at the special hardships faced by the poor in the area of
consumer purchasing.

PolS-S-13
ROSEDALE: THE WAY IT IS   SCA
        16mm   Sd   C   1976
        INUAVC   57min
Documents the racial tensions stemming from one incident in the Rosedale section
of Queens, New York, and records the bitterness and hostility of white adults and
children toward the presence of blacks in Rosedale.

PolS-S-14
TWO FACES OF DEMOCRACY   CA
        audio cassette   1982
        NPR   29min
Producer Art Silverman presents two illuminating examples of participatory
democracy--one urban, one rural. Part I goes inside a Pittsburgh steel mill. Part II
visits Stratford, Vermont, to record a traditional town meeting held in a one-room
meeting house built in 1799.

PolS-S-15
WHAT ARE WE GOING TO DO ABOUT THE CITIES?   CA
            Audio-cassette   1978
            NPR   59min
This panel discussion looks at the future of large American cities and programs to
solve their problems and reverse their decline.

Popular Culture

Lawrence E. Mintz

In addition to the numerous commercial catalogues and standard media guides, this compilation was aided by the special catalogues and indexes at the Library of Congress in the Motion Picture, Broadcasting and Recorded Sound Division, and in the Prints and Photographs Division. Popular culture materials are archived extensively at Bowling Green State University (Popular Culture Archive), the New York Public Library Performing Arts Division, the Smithsonian Institution, the UCLA Library and in several other major university collections. Attention is to be called to a catalogue entitled <u>Films About Motion Pictures and Television</u> (number 13, American Film Institute Fact File Series), a listing of nearly two hundred and fifty sources. Librarians and curators at the above institutions are most helpful and knowledgeable concerning the availability of media resources for the study of Popular Culture and American society.

POPULAR CULTURE (PopC)

PopC-A	Music
PopC-B	Film
PopC-C	Radio and Television
PopC-D	Comic Strips, Comic Books, Cartoons and Other Graphic Arts
PopC-E	Other Popular Arts
PopC-F	Sports, Recreation, Leisure Activity
PopC-G	Everyday Life, Lifestyles, Cultural Phenomena

Popular Culture: Music

PopC-A-1
AFTER THE BALL: A TREASURY OF
  TURN-OF-THE-CENTURY POPULAR SONGS   SCA
          Phonodiscs
          Nonesuch Records
Anthology of pre-Tin Pan Alley popular music.

PopC-A-2
AMERICAN MUSIC: FROM FOLK TO JAZZ AND POP   SCA
          16mm   Sd   B   1967
          MGHT   51min
The United States enjoys two musical cultural heritages, European and African.
Traces the development of both musical traditions through clips of performances
and interviews with musical personalities: the Supremes, the Beatles, Dave Clark
Five, Cousin Brucie, Richard Rodgers, the Temptations, Earl Scruggs, Billy Taylor,
Bix Beiderbecke, Benny Goodman, the Carter family, Tex Ritter, Peter, Paul and
Mary, Tony Bennett, Duke Ellington. The film is dated, but still useful to students
of musical history and popular culture.

PopC-A-3
ARETHA FRANKLIN: SOUL SINGER   SCA
          16mm   Sd   C   1969
          MGHT   25min
Occasionally television focuses on black artists, especially those who have
captured a large following among the record-buying public. Here soul singer
Aretha Franklin talks about her church and gospel-singing family background,
intercut with scenes of performances and a recording session where we see the
collaboration of singer, musicians, producer and husband-manager.

PopC-A-4
BLACK MUSIC IN AMERICA: FROM THEN TIL NOW   SCA
          16mm   Sd   C   1971
          LCA   38min
Traces the history of black music with film clips of performances by Louis
Armstrong, Nina Simone, Mahalia Jackson, B. B. King, Count Basie, Duke
Ellington, Cannonball Adderly, Sly and the Family Stone, as well as a sequence
from the only film made by Bessie Smith and a rare television appearance by
Billie Holiday with Roy Eldridge, Coleman Hawkins, and Lester Young.

PopC-A-5
BLACK MUSIC IN AMERICA, THE SEVENTIES   SCA
          16mm   Sd   1971
          LCA   32min
Black music in the 70s from Diana Ross to Donna Summer.

PopC-A-6
BLUES ACCORDIN' TO LIGHTNIN' HOPKINS, THE   SCA
          16mm   Sd   C   1968
          New Yorker Films   31min
Captures the flavor of black life in rural Texas, the region which nourished the
country music of blues singer Lightnin' Hopkins, whose music is featured.

PopC-A-7
BODY AND SOUL, PART II: SOUL   SCA
     16mm   Sd   C,B   1968
     BFA   25min
Singer Ray Charles provides an insight into the attitudes and experiences of many
Negro performers. He explains what "soul" music is, and an interpretation of its
development is illustrated by performances by Billie Holiday, Mahalia Jackson,
Duke Ellington, Count Basie, and Aretha Franklin.

PopC-A-8
CALL IT BLUEGRASS   SCA
     16mm   Sd   C   1975
     WKYC-TV Cleveland   25min
Tells the history of the Appalachian mountain music.

PopC-A-9
CONTINUING HISTORY OF ROCK, THE   SCA
     16mm   Sd   C   1973
     Rick Trow Productions   35min
Past - present - future of rock and roll music; interviews with producers,
publicists, performers, packagers.

PopC-A-10
COUNTRY GOLD   SCA
     16mm   Sd   C   1972
     MONTEB   23min
Presentation of a country music variety show.

PopC-A-11
CRADLE IS ROCKING, THE   SCA
     16mm   Sd   B   1968
     USIA   12min
Traces the origins of jazz and its continuing vitality in the city of its birth, New
Orleans.

PopC-A-12
DISCOVERING COUNTRY AND WESTERN MUSIC   SCA
     16mm   Sd   C   1977
     BFA   24min
Traces the development of country and western music from its origins in the folk
music of Southern mountain dwellers to current popular forms.

PopC-A-13
EVERYBODY LIKES JAZZ   SCA
     16mm   Sd   C   1977
     WGBH-TV   10min
In this film we see two kinds of traditional jazz. Dixieland: Dwight Perris is a
drummer for his church band in New Orleans. He likes his neighborhood because
the old people help the young people with their music. Ragtime: Chris Brashear of
St. Louis plays the music of his favorite composer, Scott Joplin, and discusses the
personal rewards of playing stride piano.

PopC-A-14
FANNIE BELL CHAPMAN: GOSPEL SINGER   SCA
         16mm   Sd   1975
         Center for Southern Folklore   42min
Fannie Bell Chapman is a gospel singer, family leader and faith healer in
Centreville, Mississippi. This film intimately presents Mrs. Chapman's religious
tradition as three generations of her family discuss her music and healing power.
The film concludes in a prayer service at the Chapman home with a meeting of
her missionary praying band where members sing, speak in tongues, and perform
the Holy Ghost Dance.

PopC-A-15
FESTIVAL!   SCA
         16mm   Sd   B   1966
         Patchke Productions   95min
Filmed at the Newport Folk Festivals from 1963-1966. Features performances by
Howlin' Wolf, Odetta, Sonny Terry, John Hirt, Paul Butterfield, Bob Dylan, Joan
Baez and many others.

PopC-A-16
FLACK,ROBERTA   SCA
         16mm   C   1971
         INUAVC   30min
Focuses on another popular black singer in performance and in informal
conversation aabout her life and career.

PopC-A-17
FOOT STOMPIN MUSIC   SCA
         16mm   Sd   C   1977
         Films, Inc.   12min
Focuses on two young country music performers.

PopC-A-18
GIMME SHELTER   SCA
         16mm   Sd   C   1970
         Cinema 5   90min
Follows the Rolling Stones on a U.S. tour, beginning with a concert in Madison
Square Garden and climaxing with the notorious free concert at Altamont,
California, during which one of the 300,000 member audience stabbed another in
front of the stage with the camera recording the entire incident. A powerful
evocation of rock culture at its height, featuring the magnetic performances of
Mick Jagger and the Stones, as well as performances by the Jefferson Airplane
and Ike and Tina Turner.

PopC-A-19
GOOD MORNING BLUES   SCA
         16mm   Sd   C   1978
         MAETEL   59min
Follows the growth of Mississippi Delta Blues from agrarian roots through the trip
northward to Memphis and Chicago.

PopC-A-20
GOSPEL TO POP   SCA
         BVU   Sd   C   1979
         Maryland Center for Public Broadcasting
Explores gospel music as a religious form and an art form.

PopC-A-21
IT AIN'T CITY MUSIC   SCA
    16mm   Sd   C   1973
    Tom Davenport   15min
Presents a look at the meaning of country music to rural America.

PopC-A-22
JAZZ MILESTONES: A HISTORY OF THE
   AMERICAN ART FORM   SCA
    FS   1976
    INUAVC   55-64 frs
A history of jazz and it's influence on the musical world in five parts.

PopC-A-23
GLADYS KNIGHT AND THE PIPS WITH RAY CHARLES   SCA
    UBV   Sd   C   1980
    Time-Life Video   75min
Knight and the "Pips" sing their popular hits and Charles makes a surprise
appearance.

PopC-A-24
LOUIS ARMSTRONG   SCA
    16mm   Sd   C   1978
    Counselor Films   12min
Portrays Armstrong whose innovations changed the course of American music.

PopC-A-25
MONTEREY POP   SCA
    16mm   Sd   C   1968
    Pennebaker Inc.   80min
The "love generation" gathers at Monterey, California, for a pop music festival.
Features performances by many of the top recording stars of the 1960s: Mamas
and the Papas, Simon and Garfunkel, Jefferson Airplane, The Who, Otis Redding,
Jimi Hendrix, Janis Joplin, among others, climaxing with a brilliant musical
"conversation" between Ravi Shankar on the sitar and Ali Akbar Khan on the
tabla that alone is worth the film rental. Effectively captures the sounds and
sights (manner of dress, attitude of young people) of the 1960s. Unlike many music
films, this one shows a respect for the music; the transitions from one group to
the next are nicely handled, and each number is allowed to play through without
interruption.

PopC-A-26
NEW ORLEANS AND ALL THAT JAZZ   SCA
    16mm   Sd   C   1973
    ABC News   8min
Shows jazz as America's music in its homeland of New Orleans.

PopC-A-27
THE POETRY OF ROCK:
   A REFLECTION OF HUMAN VALUES   SCA
    FS   4 cassettes   C   1978
    Center for the Humanities
Lyrics of rock music as today's popular poetry and as a reflection of American
social values.

PopC-A-28
POP MUSIC IN THE TWENTIETH CENTURY   SCA
            FS, Cassettes (6)   C   1973
            EAV
History, criticism and overview of American Popular music.

PopC-A-29
RED, WHITE, AND BLUE GRASS   SCA
            16mm,B   Sd   C   1974
            Time-Life Multimedia   25min
A visit to the heartland of America and its music.

PopC-A-30
CAROLINA AND RED, WHITE, AND BLUE GRASS   SCA
            16mm   Sd   C   1974
            Time-Life Films   27min
Includes the music of the Little family of Claremont, North Carolina, the Brushy
Mountain Boys, and the Gritz Band.

PopC-A-31
ROCK A BYE   SCA
            16mm   Sd   C   1974
            NFBC   50min
Examines the rock music phenomenon since 1950s, history, criticism.

PopC-A-32
RY COODER AND THE CHICKEN SKIN BAND   SCA
            VB   Sd   C   1979
            Time-Life Multimedia
Guitarist, singer Ry Cooder and the band singing and playing their best music.

PopC-A-33
SHEPHERD OF THE NIGHT FLOCK   SCA
            16mm   Sd   B   1977
            MOMA   57min
A biography of Father John Gensel, founder of the Jazz Ministry at St. Peter's
Lutheran Church in New York City, filmed over a five-year period when this
congregation was in crisis. It records Duke Ellington's last concert, his funeral
and performances by Joe Newman, Billy Taylor, Zoot Sims, Ruth Bisbane, Paul
Knopf, Evelyn Blakey, Howard McGhee and more.

PopC-A-34
SITTIN' ON TOP OF THE WORLD   SCA
            16mm   Sd   C   1974
            Phoenix Films   24min
Filmed at the 49th Old Time Fiddlers Convention at Union Grove, North Carolina.

PopC-A-35
SMITHSONIAN COLLECTION OF CLASSICAL JAZZ, THE   SCA
            35mm, Cassette
            The Smithsonian Institution   12 slides
Anthology of various great jazz performers, 1916-1966.

PopC-A-36
SOUL MUSIC   SCA
          16mm   Sd   1979
          EAV
Acquaints viewers with the origins, background, development, and influences of
soul music, relating them to the changing experiences of Black Americans from
slavery to today.

PopC-A-37
THE COMPANY   SCA
          16mm   Sd   C   1962
          WDEMCO
A look at popular songs and how they change over time.

PopC-A-38
THAT'S BLUEGRASS   SCA
          16mm, UV   Sd   C   1978
          Montage Films   56min
Examines the music and culture and includes interviews with the musicians and
their performance.

PopC-A-39
UNCLE DAVE MACON SHOW, THE   SCA
          UBV   Sd   C   1980
          Korine-Dunlap   58min
The life and times of early country music's most popular performer, Uncle Dave
Macon, is explored in this "docu-tainment" show. Vintage footage, interviews,
interpretive sequences and performances by Roy Acuff, Pete Seeger and others
help resurrect Uncle Dave.

PopC-A-40
WOODSTOCK I   SCA
          UBV   Sd   C   1970
          Warner Home Video   90min
Rock and roll counter culture lifestyle elaborated at first great outdoor rock
concert.

PopC-A-41
WOODSTOCK   SCA
          16mm   Sd   C   1970
          Warner Home Video   180min
A chronicle of the great Woodstock rock concert in 1969.

Popular Culture: Film

PopC-B-1
AMERICAN FILM GENRE: THE COMEDY FILM   SCA
          16mm   Sd   B   1975
          Films, Inc.   30min
Excerpts illustrate American comedy film genre.

PopC-B-2
AMERICAN FILM GENRE: THE GANGSTER FILM   SCA
    16mm   Sd   B,C   1975
    Films, Inc.   33min
Excerpts illustrate American gangster film genre.

PopC-B-3
AMERICAN FILM GENRE: THE MUSICAL FILM   SCA
    16mm   Sd   B,C   1975
    Films, Inc.   30min
Excerpts illustrate American musical film genre.

PopC-B-4
BLACK SHADOWS ON A SILVER SCREEN   SCA
    16mm   Sd   B,C   1973
    Lucerne Films   51min
Throughout most of cinema history, blacks have been portrayed on the screen as
"toms, coons, mulattos, mammies and bucks" (the title of Donald Bogle's history of
blacks in American films). This compilation film, written by Thomas Cripps, author
of Slow Fade to Black: The Negro in American Film, 1900-1942, traces the history
of blacks in films, from turn-of-the-century vaudeville routines through the early
1940s. Includes clips from well-known films, such as those starring Paul Robeson,
and from lesser known works, such as the black-produced films that began in
reaction to the blatant racism of D.W. Griffith's Birth of a Nation. Narrated by
Ossie Davis. Useful for opening a discussion of media-created images of minorities.

PopC-B-5
CHAPLIN: A CHARACTER IS BORN   SCA
    16mm   Sd   C   1976
    S-L Film   19min
Traces the career of Chaplin through the vaudeville years and his entry into
films.

PopC-B-6
CLOWN PRINCES, THE   SCA
    16mm   Sd   B   1963
    KILLIS   27min
Explains that some of the early comedians like Charlie Chaplin and Harold Lloyd
became Hollywood royalty, while others who made audiences laugh but never
reached the top of the ladder were dubbed "clown princes." Uses original silent
footage to examine the different styles and personalities of some of the
comedians, including Charlie Chaplin, Harold Lloyd, Larry Semon, Charlie Case,
Laurel and Hardy, Ben Turpin, and Billy West.

PopC-B-7
THE CRITIC   SCA
    16mm   Sd   C   1963
    LCA   4min
Mel Brooks, in voice over, provides a personal analysis of the nonsensical,
animated images on the screen.

PopC-B-8
DIRECTED BY JOHN FORD   SCA
    16mm   Sd   C   1972
    Films, Inc.   92min
John Ford is as much a creator as an interpreter of American history. His films

have done as much to alter the way the average American views the past.
Bogdanovich presents a chronology of American history through the eyes, ears,
and craft of John Ford. Includes sequences from Drums Along the Mohawk, Young
Mr. Lincoln, Straight Shooting, The Prisoner of Shark Island, My Darling
Clementine, Fort Apache, The Grapes of Wrath, The Battle of Midway, They Were
Expendable, She Wore a Yellow Ribbon and many others. Interviews with John
Wayne, Henry Fonda, James Stewart and Ford himself focus on Ford's directing
technique.

PopC-B-9
FUN FACTORY   SCA
        16mm   Sd   C   1961
        KILLIS   27min
Discusses Mack Senett's rise from a movie extra to a producer who developed
slapstick as a comedy form and created such stars as Ben Turpin, Carole Lombard,
Charlie Chaplin, and Marie Dressler.

PopC-B-10
THE GOLDEN AGE OF COMEDY   SCA
        16mm   Sd   B   1958
        Carousel   86min
A documented insight into the history of comedy-making films in Hollywood from
the early 1900s to the present. Includes sequences showing Laurel and Hardy, Will
Rogers, Jean Harlow, Carole Lombard, Ben Turpin, Harry Langdon, and the
Keystone Cops.

PopC-B-11
THE GOLDEN AGE OF HOLLYWOOD   SCA
        16mm, UBV   Sd   C   1976
        Time-LifeFilms   34min
Examines and illustrates Depression era movies.

PopC-B-12
GREAT MOVIE STUNTS: RAIDERS OF THE LOST ARK   SCA
        16mm   Sd   C   1981
        Lucas Film Ltd.   49min
Harrison Ford, star of Raiders of the Lost Ark, leads us through a snake pit,
great walls of fire, high falls, exploding trucks and airplanes, and bullwhip fights.
Tracing the origins of these stunts, the film also offers action sequences from
early Saturday matinee cliff-hangers. Stunts, their hazards, and difficulties are
the real stars in this fascinating and entertaining film.

PopC-B-13
HOLLYWOOD: THE DREAM FACTORY   SCA
        16mm,BV   Sd   C   1972
        Films, Inc.   52min
Before the sixties, most American movies were really made in Hollywood. Part of
the "look" and polish of the movies came from the control that resulted when
virtually any place in the world was constructed on the "back lot". In the sixties
various economic forces plus the development of lightweight portable equipment
resulted in movies being made in real locations.

PopC-B-14
HOLLYWOOD: THE SELZNICK YEARS   SCA
    16mm   Sd   C   1969
    Films, Inc.   53min
David O. Selznick founded his own film company in 1938 after producing for RKO
and MGM. His films had a reputation for quality. This film, narrated by Henry
Fonda, mixes clips from Selznick's greatest productions (Intermezzo, David
Copperfield, The Prisoner of Zenda, Gone With The Wind) with reminiscences by
Ingrid Bergman, Janet Gaynor, Gregory Peck and Joseph Cotton. It also includes
screen tests for Scarlett O'Hara.

PopC-B-15
HOW THE MYTH WAS MADE   SCA
    16mm, BV   Sd   C   1978
    Films, Inc.   59min
In 1977 filmmaker George Stoney returned to the Aran Islands where in 1931
famed documentarian Robert Flaherty filmed Man of Aran. We follow him as he
revisits the scene of the movie. He finds many of the original cast and Flaherty's
moldering equipment. Stoney raises serious questions about whether Aran was
really as primitive as Flaherty portrayed it. This is a fascinating look at the
documentary process.

PopC-B-16
THE LOVE GODDESSES   SCA
    16mm   Sd   C,B   1963
    Janus Films   87min
A history of sexuality on the screen, with a focus on the woman's role from 1900
through the 1960s. Covers sex and violence, sex and comedy, sex in the silents,
sex in sound, nudity, Busby Berkeley, and stars from Gish to Monroe. Also covers
child stars, the production code and censorship, and changing values as reflected
on the screen.

PopC-B-17
THE MAKING OF BUTCH CASSIDY
   AND THE SUNDANCE KID   SCA
    16mm   Sd   C   1970
    Crawford Productions   43min
This is a definitive film about the modern process of making a "Hollywood"
feature film. Director George Roy Hill, Paul Newman and Robert Redford talk
about what they are doing. How do you shoot the scene where the real Cassidy
used too much dynamite to blow up a railroad car safe? How do they safely drop
Redford and Newman off the cliff?

PopC-B-18
THE MAKING OF STAR WARS   SCA
    16mm, BV   Sd   C   1977
    LCA   52min
This is a fascinating behind-the-scenes account of how this most successful movie
was made. Hosted by robots C-3PO and R2-D2, it features the techniques used to
obtain the amazing special effects. Visits to location sets in Tunisia, and
appearances by Mark Hamill, Carrie Fisher, Harrison Ford and Sir Alec Guiness
round out this entertaining look at the film process.

PopC-B-19
MOVIES TODAY   SCA
          16mm   Sd   C   1976
          Time-Life   37min
Film clips, photos and narratives that examine 20th century pop culture.

PopC-B-20
NORMAN NURDELPICK'S SUSPENSION:
  A TRIBUTE TO ALFRED HITCHCOCK   SCA
          16mm   B   1975
          Campus Film Distrib.   32min
A tribute to Hitchcock's genius and ingenuity. Tells the story of a businessman
who becomes involved in Hitchcock-type adventures after a murder is committed.

PopC-B-21
SAD CLOWNS   SCA
          16mm   Sd   C   1961
          Killis   27min
Discusses the widely differing styles and techniques of Charlie Chaplin, Buster
Keaton, and Harry Langdon, showing examples of their comedy, both slapstick and
subtle.

PopC-B-22
SP FX: THE EMPIRE STRIKES BACK   SCA
          16mm, BV   Sd   C   1980
          Lucas Film, Ltd.   52min
The art of creating film illusions--special effects-- is best understood by seeing
what is done and the end result. Although this film primarily focuses on effects
achieved in The Empire Strikes Back, it also offers an historic overview and clips
from other milestone films. Among the techniques covered are stop motion,
miniatures, mechanicals, and blue screen mats.

PopC-B-23
THAT'S ENTERTAINMENT, PART I   SCA
          16mm   Sd   C,B   1974
          Films, Inc.   131min
Movie star narrators--Liza Minnelli, Elizabeth Taylor, Frank Sinatra, Donald
O'Connor, Gene Kelly, and others--put the genre into historical perspective.

PopC-B-24
THE "WHAT DID YOU THINK OF THE MOVIE" MOVIE   SCA
          16mm   Sd   C   1973
          Time-Life Films   15min
Shows that, if given half a chance, everybody loves to be a movie critic. Here,
the filmmaker prods comments from filmgoers as they leave various New York
City theaters. In the process, verbal battles ensue, jokes abound, someone gives
her impression of Streisand, and intellectuals verbalize their thoughts. Meanwhile,
a psychiatrist analyzes the film experience. A montage of off-the-cuff,
light-weight "critiques," which prove one thing--each individual sees what he
wants to see in those darkened theatres.

PopC-B-25
STRINGER--PORTRAIT OF A NEWSREEL CAMERAMAN   SCA
          16mm   Sd   C   1979
          Films, Inc.   28min
From 1928 until 1940, Mike Gittinger was a "stringer," a freelance cameraman for

the major newsreels. Since he was only paid for film that was used, when no news
was happening, he would search for the absurd or stage fictional events. He gave
the world the cat that nursed a litter of chicks, and the skater who tied rockets
to his back and caught fire. Mike talks about his exploits.

PopC-B-26
WHEN COMEDY WAS KING   SCA
        16mm   Sd   B   1960
        Carousel   90min
Comedy classics from the silent era are presented. Included are performances by
Chaplin, Keaton, Laurel and Hardy, Turpin, Arbuckle, and many more.

PopC-B-27
WILLIAM THOMAS   SCA
        16mm   B   1954
        University of S. California   28min
Hollywood producer William Thomas lectures an audience of students on the
distribution and exploitation of feature films, focusing on the difference between
studio producing and independent producing and the techniques required to
merchandise a picture around the country. The sixth installment of the "Theatrical
Film Symposium" series (sponsored by the U. of Southern California and filmed
during the 1952-53 semester) is included here because Thomas is a lively,
interesting and watchable speaker who says much that is still relevant.

PopC-B-28
WOMEN IN COMMUNICATIONS   SCA
        16mm   Sd   C   1975
        BFA   15min
Free-lance cinematographer Emiko Omori steps in front of the camera to talk
about her work within an industry dominated by men. She goes on to film
interviews with Carol Pogash, a reporter, and Kathy Gori, a disc jockey. Candidly
and articulately, they discuss how they got their jobs and what problems they
encounter, especially with discrimination. For students this is an interesting
career film.

PopC-B-29
WOODY ALLEN: AN AMERICAN COMEDY   SCA
        16mm, VB   Sd   1977
        Films for the Humanities
Allen reveals how and why he writes and what he reads, clips from his best
movies show his style.

                Popular Culture: Radio and Television

PopC-C-1
BUY, BUY   SCA
        16mm   Sd   C   1973
        Churchill Films   20min
Takes a hard look at the world of TV commercials as the viewer observes the
shooting of a Phillips Milk of Magnesia commercial and listens to the views of
several key ad men and directors. One director's warning that "we are leaving the
judgment of what is good for us up to the people who are selling the goods to us"
is confirmed by another's belief that "we are much more sophisticated than our
audience.... everything they learn about buying they learn from us." Good
eye-opener for general audiences.

PopC-C-2
COMMUNICATIONS AND MASS MEDIA   SCA
          FS, Cassette   C   1975
          BFA   78 frs
Examines media and value-formation, depersonalization.

PopC-C-3
COMMUNICATION IS POWER:
  MASS MEDIA AND MASS PERSUASION   SCA
          35mm   1975
          Center for the Humanities   240 slides
Examines techniques and impact of mass media.

PopC-C-4
DEAL   SCA
          16mm   Sd   C   1977
          Document CB   95 min
In day-to-day commerce, television is not so much interested in the business of
communications as in the business of delivering people to advertisers. People are
the merchandise, not the shows. The shows are merely the bait....The consumer,
whom the custodians of the medium are pledged to serve, is in fact served up"
(Les Brown, Television). The above quote opens this behind-the-scenes look at the
phenomenally successful game show, "Let's Make a Deal," which ran for 14 years.

PopC-C-5
A DOCUMENTARY HISTORY OF BROADCASTING   SCA
          Phonodiscs   1963
          Folkways
Anthology of radio and TV programs during years covered.

PopC-C-6
THE ELECTRIC FLAG   SCA
          16mm   C   1972
          Pyramid Films   12min
Behind-the-scenes of the feature film, The Candidate, starring Robert Redford as
a political hopeful, and directed by Michael Ritchie. Points out the manipulation
of the TV medium in order to sell a political candidate, and questions the media's
control over the candidate as well. A somewhat schizophrenic production, both
about the selling of a candidate and the making of a film; in effect, an example
of the overlap of the TV and film mediums.

PopC-C-7
ELECTRIC RAINBOW, THE   SCA
          16mm   Sd   C   1977
          Pyramid Films   20min
A clear and lively explanation of television and its technology, that traces the
invention of television equipment, the phenomenal growth of sets in use from one
million in 1949 to one-half billion worldwide in 1971, and the span of programming
from Milton Berle to the landing on the moon. An animated section illustrates the
basic workings of television transmission and reception in terms easily understood
by a general audience and offers an especially clear visual explanation of how
television images are built up line by line. Narrator Leonard Nimoy briefly
introduces different kinds of TV systems: broadcast, microwave, cable, and closed
circuit. The film ends with a look at video artist Steve Beck's fascinating
feedback creations.

PopC-C-8
GREAT RADIO COMEDIANS, THE   SCA
   16mm   Sd   C,B   1972
   MGHT   88min
This memory and memorabilia-filled film features Jack Benny, George Burns and
Gracie Allen, and Edgar Bergen and Charlie McCarthy, who developed their
starring personae in radio and moved them easily into TV. Some rarely seen film
footage is a delight. For a look at another type of comedian who never made it
past the early TV.

PopC-C-9
I'M ON THE WALTONS   SCA
   16mm, UBV   Sd   C   1977
   Films,Inc.   7min
Mary McDonough of Los Angeles plays the role of Erin on the weekly TV series.
She tells how she got the job and shows a clip from one of the episodes. Mary has
mixed feelings about being a very young television star.

PopC-C-10
IS EVERYBODY LISTENING?   SCA
   16mm   Sd   B   1947
   Time-Life Films   20min
A 1947 newsreel from "The March of Time" employs the series' format of forceful
narration and staged reenactments to appraise the overall content and inner
workings of the mass medium of the time--radio. Scenes of script conferences,
sponsor meetings, performances by famous radio personalities, and interviews with
such figures as inventor Lee De Forest. Concludes that "the sponsor exerts
virtually complete control." Although the presentation seems quaint and
old-fashioned, its major points of criticism can be applied to today's television
industry.

PopC-C-11
LENNY BRUCE ON TV   SCA
   16mm   Sd   B   1971
   New Yorker Films   35min
Here, two appearances on the "Steve Allen Show" indicate Allen's daring support
of Bruce, especially daring for 1959, and Bruce's desperate attempt to buck the
status quo. Fascinating to view in today's era of Norman Lear.

PopC-C-12
MAKING OF A DOCUMENTARY, THE   SCA
   16mm   Sd   C   1971
   Carousel Films   22min
CBS ostensibly explains its techniques and policies for making documentaries on
controversial subjects. Focusing on a 1970 program entitled "The Catholic
Dilemma," the narrator relates how decisions are made to cut or retain footage so
as to preserve the integrity of the show's subject. Emphasizes such obvious and
uncontroversial reasons for cutting as the need to drop out-of-focus shots and
scratched footage. More sophisticated ways of editing--ways that can greatly
influence the bias of a finished program--are not demonstrated. The narrator
points out that a hierarchy of network executives must approve a documentary
before it is aired, but the criteria executives use are not discussed. By skirting
its own stated investigation, this film gives the impression that CBS
documentaries try hard to avoid controversy, and that CBS does not want to
divulge its decision-making processes.

PopC-C-13
NETWORK   S C A
        16mm   Sd   C   1976
        United Artists   121min
The Oscar-winning feature about a fictional TV network's scramble for ratings
remains the only film ever made that depicts the functions and activities of the
television industry's programming executives. Despite the movie's farcical aspects,
the characterizations seem quite believable and the overall tone is somewhat
prophetic.

PopC-C-14
PROMISES   S C A
        16mm   Sd   C   1977
        Ramsgate Films   21min
Explores advertising and its pervasive influence on our lives through a series of
satires on television commercials. Analyzes a variety of techniques used by
advertisers to sell products.

PopC-C-15
QUESTION OF TELEVISION VIOLENCE, THE   S C A
        16mm   Sd   C   1973
        Phoenix films   55min
Edited version of the four-day, 1972 U.S. Senate Hearings on Television Violence.
Testimony is given by such notables as Peggy Charren (Action for Children's
Television), Dean Burch (FCC Chairman), Julian Goodman.

PopC-C-16
SCHLOCK IT TO 'EM   S C A
        16mm   Sd   C   1976
        CTV Television Network   25min
Focuses on violence, sex, "cultural mindlessness" of American film, TV. Sees TV as
a reflection of general social malaise.

PopC-C-17
SELLING OF THE PENTAGON, THE   S C A
        16mm   Sd   C,B   1971
        Carousel Films   52min
This CBS-TV News investigation of the Pentagon's press relations activities was
controversial enough to arouse then Vice-President Spiro Agnew.

PopC-C-18
REBUTTAL OF THE SELLING OF THE PENTAGON, THE   S C A
        16mm   B   1971
        Carousel Films   22min
CBS gave airtime to Agnew and two other critics of the program: F. Edward
Hebert, Chairman of the Armed Services Committee, and Secretary of Defense
Melvin Laird. Richard Salant, president of CBS News, answers their attacks.

PopC-C-19
SIX BILLION $$$ SELL, THE   S C A
        16mm, UBV   Sd   C   1976
        Films,Inc.   15min
A lively combination of comedy, animation, and an original pop theme song is used
to expose the questionable techniques of TV commercials. The film makes the
viewer aware of how advertising can influence attitudes, values, and expectations
and helps consumers develop a healthy skepticism about advertising claims. Scenes

of young people talking about their experiences are contrasted with clips from commercials.

PopC-C-20
SPOTS: THE POPULAR ART OF AMERICAN
    TELEVISION COMMERCIALS   SCA
            U   Sd   C   1977
            Arts Communications   60min
An examination of television commercials as a popular art form. Includes four ad spots and interviews with the directors who created them. Discussion covers the aesthetics of commercials and comments on their social function.

PopC-C-21
TELEVISION: AN INSIDE VIEW   SCA
            FS, Cassette (3)   C   1976
            EAV
Part 1. "On the Air" (127 frames, 15min), covers production of a soap opera, football game, and ABC evening news show. Illustrates the definitions of various jobs and technical processes.
Part 2. "The History of Television" (89 frames, 18min), traces the evolution of television technology.
Part 3. "The Business of Networks" (92 frames, 18min), relates the early history of the three television networks, covers the influence of advertisers, the economic reasons for de-emphasizing live productions, and the use of rating services.

PopC-C-22
TELEVISIONLAND   SCA
            16mm   Sd   C,B   1971
            Pyramid Films   12min
Vintage TV shows, commercials, performers, and news events crowd this brief video time capsule. Reaches back to TV's earliest years--from "I Remember Mama" and Milton Berle to the Kennedy funeral, our men on the moon, and our men in Vietnam.

PopC-C-23
THIS IS EDWARD R. MURROW   SCA
            16mm   Sd   B   1976
            Carousel Films   44min
Moving, informative profile of Murrow, highlighting his fine radio work during the war and his ultimate stardom on early television ("See It Now" and "Person to Person"). Stresses his aim for objectivity and the importance of his groundbreaking programs, e.g., "Harvest of Shame," and his broadcast on McCarthy, the McCarthy rebuttal, and Murrow's reply, as well as his interviews with world leaders.

PopC-C-24
POINT OF ORDER   SCA
            16mm   Sd   B   1963
            New Yorker Films   97min
Covers a good portion of the Army-McCarthy Hearings as they were televised during the 1954 proceedings. The excitement and drama of this event still holds up today, especially in the shadow of Watergate. Pinpoints TV's beginning role as a major journalistic medium.

PopC-C-25
TV NEWS: BEHIND THE SCENES   SCA
    16mm   C   1973
    EBEC   27min
Objective, straightforward, and informative account of a day in the life of
Channel 7's Eyewitness News Team in New York.

PopC-C-26
TV, THE ANONYMOUS TEACHER   SCA
    16mm   C   1976
    Mass Media Ministries   15min
We see children watching TV programs and commercials and subsequently imitating
the violent behavior they see on screen. Various professionals note the effects of
this violence, as well as the values learned from TV commercials and series, i.e.,
sexual, ethnic, and racial stereotypes.

Popular Culture: Comic Strips, Comic Books, Cartoons and Other Graphic Arts

PopC-D-1
AMERICA'S FUNNY FOLK: A COMIC STRIP HISTORY   SCA
    FS, Cassettes (4)   C   1976
    Audio Visual Narrative Arts
Examines the political cartoon before, during and after the American Revolution.

PopC-D-2
COMICS, THE: A CULTURAL HISTORY   SCA
    FS, Cassettes (5)   C   1976
    EAV
Traces the origins of the comics and their introduction and development in
America, 1930 to the present. Examines comics as art, literature, social
communication.

PopC-D-3
COMIC PAPER, THE   SCA
    FS, Cassette   C   1976
    McIntyre Visual Publications
Explores the work of English and American caricaturists.

PopC-D-4
DISTORTED IMAGE, THE: STEREOTYPE AND
  CARICATURE IN AMERICAN POPULAR GRAPHICS   SCA
    35mm   C
    Anti-Defamation League   60 slides
Examples of cartoons and caricature from 1850-1922 as a commentary on
American attitudes toward immigration.

PopC-D-5
A DOONESBURY SPECIAL   SCA
    16mm   Sd   C   1977
    Pyramid Films   26min
Based on one of the best U.S. satire comic strips.

PopC-D-6
FASHION IN THE MAKING   SCA
        16mm, UBV   Sd   C
        Perspective   10min
Come along with a real live magazine crew on location down in the Bahamas.
Assignment: bring back the most incredible, eye-catching, attention-riveting
fashion photos ever for the upcoming pages of Gentlemen's Quarterly.

PopC-D-7
FRANK AND OLLIE: FOUR DECADES OF
        DISNEY ANIMATION   SCA
        16mm   Sd   C   1978
        WDEMCO   21min
Frank Thomas and Ollie Johnston discuss Disney's contributions to the art of
animation.

PopC-D-8
GENE DEITCH, ANIMATING PICTURE BOOKS   SCA
        FS,Cassette   C   1980
        Weston Woods Studios   13min
Deitch reveals his technique, purpose and art in adapting picture books.

PopC-D-9
IMOGEN CUNNINGHAM, PHOTOGRAPHER   SCA
        16mm   Sd   C   1970
        Time-Life Films   20min
Salty octogenarian Imogen Cunningham still supports herself financially with her
camera, zipping around photographing portraits, nudes, and flowers, printing
photos taken 40 and 50 years ago, collecting honors and meriting retrospectives of
her work. Her whole life lived in pursuit of her art, she continues to break the
rules and to be funny, sharp, and in command of this warm profile.

PopC-D-10
OTTO MESSMER AND FELIX THE CAT   SCA
        16mm   Sd   C   1978
        Phoenix Films   25min
The creator of the cartoon talks about how Felix developed his remarkable
personality. Excerpts from five shorts demonstrate his skills.

PopC-D-11
POLITICAL CAMPAIGNERS AND LICENCED JESTERS   SCA
        FS, Cassette   C   1976
        McIntyre Visual   32 frs
Explores the art of the political cartoonist.

PopC-D-12
REAL WEST, THE   SCA
        16mm   B   1961
        MGHT   54min
A photo-montage evocation of the West through the faces of immigrants,
migrants, wagon train passengers, cowboys, lawmen, and legendary heroes.

PopC-D-13
REMEMBERING WINSOR MCCAY   SCA
            16mm, UBV   Sd   C   1978
            Phoenix Films   20min
A profile of the American animation pioneer. Three of his classics are highlighted.

PopC-D-14
SCHIZOPHRENIC SUPERMAN   SCA
            16mm   Sd   C   1973
            Canadian Filmmakers Distr. Center   5min
Focuses on sex and violence in North American comic books.

PopC-D-15
SIXTY YEARS OF MAGAZINES   SCA
            16mm   Sd   B   1961
            INUAVC   29min
Traces the changes in American attitudes and tastes as reflected in publishing
since 1900.

                        Popular Culture: Other Popular Arts

PopC-E-1
AMERICA'S HUMOR, 1647-1900   SCA
            FS   Sd   1975
            BFA
Presents 45 jokes by 19 American humorists combined with illustrations which
reveal the social history of the U.S. during the past 200 years.

PopC-E-2
AMERICAN HUMOR   SCA
            FS   Sd   C   1973
            Audio-Visual Instr. Devices
Presents samplings from some of America's best known humorists.

PopC-E-3
CAMPAIGN: AMERICAN STYLE   SCA
            16mm   Sd   C   1969
            BFA   29min
Shows the "real life" packaging of a candidate in Nassau County, New York. The
candidate is told by his advertising agency how to dress, what to say, where to
campaign, and what issues to raise in order to attract the attention of the media
and thereby manipulate the coverage.

PopC-E-4
COMIC IMAGINATION IN AMERICAN LITERATURE   SCA
            35mm, Cassette   C   1977
            Center for the Humanities   160 slides
Explores the history of comedy and focuses on traditional comic situations.

PopC-E-5
FOXFIRE   SCA
            16mm   Sd   C   1974
            MGHT   21min
In an attempt to rekindle the fading fire in his disenchanted high school magazine,

English teacher Eliot Wigginton initiated the student magazine, Foxfire. Entirely researched, written, and composed by his students in the Appalachian community of Rabun Gap, Georgia, Foxfire soon blossomed into an international bestseller in book form and a model for other school folklore publications across the nation. Here, Wigginton's students are shown working up issues of Foxfire and out in the field interviewing the mountain craftspeople and folklorists who are the focus of the copy. The students discuss their new attitudes toward their Appalachian heritage, their elders, and their now-prospering academic careers.

PopC-E-6
LEGEND OF JOHN HENRY, THE   SCA
    16mm   Sd   C   1974
    Pyramid Films   11min
Bold colors, changing camera angles, double images, a heightened sense of depth and space combine with the voice of Roberta Flack to paint a larger-than-life image of John Henry in this animated folk story. Should be shown with The Legend of Paul Bunyon.

PopC-E-7
LEGEND OF PAUL BUNYON, THE   SCA
    16mm   Sd   C   1973
    Pyramid Films   13min
An animated folktale known as a "tall tale".

PopC-E-8
NO MAPS ON MY TAPS   SCA
    UBV   Sd   C   1978
    Direct Cinema Limited   59min
A performance documentary on black jazz tap dancing. Through the lives of three renowned dancers today, the film shows tap dancing as an art form created and developed by black Americans and deeply rooted within their culture. We learn about the history of tap but most importantly we feel the spirit and love of the artists who are struggling to keep their art form alive in the best way they know how—by dancing. Music performed by Lionel Hampton. Dancers: Chuck Green, Sandman Sims, Bunny Briggs.

PopC-E-9
POPULAR ART IN THE UNITED STATES   SCA
    FS, Cassette   C   1975
    Photo Lab   40 frs
Examples of popular, decorative arts in the U.S. 18th and 19th centuries, artifacts.

PopC-E-10
PUPPETS   SCA
    16mm   Sd   C   1967
    Oxford Films   15min
Presents a variety of methods for making puppets, beginning with simple stick puppets and progressing to more technically involved processes including the use of sawdust and glue, shaped cloth, and papier-mache. Indicates the wide range of materials which may be imaginatively used in fashioning puppet heads and costumes, and emphasizes the importance of individual inventiveness.

PopC-E-11
RICHARD PRYOR LIVE IN CONCERT   A
        BV   Sd   C   1979
        Vestron Video   79min
Pryor demonstrates his unique brand of humor.

PopC-E-12
SIXTY YEARS OF SATIRE   SCA
        16MM   Sd   B   1961
        INUAVC   29min
Analyzes American satire during the past half-century and probes the relationship
between satirical form and content and the life and culture of the times.

PopC-E-13
STORIES EVERYWHERE   SCA
        UBV   Sd   C   1982
        Adair Films   25min
Presents an overview of the story-teller's art. Through example, viewers see
informal storytelling, traditional or ethnic storytelling, and the revivalist art. The
film features two of the most famous storytellers in America today, Jackie
Torrence and Ray Hicks.

PopC-E-14
STORY OF A WRITER, THE   SCA
        16mm   Sd   B   1963
        Sterled   25min
Reveals the working habits of creative writers by showing how the American
science fiction writer Ray Bradbury conceives and finally produces his various
stories.

PopC-E-15
WILL ROGERS' 1920S: A COWBOY'S GUIDE TO THE TIMES   SCA
        16mm   Sd   C   1976
        Churchill Films   41min
Cowboy philosopher, commentator on the big and little events of his day, Will
Rogers was a perceptive critic of his time and the voice of the common man.
Radio broadcast tapes, sepia-toned feature film clips of Rogers, and archival
period footage create a sociopolitical history of the 1920s. Victims of Rogers
deadly aim include Henry Ford and the Model T, Calvin Coolidge, FDR, and
Congress. Other vignettes: Lindbergh, bread lines, and the Oklahoma dust bowl.
Interviews round out the portrait of the man who kidded presidents.

Popular Culture - Sports, Recreation, Leisure Activity

PopC-F-1
AMUSEMENT PARK   SCA
        16mm   Sd   C   1981
        Ifex Films   6min
The thrill rides and exciting attractions of an amusement park are transformed
through pixillation (the art of animating inanimate objects) into brilliantly-colored,
starkly different images, with the total effect heightened by a driving modern
jazz/rock score.

PopC-F-2
BILLIE JEAN KING   SCA
    16mm   Sd   C   1972
    Oxford Films   22min
Brief profile of King at 28. Includes footage of a young Billie Jean, but mostly
follows an exhausted King as she loses to Chris Evert in Fort Lauderdale, as she
signs autographs at a sports show, discusses her commitment to her career, and
comes back to beat Evert in a particularly brutal tournament.

PopC-F-3
BILLIE JEAN: A STUDY IN MOTION   SCA
    16mm   Sd   C   1974
    Macmillan Films   10min
Her moves are set to music and filmed in slow motion. A non-narrated, visual
lesson in championship form.

PopC-F-4
BODY AND SOUL, PART I: BODY   SCA
    16mm, UBV   Sd   C   1968
    BFA   25min
Studies the history of the Negroes in the field of sports in the U.S. Brings up
questions about the fairness of treatment that the Negro athletes have received
from their managers, spectators, and country.

PopC-F-5
THE FEATHERED WARRIOR   SCA
    16mm, UBV   Sd   1973
    Appalshop Films   12min
The film consists of a non-judgmental portrayal of the widely-practiced but illegal
game of cockfighting. Troy Muncie, a seasoned cock breeder and fighter, outlines
the rules, describes the breeding techniques and fighting skills, and talks about
why people enjoy cockfighting.

PopC-F-6
FLASHETTES, THE   S
    16mm   Sd   C   1977
    New Day Films   20min
The positive use of sports to redirect inner city adolescents—in this case, girls. A
young black man returns to Brooklyn's Bedford-Stuyvesant after college and starts
a track club for the girls in the neighborhood. The girls now have Olympic
possibilities. Shows the coach's interaction with the girls, his pep talks, their
losses and wins, and their complete devotion to the sport. The girls have new
priorities, and their parents see the club as a lifesaver. Upbeat look at the
enjoyable and rewarding experiences that sports can provide for children.

PopC-F-7
FOUR DAY WEEK, THE   SCA
    16mm   Sd   C   1968
    MGHT   26min
Apparently one of the more pleasant problems of the future will be what to do
with our expanded leisure time. Discusses our concepts of work (work is
necessary) and leisure (leisure is a reward for work) and suggests that we will
have to alter those concepts because overproduction and automation are making
work unnecessary. Some people who have a psychological need to work may even
have to pay for the privilege.

PopC-F-8
GLORIOUS GAME, A   SCA
        16mm   Sd   C   1974
        Time-Life Films   25min
NFL footage of big teams and superstars in action, e.g., Joe Namath, who is
termed a "national hero." A team game, pro football is also dependent upon super
talents like Namath to put the team over the top. Low angle shots and slow
motion photography give the players a godlike status.

PopC-F-9
JACK JOHNSON   SCA
        16mm   Sd   B   1970
        Macmillan Films   90min
Brilliant documentary recounts the phenomenon of Jack Johnson, who held the
heavyweight title from 1980 to 1915. A black, Johnson courted and married white
women, traveled the world, raced cars, fought bulls, and dressed like a fashion
plate. The subject of much controversy, he made and spent thousands of dollars in
his heyday, and had the chutzpah to make star-like movies in and out of the ring
before it was expedient for a black to do so. Great stills of the period are well
integrated with fight footage; Brock Peters is Johnson in voice over.

PopC-F-10
JACKIE ROBINSON   SCA
        16mm, BVU   Sd   B   1966
        Sterled   30min
The career of Jackie Robinson, the first black major league baseball player, is
documented.

PopC-F-11
LAST AMERICAN HERO, THE   SCA
        16mm   Sd   C   1973
        Films, Inc.   97min
Jeff Bridges portrays a country boy who makes it the hard way as a dirt
racetrack driver. Good depiction of the pop culture world of auto
racing--small-town style.

PopC-F-12
MUHAMMAD ALI--SKILL, BRAINS, AND GUTS!   SCA
        16mm   Sd   C   1975
        Macmillan Films   90min
In this sometimes funny, consistently entertaining, and slick biography of Ali, we
see that Ali's brassiness, verbal prowess, and talent to be a star were evident
from his first big win--the Olympic Gold Medal at age 18. Through the fight
sequences, the taunting of his opponents before a match and his loss and
recapture of his boxing license, he shows himself to be quick and strong in the
ring and full of chutzpah outside the ring.

PopC-F-13
ONLY THE BALL WAS WHITE   SCA
        16mm   Sd   C   1980
        VERVE Films   30min
Documentary of negro baseball league.

PopC-F-14
RAFER JOHNSON STORY, THE   SCA
      16mm   Sd   1964
      Sterled   55min
Black U.S. decathlete (gold medalist), peace cosponsor, friend of JFK and RFK,
his story.

PopC-F-15
SOCCER U.S.A.   SCA
      16mm   Sd   C 1981
      LCA   25min
From the opening scene--70,000 soccer fans in a huge stadium root for their
teams while cheeleaders and an electron scoreboard coordinate the cheers--Soccer
U.S.A. presents an American view of the fastest-growing spectator and participant
sport in this country.

PopC-F-16
SPORT AS A MIRROR OF SOCIETY   SCA
      FS, Cassette   C 1974
      Multimedia Productions   60 slides
Shows how aspects of U.S. culture are reflected in sports activities.

PopC-F-17
WEEKEND ATHLETE, THE   SCA
      16mm   Sd   C 1978
      Best Films   48min
"If you only exercise on the weekend...you're going to die on the weekend." This
statement sums up a basic thesis of the film which addresses such questions as the
effect of exercise on the heart, bones, muscles, tendons as well as suggesting
some solutions to the problems. It travels the U.S. and interviews almost every
"star status" medical authority.

PopC-F-18
WILD RIDES   SCA
      UBV   Sd   C 1982
      Nickelodeon   30min
A video vision of the roller coaster experience, hosted by screen idol Matt Dillon.
Capturing the physical thrill of careening with sensurround impact, it also
documents the symptoms of "roller coaster madness," and some bizarre things that
have taken place "under the spell."

PopC-F-19
WILDERNESS NOMADS   SCA
      16mm   Sd   C 1976
      LCA   18min
A group of teeange students who call themselves the "Wilderness Nomads" takes a
4-week canoe trip through the woods of northern Canada with their teacher. An
intrepid cameraman records their exhilarating journey far from the confines of
civilization as they go camping, portaging and shooting the rapids. Along with an
appreciation for the unspoiled beauty of natural surroundings, the viewer gains
some interesting insights into the basics of pitching tents, packing and outdoor
cooking, and an awareness of the sense of responsibility developed by such
outdoor pursuits.

PopC-F-20
WOMEN IN SPORTS   SCA
    16mm   Sd   C   1976
    Altana Films   28min
With New York City's 26-mile Marathon Race as the backdrop, the film gives an
overview of women's roles in sports, past and present. Stress is on women's true
strength and stamina as opposed to the traditional role of passivity that women
have been unrealistically forced to play. Good film, with well researched capsule
history and coverage of early sports stars. Highlights every possible sports arena,
from skating and roller derby to tennis and horse racing.

Popular Culture - Everyday Life, Lifestyles, Cultural Phenomena

PopC-G-1
ALTERNATIVE LIFESTYLES IN CALIFORNIA:
    EAST MEETS WEST   SCA
    16mm   Sd   C   1978
    Time-Life Multimedia   52min
Ronald Eyre, host of The Long Search series, introduces us to Californians who,
brought up mainly in a Christian culture, now look to Taoism and Hinduism for
inspiration. They are preoccupied with the search for a saner, healthier life in
which ecology is sacred.

PopC-G-2
AMERICA: EVERYTHING YOU'VE EVER DREAMED OF   SCA
    16mm   Sd   C   1973
    Films, Inc.   26min
Through interviews with sincere believers of each practice, examines four aspects
of modern American culture: Sun City, Arizona, a self-contained retirement
haven; honeymoon hotels, complete with heart-shaped, bubble-filled tubs and red
velvet bedrooms; Campus Crusades for Christ whose members use "modern
technology to help saturate the world with the word of Christ by 1980"; and
Muzak, that ever-present musical system we hear at airports, doctor's offices, in
elevators and stores.

PopC-G-3
CROCK OF GOLD   SCA
    16mm   Sd   C   1976
    Dennis Lanson   19min
Fast-food hamburger restaurants are an increasingly popular phenomenon in our
culture. This pseudo-documentary is a satirical glimpse at the institution.
"Interviewed" about the work ethic and his rapid rise to success is Jim Krauss,
founder of this empire.

PopC-G-4
GOLDEN TWENTIES   SCA
    16mm   Sd   B   1952
    MOT   68min
The fabulous Jazz Age, the age of the lost generation, is pictured through
newsreel shots of the time. The narrators are Red Barber, Elmer Davis, Robert Q.
Lewis, and Frederick Lewis Taylor. Ranges over the fields of politics, sports,
business, entertainment, and ordinary living. President Harding, Red Grange,
Bobby Jones, Rudolph Valentino, and Sinclair Lewis are a few of the many
personalities here.

PopC-G-5
LET'S EAT FOOD   SC
         16mm   Sd   C   1976
         MGHT   35min
A close look at our food, environment, eating habits, the possible link between
diet and disease, and advertising and marketing techniques used to influence our
food buying. Several health and nutrition experts report their critical findings and
latest research. Narrated by Tony Randall.

PopC-G-6
MOST, THE   SCA
         16mm   Sd   B   1962
         Pyramid Films   27min
Hugh Hefner epitomizes the Horatio Alger success story: a farm boy from
Nebraska who grew up on Chicago's West Side, started his own business with a
few thousand dollars capital, and developed it into the multi-million dollar
Playboy Enterprises. This cinema verite' documentary takes us to a party at the
Chicago Playboy mansion, where relatives and associates discuss Hefner's
personality and lifestyle. Hefner himself comes across as rather shy, ambitious,
industrious, and enormously pleased with his success, "like a child with a new
toy." The film implicitly questions the seeming shallowness of the way of life
depicted; nevertheless it appears to be very satisfying to Mr. Hefner.

PopC-G-7
NASHVILLE   A
         16mm   Sd   C   1975
         Paramount Home Video   159min
Lives of 24 people during a five-day country music festival at the "Grand Ole'
Opry" provide a portrait of America.

PopC-G-8
NATIVE AMERICAN ARTS   SCA
         16mm   Sd   C   1974
         NAVC   20min
Contemporary artists and craftsmen of Native American descent—Indian, Eskimo,
Aleut—are making unique and significant contributions to the cultural life of the
United States. This film provides the viewer with a rich and vivid impression of
the unique historic and esthetic values, images, and traditions that are being
maintained and rigorously developed by Native Americans in virtually every art
form today.

PopC-G-9
ONE MORE YEAR ON THE FAMILY FARM?   SCA
         UBV   Sd   C   1977
         Coronet Films   21:30min
An interview approach is used to expose viewers to the opinions and values of
two families that represent the dramatic changes occurring in farming today. One
family, despite high taxes and other obstacles, decides to keep their small farm.
Another family explains the success of their large, modernized farm.

PopC-G-10
THE PURSUIT OF EXCELLENCE   SCA
         16mm   Sd   C   1978
         WQED, Pittsburgh   50min
A PBS television pilot film for a series about people of all walks of life who are
the best at what they do. This pilot profiles top long distance runners Frank

Shorter and Bill Rodgers, examining their lifestyles and motivations. Concludes with the 1978 Boston Marathon.

PopC-G-11
REPLAY   SCA
    16mm   Sd   C   1971
    MGHT   8min
A humorous commentary on the generation gap which makes the point that the present may be no better or worse than the past. Street interviews elicit remarks on music, dress, sex, and movies, intercut with film clips of the comparable follies of earlier generations.

PopC-G-12
STRIPTEASE   SCA
    16mm   Sd   C   1980
    Serious Business Company   24min
Examines an aspect of the role of working women and raises questions of sexuality and society's notion of the human body. Examines the world of the stripper--as a human being and as a worker. The dancers discuss their lives as entertainers and the feelings of friends and audiences towards their chosen profession.

PopC-G-13
STYLES THAT MADE A SPLASH   SCA
    16mm   Sd   C   1968
    Association Films   20min
A history of women's bathing costumes and swim suits. The changes in attire from the ankle-length bathing dress with long sleeves, stockings, and cap, to today's fashion bikinis and "le minimum" swim suits are shown to be a result of women's persistent efforts to have a more attractive and functional suit.

PopC-G-14
SUNNY MUNCHY CRUNCHY NATURAL FOOD STORE   SCA
    16mm   Sd   C   1973
    NFBC   10min
For a variety of reasons, many Americans are turning away from the junk foods and chemical concoctions that are a major part of our national diet. This is a lighthearted look at a health food store whose proprietor is a dropout from the advertising world. More of a human interest film than an exploration of the health food movement, but is useful for opening a discussion about the current interest in natural foods.

PopC-G-15
THERAPEUTIC TOUCH, THE:
  HEALING IN THE NEW AGE   SCA
    16mm   Sd   C   1979
    Hartley Film Foundation   35min
Research in paranormal healing has been carried on by a few dedicated scientists--Drs. Elmer and Alyce Green, Dr. Justa Smith, Dr. Bernard Grad and Dr. Dolores Krieger. This film deals in brief with the work of the first four and in detail with the work of Dolores Krieger--a professor of Nursing at NYU who has trained more than 4000 health professionals in the use of what she calls "the therapeutic touch."

PopC-G-16
YOU IRRESISTIBLE YOU   SCA
     16mm   Sd   C   1975
     Benchmark Films   11min
A humorous look at the suggestions of sexual prowess promised by the
manufacturers of waterbeds, hygenic products (soaps, sprays, and deodorants for
all parts of the body), tanning lotions, and creams available to the men in our
culture. Features Marshall Efron as the "sensitized," "pleasure-seeking" male.

Science and Technology

George Basalla

The study of the history of American science and technology is a relatively new, but vigorously pursued, scholarly activity. Each year brings more books and articles on notable American scientists and engineers; each year scholars investigate new archival and manuscript sources that throw new light on the complex interrelationship between science, technology and culture. The scholarship that emerges from these studies is not so much a celebration of American achievements in science and technology as it is critical, interpretive investigations of the work and ideas of American mathematicians, scientists, and engineers over the past two centuries. Although there are many gaps in the story of the growth of our science and technology, the main trends have been uncovered and a general overview of the subject is now available for the interested reader.

Unfortunately the above cannot be said for the presentation of American science and technology on film. The achievements of prominent Americans have not yet been recorded on film nor have the histories of scientific disciplines been retold using visual imagery. There are several reasons for this situation. First, the history of science, since it is in large part the history of ideas, does not lend itself readily to cinematic presentation. There are not many good films on the history of science, for it is all too easy to descend to the level of the anecdote in making such films.

Second, since it is cheaper to write a book or an article than it is to make a 16mm sound–color film on a topic, we have many more books than films on science and technology. The bibliographical analogue of this catalogue is as rich as this work is lean.

Third, because of their high cost, films are produced for very special occasions by corporate, academic, and independent producers who are reasonably certain that their finished product will have a wide distribution. For, example, educational films are often made to appeal to the lower levels of the school system. These are not suitable for a more general, educated audience.

Because of all this the list that follows here is rather short when one compares it to the vast possibilities inherent in the subject. Major figures and themes are missing while minor individuals and topics appear several times. In compiling this list we have aimed at the creation of a list of the –best available– materials in the category. We believe this list presents a fair sample of them. There are no vast hidden treasures of audiovisual materials on the history of American science and technology that are as yet untapped. However if the user wishes to peruse some other similar compilations he or she might look at the following publications:

Bruce Eastwook, ed. Directory of Audio–Visual Sources, History of Science, Medicine, and Technology. Science History Publications, New York, 1979.

Kay Salz, ed.<u>Craft Films: An Index of International Films on Crafts.</u>
Neal-Schuman Publishers, Inc.
New York, 1979.

Educational Film Library Association, ed.<u>Connections: Technology</u>
<u>and Change (An Annotated List of</u>
<u>Films).</u> Educational Film Library
Association, New York, 1979.

SCIENCE AND TECHNOLOGY (ST)

ST-A   General Issues
ST-B   Agriculture
ST-C   Crafts and Trades
ST-D   Transportation
ST-E   Industry
ST-F   Invention and Exploration
ST-G   The Nuclear Age
ST-H   New Frontiers

Science and Technology - General Issues

ST-A-1
DARROW VS. BRYAN   SCA
        16mm   Sd   B   1964
        Films, Inc.   25min
The eloquence of Darrow and Bryan helped to make the famous "monkey" trial
still more famous. The results and findings of the trial contributed a great deal to
public education, both in science and religion. Narrator: Edmund O'Brien.

ST-A-2
MARGARET MEAD: TAKING NOTE   SCA
        BV   Sd   C   1981
        PBS Video   58min
This profile chronicles Mead's life and career, as a humanist, scholar and
scientist, and her qualities as a researcher, thinker, teacher, friend, wife and
mother. From her pioneering studies of children to her campaigns on behalf of the
environment, Mead was both a student of the world and its teacher.

ST-A-3
OTHER PEOPLE'S GARBAGE   SCA
        BV   Sd   C   1980
        PBS Video   58min
Historical anthropologists are uncovering more clues to America's 350 year past
than the written documents left behind by mainly "wealthy, white, middle-class
males." The documentary looks at the work going on at three different sites
across the U.S. Charles G. Fairbanks, Univ. of Florida at Gainesville, excavates
slave quarters in Georgia in order to verify and correct written documents of
slave life. James Deetz, Univ. of California at Berkeley, conducts an intensive
search into the roots of a multi-ethnic community which briefly flourished in a
19th century town near N. Calif. coal mines. Several urban archaeologists in the
Boston area are using legislative and bureaucratic means to salvage valuable sites
from subway excavation and construction, to learn about the lives of early city
dwellers. Using both written records and seemingly mundane objects, historical
archaeologists are putting together a more accurate picture of our past.

ST-A-4
RIVER, THE   SCA
        16mm   Sd   B   1937
        NAVC   30min
Pare Lorentz' classic 30s documentary that follows the Missippi from its source to
the sea; and studies the industry, life, and trade that depend on the river and the
hardships caused by the river. A beautiful buildup to some propaganda for the
TVA, the government-financed corporation that harnessed the energy of the
Tennessee River and converted it into electrical power.

ST-A-5
VALLEY OF THE TENNESSEE   SCA
        16mm, BV   Sd   B   1944
        NAVC   29min
This film explores in depth the role of the Tennessee Valley Authority in
reclaiming the ruined Tennessee Valley. The TVA overcomes decades of prejudice
and suspicion by the residents of the area, and shows them how to harness nature
for their own benefit.

ST-A-6
WORLD OF DIFFERENCES, A:
  B.F. SKINNER AND THE GOOD LIFE   C A
      16mm, BV   Sd   C   1979
      Time-Life Films, Time-Life Video   57min
An intimate, biographical film that traces the life of this behavioral psychologist
who believes that environment alone molds behavior. Skinner claimed that humans
are different from animals only because our environment is more complex. by
insisting on man's lack of free will in shaping his own behavior, Skinner
established himself as the lonely, central figure in the ensuing furor over
behaviorism. Skinner's belief that a better society shaped by positive personal
reinforcement (as expressed in his Walden Two) was put into practice at a rural
cooperative, Twin Oaks. With Skinner, we visit Twin Oaks and learn first hand
that his system works better in theory than in practice.

Science and Technology – Agriculture

ST-B-1
DR. GEORGE WASHINGTON CARVER   S C A
      16mm   Sd   B   1966
      Kent State University   11min
Using historic footage of Dr. Carver at work in his laboratory during the early
1930s, the film gives a documented account of the achievements of this great
Negro American who devoted his life to agricultural research, developing over 300
by-products from the peanut.

ST-B-2
GATECLIFF: AMERICAN INDIAN ROCK-SHELTER   S C A
      16mm   Sd   C   1974
      NGS   24min
Led by Dr. David Hurst Thomas, amateur archaeologists attempt to discover the
identity of ancient inhabitants of this shallow rock-shelter in Monitor Valley,
Nevada.

ST-B-3
LOGDRIVERS   S C A
      16mm   Sd   C   1982
      Beacon Films   15min
On the last river in North America where white pine is driven as it was 100 years
ago, rivermen herd the logs downstream, poking, prodding, and sometimes
dynamiting until they reach the mill. Up at 5 a.m. for breakfast, they have first
lunch at 11, second lunch at 3, dinner at 7 and bed down at 8. A saga from
another time still carried on today.

ST-B-4
MAC'S MILL   S C A
      16mm   Sd   C   1976
      Bulldog Films, Inc.   12min
Mac Armstrong farms 2000 acres of healthy woodland, and uses the free-flowing
energy of a stream to power his sawmill. His way of life is hard but satisfying and
environmentally sound. The stream could support many other small independent
mills. As fossil fuels begin to reveal their true price, older technologies show
their inherent good sense.

ST-B-5
PLOW THAT BROKE THE PLAINS, THE   SCA
    16mm   Sd   B   1936
    NAVC   25min
Traces the social and economic history of the Great Plains from the time of the
settlement of the prairies by cattlemen and farmers throughout the World War I
boom to the years of depression and drought.

ST-B-6
POWER AND THE LAND   A
    16mm, BV   Sd   B   1940
    NAVC   41min
A typical day on the Bill Parkinson farm is shown without--and later, with--the
benefits of electricity. In both instances, the film makes no attempt to conceal
the fact that farm life is an endless routine of chores that will repeat themselves
throughout the seasons. Made by Joris Ivens for the Rural Electrification
Administration.

ST-B-7
RISE AND FALL OF D.D.T., THE   SCA
    16mm   Sd   C   1975
    Time-Life Films   18min
This film deals with the pros and cons of D.D.T., both in this country and abroad.
This history of D.D.T. is traced from when it was first synthesized in 1874 to the
present. Involved in the history is the story of D.D.T.'s use in farming and the
control of tropical diseases; also, the concerns of environmentalists are explored.
The film explores the question of D.D.T. and its link with cancer. A NOVA
program.

ST-B-8
WHEN WE FARMED WITH HORSES   A
    16mm   Sd   C   1979
    Iowa State Univ.   25min
Centers on the draft horse, around which the agricultural practices of the
midwest developed in the late 19th and early 20th centuries. Comments on the
evolution of equipment, seasonal activities, and the combination of frustrations
and pride in workmanship which characterized farming during that period.

Science and Technology - Crafts and Trades

ST-C-1
ALEX STUART, COOPER   SCA
    16mm   Sd   C   1973
    Tennessee State Museum   13min
Alex Stuart learned his craft from his father. He works with non-powered tools to
make churns, buckets, and barrels.

ST-C-2
ALICE ELLIOTT   SCA
    16mm   Sd   C   1975
    Media Generalists   11min
The Pomo Indians are among the world's finest basket-makers. Alice Elliott is one
of the few Pomos continuing that centuries-old tradition.

ST-C-3
AMERICA, BE SEATED   SCA
    16mm   Sd   C   1976
    Fenwick Productions   14min
Story of the birth, demise, and ressurrection almost a century later of
Connecticut's famous Hitchcock chair factory. Shows ancient art of stencilling
and producton methods used today to maintain the 19th century tradition.

ST-C-4
AMERICAN CRAFTSMAN: 17TH AND 18TH CENTURIES   SCA
    FS, Cassette   C   1972
    EDDIM   89 frs
Examines the simple necessary crafts of early America, including popular and folk
objects.

ST-C-5
BASKETMAKING IN COLONIAL VIRGINIA   SCA
    16mm   Sd   C   1968
    Colonial Williamsburg   28min
Depicts the steps in the handweaving of a basket, from the splitting of an oak log
to the completion of the basket. An ax and a sharp knife are the basketmaker's
chief tools. The camera follows Mr. and Mrs. Cody Cook of Colonial
Williamsburg's craft department in creating utilitarian beauty.

ST-C-6
BEFORE THE INDUSTRIAL REVOLUTION   SCA
    16mm   Sd   C   1974
    Vedo Films   17min
Dramatizes scenes of the trades, crafts, and industries of rural America before
the Industrial Revolution. Soap making, bread baking, wool and flax spinning,
quilting, woodworking, and pottery throwing are shown.

ST-C-7
BEN'S MILL   SCA
    BV   Sd   C
    PBS Video   58min
In northeastern Vermont, Ben Thrasher operates his nineteenth century
water-powered mill to provide tubs, sleds and tools needed by local farmers.
Almost a century and a half old, Ben Thrasher's mill and mill technology were
critical to America's settlement. The program examines how Ben's mill is still
today serving the needs of the community, forging an old silage fork into a
sod-lifting tool, a new tub for watering livestock, a new sled for a neighbor and
other unique hand-made items.

ST-C-8
BLACKSMITH   SCA
    16mm, UBV   Sd   C   1979
    EBEC   10min
Viewers see a blacksmith in the Missouri Osarks at work and learn about the
historical role of the blacksmith as craftsman and inventor.

ST-C-9
COOPER, THE   SCA
     35mm   S   C
     Colonial Williamsburg   38 slides
This film shows in detail the manufacturing of a colonial watertight cask. Detail
of the history of barrel-making as well as the tools and methods of the cooper.

ST-C-10
COOPER'S CRAFT, THE   SCA
     16mm   Sd   C   1967
     Colonial Williamsburg   39min
Depicts the steps in making of a barrel--from the felling of an oak tree to the
application of the craftsman's mark to the finished product. The camera follows
the work of cooper George Pettengell, formerly of London, as he reenacts the
activity of a small colonial cooperage in eighteenth century Williamsburg.

ST-C-11
CRAFTSMAN IN COLONIAL VIRGINIA, THE   SCA
     FS, Cassette   C   1957
     Colonial Williamsburg   8:50min
This filmstrip gives a broad picture of the craftsmanship that was so important in
colonial days. It outlines the basic tools, materials, and methods of work for a
variety of craftsmen as they relate to the economic and social role of both the
plantation frontier and urban center. A detailed picture is given of a colonial
bootmaker as an example of the colonial craftsman.

ST-C-12
GUNSMITH OF WILLIAMSBURG   SCA
     16mm   Sd   C   1969
     Colonial Williamsburg   58min
The film traces the manufacture of a colonial gun by Master Gunsmith Wallace
Gusler, from the iron that has to be mined, to smelting, to the forming and
welding of the barrel, drills, lock, casting brass parts, to the finished gun.

ST-C-13
HAMMERMAN IN WILLIAMSBURG,
     AN EIGHTEENTH CENTURY BLACKSMITH   SCA
     16mm   Sd   C   1972
     Colonial Williamsburg   37min
This film traces the progress of the blacksmith in the colonial community. From
his basic repairs of necessary farm and household objects to the manufacture of
axes and nails. The ornamental manufacture of chairs and the ware for a
fireplace. Included is the repair of a cannon.

ST-C-14
HOMESPUN   SCA
     16mm   Sd   C   1952
     IFB   22min
A robust, elderly Minnesota farm wife uses relic tools and methods native to her
Swedish homeland to highlight each step in the weaving process--from shearing
her Angora goat, carding the wool, spinning the wool on an old wheel, washing
and dyeing (natural) and drying (sun) the wool, weighing and winding the yarn, and
finally weaving. In the end, various woven goods are displayed with much pride.

ST-C-15
MALCOM BREWER: BOAT BUILDER   SCA
         16mm   Sd   C   1976
         EBEC   18min
Portrait of a seventy-seven year old New Englander who builds wooden boats
much as they were built in colonial times. Stresses the traditional American
values of integrity, craftsmanship, and self-sufficiency that he embodies. A rather
nostalgic view of a kind of life and work that predates the Industrial Revolution.

ST-C-16
MOHAWK BASKETMAKING: A CULTURAL PROFILE   SCA
         16mm   Sd   C   1979
         Image Films   28min
Documents the traditional art of basket-making on the St. Regis Reservation in
northern New York State and explores its relationship to the Mohawks who live
there.

ST-C-17
PIONEER AXE   SCA
         16mm   Sd   B   1975
         Peter Vogt & Associates   12min
A documentation of axe making on the trip hammer and anvil dating from the turn
of the century. Only one measurement is made and the rest of the process
depends on the unerring eye and skilled hand of the craftsman.

ST-C-18
SENECA GLASS   SCA
         16mm   Sd   C   1975
         Harper's Ferry Historical Association   24min
Follows the production of handblown glassware at Seneca Glass in Morgantown,
West Virginia. The film was produced as documentation for the American
Engineering Record.

ST-C-19
SILVERSMITH OF WILLIAMSBURG   SCA
         16MM   Sd   C   1971
         Colonial Williamsburg   44min
This film is believed to be the most complete existing visual treatise on
silversmithing. In his shop, Williamsburg's present-day master silversmith, William
de Matteo, and his journeyman, Philip Thorp, fashion two pieces using ancient
tools and methods centuries old. A coffee pot of the 1765 period and a cann
(small mug) commence with the pouring of a thick silver ingot. This is beaten to
sheet and then the many steps of forging and raising begin. The film reenacts
every major step in the handcrafting of silver, including the casting and soldering
of the spout, sockets, and finial.

ST-C-20
YANKEE CRAFTSMAN   SCA
         16mm   Sd   1972
         Syracuse University   18min
Follows the craft of a New England cabinet-maker with a trained eye and a keen
instinct for quality. Through the 18th century, furniture making was the most
highly developed of any art in America. With the coming of the machine-age, the
personality and the individuality of the maker disappeared, and we gained in
quantity what we lost in quality. Film contrasts the way furniture is
mass-produced today with the older cabinet-making history of American furniture
styles.

Science and Technology – Transportation

ST-D-1
AMERICA'S WINGS   SCA
         16mm   Sd   C   1976
         NASA   28min
The airplane did not simply evolve. Everything that happened since Kitty Hawk, happened because somebody had an idea. "America's Wings" looks at some of these ideas, and "somebodies." They include: Igo Sikorsky who invented the helicopter, James Osborne whose small suggestion helped make jet transports flyable, Eastman Jacobs whose wind tunnel work in the 30s established the shape of airfoils, Adolph Busemann who thought of the sweptwing, Kelly Johnson who designed some 40 airplanes and Richard Whitcomb who thought of the supercritical wing, the "coke-bottle" fuselage and the winglet.

ST-D-2
BALLAD OF THE IRON HORSE   SCA
         16mm   Sd   C   1970
         LCA   29min
From Peter Cooper's steam locomotive in 1829 to the eclipse of the railroad by automobile and airplane.

ST-D-3
EARLY BALLOONS   SCA
         16mm, V   Sd   B   1981
         NAVC   29min
Describes the use of balloons during the Civil War and development of the steerable balloon during the latter part of the 19th century.

ST-D-4
FROM THESE BEGINNINGS   SCA
         UB   Sd   1981
         NAVC   23min
Discusses the heritage of Black Americans in the history of American aviation.

ST-D-5
HENRY FORD'S AMERICA   SCA
         16mm   Sd   C   1977
         NFBC   57min
Traces the history of the car and its mass appeal from its Model T ("the little black box that could run forever") origins to its present day ten-million-cars-a-year production level. Somewhere along the way, the puritan ethic behind Henry Ford's idea to manufacture a practical, economical means of transportation which would put the country on wheels, got side-tracked by an obsession with the profit motive. The utility of the car got confused with glamour and other indicators of upward mobility. The assembly line got drearier and more demeaning and laborers organized. Henry Ford II revived the Ford Motor Co. and pushed it into high-scale production and a competitive position with GM. But with increased production came problems – consumer complaints and warnings about the safety hazards of the auto. Includes a satirical look at custom-made cars and a church service at a Drive-In Sanctuary that only Evelyn Waugh could have invented.

ST-D-6
KITTY HAWK TO PARIS, THE HEROIC YEARS   SCA
        16mm   Sd   C   76
        LCA   30min
Depicts the first chapter in the continuing story of men who fly, their successes,
failures and sacrifices.

ST-D-7
LINDBERG'S FLIGHT   SCA
        16mm   Sd   B   1927
        Museum of Modern Art   13min
One of the very first of the sound newsreels, this record of Lindbergh's historic
flight did much to establish the new form of pictorial reporting, with emphasis on
natural sound.

ST-D-8
A PLACE OF DREAMS   SCA
        16mm   Sd   C   1978
        LCA   58min
Explores the fascinating contents of the National Air and Space Museum,
Washington, D.C. and reveals the human stories behind the artifacts. Host Cliff
Robertson shares the thrill of flying and with help of archival footage tells the
story of manned, powered flight from the Wright brothers to the Apollo missions
to the moon and beyond.

Science and Technology – Industry

ST-E-1
AMERICAN PARADE: THE SECOND REVOLUTION   SCA
        16mm   Sd   C   1977
        Syracuse University   28min
Narrated by Tony Randall, this CBS News production records the American
Industrial Revolution which began in 1789 when Samuel Slater brought the secret
British textile spinning design to America and started the first large scale
production of textiles here. After Eli Whitney invented the cotton gin and Francis
Lowell built the first self-contained factories, the textile industry expanded even
more. Soon 19th century America was booming with new industries and inventions.
By 1876, the Centennial Exposition in Philadelphia demonstrated that America's
character was shaped as much by the 2nd revolution as by the first. Uses both
live dramatization and animation for emphasis.

ST-E-2
BROOKLYN BRIDGE, THE   SCA
        16mm   Sd   1981
        Florentine Films   59min
New York City's Brooklyn Bridge is the feature of a documentary film, produced
for the bridge's centennial celebration in 1983. The film documents the
engineering and construction of the bridge and traces its transformation from a
spectacular and heroic civil engineering feat to a symbol of American culture,
strength and promise. Meant to be lively and entertaining, it includes old movie
clips, time lapse photography, rare archival material, and an original score. Much
of the narration is by David McCullough, whose book, The Great Bridge, inspired
the film.

ST-E-3
COKE MAKING IN THE BEEHIVE OVEN   C A
    16mm   Sd   C   1976
    NAVC   18min
The early American industrial process of making blast furnace coke using
techniques and equipment from the 19th century.

ST-E-4
HENRY FORD   SCA
    16mm   Sd   C   1976
    Show Corp.   25min
Examines the life and work of Henry Ford, visiting replicas of his homes, school
and factory, and highlighting the important inventions of his time.

ST-E-5
INDUSTRIAL REVOLUTION, THE:
  BEGINNINGS IN THE UNITED STATES   SCA
    16mm   Sd   C   1968
    EBEC   23min
Covers the importance of water power, Samuel Slater's first textile mill (from his
British model), and Eli Whitney's innovation of interchangeable parts (muskets) in
the move from a bucolic farming nation to a land of cities and factories in the
space of 50 years.

ST-E-6
LOUISIANA STORY   SCA
    16mm   Sd   B   1948
    MGHT   77min
Robert Flaherty's classic documentary of a young Cajun boy's life in the
Louisiana Bayou country and the changes brought about by oil exploration there.
Particularly excellent sequences include the installation of the drilling derrick and
the boy's capture of a large alligator.

ST-E-7
MODERN TIMES   SCA
    16mm   Sd   B   1936
    Paramount Pictures Corp.   89min
Perhaps Chaplin's finest social comment, this satire exposes the effects of mass
production--automation, assembly-line technology--on the sanity of the factory
worker. The imaginative worker who tries to project a bit of his own personality
"on the line" is quickly and literally chewed up and spit out by the system, while
the worker who marches in step with the rest of the flock has an easy, if dull,
time of it.

ST-E-8
WATERGROUND   SCA
    16mm, BV   Sd   C   1977
    Appalshop Films   16min
A tribute to a 100-year-old water-powered North Carolina grist mill, operated by
a descendant of the original operator. Walter Winebarger talks about his work,
the natural flour he provides (no bleach, no chalk), and his business today vs. the
mill's 24-hour-a-day, six-day-a-week business in the Twenties. He grinds flour and
meal using a method little changed from the process used by five generations of
Winebargers. The mill operates in a lush, natural setting, which is contrasted with
the interior of an automated General Mills plant in Johnson City, Tennessee.

ST-E-9
WORKING PLACES   SCA
        16mm   Sd   C   1974
        Society for Industrial Archeology   23min
A seminal presentation on the adaptive re-use of early industrial structures.

Science and Technology – Invention and Exploration

ST-F-1
ADMIRAL BYRD   SCA
        16mm   Sd   B
        Macmillan Films   26min
Richard Evelyn Byrd, the American explorer, was the most renowned explorer of
his age. He was the first man to fly over the North Pole before turning his
attention to Antarctica, which was his life's work. He led five explorations to
Antarctica, and although he had been educated at Annapolis as a naval officer,
carried out many valuable scientific experiments and is credited with opening the
polar frontiers.

ST-F-2
ADMIRAL RICHARD E. BYRD   SC
        16mm   Sd   B   1954
        Star Film Co.   15min
The first human to reach the North Pole by airplane. Flight over the South Pole.
Hardships of "Little America."

ST-F-3
ALBERT EINSTEIN   SCA
        16mm   Sd   1970
        MGHT   16min
More than any other single man of our time, Albert Einstein changed our ideas
about the universe. Yet, as a schoolboy in Germany, his teachers thought him
slow, perhaps mentally retarded, because he would not answer rapidly on command
as the other students. At the age of 26, he published 3 theories that were to
change the world--making possible a number of inventions and the harnessing of
atomic energy. The film offers an interesting analogy of Einstein's famous formula
$E=MC^2$, along with discussion of his other theories and their implications.

ST-F-4
ALBERT EINSTEIN, THE EDUCATION OF A GENIUS   SCA
        16mm   Sd   1974
        Films for the Humanities   44min
The film explores the youth and early development of Einstein, using his own
recollections and rare historical footage. It retraces his school days and the
influences of such men as Ernst Mach and August Toppl. Of special interest is the
year 1905, when, working at the Swiss patent office in Berne, he astonished the
scientific world with his four monumental papers. Special time is given to the
impact of the theory of relativity, as Einstein himself describes the theory and its
implications.

ST-F-5
AMERICA, BE SEATED   SCA
        16mm   Sd   C   1976
        Fenwick Productions   14min
Story of the birth, demise, and ressurrection almost a century later of
Connecticut's famous Hitchcock chair fastein and discusses the meaning
and implications of Einstein's contributions, including his theory of relativity.

ST-F-6
AUDUBON   SCA
        UBV   Sd   C   1969
        INUAVC   58min
Traces the travels of John James Audubon throughout Europe and North America.
Includes scenes taken from his book, The Birds of America.

ST-F-7
AUDUBON'S FLORIDA WILDLIFE   SCA
        16mm   Sd   C   1977
        INUAVC   16min
Explores the relationships that connect several species of predatory birds and
animals living in the Florida Everglades as described in Audubon's Ornithological
Biography. Depicts bird paintings melded with action photography.

ST-F-8
BENJAMIN BANNEKER, THE MAN WHO LOVED THE STARS   SCA
        16mm   Sd   1981
        BFA   58min
Docu-drama that provides a look at the life and work of Benjamin Banneker, a
black man born in 1731 who overcame racial barriers to become an accomplished
mathematician, surveyor and astronomer.

ST-F-9
BENJAMIN FRANKLIN: SCIENTIST, STATESMAN,
    SCHOLAR AND SAGE   SCA
        16mm   Sd   C   1969
        Handel Film Corp.   30min
Serves as an introduction to the multi-faceted life of Franklin. He was a signer of
the Declaration of Independence, an ambassador, a printer, author of Poor
Richard's Almanac, and an inventor. He developed the lightning rod, bifocal
glasses, the Franklin stove, and scores of utilitarian products, but he never earned
money from them; he donated them for the public good. Uses authentic sites,
memorabilia, and stills for the visuals.

ST-F-10
CHARLES PROTEUS STEINMETZ   SCA
        16mm   Sd   B
        General Electric Education Films   15min
His life is shown by means of actual photographs, made by the motion picture
camera. It is a sentimental, yet honest story.

ST-F-11
CHARLES SANDERS PEIRCE   SCA
        UBV   Sd   B   1970
        Ontario Education Communications Authority   28min
Produced by Kenneth O. May, Department of Mathematics, University of Toronto,
for broadcast on ETV, Toronto. Pictures and models used. In series Rebels Who
Count.

ST-F-12
EDISON, PERSISTENT GENIUS   SCA
          16mm   Sd
          AIMS
The basics of scientific problem-solving: experimentation, persistence, note-taking,
and viewpoint. The role of science and research to bring about change in our way
of life. Dramatizes Edison's development of electric lighting, the research and
investigation involved, and his persistence in meeting the challenges and problems.

ST-F-13
EDISON THE MAN   SCA
          16mm   Sd   B   1940
          Films, Inc.   107min
The story begins with Thomas Edison, aged 82, portrayed by Spencer Tracy, on
the night of the celebration of the 50th anniversary of the electric lamp, then
flashes back to the years when he was an unknown inventor. Includes his
fortuitous invention of the phonograph, and his ordeal with the incandescent lamp.

ST-F-14
EINSTEIN: THE STORY OF THE MAN TOLD BY HIS FRIENDS   CA
          16mm   Sd   B
          Time-Life Films   42min
Interviews with friends and colleagues of Einstein. They tell of the theory of
relativity, the atomic bomb, and other events concerned with Einstein's life.

ST-F-15
ELI WHITNEY INVENTS THE COTTON GIN   SCA
          16mm   Sd   1956
          Syracuse University   28min
Reconstructs the events of May 27, 1793, as attention is focused on Eli Whitney
who has just completed the successful working model of his cotton gin, giving U.S.
economic independence from Great Britain.

ST-F-16
FOR YOU, MR. BELL   SCA
          16mm   Sd   C   1973
          LCA   16min
This warm portrait of the inventor of the telephone, Alexander Graham Bell,
emphasizes his work with the deaf amd his founding of the National Geographic
Society.

ST-F-17
GOTTINGEN AND NEW YORK--REFLECTIONS
  ON A LIFE IN MATHEMATICS   SCA
          16mm   Sd   C   1965
          Modern Learning Aids   43min
An intimate overall survey of the career of one of the great "builders" of modern
times in mathematics, Professor Courant. His colleagues describe his influence and
work, and he himself lectures on soap bubbles and minimal surfaces. A large part
of the film consists of reminiscences of the formative years of the Institute at
Gottingen and N.Y.U. The film includes rare old footage of the giants of
Gottingen.

ST-F-18
INDOMITABLE BLACKSMITH, THE: THOMAS DAVENPORT   SCA
        16MM   Sd   B   1953
        INUAVC   20min
Dramatization of blacksmith Tom Davenport's discovery in the 1830s of the
principle behind the electric motor, and his efforts to develop a practical,
working model. The moment of discovery is shown as accidental: a spinning wheel
that Davenport repaired with an iron patch moves when it comes in contact with
an electromagnet. Observes that industrialists of the period, committed to steam
power, remained unconvinced of the potential of Davenport's invention.

ST-F-19
INVENTIONS IN AMERICA'S GROWTH, 1750-1850   SCA
        16mm   Sd   1956
        Syracuse University   11min
Discusses, through the recollections of an old settler, the contributions of
inventions to the growth of America prior to 1850. Shows the use made of such
inventions as the Franklin Stove, Sam Slater's spinning machine, Eli Whitney's
cotton gin, etc.

ST-F-20
INVENTIONS IN AMERICA'S GROWTH, 1850-1910   SCA
        16mm   Sd   1956
        Syracuse University   11min
Photographs, reconstructed models, and the recollections of Jonathan Sharpe,
editor of Scientific America, are used to show the impact of inventions on life in
America during the age of miracles, 1850-1910. Explains the influence of railroads
and farm machinery on the economy.

ST-F-21
JOHN WESLEY POWELL: CANYON GEOLOGIST   SCA
        16mm   Sd   1968
        NAVC   20min
Reviews Powell's 1869 exploration of the Colorado River and Grand Canyon, using
excerpts from his diary and explanations of geologic phenomena he encountered.

ST-F-22
LEGACY OF GENIUS:
    THE STORY OF THOMAS ALVA EDISON   SCA
        BV   Sd   1979
        PBS Video   59min
The extraordinary life and career of Thomas Alva Edison, America's most prolific
inventor, is chronicled in this program narrated by veteran broadcaster Eric
Sevareid. Visiting Edison exhibits at Greenfield Village in Michigan, the
Smithsonian Institution in Washington,D.C. and the Edison National Historic Site at
West Orange, N.J., Sevareid traces the development of some of Edison's greatest
inventions. He also looks at the personality of the man who gave the world the
light bulb, phonograph, movie camera and over a thousand lesser-known inventions.
The impact of Edison's work on the world and tomorrow's inventors is examined in
interviews with Reginald Jones, former Chairman of the board of General Electric
(which Edison helped found), the late Dr. Philip Handler, former President of the
National Academy of Sciences, and others.

ST-F-23
PROPHET FOR ALL SEASONS, A: ALDO LEOPOLD   SCA
          BV   Sd
          PBS Video   59min
Actor Lorne Greene narrates this biography of Leopold, following his life and
career as a naturalist, biologist and agriculturalist. Beginning with the study of
plants and animals at a young age, Leopold soon became a recognized authority in
soil conservation, contour plowing, renewable forests, game restoration and
wildlife management. The program re-introduces many of Leopold's contributions
and his concept of the "land ethic." Nearly 35 years after their original
publication, his writings are still the best expression of the philosophy needed for
a new era of living in balance with the rest of nature.

ST-F-24
THOMAS ALVA EDISON   SCA
          16mm   Sd   B   1963
          Univ. of Southern California   26min
Traces the life of the inventor Thomas Alva Edison from his early boyhood until
his death in 1931. Provides historical scenes of early lighting and transportation
systems, and of the customs and costumes of the time.

ST-F-25
WIZARD WHO SPAT ON THE FLOOR, THE:
    THOMAS ALVA EDISON   SCA
          16mm   Sd   C   1974
          Time-Life Films   60min
Study of the life of Thomas A. Edison, including rare interviews with his only
living daughter and actual footage of famous moments with the great inventor.
Shows several inventions including light bulb, phonograph, the storage battery, the
fluoroscope, and the kinetoscope.

ST-F-26
YOUNG TOM EDISON   SCA
          16mm   Sd   B   1940
          Films, Inc.   86min
Mickey Rooney portrays Thomas Edison as a young man in this biography that
covers the young inventor's Port Huron years, during which time most of the
townfolk, his father among them, thought there was something strange about
young Edison. He spent his pocketmoney on chemicals, almost blew up the
schoolhouse with an experiment, nearly wrecked a train with a bottle of
home-made nitroglycerine, among other apocryphal things.

              Science and Technology – The Nuclear Age

ST-G-1
BUILDING OF THE BOMB, THE:
    THE RACE TO BEAT HITLER   SCA
          16mm   Sd   B   1967
          Time-Life Films   72min
This film tells the complete story of the race to beat Hitler to an atomic bomb,
including the early work in the U.S., the fantastic cost, and, finally, the decision
to use it against Japan. The film makes use of contemporary newsreel film and
interviews with scientists involved with the bomb.

ST-G-2
DAY AFTER TRINITY, THE   SCA
    16mm, UBV   Sd   C   1981
    Pyramid Films   88min
A journey through the dawn of the nuclear age, focusing on the dramatic events
preceeding July 16, 1945--the day the first atomic bomb exploded in New Mexico.

ST-G-3
DAY TOMORROW BEGAN, THE   SCA
    16mm   Sd   C   1967
    NAVC   30min
The historical film tells the story of the building and testing of CP-1 (Chicago
Pile-1), the first atomic pile...behind cloak of wartime security under the stands
of Stagg Field, Chicago, Dec. 2, 1942...Interviews are conducted with some of the
members of the team and people closely associated with them--John Wheeler, Mrs.
Laura Fermi, Glenn Seaborg, Leslie Groves.

ST-G-4
ENRICO FERMI   SCA
    16mm   Sd   1970
    MGHT   15min
The film traces Fermi's life and his work from his childhood in Italy to his
acceptance of the Nobel Prize at the age of 37 to his achievement of the first
controlled nuclear reaction--the beginning of the atomic age.

Science and Technology - New Frontiers

ST-H-1
AMERICA IN SPACE, THE FIRST DECADE   SCA
    16mm   Sd   C   1968
    NASA   28min
A pictorial history of NASA's role in space and aeronautics research from 1958
through 1968. The film presents a broad nontechnical review of major areas of
NASA study and emphasizes the contribution of industry and educational
institutions to the success of the first decade. The film briefly shows major
accomplishments in aeronautics, atmospheric research, the use of scientific
applications of satellites, studies of the moon and planets, and space flight prior
to the Apollo 8 mission.

ST-H-2
APOLLO 11   SCA
    16mm   Sd   C
    Harper & Row   3:40min
Four films, each the same length, of four stages of the Apollo 11 trip: (1) leaving
the earth, (2) landing on the moon, (3) exploring the moon, and (4) returning to
earth. Each may be ordered separately. Produced by NASA. Each is in cartridge.

ST-H-3
APOLLO 16: NOTHING SO HIDDEN   SCA
    16mm   Sd   C   1972
    NASA   28min
"There is nothing so far removed from us to be beyond our reach, or so hidden
that we cannot discover it." - Rene' Descartes. The film is a visual documentary
account of the Apollo 16 lunar landing mission, and exploration in the highland

region of the Moon, near the crater Descartes. Through the use of cinema verite'
techniques, the real time anxieties and lighter moments of the support teams were
captured in Mission Control and the Science Support Room. The film includes
some of the most spectacular lunar photography of any Apollo mission.

ST-H-4
DREAM THAT WOULDN'T DOWN, THE   SCA
        16mm   Sd   B   1965
        NAVC   27min
Robert Goddard and his rocketry experiments. Commentary by Mrs. Goddard.

ST-H-5
THE EAGLE HAS LANDED: THE FLIGHT OF APOLLO 11   SCA
        16mm   Sd   C   1969
        NASA   28:30m in
The story of the historic first landing of men on the moon in July 1969. Depicts
the principal highlight events of the mission from launching through post-recovery
activities of Astronauts Armstrong, Aldrin and Collins. Through television, motion
picture and still photography, the film provides an "eyewitness" perspective of the
Apollo 11 mission.

ST-H-6
FOUR DAYS OF GEMINI, THE   SCA
        UBV   Sd   1979
        NAVC   28min
Documents the Gemini-Titan 4 mission of astronauts James McDivitt and Edward
H. White. Includes White's "space walk" and the actual voice communications of
the astronauts inside the spacecraft. Shows White's space suit and "space-gun."

ST-H-7
GREATEST ADVENTURE, THE
  --THE STORY OF MAN'S VOYAGE TO THE MOON   SCA
        16mm   Sd   C   1981
        ABC Wide World of Learning   51min
An account of America's race for the moon, from the first orbital flight to Neil
Armstrong's landing.

ST-H-8
ONE SMALL STEP   SCA
        16mm, BV   Sd   C   1972
        Time-Life Films   57min
The race for space officially ended in July 1975, when the Soviet Soyuz and the
American Apollo rendezvoused and docked in space. Examines the history of space
exploration up to that point and the vistas that remain ahead.

Sociology

Nancy W. Stein

This listing includes materials from a variety of sources, covering a wide range of topics that illustrate social and psychological aspects of life in the U.S. It should be noted, however, that unlike a print bibliography of materials about U.S. society, most of the items included here were <u>not</u> produced by sociologists or psychologists, but rather film makers and mass media organizations who focused on topics of interest to those studying society. Thus, this bibbliography does not reflect the same emphases as the disciplines themselves would. In fact, some topics are clearly more popular with producers of audiovisual materials than others - note the large numbers of items on family and sex and gender roles; while on the other hand social stratification is less well documented in such materials. Nevertheless, the audiovisual materials included here serve effectively to illustrate major points about American society.

This listing of materials is divided into several major categories to aid the user - classifications that represent the major focuses of sociology and psychology used in studying society.

SOCIOLOGY (Sy)

Sy-A - Community, Town, City, and Region - includes materials that deal both with the general concept of community as well as illustrations of specific geographical areas.

Sy-B - Race and Ethnicity - is further subdivided to focus on specific groups: Native Americans, Black Americans, Hispanic Americans, and other ethnic groups.

Sy-C - Family, Education and Youth, Lifecycles - deals with aspects of domestic life and changes taking place in some social institutions. It is also divided so items on family appear in one section, education and youth in another, and lifecycles (including aging) in a final section.

Sy-D - Sex and Gender Roles - includes materials both on the topic in general, and male and female lifestyles in specific.

Sy-E - Personality and National Character - includes items which illustrate how values affect the behavior of individuals in U.S. society.

Sy-F - Social Class (and work and occupations) - deals with stratification in general and also some specific examples of class and work in the U.S.

Sy-G - General Studies and Commentaries - includes both historical materials, tracing trends and developments in U.S. society, and materials illustrating various aspects of U.S. society that are not covered in other sections.

Sy-H - Social Problems (Deviance, Criminal Justice, War) - includes such social problems as deviance and abnormal behavior that do not fit neatly in the other sections.

Sy-I - Lifestyles - includes materials that generally focus on a given group or individual's manner of arranging their life priorities and activities. Many of these items could also be considered illustrations or case studies for understanding community or social stratification.

Sociology -   Community, Town, City, and Region

Sy-A-1
APPALACHIA: NO MAN'S LAND   SCA
          16mm   Sd   C   1980
          Maryknoll Communications   27min
A highly personalized account of the effects of coal mining on several
communities on the West Virginia/Kentucky border. Based entirely on inteviews
with long-time Appalachians -- many of whom have worked for the coal companies
-- the film chronicles the effects of coal mining on the schools, communities,
environment, and economy of the region.

Sy-A-2
ARE YOU FROM DIXIE?   SCA
          16mm   Sd   C   1981
          Fore Head Productions
Explores the unique character of three counties in northeastern North Carolina
where the filmmaker grew up. It gives the viewer insight into a typical rural
southern community, hopefully providing a more accurate picture of an often
misunderstood part of the country. Focuses on agriculture, small town life, local
artisan Willie Baker, the annual herring migration, general stores, and historic
preservation.

Sy-A-3
BALTIMORE   S
          Audio-cassette   1979
          NPR   20min
A revitalized Baltimore, Maryland is the focus of this program. Where once it was
mostly tenements with absentee landlords, the tenth largest U.S. city now has 50%
home ownership. The mayor, bank officials, community groups, and residents tell
the story of Baltimore's success, and some adverse effects of this success..
Produced by Jackie Judd.

Sy-A-4
CONFRONTATION   SCA
          16mm   Sd   C   1969
          Films, Inc   81min
This film uses a 1968 student strike at San Francisco State College as a classic
example of confrontation in contemporary urban America. It shows in personal
terms how members of various groups act and react until all segments of a city's
society are involved in the issue.

Sy-A-5
CALIFORNIA'S CHALLENGE   SCA
          16mm   Sd   C   1981
          Lucerne Films   15min
This contemporary look at the most populous state in the United States and its
citizens gives a variety of reasons for living in California. Raises the question of
how the state can maintain its present level of "good living" without depleting
natural resources or seriously damaging the environment.

Sy-A-6
COMPANY TOWN   SCA
        16mm   Sd   C   1979
        Pennsylvania State Univ.   45min
Recounts the closure (1977) of Hines mill, Westfir, Oregon, its devastating effect
on the town, and the workers' attempt to buy the mill and run it as a
cooperative. Footage from Astoria, Plywood Co-op (1950's) shows workers in
towns with closing plants the importance of the workers' co-op as a possible
solution in these situations.

Sy-A-7
DELTA UTAH: A Portrait of Change   S
        Audio-cassette   1981
        NPR   28min
Highrise condominiums and commercial buldings are visible proof that the small
farming commuity of Delta, Utah is changing. Less visible proof are the changes
wrought by the construction of a major coal power plant. This intimate sound
portrait shares the feelings of residents, a professor of sociology, a clinical
psychologist, a newspaper editor, and power plant personnel about the impact of
growth on this community. Produced by Art Silverman.

Sy-A-8
DAIRY QUEENS   A
        UBV   Sd   C   1983
        Minnevideo   27min
The story of three Minnesota women who are fighting to save their farms from
economic crisis and urban-oriented destruction of farmland. Focuses on the
seriousness of the current economic crisis for American family farms, how that
crisis has affected three farm families, and what three farm women are doing to
change the situation as they organize other farmers.

Sy-A-9
HELLO NEW YORK   SCA
        16mm   C   1980
        New York Times   16min
Examines little known ironies of New York, its history and the dynamic people
that make the city unique.

Sy-A-10
MOUND BAYOU   S
        Audio-cassette   1982
        NPR   29min
In 1965, Mound Bayou, a poor, all-black Mississippi delta town, became a
showcase for President Lyndon Johnson's "War on Poverty", and tens of millions
of dollars were pumped into Boliver County. NPR reporter Alan Berlow visits
Mound Bayou almost 20 years later to find out what this federal aid has bought.
He interviews the town's black activist mayor, personnel at a federally-funded
health center, a private doctor who opposes the center, states' rights advocates,
and residents who discuss President Reagan's "New Federalism."

Sy-A-11
PARADOX ON 72ND STREET   S
        16mm   Sd   C   1982
        Films, Inc.   60min
An amusing and insightful look at how the goings-on at one intersection --72nd
Street and Broadway — in New York City can reflect the larger society.

Voice-overs by Philip Slater and Lewis Thomas discuss the American conflict between individual freedom/expression and social harmony/equality.

Sy-A-12
POLETOWN LIVES!   SC
       Video-cassette   C   1982
       Information Factory   56min
Documents community resistance and lessons learned from forced relocation to make room for an auto plant in Detroit. Follows middle aged Americans who raised families, paid taxes and fought in wars as they became involved in trying to save their neighborhood. Vivid footage of arson, demolition and destruction of homes and churches. Tracks evolution of political awareness from project inception to end.

Sy-A-13
TAKING BACK DETROIT   S
       16mm   C   1980
       ICARUS Films   55min
Detroit is the only major American city to elect socialists to citywide office. Taking Back Detroit is a look at those people and the organization behind them, against the backdrop of a city in extreme economic crisis. It provides a realistic look at the nuts and bolts of urban organizing, and it also documents an important trend in urban politics. But maybe even more than that, it presents a positive and moving portrait of the people who live in, and are, the city of Detroit.

Sy-A-14
THROUGH ALL TIME: THE AMERICAN SEARCH FOR
COMMUNITY: PART I: PLEASURE DOMES AND MONEY   SCA
       16mm   C   1977
       University of California EMC   28min
This film examines resort and recreation towns through observations from townspeople and sociologists. This is also a useful movie for discussions on the sociology of leisure.

Sy-A-15
THROUGH ALL TIME: THE AMERICAN SEARCH FOR
COMMUNITY: PART II: TRADITIONAL SMALL TOWNS   SCA
       16mm   C   1977
       University of California EMC   28min
With scenes of many towns throughout America and the comments of townspeople and sociologists, this film views the strengths and weaknesses and future changes in the small town.

Sy-A-16
TWO FACES OF DEMOCRACY   SC
       Audio-cassette   1982
       NPR   29min
Producer Art Silverman presents two illuminating examples of paticipatory democracy -- one urban, one rural. Part I goes inside a Pittsburgh steel mill, where blue-collar workers read poetry they have written to capture their factory experiences. Part II visits Stratford, Vermont to record a traditional town meeting held in a one-room meeting house built in 1799. Members vote on everything from electing a new town constable to calling for a freeze on nuclear weapons.

Sy-A-17
THE UNINVITED: THE HOMELESS OF PHOENIX   SCA
          16mm   Sd   C   1983
          Public Media, Inc.   28min
Fear and hostility are expressed by residents and businessmen about the thousands
of impoverished individuals who have settled in a "tent city" around Phoenix,
Arizona. Interviews raise questions about our attitudes toward the poor and
toward government's role in creating a new class of two million homeless
Americans.

Sy-A-18
WASHINGTON: A TALE OF TWO CITIES   S
          Audio-cassette   1981
          NPR   59min
The Washington, D.C., of politics and government has obscured a second city of
diverse cultures and peoples. Producer Carolyn Jensen provides an historical
pespective to the city. She takes listeners on a tour into the homes, streets, and
workplaces of people who call the nation's capital "home."

Sy-A-19
WHAT ARE WE GOING TO DO ABOUT THE CITIES?   S
          Audio-cassette   1978
          NPR   59min
This panel discussion looks at the future of large American cities and programs to
solve their problems and reverse their decline. Panelists include Congressman
Henry Reuss (D-WI); Bob Kuttner, of the National Commission on Neighborhoods;
and Anthony Downes, of the Brookings Institution. Topics include federal aid to
the cities, federal programs which encourage urban flight, and the changing role
of the city.

                    Sociology - Race and Ethnicity

                    Native American Indians

Sy-Ba-1
THE AMERICAN INDIAN IN TRANSITION   SCA
          16mm   C   1975
          Atlantis Productions   22min
A middle-aged North American Indian mother and grandmother reflects upon the
changing "white" lifestyle that her family is forced to live, as well as the
psychological and economic realities of reservation life that lead most Indian men
to go on welfare and become alcoholics and that also push many young Indians off
the reservation into white man's slums. A sensitive film, especially unique becaus
of its Indian point of view -- three generations of one Indian family are captured
through a mother's eye.

Sy-Ba-2
BLACK SEMINOLES: A CELEBRATION OF SURVIVAL   S
          Audio-cassette   1981
          NPR   29min
Black Seminoles are the descendants of West African blacks who settled among
the Creek Indians in Florida more than two centuries ago. Producer Betty Rogers
focuses on a 1981 reunion of two Black Seminole tribes who met to learn more
about their unique cultural heritage. An author and an historian discuss the

history of the tribes, attempts to preserve their rich tradition and language, how the tribes have retained West African ways, and the problems they have had in joining mainstream black America.

Sy-Ba-3
BROKEN TREATY AND THE LONGEST WAR   C A
    16mm   C   1974
    University of Minnesota   73min
These are two of the most important documentaries on native American struggles. The Longest War was filmed from inside the compound during the historic Indian takeover at Wounded Knee, South Dakota, on March 8, 1973. -Broken Treaty- portrays the struggle of the Western Shoshoni Indians of Nevada to retain their culture and their land. The films are narrated by Robert Redford.

Sy-Ba-4
THE DIVIDED TRAIL   S C A
    16mm   C   1978
    Phoenix Films   33min
Various audiences will welcome a film that realistically portrays some of the problems of contemporary American Indians without being inappropriately romantic, mawkishly sentimental, or shrilly polemical. By focusing on changes in the lives of three individuals between 1970 and 1978, this film conveys a vivid sense of the ways in which ethnic consciousness is raised, political activism is changed, and the needs and goals of dynamic people are reoriented. The contrast between the Wisconsin lake country, where the Chippewa were encouraged to sell their land, and the slums of Chicago, where they found frustrations rather than the opportunities touted by officials, shows why Indian distrust endures.

Sy-Ba-5
THE INDIAN EXPERIENCE   S C A
    16mm   C   1975
    Journal Films   19min
Scientific evidence -- actual human remains dated scientifically -- tells us that Homo sapiens existed in North America for thousands of years. Who were the first people? Were they the ancestors of the American Indians? In 1500 A.D. several million Indians lived on this continent. Later, when Europeans came to live in the New World, the Indians' lives were changed dramatically. These changes are traced from initial contact with the Europeans to the present. It is an important contrast to the movies' "cowboys and Indians" representation. Students who do not live in areas with an Indian population might ask, "Where are the Indians today?", and this question is a good basis for discussion. Over 400 years of contact with whites has produced a pattern of white domination with many destructive consequences.

Sy-Ba-6
LUCY COVINGTON: NATIVE AMERICAN INDIAN   S C A
    16mm   Sd   C   1978
    EBEC   16min
As an active leader and spokesperson for the Colville Indians, Lucy Covington retells the history of her people as it has been handed down through oral tradition. The Indian language, ritual music, rare historical photographs, and on-location shots of the Colville Reservation in northern Washington enrich the portrayal of these native Americans who valued the land they were born to and the heritage which gave them their identity.

Sy-Ba-7
MEET THE SIOUX INDIAN   SCA
        UBV   C   1956
        IFB   11min
Shows how the Sioux Indians adapted to their environment and found food, shelter,
and clothing on the western plains. Provides insights into the Indian way of life.

Sy-Ba-8
NATIVE AMERICAN ALCOHOLISM: Folklore or Fact?   SCA
        Audio-cassette   1980
        NPR   29min
Producer Candy Hamilton looks at Native American alcoholism -- its social and
economic causes and its effects. Focusing on the Pine-Ridge Indian Reservation in
South Dakota, she interviews social workers, law enforcers, and victims, and
explores current rehabilitation programs and educational projects for the young.

Sy-Ba-9
NAVAJO COUNTRY   SCA
        16mm   C   1951
        IFB   10min
Nomadic Navajos depend on sheep and goats to supply food and wool for clothing
and marketable rugs and blankets. Some of the 60,000 Navajos card wool, spin
yarn, and weave patterns of religious meaning using only primitive tools. Others
make jewelry with semi-precious stones and silver from Mexico acquired in their
ceaseless journeying.

Sy-Ba-10
THE NAVAJO WAY   SCA
        16mm   C   1974
        Films, Inc.   52min
The Navajo, the largest American Indian tribe, have survived a history of
deprivation and injustice because they've held fast to their traditions.   The
traditions that have kept them from being swallowed up by white society, as well
as past and present injustices, are examined, with focus on a leading symbol of
Navajo continuity, an 85-year-old medicine man.

Sy-Ba-11
PUEBLO OF LAGUNA: Elders Of The Tribe   SCA
        16mm   Sd   C   1981
        USIA   141/4m in
Pursuant to several decades of tribal planning, the Laguna Indians of New Mexico
have recently opened their Elderly Care Center ... a model of comprehensive
service to their elderly including housing, nutrition, health, transportation,
recreation cultural and social services.

Sy-Ba-12
RIGHT TO BE DIFFERENT: Culture Clashes   SCA
        16mm   Sd   C   1972
        Xerox Films   29min
An ABC-TV production, the film examines the relationship of various cultural
minorities in the United States with the dominant Anglo-Saxon culture. Shown are
the black community in Detroit, Chicanos in the Southwest, Navajos in New
Mexico and Arizona, the Amish in Pennsylvania, and young people in communes.

Sy-Ba-13
SEMINOLE INDIANS   SCA
    16mm   Sd   C   1951
    Univ. of Minnesota   11min
These Semonole Indians live in the Florida Everglades. Shows their open-sided
houses with raised floors which offer protection against floods and snakes. Women
create souvenirs for tourists, do washing and sewing, paddle dugout canoes, make
sweetgrass baskets and ornaments of silver and beading. Men hunt, fish, and skin
the frogs they will sell. A family eats around an open fire.

Sy-Ba-14
WALKING IN A SACRED MANNER   SCA
    16mm   C   1983
    IFB   23min
A moving exploration of the profound respect and appreciation of the Indians for
the natural world and its importance to the physical, spiritual, and psychological
well-being of man. The famous photographs taken by Edward S. Curtis between
1896 and 1930 are combined with authentic Indian songs and commentary. Live
landscapes, and phenomena of the northwestern plains and mountains of the U.S.A.
provide the contest. A unique record of cultures forever altered by European
civilization.

Black Americans

Sy-Bb-1
BLACK ROOTS, BLACK IDENTITY   SCA
    FS, Cassette - Series
    Guidance Associates
This series traces the cultural origins of black Americans, explores the lives of
two major black leaders and investigates the ghettos that have held millions of
black Americans captive. The programs put the black experience in perspective
for all young people.

Martin Luther King, Jr.: The Search for Black Identity (2 pts)
Malcolm X: The Search for Black Identity (2 pts)
The Black Odyssey: Migration to the Cities
Proud Heritage from West Africa

Sy-Bb-2
THE COLOR OF FRIENDSHIP   SCA
    16mm   Sd   C   1982
    LCA   47min
Joel Garth is the first black student in David Bellinger's class at recently
integrated Nichols Junior High School. At first unsure of each other, the boys
soon become good friends -- a bond that is strengthened when Joel becomes the
target of classroom prejudice. But their friendship is put to the test when racial
strife breaks out in their town.

Sy-Bb-3
CIVIL DISORDER: The Kerner Report   SCA
    16mm   B   1968
    INUAVC   80min
This three-part film investigates the ghetto riots in the 1980s. The report
analyzes the symptoms and probable future of racism in the United States. It

speaks of the "polarization of the American community" along racial lines. Major civil rights leaders comment on the adequacy of the report, what its impact can be, and whether it is, in fact, a political document. This is a good backdrop for a discussion on race relations in the present and what has or has not changed.

Sy-Bb-4
EVERYBODY NEEDS A FOREVER HOME — REALITIES
OF BLACK ADOPTION   SCA
        16mm   Sd   C   1979
        Texas Department of Human Resources, Region Six   21min
By witnessing aspects of the lives of four black families with adopted children, the viewer better understands the realities of black adoption in America today, and feels the love and happiness that grows by giving a needy child a "forever home."

Sy-Bb-5
NO MORE FIELDS TO PLOW   SCA
        Audio-cassette   1980
        NPR   29min
By 1910, black farmers had accumulated some 15 million acres of land. With new agricultural technology, however, most found their plots too small to be economical. Consequently, by 1969, blacks owned only an estimated six million acres. To combat this trend, activists formed the Emergency Land Fund and the National Association of Landowners. This program focuses on the effects of these initiatives.

Sy-Bb-6
WE SHALL OVERCOME: The Struggle for Equality   SCA
        FS, cassette — Series   1980
        SSSS
Did the activism of the 1960s help or hinder the advancement of rights for Blacks? The freedom marches and sit-ins of 1963, the riots of 1964-5, the rise of "Black Power" in new leaders such as the Rev. Jesse Jackson and Julian Bond are all portrayed in this moving account of the Black struggle for equality. The program also traces apparent challenges to Black progress during the late 1970s: the Bakke decision, cutbacks in welfare, and clashes with Affirmative Action laws.

                            Hispanic Americans

Sy-Bc-1
BLACK LATINOS: A DOUBLE MINORITY   SCA
        Audio-cassette   1981
        NPR   29min
Producer Jose McMurray focuses on the special problems of black Latinos in the U.S. He interviews Congresswoman Shirley Chisholm (D-NY) and black Latinos including a journalist.

Sy-Bc-2
LATINO BUSINESS: FROM BODEGAS TO BANKS   SCA
        Audio-cassette   1981
        NPR   29min
This program examines the growth of Hispanic-owned business in the United States. The "bodegas" or neighborhood grocery store, remains the social hub of

the Hispanic community and the backbone of the Latino economy. Through interviews with business people, producer Elizabeth Perez-Luna explores both large and small scale Latino businesses and the impact they are having on the American market.

Sy-Bc-3
LOS SURES   SCA
            16mm   Sd   C   1983
            Terra Productions   57min
Provides an inside look at the poorest Puerto Rican neighborhood in New York City from the perspective of five men and women who live there. A portrait of a neighborhood and a people on the economic and cultural margins of American society in the 1980s.

Sy-Bc-4
MEXICAN COLONIES IN THE RIO GRANDE   SCA
            Audio-cassette   1981
            NPR   29min
"Colonias" are closely-knit communities of poor Mexican migrants in south Texas. Living conditions there are harsh; water, electricity, and sewage systems are often lacking. This program looks at these communities and efforts underway to improve them. It features interviews with residents, developers, and members of advocacy groups who are helping the "colonias'" approximately 75,000 inhabitants.

Sy-Bc-5
NEW YORK CITY TOO FAR FROM TAMPA BLUES   SCA
            16mm   C   1979
            Time-Life Multimedia   47min
A music-filled comedy-drama focusing on the problems encountered by a Puerto Rican boy and his family when they move from Tampa, Florida to New York. As a newcomer, Tom must deal with many challenges -- new friends, an intimidating street gang and the need to make money. While shining shoes, Tom forms a musical partnership with another shoe shine boy. Their musical act is overwhelmingly sucessful; but, their success brings about a revealing confrontation with Tom's father.

Other Ethnic Groups

Sy-Bd-1
BIRTH OF A COMMUNITY   SCA
            Audio-cassette   1980
            NPR   29min
Many Vietnamese refugees now live in Arlington, Virginia, near Washington, D.C. Producer Geraldine Calkins looks at this ethnic community, the refugees' adjustment to American life, changes in family life, and the role of the local county government.

Sy-Bd-2
GUM SAHN: Changing Values in the Chinese-American
Community   SCA
            Audio-cassette   1980
            NPR   59min
From as early as 1848, the legend of the Gum Sahn, or gold Mountain, attracted hundreds of Chinese to California despite discrimination and strong immigration

laws. Producer Leo Lee of Western Public Radio explores America's impact on Chinese tradition and values and the renewed interest among Chinese-Americans in their heritage.

Sy-Bd-3
THE JAPANESE-AMERICAN: Four Generations of Adaptation   SCA
                    Audio-cassette   1979
                    NPR   59min
Producers Leo Lee and Zane Blaney of Western Public Radio look at four generations of Japanese-Americans and explore cultural adaptation, relocation camps, and ethnic suicide. Lay persons and professionals compare the generations and discuss the Japanese-American culture.

                 Sociology - Family, Education and Youth, Lifecycles

                                  Family

Sy-Ca-1
ALICE DOESN'T LIVE HERE ANYMORE   SCA
        16mm   Sd   C   1974
        Swank Motion Pictures   112min
A young widowed mother and her adolescent son travel west in hopes of starting a new life. Stopping briely in Phoenix for a waitressing gig to finance further travelling, she meets a young rancher who offers security and love. Warm, funny depiction of a single mother/only child relationship. Stars Ellen Burstyn, Alfred Lutter, and Kris Kristofferson.

Sy-Ca-2
THE AMERICAN FAMILY: An Endangered Species?   SCA
        16mm, series   Sd   C   1979
        Films, Inc.   9min each
The traditional American family as an institution is in a state of flux. Social trends have caused a revolution in family living and in the makeup of families. This series of ten films focuses on a variety of family units through a series of intimate film essays. Covering a wide social, economic, racial and geographic range, these film portraits reveal significant factors in the changing family compositions.

THE MARINOS (Divorcing Parents)
The parents of three children are divorcing and are in the midst of a bitter custody fight.

THE EDHOLMS (Blended Family)
A blended family, where husband and wife live together with children from their former marriages.

SEAN'S STORY (Divided Custody)
Twelve-year-old Sean divides his time between his divorced parents.

THE HARTMANS (Mother Returns to Work)
Mother returns to work out of financial necessity.

THE GLEGHORNS (Unemployed Father)
The effect on a family when the father loses his job.

PEGGY COLLINS (Single Mother)
A divorced mother raising her children alone.

SHARE-A-HOME (Group Home for the Elderly)
The concept of group homes for the elderly is explored.

THE KREINIK AND BOSWORTH FAMILIES (Single Adoptive Parents)
An unmarried man and an unmarried woman have each adopted children.

THE SORIANOS (Extended Family)
The study of an extended family.

THE SCHUSTER/ISSACSON FAMILY (Lesbian Mothers)
Two lesbian mothers living with their six children.

Sy-Ca-3
BUILDING FAMILY RELATIONSHIPS   SC
        16mm   Sd   1980
        Films, Inc.   30min
Family relationships are fundamental in shaping the adult the child will become,
building trust, confidence, and a sense of belonging and security. Inclusion in
family projects depicted in the film gives children positive images of themselves.
A trip to the beach and dramatization of a day at the zoo emphasize the need for
patience and flexibility on the part of parents.

Sy-Ca-4
CAREERS AND BABIES   CA
        16mm   Sd   C   1976
        Polymorph Films   20min
Four women, two of whom have children and two of whom do not, who have made
decisions about careers and/or babies talk about schedules, priorities, and values.
The issues are strongly emotional, and it is difficult to get a broad view of the
possibilities because of the intense feelings of the four women.

Sy-Ca-5
CHANGING COURSE: A Second Chance   CA
        16mm   Sd   C   1981
        PTV Productions, Inc.   28 1/2min
Recently divorced and widowed women who had been homebound learn about new
educational and job opportunities at the Displaced Homemakers Center in Oakland,
Ca.   Other women in similar circumstances develop electronics skills in a special
program for women in Boston. All lead new and different lifestyles because of
their changed roles in society.

Sy-Ca-6
CHILDREN OF PRIDE   SCA
        16mm   Sd   C   1983
        Carole Langer Productions   60min
A single Black man adopts 23 handicapped kids and helps them achieve
extraordinary things.

Sy-Ca-7
FAMILY LIFE: Transitions in Marriage (A Case History)   SCA
        FS, series (3 PT)
        Coronet   43 1/2min
The three new dramatic motion pictures in this series form a continuum, depicting

parents and children passing through the trauma of divorce, the single custodial parent household, and eventual remarriage and readjustment. Each film contains a wealth of ideas for discussion and analysis.

Divorce

From the opening scene, it is clear that Helene and Alan have reached the crisis point in their marriage. Their three children, Kathy, Bobby and Christine, are upset over the continual bitter arguments between their parents. Inevitably, the mother and father call the children together to announce their intention to separate. The children's reactions range from fear to guilt to anger. The children are torn by uncertainty over what the future holds for them and for their relationship to each of their parents. As the children struggle to adjust to the new realities of their family life, the parents must deal with the divorce issues of child support, property settlement, and visiting rights.

The Single Parent Family

The divorce between Helene and Alan is now final. Helene has custody of the children. She must grapple with raising them while holding down an unfamiliar job to try to augment the limited financial support they receive from Alan. On his visiting day, Alan takes the children for a jaunt on a rented sailboat with his new girlfriend. Meanwhile, Helene attends a Parents Without Partners meeting where she gains some insights into her situation and meets Ray, a pleasant man who takes an interest in her. Helene's day ends bitterly as the children gush about how much they like their dad's new girlfriend, and mention that Alan is considering buying the sailboat they rented for the day.

Step Family

Helene has now married Ray, the man she met in the previous film. Their relationship is warm and caring, but is strained by the squabbles between Helen's children and Ray's son. Alan has also remarried, and he and his wife have a new baby. The wife resents the extra work involved in the regular Saturday visits from Alan's children. Alan is worried that he's losing contact with his children. Helene is buoyed to find that some of her old friends who avoided her after the divorce are interested in seeing her again now that she's "respectably" remarried. The film ends on an upbeat note as Ray and Helene vow to work through their problems together.

Sy-Ca-8
FATHERS   SCA
          16mm   Sd   C   1980
          ASPO/ Lamaze   29min

Examines, through interviews with new and expectant fathers, the role of men during pregnancy and childbirth; aspects of the changing role in child care, the importance of the father/child bond and the important role of the father in child-rearing.

Sy-Ca-9
I ONLY WANT YOU TO BE HAPPY!   SCA
          16mm   Sd   C   1975
          MGHT   16min

Helen, an ambitious college graduate, is about to enter medical school. Her sister, Dru, has decided to remain in their hometown, work in a nursery, and probably marry "the boy next door." Their mother is a traditional, contented housewife in her mid-forties. The interactions among these three women and their conflicting points of view on the "female role" create a tension as revealing as it is educational.

Sy-Ca-10
JOE AND MAXI   SCA
      16mm   Sd   C   1978
      Maxi Cohen   90min
An autobiographical exploration of a daughter/father relationship. Eight months
after her mother died, Maxi began to make this film, trying to get closer to her
father through the filmmaking process. While making the film, her father, Joe,
discovers he has cancer. The film explores what happens to Joe, Maxi, and her
two younger brothers during this time.

Sy-Ca-11
LEAVING HOME: A Family In Transition   SCA
      16mm   Sd   C   1981
      Direct Cinema Limited   28min
This cinema verite profile of the filmmaker's family shows the conflicts which
arise when two of her four daughters decide to move away from their parents'
home. The ways the family struggles with the inevitable rites of passage reflect
the changing roles of women in our society.

Sy-Ca-12
MARRIED LIVES TODAY   SCA
      16mm   Sd   C   1975
      BFA   19min
Examines the views of three young, middle-class couples -- a black couple with
two children; a white couple, separated with one child; and a white couple who
run a haircutting salon together and who have no children. All provide their
private theories on what makes their marriages work/fail and what role each
partner should and does play.

Sy-Ca-13
MARRIED LIVES TOGETHER   CA
      16mm   Sd   C   1975
      BFA   19min
This film about three couples who have very different marital lifestyles suggests
that marrige today is a flexible and important institution.

Sy-Ca-14
NEW MAID, THE   SCA
      16mm   Sd   1982
      LCA   35min
Maria, a recent Central American immigrant, is hired by the McGraths, a
well-to-do Los Angeles couple with two mischievous boys, to be their new maid.
The story focuses upon the complex relationship which develops between Maria,
the younger boy Joey, and Mrs. McGrath. The situations and mishaps that occur
provide a very human and warm look at a contemporary family and its reaction to
change.

Sy-Ca-15
NEW RELATIONS: A Film About Fathers & Sons   CA
      16mm   Sd   C   1980
      Ben Achtenberg   34min
The filmmaker explores the costs as well as the rewards of becoming a father in
his thirties, and of choosing to share child care responsibilities with his wife, who
also has a career.

Sy-Ca-16
OF BIRTH AND FRIENDSHIP   A
         16mm   Sd   C   1981
         Environmental Films   29min
The story of Susan, who chooses to have her baby at home with 80 of her friends
present. It is also a deeply moving account of friendship and support between
people who live in a new, exciting and courageous lifestyle.

Sy-Ca-17
PATRICIA'S MOVING PICTURE   SCA
         16mm   Sd   C   1978
         NFBC   27min
An extraordinary ordinary middle-aged woman goes through a mid-life crisis,
which changes her view of herself and her relationship with her family.

Sy-Ca-18
RELATIONSHIPS   SCA
              Audio-cassette   1979
              NPR   59min
Producer David Selvin examines recent changes in the way American society
defines and accepts relationships. He focuses on couples who live together without
marrying, housewives and mothers who work and gay couples who no longer hide
their relationships.

Sy-Ca-19
SIX AMERICAN FAMILIES   CA
         16mm   Sd   C   1976
         Carousel Films   58min
Filmed for television, this series of vignettes shows six very different American
families:

-- The George family of New York City (upwardly mobile black family)
-- The Stephens family of Villisca, Iowa (Midwestern farm family)
-- The Pasciak family of Chicago (second generation Polish-Americans)
-- The Greenberg family of Mill Valley, California (an upper-middle-class Jewish
family)
-- The Kennedy family of Albuquerque, new Mexico (interactions between parents
with high achievement orientation, a teen-age daughter, and a mongoloid son)
-- The Burk family of Dalton, Georgia (a poor, clanlike family)

Sy-Ca-20
STEPPING OUT: The Debolts Grow Up   SC
         16mm   Sd   C   1980
         Pyramid Films   52min
The DeBolt family, whose own and adopted children eventually numbered 21 —
with blind, paraplegic and fully healthy children from many countries -- celebrate
a long Christmas reunion, as several now self-supporting young DeBolts return for
a loving renewal of their lifestyle and affirmations reinforcing each other. See
also: Who Are The DeBolts? Sy-Ca-21.

Sy-Ca-21
TWO TO GET READY   CA
         16mm   Sd   C   1980
         NAVC   281/2m in
Examines ways parents get ready for parenthood, focussing on their psychological
preparation including the many emotions prospective parents have during
pregnancy and the ways to resolve these feelings.

Sy-Ca-22
WHO ARE THE DEBOLTS AND WHERE DID THEY
GET 19 KIDS?   SCA
     16mm   Sd   C   1977
     Pyramid Films   72min
A couple expands their family to nineteen children by adding many war-orphaned
or handicapped children. This film won many awards for its poignant portrayal of
the fine yet not falsely congenial relationships among the family members.

Education and Youth

Sy-Cb-1
A GANG AIN'T NOTHIN' BUT FRIENDS   SCA
     16mm   Sd   B
     WCAU-TV   29min
Gang members discuss their life-styles in the group while being filmed on the
streets and in the meeting places of the gangs.

Sy-Cb-2
ADOLESCENT RESPONSIBILITIES: Craig and Mark   SCA
     16mm   Sd   C   1973
     EBEC   28min
Teenagers Craig and Mark seek more independence as their California family
considers the pros and cons of a move to Colorado.

Sy-Cb-3
CHILDREN OF VIOLENCE   SCA
     16mm   Sd   C   1982
     Quest Productions   58min
A Chicano family's life is penetrated by adolescent violence. Strong familial bonds
evident in their celebrations and suffering guide the family through the death and
burial of their own son and brother. Depicts the psychological and social
entrapment/dilemma of the well-meaning mother, the frustration of the
adolescents and the overwhelmed juvenile justice systems.

Sy-Cb-4
COMING OF AGE   CA
     16mm   Sd   C   1982
     New Day Films   60min
180 young people of different racial backgrounds and diverse cultures gather
together with 25 counselors to confront vital interpersonal and social issues. The
lush mountain setting bristles with the participants' emotional responses to such
charged topics as racial attitudes, sexual identity and other related issues
important to both young and old in today's world.

Sy-Cb-5
GOOD GIRL: Exploring an Awkward Age   SCA
     16mm   Sd   C   1982
     Filmmakers Library   45min
Good Girl is a re-enactment of a diary kept by the filmmaker during her
thirteenth year. The cheerful entries reflect her everyday life: a proper girls'
school, a summer at the Cape, sports, exams.
      But the real impact comes from the film's ability to read between
the lines, revealing her unexpressed loneliness and self-doubt. When the filmmaker

interviews today's schoolgirls, she learns that this generation too feels awkward, unsure and confused.

Sy-Cb-6
IN THE BEST INTERESTS OF THE CHILDREN   SCA
        16mm   Sd   C   1976
        Iris Films   53min
Eight lesbian mothers and their children, along with two professionals, discuss the realities, joys, and problems of being lesbian mothers or having a mother who is a lesbian. Particular focus on the issue of child custody and the special problems these mothers face if they have to go to court to fight for the custody of their children. Shows much interaction between the mothers and children.

Sy-Cb-7
HIGH SCHOOL   SCA
        16mm   Sd   B   1969
        Zipporah Films   75min
This is a documentary study of the high school, an institution familiar to every American. Frederick Wiseman examines the ideology and values of a large urban high school as seen through encounters between students, teachers, and parents in guidance sessions, college counseling, discipline, faculty meetings, corridor patrol, and gymnasium and classroom activities.

Sy-Cb-8
SOCIAL STUDIES SOCIOLOGY: U.S./Minorities   SC
        16mm   Sd   B
        Benchmark Films   51min
My Childhood (2 parts)
A powerful, absorbing study of contrasts in the recreated childhoods of two famous Ameicans - one white, small town, loved ... the other black, urban ghetto, rejected.

Part 1. Hubert Humphrey's South Dakota
"My childhood was as American as apple pie - really as the 4th of July. It was a wonderful time of life and I loved it". Hubert Humphrey recalls his childhood in a small town and his appreciation of what home and the influence of his father meant to him.

Part 2. James Baldwin's Harlem
My life had begun "... in the invincible and indescribable squalor of Harlem ... here in the ghetto I was born". Now James Baldwin speaks of the grinding poverty, despair, and his father's hatred which led him to despise both white and black people alike.

Sy-Cb-9
ROMANCE, SEX, AND MARRIAGE: All the Guys Ever
Want is S.E.X.   SCA
        16mm   Sd   C   1976
        Hobel-Leiterman productions   26min
Young people from a variety of ethnic, educational, and economic backgrounds tell of their attempts to straighten out what they feel and think about their physical well-being and sexual experiences. A psychiatrist comments on the stressful aspects of teen-age sexuality.

Lifecycles

Sy-Cc-1
ELDERHOSTELS   SCA
            Audio-cassette   1981
            NPR   59min
"Elderhostels" are special educational programs which offer people between the
ages of 60 and 95 a week of dorm living, cafeteria food, and the chance to learn
about everything from the mysteries of the universe to Shakespearian tragedy.
Elderhostel co-founder Martin Knowlton and gerontologist Paul Kershner discuss
the idea of learning difficulties for people over 60.   Producers Barbara
Schelstrate and Rebecca Goldfield interview both Elderhostel teachers and
students.

Sy-Cc-2
CHILLYSMITH FARM   SCA
            16mm   Sd   C   1981
            Filmmakers Library   55min
Chillysmith Farm was the home of Gramp, whose last years so memorably
documented by his grandsons in the photo-essay Gramp. This book had an
enormous impact as people responded to its example of intergenerational caring
and were moved by Gramp's poignant death at home. In this extraordinary film, 10
years in the making, we recall Gramp and meet the other members of his
remarkable family. Nan, Gramp's delightful wife, presents an eloquent example of
how to live and how to die. We watch her aging in the bosom of her family, and
see her peacefully die, her young great-grandchildren at her side.   Four
generations are bound with loving ties.

Sy-Cc-3
FOREVER YOUNG   SCA
            16mm   Sd   C   1980
            LCA   59 1/2m in
Ranging in age from 70 to 100, active older people discuss their views on life,
death, sex, love, on being active, and aging itself. We learn what good things are
in store for us as we grow older, and how these people have achieved their goal
of living longer and loving it.

Sy-Cc-4
GROWING OLD IN CALIFORNIA: Life, Not Death, In Venice   SCA
            Audio-cassette   1980
            NPR   29min
Producer Connie Goldman visits the Israel Levin Center for Senior Citizens in
Venice, California, where elderly Jewish people gather daily for companionship,
camaraderie, and activism. She also interviews anthropologist Barbara Meyerhoff.

Sy-Cc-5
LILA   SCA
            16mm   Sd   1981
            Ideas and Images, Inc.   28min
Lila is a film about being 80 and liking it, about continuing to work and to
create, to give and to fight to do your part in the world whatever it is.   Lila
Bonner Miller is, at 80, a doctor, a great-grandmother, a church leader, a
psychiatrist, an artist, an independent woman, and a remarkable example to all
who know her. Lila's compassion, intelligence, humor and freedom of thought and
expression are an experience for all to share.

Sy-Cc-6
MATTER OF INDIFFERENCE   SCA
    16mm   Sd   B   1974
    Phoenix Films   45min
Bombards the viewer with the inequities of old age. Senior citizen activists --
especially Gray Panther leaders Maggie Kuhn and Hope Bagger -- discuss the
physical, social, and psychological problems of growing old in America. The women
aim for the politicization of the elderly.

Sy-Cc-7
MIDDLE YEARS   SCA
    16mm   Sd   C   1976
    Films, Inc.   22min
The film consists of interviews with men and women who have reached middle age
and may be experiencing a personal crisis. It explores the people's recognition of
their mortality and their decisions about how to live the rest of their lives. It
illustrates the importance of the ideas of family life cycle and adult development.

Sy-Cc-8
NO PLACE LIKE HOME   SCA
    16mm   Sd   C   1981
    Films, Inc.   28min
Actress Helen Hayes, who has long been an outspoken advocate for the elderly,
travels throughout the U.S., reporting on nursing homes and on a range of
alternative approaches to long-term care for the aged. These include home care,
day care, and congregate living.

Sy-Cc-9
OTHER GENERATION GAP, THE   CA
    Audio-cassette   1978
    NPR   59min
Dr. Steven Cohen, author of The Other Generation Gap: The Middle-Aged and
Their Aging Parents, discusses responsibility for one's parents and distinguishing
between a parent's needs and wants. Maggie Kuhn of the Gray Panthers talks
about the media's portrayal of older people, the demographic changes of society,
using drugs to ease the pain of dying, and the problems of nursing homes.

Sy-Cc-10
SEE NO EVIL: A Late-Life Relationship   A
    16mm   Sd   B   1976
    Filmmakers Library   15min
This documentary underscores some of the problems that occur in later life:
failing health, loneliness, a different life style. A useful film for programs on
adjustment to aging, marriage in later life and counseling.

Sociology - Sex and Gender Roles

Sy-D-1
AMERICAN PARADE: We The Women   A
    16mm   Sd   C   1974
    BFA   30min
This film, narrated by Mary Tyler Moore for a television special, shows vignettes
of prominent feminists in American history. It analyzes the causes of increasing
feminism in America and chronicles the successes and failures of the women's

movement from its earliest times to the present. It gives students an historical perspective on feminism.

Sy-D-2
BEAUTY KNOWS NO PAIN   SC
    16mm   Sd   C   1982
    Benchmark Films   25min
Each year for two weeks, new co-eds who aspire to join the Kilgore College Rangerettes, and share in the glamour of marching on football fields between halves, submit to an incredible, torturous ordeal of training and testing.

The value of the Rangerette ideal holds for them is unforgettably demonstrated in scenes of hysteria when the results are posted. The winners and losers embrace with uncontrollable tears and sobs to console or congratulate each other.

Whether the film appears cynical or sentimental about these values, is in the eye of the beholder.

Sy-D-3
THE CONTINUOUS WOMAN   CA
    16mm   Sd   C   1973
    University of Minnesota   26min
This series of short interviews takes a personal look at the development of women in our society today. The combination of excellent photography and animation, honest interviews, and personality create a moving women's film for all viewers. Those interviewed include a black teacher who ascribes her success to her belief that she is "a very special person" and poet Meridel LeSueur, her daughter, and granddaughter, who talk about womanhood. In the best segment, Sherrie, a clinical psychologist, tells how she came to terms with her lesbianism.

Sy-D-4
GROWING UP FEMALE: As Six Become One   SCA
    16mm   B   1971
    New Day Films   50min
The sexist indoctrination of American women through home, media, and marketplace, from preschool on up is delineated in this feminist film. Focuses on six females, both black and white, of varying ages (four to thirty-five) and economic positions. Excellent companion piece to Men's Lives, which examines the forces that shape American boys into sexist America men. Exposes the stereotypic male role model, as molded at school, in the home and by the media, and whose force is felt from early childhood on.

Sy-D-5
LIFE AND TIMES OF ROSIE THE RIVETER   SCA
    16mm   Sd   C   1980
    Clarity Educational Productions   60min
A documentary of the experience of women workers during World War II. After women had been swiftly trained to take over jobs held by men leaving for military duty, they surpassed work quotas in most industries. When the war was over and "Rosie" wanted to stay, neither the structure of the American economy nor the dominant view of women's place in society sustained such hopes. The story is told by the women themselves — five former "Rosies." Their testimony is interwoven with rare archival recruitment films, stills, posters, ads, and music from the period, which contrast their experiences with the popular legend and mythology of Rosie the Riveter. Useful in units on ideology, occupational segregation, and working women.

Sy-D-6
MAN'S PLACE   SCA
   16mm   Sd   C   1979
   CASE/Institute for Research and Development   27min
   in Occupational Education
Documents the lives of men who live and/or work in a setting that requires them
to expand their conception of the traditional male role. The film focuses on five
men: a homemaker, a nurse, a father raising an infant, a man sharing household
responsibilities with a working wife and, lastly, a man in equal work and home
participation with a woman. These sequences are alternated with
man-on-the-street interviews which address the issues raised by the lifestyles of
the five men.

Sy-D-7
MEN'S LIVES   A
   16mm   Sd   C   1974
   New Day Films   45min
The process of socialization into male sex roles from childhood through adulthood
is followed and tied into education, relationships with women, work, and society.
The film includes some excellent interviews. One interview with an Antioch
professor suggests that achieving "success" is a myth -- there is no top -- which
creates a lot of anxiety and frustration, but keeps us competing because there is
always somebody better than we are. The film concludes that men are socialized
into a hard, machine-like existence to fit a competitive society, which is not in
the best interests of the humans involved; therefore, society should be changed.
This film is helpful in diffusing the defensiveness frequently found in male
students when the sex-role material seems to focus on women. It also helps define
sex-role stereotypes as being an issue for both sexes.

Sy-D-8
SEX ROLE DEVELOPMENT   A
   16mm   Sd   C   1974
   MGHT   23min
This film examines the influence that sex roles and stereotypes have on almost
every facet of people's lives, the ways they are instilled in successive generations
of Americans, and the ways in which some people are currently trying to find
some better models for human behavior. The film opens with some examples of
common sex-role stereotypes and then illustrates several of the ways in which
these roles are taught to children, including the influences of the media, toys,
peers, and adult expectations. In an interview sequence, Peter Bentler, a
psychologist from UCLA, discusses the consequences of sex-role stereotyping,
pointing out that one of the more important ideas stemming from sex-role
research is the concept of androgyny (the idea that the best of the male and
female sex roles can be combined so that people can behave flexibly and
effectively in any given situation). The remainder of the film is devoted to two
examples in which nontraditional sex-role philosophy pervades the socialization of
particular children.

Sy-D-9
THE SEXES: What's The Difference. THE SEXES: Roles   SCA
   16mm   Sd   C   1983
   Filmmakers Library   28min
The Sexes: What's the Difference addresses the sensitive question: Are "male" and
"female" traits inborn or are they learned in childhood?

The Sexes: Roles, surveys the evolution of male-female roles from pre-history to our current industrial age.

Both films incorporate cross-cultural material; Roles also utilizes findings from animal behavior studies. The films can be shown independently or used in sequence for a comprehensive survey of the psychology and sociology of male and female behavior.

Sy-D-10
TO BE A MAN   C A
    16mm   Sd   C   1980
    Perspective Films   43 1/2 min
Through profiles and interviews with prominent men and women, examines the wide range of contemporary attitudes toward the shifting masculine role in society.

Sy-D-11
VERY ENTERPRISING WOMEN   C A
    16mm   Sd   C   1980
    Small Business Administration   15min
Profiles of five women-owned businesses.

Sy-D-12
WOMAN'S PLACE   C A
    16mm   Sd   C   1973
    Xerox Films   52min
Bess Myerson narrates this film, which examines the creation and perpetuation of sex-role stereotypes. It also explores women's questioning of their roles and how the roles can be changed. It is a good overview of the range of influences (children's literature, media images, parental messages, movies, and job counselors) by which women are socialized into traditional roles.

Sy-D-13
WHY NOT A WOMAN?   C A
    16mm   Sd   C   1977
    NAVC   26min
Shows women working successfully in nontraditional jobs like welder, carpenter, and mechanic. Explores the attitudes of their male co-workers, supervisors, personnel managers, and teachers. Demonstrates the wide range of job options and training available to girls and women. Presents audiences with a realistic and entertaining argument against the long-standing myths about women and work. Attempts to direct audiences to reassess their deep-seated attitudes about working women.

Sy-D-14
THE WILLMAR 8   A
    16mm   Sd   C   1980
    California Newsreel   51min
This is the inspiring story of eight women bank workers in the small town of Willmar, Minnesota, who suddenly found themselves in the forefront of the fight for working women's rights. When a young male trainee was hired at almost twice their starting salary, and the women were required to "train him in," they complained to the bank president, who told them, "We're not all equal you know." That comment led eight unassuming and apolitical women to take the most unexpected step of their lives. They formed a union and started the first bank strike in the history of Minnesota.

Sociology – Personality and National Character

Sy-E-1
AMERICANS ON AMERICA: Our Identity and Self-Image   SCA
      FS, Cassette(2)
      Guidance Associates
Traces the twin concepts of freedom and equality as they appear time and again
in American history and literature. Describes the forging of these ideals by the
American colonists and later immigrants.

Sy-E-2
CONFLICTS IN AMERICAN VALUES:
Individualism vs. Conformity   CA
      16mm   Sd   C   1974
      BFA   15min
The desire for individual freedom shapes the values of most Americans and has
created a national mythology of rugged individualism. Yet society's needs for
conformity also shape our values. Recognition of the complexity of our value
structure can lead to more creative solutions to conflicts in America.

Sy-E-3
LEARNING TO COPE   CA
      16mm   Sd   C   1979
      Screenscope, Inc.   25min
To help people of all ages deal with the kind of stress they have felt and will
continue to feel, successful strategies people use to master the events in their
lives, the transitions, and the painful times are shown.

Sy-E-4
VALUES IN AMERICA (2 Parts)   CA
      FS, cassette series
      Guidance Associates
This series analyzes the many sources of America's system of values and provides
an historical viewpoint on growth and change in Ameican standards. Students
investigate the roots of American attitudes, see the panorama of American
society and meet Americans with diverse life-styles that promise fulfillment.

1. THE ORIGINS OF AMERICAN VALUES:
The Puritan Ethic to the Jesus Freaks
Explores the wide range of life styles pursued in America. Examines the causes of
diversity and the conflicts that can arise between independent life-styles and the
ideals of unity, harmony and a rising standard of living. Explores the nature of
subcultures and focuses on individuals who have established distinctive life-styles
for themselves.

2. CONFLICT IN AMERICAN VALUES:
Life-Style vs. Standard of Living
Traces the evolution of the American value system, giving particular attention to
controversies over life-styles that differ from the American norm. Focuses on
important stages in the growth of American values, relating each stage to
historical conditions. Explores the resurgence of American Indian values, changing
aims of the black community and efforts at developing alternative life-styles.

Sociology - Social Class (Work and Occupations)

Sy-F-1
A DAY WITHOUT SUNSHINE   A
    16mm   Sd   C   1976
    ICARUS   60min
A comprehensive and penetrating documentary about America's farmworkers, A
Day Without Sunshine, focuses on the Florida citrus industry and the workers who
harvest its fruit. Reviews the farm workers seemingly perpetual plight: low wages,
poor living conditions, malnutrition, hunger and disease, and — above all -- an
overwhelming sense of powerlessness.

Sy-F-2
BETWEEN ROCK AND A HARD PLACE   A
    16mm   Sd   C   1981
    Blue Ridge Mountain Films   59min
The changing meaning of work for three generations of Appalachian coal miners is
explored in this film.

Sy-F-3
BLUE COLLAR   A
    16mm   Sd   C   1978
    Universal 16   114min
The combined pressures from the industry, the union and the economy affect the
friendship of two auto workers -- one black, one white -- and the well-being of
their families. The family scenes highlight some of the problems confronting the
American working-class home today. Stars Richard Pryor and Harvey Keitel.

Sy-F-4
THE DETROIT MODEL   A
    16mm   Sd   C   1980
    California Newsreel   45min
Workers in Detroit's auto plants are shown studying their own industry. Frederick
Taylor's strategy to transfer design and control of the job from workers to
management is illustrated as Detroit tries to build an energy-efficient world car.
The U.A.W. is shown formulating innovative programs so that the new computer
technology does not fragment their work and make their skills obsolete. The film
is useful in units on political economy and occupations.

Sy-F-5
SOCIAL MOBILITY IN THE UNITED STATES   A
    FS, cassette series   1980
    SSSS
Is the American Dream of upward mobility a reality or a myth? This filmstrip
program explores the issue of social stratification in the USA and finds that it is
more rigid than many would like to admit. 5% of the population owns 60% of the
nation's stocks and bonds. The program discusses these issues, the social restraints
imposed on minority groups, and the available means of overcoming class
handicaps in the USA.

<u>Sociology</u> – General Studies and Commentaries

Sy-G-1
THE AMERICAN EXPERIENCE: Religious Diversity   SCA
          16mm   Sd   C   1976
          BFA   18min
More than three hundred religions are practiced in America today, each with a
unique origin and each contributing in a special way to the richness of American
society. Through this film, we meet young people involved in seven of America's
major religious groups and observe some of the differences and similarities in
America's many religions.

Sy-G-2
EQUALITY   SCA
          16mm   Sd   C   1976
          Best Films   60min
An examination of the question of equality intended to stimulate new thinking on
the subject through interviews with prominent people in the struggle for equality,
and men, women and children, who reflect the difficulties of achieving equality.

Sy-G-3
FOCUS ON THE SIXTIES   A
          16mm   Sd   C   1982
          ABC Wide World of Learning   58min
The peak of the Vietnam conflict is brought to the homes of America. Political
and social unrest spreads to every facet of the American society. The Mets win
the World Series, and Carlos and Smith defiantly raise the black fist that shook
the Olympic games. 1965-1969 are years to remember.

Sy-G-4
HOSPITAL   SCA
          16mm   Sd   B   1970
          Zipporah Films   84min
This Emmy-award-winning film examines the activities of a city hospital.
Frederick Wiseman lets his camera run to present a regular day in this type of
institution.

Sy-G-5
MEASURE OF AMERICA, THE   SCA
          16mm   Sd   C   1983
          Solari Communications   26:30min
Shows working people gathered to examine the current status of the American
value system and to share their feelings about the United States.

Sy-G-6
POPULAR CULTURE IN AMERICA   SCA
          Audio-cassette, 3 parts   1978
          NPR   59min
This radio documentary explores the relationship between popular culture and the
political and social life of contemporary America, through inteviews, speeches,
and discussions with social critics throughout the U.S. Produced by Barbara Sirota
and John Weber.
          Part I examines mass culture: popular music, movies, radio,
television, advertising, sports, and the industries that produce them.
          Part II concentrates on heroism, images of women, and love and
romance in television, radio, film, and records.

Sy-G-7
STAR SPANGLED PATRIOTISM   S
        Audio-cassette   1981
        NPR Journal series   29min
Presented is a montage of "patriotism" as experienced at a parade, in music, and
on the Fourth of July. People born in America, as well as those who have
immigrated here, describe their feelings in a blend of interviews, historical tapes,
speeches, and patriotic songs.

Sy-G-8
THE SIXTIES   S C A
        16mm   Sd   C   1970
        Pyramid Films   14min
An overview of a decade of change, protests, confrontations, violence,
assassinations, and foreign war are presented in this short film. It is appealing to
students who were born in the sixties but were too young to realize the impact of
these struggles. Many aspects of the film can be analyzed in terms of discussions
of social change. Ten years of CBS news film clips are the sources for the
pictures.

        Sociology - Social Problems (Deviance, Criminal Justice, War)

Sy-H-1
ABNORMAL BEHAVIOR: A Mental Hospital   C A
        16mm   Sd   C   1971
        CRM Productions   28min
Documentary sequences filmed at Gateways Mental Hospital in Glendale,
California, present a haunting view of the pathos, tragedy, uncertainty, and terror
of mental illness. Throughout the film, the director of the hospital discusses the
problems and intricacies of running a large mental hospital, scheduling daily
activities of a large number of patients of all ages. A series of doctor-patient
interviews acquaints the viewer with the symptomology of various schizophrenic
disturbances. A patient with paranoid tendencies is shown undergoing
electroconvulsive therapy.

Sy-H-2
ALL THE PRESIDENT'S MEN   C A
        16mm   Sd   C   1976
        Warner Brothers Non-Theatrical Division   135min
Based on the book by Washington Post reporters Carl Bernstein and Bob
Woodward, this outstanding production chronicles their investigation of the
Watergate incident and the hidden circumstances leading to it. Dustin Hoffman
and Robert Redford play the leading roles.

Sy-H-3
ATTICA   A
        16mm   Sd   C   1974
        Tricontinental Film Center   80min
Carefully researched documentary of the events in Attica prison, before, during
and after the take-over by inmates in 1971. Includes newsreel footage of the
events and interviews with inmates and members of the McKay Commission
hearings that followed the rebellion. Powerful documentary that gives insights
into the conditions in many large penal institutions.

Sy-H-4
EAST 103RD STREET   A
     16mm   Sd   C   1981
     Institute for the Study of Human Issues   70min
An intimate exploration of the complexities of life facing a group of heroin users
on the streets of New York. Shows how they view their world; their problems,
hopes, and fears; the ways in which they cope with the challenges and threats of
daily existence.

Sy-H-5
FIFTH STREET: Skid Row   A
     16mm   Sd   C   1973
     MGHT   28min
This film candidly portrays life on Fifth Street in downtown Los Angeles. Through
unrehearsed vignettes and short interviews with these men, viewers learn what
life is like on skid row. The language is explicit; the subject matter may be
shocking to some viewers. However the camaraderie between friends is genuine
and provides a poignant counterpoint to their degrading physical environment.

Sy-H-6
GETTING STRAIGHT   SCA
     16mm   Sd   C   1982
     Films, Inc   26min
The adolescent death rate has risen 16% in the last decade and it is estimated
that 45% of all teenagers in the U.S. are using drugs in high school. Dr. Miller
Newton, founder and director of Get Straight, Inc., is fighting this epidemic of
teenage drug abuse with a very successful program in which teens receive
constant support from both peers and parents and are forced to the truth about
their lives.

Sy-H-7
HARD WORK   CA
     16mm   Sd   C   1977
     Durrin Films, Inc.   29min
Focuses on the efforts of Margo St. James, an ex-hooker, to decriminalize
prostitution. Filmed during the Second Annual Hookers Convention in Washington,
DC, it raises the complex social, moral, and legal issues of prostitution.

Sy-H-8
I AM SOMEBODY   A
     16mm   Sd   C   1970
     ICARUS   30min
When 400 poorly paid black women—hospital workers in Charleston, S.C.—went on
strike in 1969 to demand union recognition and an increase in their hourly wage,
they soon found that they were confronting the National Guard and the power of
the State Government, as well as their employers. This classic labor film presents
the dramatic story of their 113 days long strike.

Sy-H-9
JUVENILE COURT   SCA
     16mm   Sd   B   1974
     Grove Press Films/Zipporah Films   144min
Another of Frederick Wiseman's cinema verite' documentaries, this film focuses on
the processing of juveniles who have somehow offended either the legal
authorities or their parents. The emphasis is on the daily routine of the juvenile
court. The effect is all the stronger because it is obvious that the cases

portrayed in the film are neither unusual nor rare. Filmed in a court in Memphis, Tennessee, this is a useful example of how definitions of deviance are socially constructed and differentially applied.

Sy-H-10
ODDS AGAINST, THE   SCA
    16mm   Sd   B   1966
    U. of California at Los Angeles   32min
Following one convicted burglar through the criminal justice system, this film shows the American correctional system and compares older facilities and programs to more modern ones.

Sy-H-11
THINKING TWICE   SCA
    16mm   Sd   C   1981
    Skye Pictures, Inc.   29min
Captures one family's coming to grips with the arms race and national security in their lives. By sharing dinner with a survivor of Hiroshima and a picnic with a Russian family now living in the United States, going to community events and viewing recent film and TV programs, the children and parents come to their own decisions about the issue.

Sy-H-12
VIOLENT YOUTH--THE UNMET CHALLENGE   SCA
    16mm   Sd   C   1975
    Altana Films   23min
Interviews with two boys convicted of armed robbery. Also includes reactions from officials on the rise in juvenile crimes of violence and the failure of the present system of corrections to change these offenders.

Sy-H-13
WAR WITHOUT WINNERS   SCA
    16mm   Sd   C   1979
    Films, Inc.   28min
American people and Russian people--auto workers, bomb assemblers, ballerinas, fruit vendors, space museum tour guides and retired government officials--express their fears, thoughts, and hopes about the future in an age of nuclear weapons that can incinerate civilization in minutes.

Sy-H-14
WOMEN IN PRISON   CA
    16mm   Sd   C   1974
    Carousel Films   54min
This ABC documentary portrays the brutality of the women's prison and suggests structural alternatives. The Des Moines, Iowa, project allows women to stay home, to be employed, and to care for their children. This one alternative is shown to be not only more humane, but also very cost-effective.

Sociology – Lifestyles

Sy-I-1
ALTERNATIVE LIFESTYLES IN CALIFORNIA:
  EAST MEETS WEST   SCA
      16mm   Sd   C   1978
      Time–Life Multimedia   52min
Ronald Eyre introduces us to Californians who, brought up mainly in a Christian
culture, now look to Taoism and Hinduism for inspiration. They are preoccupied
with the search for a saner, healthier life in which ecology is sacred.

Sy-I-2
AUNT ARIE   SC
      16mm   Sd   C   1975
      EBEC   18min
This film pays tribute to an authentically American cultural region and documents
the life of a passing generation. Spry and independent Aunt Arie Carpenter, who
is nearly 87, lives in the Blue Ridge Mountains of North Carolina. In the
characteristic idiom of Appalachia, she tells of her childhood, her marriage, and
how she helped her husband build their house and farm the red clay soil near
Coweeta Creek.

Sy-I-3
EARLY MORNING   S
      Audio–cassette   1979
      NPR   59min
Producer David Selvin explores the lives of people who sleep during the day and
stay awake at night. He traces the daily routine of a paper deliverer, then
interviews coffee shop patrons, insomniacs, and bus drivers, who discuss the pros
and cons of being morning people. Music highlights the program.

Sy-I-4
EMPIRE OF THE SUN   CA
      16mm   Sd   C   1974
      U. of California EMC   25min
Documents the beliefs and daily life of the young men and women from the
Brotherhood of the Sun commune near Santa Barbara, California. In this
community, built around a life devoted to Christ and his teachings, the young
people plow their land, grow their own food, build their houses, raise animals,
make their own clothes and music, and celebrate their nearness to Jesus through
prayer and meditation.

Sy-I-5
CAROLINAS PEYTON: BLACK
  FARMER   SCA
      16mm   Sd   C   1978
      Simeon Hyde III   11min
A look at the lifestyle of a 94-year-old black Virginia farmer who continues to
work his land with a team of mules.

Sy-I-6
COWHAND'S SONG: CRISIS ON THE RANGE   CA
      16mm   Sd   C   1981
      Cattle Kate Communications   28 1/2min
Presents the life of family ranchers in northern California and Nevada who graze

their cattle on public rangelands.

Sy-I-7
FARMING AND THE LAND   A
    16mm   Sd   C   1978
    Image Resources   29min
Examines the current state of agriculture in southern New Hampshire by
documenting six different small family farms which are threatened by population
growth, increased taxes, and low earnings. Focuses on the need for planning and
the lack of governmental awareness and concern on the issues. Intended to inform
urban as well as rural audiences about the problems facing today's audiences.

Sy-I-8
HARVEST   SCA
    16mm   Sd   C   1979
    WNET Media Service   58min
A married couple from New York City, social workers in their early 30s, seeking a
new direction in life, take over a 430-acre farm in North Dakota. The film records
their struggle to bring in their first harvest, their adjustment to a new
community, and the preparation for the birth of their daughter. A Bill Moyers
Journal Report.

Sy-I-9
HOBO: AT THE END OF THE LINE   SC
    16mm   Sd   C   1978
    EBEC   24min
The hobo symbolizes an American romantic tradition. He lives on the road, hitches
rides on freight trains, cooks mulligan stew over an open fire, and plays the
harmonica. He "rides the rails" from season to season, job to job. He frequents the
skid row missions for a little preaching and a free meal. This film portrayal of
hobo life reveals an element of Americana approaching extinction, and considers
what values and standards dictate any person's choice of lifestyle.

Sy-I-10
HOW MUCH WOOD WOULD A WOODCHUCK CHUCK   SCA
    16mm   Sd   C   1978
    New Yorker Films   45min
The annual World Championship of Livestock Auctioneers, set in the Amish region
of Pennsylvania's Lancaster County. Records the mystique and education of the
professional auctioneer, and the high-speed incantations of the auctioneers—a
language both zany and beautiful.

Sy-I-11
IN WHITE COLLAR AMERICA   CA
    16mm   Sd   C   1974
    Films, Inc.   54min
The life-styles of white-collar workers are shown in this award-winning film. This
growing segment of the labor market has not been studied or filmed until recent
years, and this film is a fine start at documenting the particulars of this
subsection of workers.

Sy-I-12
KING OF THE HOBOS   SCA
    16mm   Sd   C   1983
    Mark Forman Films   28min
A glimpse into the life of "Steam Train" Maury Graham—historian, storyteller,

wanderer, good samaritan, and five-time King of the Hobos. A man of contradictions, Maury worked construction, raised a family, and then began a search for his youth and the lost days of the Hobos.

Sy-I-13
LA LA, MAKING IT IN L.A.   SCA
        16mm   Sd   C   1979
        Direct Cinema Ltd.   58min
Struggling performers (actors, musicians and comedians) in Los Angeles speak directly to the film audience of their goals, hopes and fears for making it in the entertainment capital of the world.

Sy-I-14
LEE BALTIMORE: 99 YEARS OF
  "WHAT MAKES A POOR MAN RICH"   SCA
        16mm   Sd   C   1976
        EBEC   17min
Lee Baltimore—farmer, philosopher and son of slaves—is 99 years old. Six days a week he rises with the sun and works his tiny farm in Jasper County, Texas. In his own words he tells of a life simple, poor, yet rich in memories and love of the land that sustains him. His wife of 68 years is dead and he is often lonely, but never despondent. He has kept his faith in the goodness of life. And he has his piano—which he taught himself to play two years ago at the age of 97.

Sy-I-15
LIVING THE GOOD LIFE   SCA
        16mm   Sd   C   1977
        Bullfrog Films, Inc.   30min
Homesteading with Helen and Scott Nearing, pacifists and vegetarians, who opted out of the market economy 45 years ago. At ages 74 and 93, their way of life has become a model for young homesteaders. Through books and public appearances, they remain effective social critics.

Sy-I-16
MALCOLM BREWER: BOAT BUILDER   SC
        16mm   Sd   C   1976
        EBEC   18min
Malcolm Brewer, 77 years old, still practices the craft he has toiled at all his life: building boats by hand in his shop on the coast of Maine. As he works, he tells of a life built on self-reliance and joy in hard work. As he talks, Malcolm Brewer, son of a lobster fisherman, single-handedly recreates the generations of stolid New Englanders who helped set this country on its course toward greatness.

Sy-I-17
MOUNTAIN PEOPLE   SCA
        16mm   Sd   C   1978
        Wombat Productions   52min
Examines a disappearing way of life in rural West Virginia.

Sy-I-18
NOW WE LIVE ON CLIFTON   SCA
        16mm   Sd   C   1974
        Kartemquin Films   26min
The Taylor family, white and working-class, live on the north side of Chicago in a multi-racial neighborhood. The Taylor children—Pam, age 10, and Scott, age 12—reflect on the changing state of their neighborhood, their family, and their

racially-mixed friends. A great film because it's totally from the point of view of the children who have adjusted to the realities of urban living and who love it despite its drawbacks.

Sy-I-19
PEOPLE OF PRESERVATION: THE AMISH   SCA
     16mm   Sd   C   1978
     EBEC   28min
Filmed in Lancaster County, Pennsylvania, this documentary captures the sensitivity and humility of the Amish people, while examining their religious beliefs, closeness to nature, and strong sense of community. The film invites students to evaluate the consequences of choosing a simple life and resisting "too much progress" in the modern world. Viewers get an intimate look at a people who differ from most of society in fundamental ways, while proudly preserving their own values.

Sy-I-20
POLICEMAN'S FAMILY, THE   SCA
     16mm   Sd   C   1976
     Harper & Row Media   20min
The family stresses that may arise in a policeman's household due to the element of danger inherent in his work.

Sy-I-21
POPOVICH BROTHERS OF SOUTH CHICAGO, THE   A
     16mm   Sd   C   1978
     Ethnic Folk Arts Center   60min
A musical portrayal of the small, blue-collar Serbian-American community of South Chicago as seen through the lives of The Popovich Brothers—one of the best of old-time "tamburitza" orchestras. Stresses the role of traditional music as a cohesive force in family and community life and examines the possibility for survival of immigrant cultural heritage in succeeding generations.

Sy-I-22
PROUD PENSIONER LIVES HIS LIFE IN THE CHICAGO
  NEIGHBORHOOD HE CANNOT SEE   SCA
     16mm,BV   Sd   C
     Perspective Films   13min
Sykes Williams. Gutsy. Blind. Irish. A storyteller. Sykes and his wife live in a run-down Chicago neighborhood. He plays piano two nights a week in a bar to supplement his pension. He's popular in the neighborhood. He talks about living a long time and getting along. His amiable banter is spiced with complaints about lack of respect for the elderly, poor sidewalk maintenance ("just look at this hole"), inadequate Social Security. This is more than a story about growing old. This is the story of Sykes, a proud man, living an active, meaningful life.

Sy-I-23
PURSUIT OF EXCELLENCE, THE   A
     16mm   Sd   C   1978
     WQED, Pittsburgh   50min
A PBS television pilot film for a series about people in all walks of life who are the best at what they do. This pilot profiles top long distance runners Frank Shorter and Bill Rodgers, examining their lifestyles and motivations. Concludes with the 1978 Boston Marathon.

Sy-I-24
ROCKING HORSE COWBOY   SCA
        16mm   Sd   C   1977
        EBEC   24min
The American cowboy: creature and symbol of the old West, the untamed frontier.
But how does this romantic image compare to the life of a real cowboy? This
character study captures the poignant true story of a modern-day cowboy growing
old. Vivid photography and narration in the man's own words and voice reveal the
life of a person who followed his dreams, only to find the road bittersweet. The
film offers a unique perspective on American history and contemporary society.

Sy-I-25
ROOT HOG OR DIE   A
        16mm   Sd   B   1978
        Documentary Educational Resources   58min
Filmed in Western Massachusetts and Southern Vermont, portrays the life-style,
values, character and work of rural New England. Follows the rhythm of the
seasons and the activities involved in self-sufficient family farming. The format is
cinema verite intercut with interviews.

Sy-I-26
RURAL LIVES   SC
        Audio cassette(2)   1982
        NPR   59min each
Part I. FARMING: SUN-UP TO SUN-DOWN, focuses on farming methods of the past
and present and the effects of farm life on family life. Long hours and a love of
the land are emphasized.
Part II. A QUESTION OF VALUES, presents rural people talking about their love
for the land, raising children, working in the outdoors, and the peace and quiet of
the countryside. One old-timer reminds listeners of the dependency of city folks
on food grown in the countryside.

Sy-I-27
SHANNON COUNTY: HOME
   (A PORTRAIT OF THE OZARKS, PART I)   SCA
        16mm   Sd   C   1981
        Veriation Films   67min
The first of two films of life in a remote Ozarks country of southern Missouri.
Landscape, historic setting and culture of the country are portrayed through
personal vignettes. Burial of the oldest citizen, fathers and sons hunting, rural
celebrations, brush arbor revival, night gigging on the rivers, the county
courthouse, all portray history, place, family, humanity. Conversations are open,
humorous, articulate, revealing.

Sy-I-28
SHANNON COUNTY: THE HEARTS OF THE CHILDREN
   (A PORTRAIT OF THE OZARKS, PART II)   SCA
        16mm   Sd   C   1982
        Veriation Films   57min
The second of two films of life in a remote Ozarks county of southern Missouri.
Old and young alike are concerned for the future, for viability of county life, for
conserving the best of the past. Newcomers from Chicago exemplify urban people
choosing a rural life. Intimate conversations with a campaigning politician,
farmers, and deer hunters reflecting on their sons' futures; and expressing quiet
anxiety.

Sy-I-29
SPEND IT ALL   C A
    16mm   Sd   C   1970
    U. of California EMC   41min
This is a documentary of the Cajun sub-culture of the Louisiana bayou country. A major cultural value of these people is the enjoyment of life in the present. After subsistence needs are met, money is freely spent to have a good time. Interviews with the residents show the daily life of this subculture in the United States that has some distinct features and yet co-exists with the dominant culture.

Sy-I-30
TRADER VIC'S USED CARS   SCA
    16mm   Sd   C   1975
    EBEC   10min
Trader Vic, self-made businessman, started out with a borrowed $800. Ten years later he was profiled in the New York Times. His business--selling used cars-- is not a trade celebrated for honest dealings. But Trader Vic rises above the stigma with a blend of honesty, shrewdness and originality that has made him one of America's most successful salesmen. In this film, he tells in his own words--and with twinkles of humor--how to win customers and keep them coming back.

Sy-I-31
UNDERGROUND   SCA
    16mm   Sd   C   1976
    Action Films/27   85min
Interviews with members of the Weather Underground (Billy Ayers, Kathy Boudin, Bernardine Dohrn, Jeff Jones, Cathy Wilkerson) were filmed in secret locations with the faces of the subjects obscured because they are still fugitives from justice. As the members of the Weather Underground discuss revolution as well as social and economic change in the United States, the film intercuts with footage of the turbulent sixties. The women also discuss their growing involvement in the movement, from performing domestic chores for their men to assuming major responsibilities and carrying out dangerous missions. The subjects reveal that they believe their choice to engage in terrorists activities was a moral decision in light of their political beliefs.

Sy-I-32
VOYAGE TO A MOUNTAIN MAN   SCA
    16mm   Sd   C   1981
    Glen Lau Films   26min
The account of a film crew's wilderness journey to locate a real mountain man--Buckskin Bill--and a tribute to the self-sufficient spirit and values of America's remaining wilderness people.

Sy-I-33
WORD IS OUT   C A
    16mm   Sd   C   1978
    New Yorker Films   130min
Interviews with 26 gay people--ranging in age from 18 to 77, in locales from San Francisco to New Mexico to Boston, in type from a beehived housewife to the sultriest drag queen--who speak frankly, amusingly and movingly about their experiences as homosexuals. That diversity, intelligence and wit help to break down the accumulated stereotypes frequently held.

Sy-I-34
YEAR OF THE COMMUNES   SCA
    16mm   Sd   C   1970
    MGHT   53min
This film examines the history of communes as an alternative style of family life
and shows the diversity of goals and rules among nine communes in the western
United States.

Sy-I-35
YELLOW CAB   A
    16mm   Sd   C   1979
    Time-Life Multimedia   47 1/2min
Two New York City plainclothes police officers, cruise the streets of Harlem in a
taxi looking for street crime. Narrated by the cops themselves and the street
people they meet, the film gives insight into their private lives, as well as their
daily routine.

Sy-I-36
YES, MA'AM   CA
    16mm, BV   Sd   C   1981
    Filmmakers Library   48min
The gracious life within the stately mansions and gardens of New Orleans is
maintained by black household workers, a vanishing remnant of the Old South.
Many have spent their whole working life in one family's employment, and strong
attachments have developed on both sides.

Appendix: Directory of Distributors

ABC Video Enterprises
825 Seventh Avenue
New York, NY 10019

ABC Wide World of Learning
1330 Avenue of the Americas
New York, NY 10019

Academy Films
Box 1023
Venice, CA 90291

ACCOD
AIDS of Cape Cod
110 Old Town House Road
South Yarmouth, MA 02646

ACI Media, Inc.
35 W. 45th Street
New York, NY 10036

Acorn Films
33 Union Square West
New York, NY 10003

Action Films/27
P.O. Box 315
Franklin Lakes, NJ 07417

Actuality Films, Ltd
47 E. 64th Street
New York, NY 10021

Adair Films
2015 Third Street
San Francisco, CA 94608

Adams County Historical Society
Box 102
Hastings, NE 68901

Adams/King Productions
2619 Garfield Street, N.W.
Washington, D.C. 20008

Aims
626 Justin Avenue
Glendale, CA 91201

Allied Film Laboratory
1322 West Belmont Avenue
Chicago, IL 60657

Altana Films
340 E. 34th Street
New York, NY 10016

Amberola Productions
259 Broadway
Cambridge, MA 02139

American Crafts Council
44 W. 53rd Street
New York, NY 10019

AMDOC
American Documentary Films, Inc.
379 Bay Street
San Francisco, CA 94133

AMEDFL
American Educational Films
Box 8188
Nashville, TN 37207

American Federation of Arts
41 E. 65th Street
New York, NY 10021

American Petroleum Institute
2101 L Street, N.W.
Washington, DC 20037

Americas in Transition, Inc.
401 West Broadway
New York, NY 10012

Amon Carter Museum
P.O. Box 2365
Fort Worth, TX 76101

Anti-Defamation League
823 United Nations Plaza
New York, NY 10017

Appalshop Films
P.O. Box 743
306 Madison Street
Whitesburg, KY 41858

Art Now, Inc.
144 N. 14th Street
Kenilworth, NJ 07033

Arthur Cantor Inc.
33 W. 60th Street
New York, NY 10023

Arts Communications
27 East 11th Street
New York, NY 10003

Arthur Mokin Productions
17 W. 60th Street
New York, NY 10023

ASPO/ Lamaze
1840 Wilson Boulevard #204
Arlington, VA 22201

Association Films
605 Market Street
San Francisco, CA 94105

ASTF
Association-Sterling Films
866 Third Avenue
New York, NY 10022

Atlantis Productions, Inc.
850 Thousand Oaks Boulevard
Thousand Oaks, CA 91360

AVDEV
Audiovisual Instructional Device
24-20 Little Neck Boulevard
Bayside, New York 11360

Audio-Visual Narrative Arts
Box 9
Pleasantville, NY 10570

Australian Film Commission
9229 Sunset Boulevard, #720
Los Angeles, CA 90069

Barbara Wilk
29 Surf Road
Westport, CT 06880

Barr Films
PO Box 5667
Pasadena, CA 91107

Bayou Films
Route 3, Box 614
Cut Off, LA 70345

Beacon Films
P.O. Box 575
Norwood, MA 02062

Bell Telephone Film Library
c/o AT&T Information Dept
195 Broadway, Room 071106
New York, NY 10007

Ben Achtenberg
47 Halifax Street
Jamaica Plains, MA 02130

Best Films
1335 Camino Del Mar
P.O. Box 692
Del Mar, CA 92014

BFA
BFA Educational Media
2211 Michigan Avenue
P.O. Box 1795
Santa Monica, CA 90406

Bill Jersey Productions, Inc.
5915 Hollis Street
Emeryville, CA 94608

Bishop Hill Heritage Association
Box 1853
Bishop Hill, IL 61419

Black Filmaker Distribution
Service
P.O. Box 315
Franklin Lakes, NJ 07417

Blackhawk Films
1235 West Fifth
Box 3990
Davenport, IA 52808

Blackwood Productions
251 W. 57th Street
New York, NY 10019

Blue Ridge Mountain Films
278 E. 10th Street, #4-D
New York, NY 10009

Blue Sky Productions
P.O. Box 548
Santa Fe, NM 87501

Bowling Green Films, Inc.
Box 384-D
Hudson, NY 12534

Brainstorm Films
2 Central Green
Winchester, MA 01890

Brigham Young University
DMDP Media Business Services
W. 164 Stadium
Provo, UT 84602

BBC
British Broadcasting Co.
630 Fifth Avenue
New York, NY 10020

Brown Bird Productions, Inc.
1971 N. Curson Avenue
Hollywood, CA 90046

Bruce Ricker
30 Charlton Street
New York, NY 10014

Bullfrog Films
Oley, PA 19547

Caedmon Records
505 8th Avenue
New York, NY 10018

California Newsreel
630 Natoma
San Francisco, CA 94103

Cambridge Media Resources
36 Shepard Street
Cambridge, MA 02138

Campus Film Distributors
Box 206
14 Madison Avenue
Valhalla, NY 10595

CBC
Canadian Broadcasting
Corporation
P.O. Box 500, Terminal A
Toronto, CANADA

Canadian Filmakers
299 Queen Street West, Suite
204A
Toronto M5V 1Z9 Ontario
CANADA

Canyon Cinema Co-Op
2325 Third Street, Suite 338
San Francisco, CA 94107

CAPCBC
Capitol Cities Broadcasting Co.
24 E. 51st Street
New York, NY 10022

Carole Langer Productions
28 Green Street
New York, NY 10013

Carousel Films
241 E. 34th Street
New York, NY 10016

Case Institute for Research &
Development in Occupational
Education
33 West 42nd Street, Room 1439
New York, NY 10036

Cattle Kate Communications
66 Broadway
San Francisco, CA 94111

CBS Fox Video
23454 Industrial Park Court
Farmington Hills, MI 48024

CBS News
524 West 57th Street
New York, NY 10019

Cecilia Conway
1720 Allard Road
Chapel Hill, NC 272514

Cecropia Films
c/o Transit Media
Box 315
Franklin Lakes, NJ 07417

Centaur Productions Inc.
P.O. Box 5108
Vancouver, B.C.
CANADA V6B 4A9

Center for Humanities, Inc.
Communications Park
Box 1000
Mt. Kisco, NY 10549

Center for Southern Folklore
P.O. Box 40105
1216 Peabody Avenue
Memphis, TN 38104

Centron Films
P.O. Box 687
1621 W. 9th Street
Lawrence, KS 66044

CBC
Children's Book Council
67 Irving Place
New York, NY 10003

Chronicle Productions
364 W. 18th Street
New York, NY 10011

Churchill Films
662 N. Robertson Boulevard
Los Angeles, CA 90069

Cine Manifest
308 11th Street
San Francisco, CA 94103

Cinema 5
595 Madison Avenue
New York, NY 10022

The Cinema Guild
1697 Broadway
New York, NY 10019

Cinetronics
304 S. Broadway, #510
Los Angeles, CA 90013

Clarity Educational Productions
4560 Horton Street
Emeryville, CA 94608

Colonial Williamsburg Foundation
A-V Section
Box C
Williamsburg, VA 23185

CBSTV
Columbia Broadcasting System
383 Madison Avenue
New York, NY 10019

Columbia Pictures Corporation
16mm Sales Division
711 Fifth Avenue
New York, NY 10022

Consumer's Union Film Library
256 Washington Street
Mt. Vernon, NY 10550

Contemporary Films
271 Central Park West
New York, NY 10024

Coronet
65 E. South Water Street
Chicago, IL 60601

Counselor Films, Inc.
2100 Locust Street
Philadelphia, PA 19103

CPB
Corporation for Public
Broadcasting
1111 16th Street, N.W.
Washington, DC 20036

Crawford Productions
2101 Hampden Drive
Lansing, MI 48910

CRM/McGraw Hill
Box 641
Del Mar, CA 92014

CRM Productions
1550 Euclid
Santa Monica, CA 90404

Crystal Productions
Box 12317
Aspen, CO 81612

CTV Television Network
42 Charles Street East
Toronto, Ontario M 441T5
CANADA

Current Affairs Films
24 Danbury Road
Wilton, CT 06897

Dallas County Community College
c/o Center for Telecommunications
4343 North Highway 67
Mesquite, TX 75150

David Deutsch
c/o WETA-TV
Box 2626
Washington, DC 20013

Dennis Lanson
313 W. 78th Street, #3F
New York, NY 10024

Direct Cinema, Ltd.
P.O. Box 69589
Los Angeles, CA 90069

Document C/B
489 Broome Street
New York, NY 10013

Documentary Educational Resources
24 Dame Street
Somerville, MA 02143

Donars Production
P.O. Box 24
407 Lincoln Avenue
Loveland, CO 80537

Doreen Moses
1730 21st Street, N.W.
Washington, DC 20009

Doubleday and Co., Inc.
Educational Systems Division
Garden City, NY 11530

Drew Associates
166 E. 66th Street
New York, NY 10021

DUART
DuArt Film Laboratories
245 W. 55th Street
New York, NY 10019

Durrin Films
4926 Sedgwick Street, N.W.
Washington, DC 20016

Eastern Educational TV Network
120 Boylston Street
Boston, MA 02116-4611

EAV
Educational Audio Visual
29 Marble Avenue
Pleasantville, NY 10570

EDDIM
Educational Dimensions
Corporation
Box 126
Stamford, CT 06904

Educational Art Transparencies
Film
27 W. Summit Street
Chagrin Falls, OH 44022

Educational Enrichment
Materials
Random House School Division
400 Hahn Road
Westminster, MD 21157

Educational Filmstrips
1401 19th Street
Huntsville, TX 77340

EBEC
Encyclopedia Brittanica
Educational Corporation
425 North Michigan Avenue
Chicago, IL 60611

Environmental Communications
64 Windward Avenue
Venice, CA 90291

Environmental Protection Agency
401 M Street, S.W.
Washington, DC 20024

Esmeralda Films
P.O. Box 4868
North Hollywood, CA 91607

Ethnic Folk Arts Center
Box 315
Franklin Lakes, NJ 07417

Eye Gate House, Inc.
146-01 Archer Ave.
Jamaica, NY 11435

Federal Reserve Bank
1700 G Street, N.W.
Washington, DC 20551

Fenwick Productions
Box 277
West Hartford, CT 06107

Film Authors
1270 Avenue of the Americas
New York, NY 10020

Film Boston
11 Sacramento Street
Cambridge, MA 02138

Film Images
17 W. 60th Street
New York, NY 10023

Filmakers Library
133 E. 58th Street
New York, NY 10022

Film Production Unit
Iowa State University
Ames, IA 50010

Films for the Humanities
P.O. Box 2053
Princeton, NJ 08540

Films, Inc.
733 Green Bay Road
Wilmette, IL 60091

Fine Line Productions
1101 Masonic Avenue
San Francisco, CA 94117

First Generation Programming
250 West 54th Street
New York, NY 10022

First Run Features
144 Bleeker Street
New York, NY 10012

Florida Folklife Program
Box 265
White Springs, FL 32096

Flower Films
10341 San Pablo Avenue
El Cerrito, CA 94530

Fogg Fine Arts Films
Fogg Museum/Harvard University
Cambridge, MA 02138

Folkways Records & Service
Corp.
43 West 61st Street
New York, NY 10023

Fore Head Productions
1510 A South Rennsselaer Pl.
Charlotte, NC 28203

Frost Media Associates
c/o Frost Productions, Inc.
1025 Connecticut Avenue, N.W.
Washington, DC 20036

Gary Goldman
Paramount Studios
5555 Melrose Avenue
Los Angeles, CA 90038

G.E. Educational Films
A-V Communications
Department 482
Cleveland, OH 44112

Gerald Ford Presidential Museum
303 Pearl Street, N.W.
Grand Rapids, MI 49504

Glen Lau Films
3211 S.W. 27th Avenue
Ocala, FL 32674

Globe Filmstrips
65 E. South Water Street
Chicago, IL 60601

GPN Educational Media
Box 80669
Lincoln, NE 68501

GPITVL
Great Plains Instructional TV Library
University of Nebraska
P.O. Box 80669
Lincoln, NB 68501

GRACU
Graphic Curriculum, Inc.
699 Madison Avenue
New York, NY 10021

Greenwood Press
88 Post Road West
Westport, CT 06881

Gretchen Robinson
P.O. Box 671
Greenville, SC 29602

Grove Press, Films Division
196 West Houston Street
New York, NY 10014

Grover Jennings Productions
P.O. Box 303
Monterey, CA 93941

Guggenheim Productions, Inc.
3121 South Street, N.W.
Washington, DC 20007

Guidance Associates
Communications Park
Box 3000
Mt. Kisco, NY 10549

Gulfsouth Films
Center for Gulfsouth
History and Culture
1220 Gayoso Street
New Orleans, LA 70119

Hagley Museum
Greenville, DE 19807

Handel Film Corporation
8730 Sunset Boulevard
West Hollywood, CA 90069

Harper & Row Media
10 East 53rd Street
New York, NY 10022

Harpers Ferry Historical
Association
Box 147
Harpers Ferry, WV 25425

Hartley Productions
Cat Rock Road
Cos Cob, CT 06807

Hearst Metrotone News
235 E. 45th Street
New York, NY 10017

Helios Film Productions
5485 Hyde Park Boulevard
Chicago, IL 60615

Hellenic American Neighborhood
Action Committee
1730 21st Street, N.W.
Washington, DC 20009

Heritage Productions, Inc.
Box 64, R.D.1
Harleysvills, PA 19438

Holt, Rhinehart, Winston
383 Madison Avenue
New York, NY 10017

Howard Street Productions
458 Broome Street
New York, NY 10013

Human Relations Media
175 Tompkins Avenue
Pleasantville, NY 10570

IBM Corporation
1133 Westchester Avenue
White Plains, NY 10604

ICARUS Films
200 Park Avenue South
Suite 1319
New York, NY 10003

IDEAL
Ideal Pictures, Inc.
SEE: McMillan Films, Inc.

Ideas and Images Inc.
P.O. Box 5354
Atlanta, GA 30307

IFB
International Film Bureau
332 South Michigan Avenue
Chicago, IL 60604

IFEX Films
159 West 53rd Street
New York, NY 10019

Image Associates
Box 40106
352 Conejo Road
Santa Barbara, CA 93103

Image Resources
53 Center Road
Eastern, CT 06612

Impact Films
144 Bleeker Street
New York, NY 10012

Independent Southern Films, Inc.
P.O. Box 2602
Greenville, SC 29602

INUAVC
Indiana University AV Center
Bloomington, IN 47440

Information Factory
3512 Courville
Detroit, MI 48224

Institute for the Study
of Human Issues
3401 Market Street, Suite 252
Philadelphia, PA, 19104

Instructional Resources Corp.
6824 Nashville Road
Lanham, MD 20706

International Historic Films
Box 29035
Chicago, IL 60629

Iowa State University
AV Department
Ames, Iowa 50011

Iris Films
Box 5353
Berkeley, CA 94705

ISHTAR
310 E. 12th Street, #41
New York, NY 10003

Jacques Bailhe
The Noble House
Acme Film Company
4967 Franklin Avenue
Hollywood, CA 90027

Jason Films
2621 Palisade Avenue
Riverdale, NY 10463

Jewish Media Service
65 William Street
Wellesley, MA 02181

John F. Kennedy Library
P.O. Box 15
Back Bay Station
Boston, MA 02117

Johnson Architectural Images
P.O. Box 5481, Hilldale Station
Madison, Wisconsin 53705

Joseph Green Pictures Co.
200 W. 58th Street
New York, New York 10019

Journal Films
930 Pitner Avenue
Evanston, IL 60202

KAIDIB
Kaidib Films International
1455 Valane Drive
P.O. Box 261
Glendale, CA 91209

Kartemquin Films
P.O. Box 1665
Evanston, IL 60204

Kaufman and Boyce Productions
P.O. Box 283
Allston, MA 02134

KCET-TV
4401 Sunset Blvd.
Los Angeles, CA 90027

Kent State University
A-V Services
330 Library Building
Kent, OH 44242

KILLIS
Killiam Shows
6 E. 39th Street
New York, NY 10016

King Features Entertainment
235 E. 45th Street
New York, NY 10017

Korine-Dunlap
Route 1, Box 64
Arrington, TN 37014

KUON
KUON-TV
University Educational TV Station
P.O. Box 83111
Lincoln, NE 68501

Lauren Productions, Inc.
12121 Pinewood, Boxx 666
Mendocino, CA 95460

LCA
Learning Corporation of America
1350 Avenue of the Americas
New York, NY 10019

LIFE
Life Filmstrips
9 Rockefeller Plaza
New York, NY 10020

Light Impressions Corporation
P.O. Box 3012
Photo Slide & A-V Department
Rochester, NY 14614

Lightworks
97 Wooster Street
New York, NY 10012

Linda Williams
1726 Franklin
Denver, CO 80218

Little Red Filmhouse, The
666 N. Robertson Boulevard
Los Angeles, CA 90069

Lucasfilm
P.O. Box 186
San Anselmo, CA 94960

Lucerne Films
37 Ground Pine Road
Morris Plains, NJ 07950

Macmillan Films, Inc.
34 MacQuesten Parkway South
Mt. Vernon, NY 10550

Magic Lantern Films
872 Winston Churchill Drive
Oakville, Ontario
CANADA

MOT
March of Time
Time Life Building
1271 Avenue of the Americas
New York, NY 10021

MAR-Chuck Film Industries, Inc.
P.O. Box 61
Mt. Prospect, IL 60056

Mark Forman Films
3159 Goddard Road
Toleda, OH 43606

Marlene Booth
23 Irving Street
Cambridge, MA 02138

Maryknoll Communications
Maryknoll, NY 10545

Maryland Center for Public
Broadcasting
11767 Bonita Avenue
Owings Mills, MD 21117

Marx-Handley Productions
600 Woodbridge
Detroit, MI 48226

Mass Media Ministries
2116 North Charles Street
Baltimore, MD 21218

Maxi Cohen & Joel Gold
31 Greene Street
New York, NY 10013

MGHT
McGraw-Hill Films
1221 Avenue of the Americas
New York, NY 10020

McIntyre Visual Productions
716 Center Street
Lewiston, NY 14092

The Media Guild
11526 Sorrento Valley Road
San Diego, CA 92121

Media Project
Box 4093
Portland, OR 97208

MCC
Mennonite Central Committee
c/o Information Service
21 South 12th Street
Akron, PA 17501

Merrimack Valley Textile Museum
800 Massachusetts Avenue
North Andover, MA 01845

MGM
Metro-Goldwyn Mayer Home Video
1350 Avenue of the Americas
New York, NY 10019

Metropolitan Museum of Art
Fifth Avenue & 82nd Street
New York, NY 10028

Michael Lawrence Films
514 St. Paul Place
Baltimore, MD 21202

Mick Molony
20 West Harvey Street
Philadelphia, PA 19144

Mid-America College Art Association
c/o Arlene Zelda Richardson
Room 2010
University of New Mexico
Albuquerque, NM 97131

Minnevideo
3817 Columbus Avenue South
Minneapolis, MN 55407

MAETEL
Mississippi Authority for
Educational TV
3825 Ridgewood Road
Jackson, MS 39205

Mississippi ETV
P.O. Drawer 1101
Jackson, MS 39205

Modern Learning Aids
P.O. Box 1712
Rochester, NY 14603

MTPS
Modern Talking Picture Service
5000 Park Street North
St. Petersburg, FL 33709

Modern Video Center
5000 Park Street North
St. Petersburg, FL 33709

Monroe County Public Library
303 E. Kirkwood Avenue
Blommington, IN 47401

MONTEB
Montbello Projects
Toronto
CANADA

Mountain Moving Picture
Company
c/o Sally Barrett-Page
Box 1235
Evergreen, CO 80439

MTI Teleprograms
4825 N. Scott Street
Suite 23
Schiller Park, IL 60176

Multimedia Productions
PO Box 5097
Stanford, CA 94305

Museum of Modern Art
Department of Film Circulating
Program
11 W. 53rd Street
New York, NY 10019

NASA
National Aeronautics and Space
Administration
CODE FAM
Washington, DC 20546

NAVC
National AudioVisual Center
c/o National Archives and Records
Service
GSA
Washington, DC 20409

National Education Film Center
21601 Devonshire Street
Chatsworth, CA 91311

NEPAHC
National Education Program
American Heritage Center
815 E. Center Street
Searcy, AR 72143

National Endowment for the Arts
2401 E Street, N.W.
Washington, DC 20015

NFBC
National Film Board of Canada
1251 Avenue of the Americas
New York, NY 10020

NGS
National Geog. Soc. Int'l.
c/o Key Book Service, Inc.
540 Barnum Ave.
Bridgeport, CT 06608, USA

NGS (for Europe)
National Geographic Society
Educational Services Dept. 83
Washington, D.C. 20036

NPR
National Public Radio
2025 M Street, N.W.
Washington, DC 20036

Native American Videotape
Archives
Institute for American Indian
Arts Museum
Cerrillos Road
Santa Fe, NM 87501

NBC News
30 Rockefeller Plaza
New York, NY 10020

NETCHE
Nebraska Educational Television
Council
P.O. Box 8311
Lincoln, NE 68501

NET Film Service
Indiana University
Bloomington, IN 47401

New Day Films
P.O. Box 315
Franklin Lakes, NJ 07417

New Line Cinema
121 University Place
New York, NY 10003

Newsweek
444 Madison Avenue
New York, NY 10022

New Yorker Films
16 W. 61st Street
New York, NY 10023

New York Times Education
Division
229 West 43rd Street
New York, NY 10036

NFL Films Video
330 Fellowship Road
Mt. Laurel, NJ 08054

Nicholls State University
University Station
Thibodaux, LA 70301

Nickelodeon
WASEC
1133 Avenue of the Americas
New York, NY 10036

Nonesuch Records
c/o Consumer Department
926 N. La Cienga Boulevard
Los Angeles, CA 90069

North Carolina Office of Folklife
Programs
Department of Cultural Resources
Raleigh, NC 27611

North State Public Video
Box 3398
Durham, NC 27702

Oak Creek Films
711 14th Street
Golden, CO 80401

Olesen Films
c/o Communication Materials
Exchange
1535 IVAR Avenue
Hollywood, CA 90028

Omnificent Systems
1117 Virginia Street East
Charleston, VA 25301

Ontario Education Committee Authority
P.O. Box 200, Station Q
Toronto, Ontario M4T2T1
CANADA

Oxford Films/Paramount
5451 Marathon Street
Hollywood, CA 90038

Pacific Street Film Library
c/o Transit Media
Box 315
Franklin Lakes, NJ 07417

Paramount Communications
5451 Marathon Street
Hollywood, CA 90038

Paramount Home Video
5555 Melrose Avenue
Los Angeles, CA 90038

Paramount-Oxford Films
SEE: Paramount Pictures, Inc.

Paramount Pictures, Inc.
Communications Department
1136 N. Las Palmas Avenue
Hollywood, CA 90038

Patchke Productions
31 W. 12th Street
New York, NY 10011

PBS Video
475 L'Enfant Plaza, S.W.
Washington DC 20024

Penn Communications, Inc.
P.O. Box 10
Erie, PA 16512

Pennebaker, Inc.
56 W. 45th Street
New York, NY 10036

Pennsylvania State University
A-V Services
Special Services Building
University Park, PA 16802

Perspective Films
369 West Erie Street
Chicago, IL 60610

Peter Vogt & Associates
1000 Wisconsin Avenue
Washington, DC 20007

Phoenix Films
470 Park Avenue South
New York, NY 10016

Photo Lab, Inc.
3825 Georgia Avenue, NW
Washington, DC 20011

Pictura Films
470 Park Avenue South
New York, NY 10016

Polymorph Films
331 Newbury Street
Boston, MA 02115

Portland Cement Association
33 West Grand Avenue
Chicago, IL 60610

Prentice-Hall Media
150 White Plains Road
Tarrytown, NY 10591

Preservation Ventures, Inc.
P.O. Box 22361
Denver, CO 80222

PTV Productions, Inc.
150 E. 52nd Street
New York, NY 10022

Public Broadcasting Associates
566 Center Street
Newton, MA 02158

Public Interest Video Network
1736 Columbia Road, NW
Washington, DC 20009

Public Media, Inc
119 West 57th Street
New York, NY 10019

PUAVC
Purdue Audio-Visual Center
Room 54 STEW
Lafayette, IN 47907

Pyramid Films
Box 1048
Santa Monica, CA 10406

Quest Productions, Inc
630 9th Avenue, Room 901
New York, NY 10036

Ramsgate Films
704 Santa Monica Boulevard
Santa Monica, CA 90401

Rand-McNally
P.O. Box 7600
Chicago, IL 60680

Red Hen Films
1305 Oxford Street
Berkeley, CA 94709

Rediscovery Productions
2 Half Mile Common
Westport, CT 06880

Refocus Films
111 Wilton Road
Westport, CT 06880

RSC
Republic Steel Corporation
1025 Republic Building
Public Affairs Department
Cleveland, OH 44115

Rick Goldsmith
1315 Grove, #4
Berkeley, CA 94709

RMI Film Productions
701 Westport Road
Kansas City, MO 64111

Robert Richter Productions
330 W. 42nd Street, 24th Floor
New York, NY 10036

Robin Films
63 E. 82nd Street
New York, NY 10028

Ron Taylor
20007 Columbine
Boulder, CO 80302

Russell and Remington
Publications Department
Amon Carter Museum of Western
Art
P.O. Box 2365
Fort Worth, TX 76113

Ruth Sproat
South Carolina ETV Network
Drawer "L"
Columbia, SC 29250

SANDAK, Inc.
180 Harvard Avenue
Stamford, CT 06902

Scholastic Magazines, Inc.
50 W. 44th Street
New York, NY 20036

Scott Education Division
Lower Westfield Road
Holyoke, MA 01040

Screenscope, Inc.
1022 Wilson Boulevard
Arlington, VA 22209

Sears Roebuck Foundation
Sears Tower
Chicago, IL 60684

Serious Business Company
1145 Mandana Boulevard
Oakland, CA 94610

Sher Films
147 Hart Avenue
Santa Monica, CA 90405

Show Corp.
10 East 49th Street
New York, NY 10017

Sidney Kirkpatrick
342 E. 76th Street, #4B
New York, NY 10021

Sidney Platt
c/o National Geographic Society
17th and M Street, N.W.
Washington, DC 10036

Simeon Hyde III
P.O. Box 879
Oak Bluffs, MA 02557

Skye Picture, Inc.
1460 Church Street, N.W.
Washington, DC 20005

Skylight Films
21 Irving Avenue
Providence, RI 02906

S-L Film Production
P.O. Box 41108
Los Angeles, CA 90041

Small Business Administration
811 Vermont Avenue, N.W.
Washington, DC 20416

Smithsonian Institution
Office of Folklife Programs
Suite 2600
955 L'Enfant Plaza
Washington, DC 20560

Smithsonian Institution
Office of Telecommunications
Washington, DC 20560

SSSS
Social Studies School Service
10,000 Culver Boulevard
P.O. Box 802
Culver City, CA 90230

Society for Industrial Archeology
Room 5220
National Museum of American History
Washington, DC 20560

SVE
Society for Visual Education
1345 Diversey Parkway
Chicago, IL 60614

Solari Communications
406 North Citrus Avenue
Los Angeles, CA 90036

Southwest Film Labs
P.O. Box 220111
Dallas, TX 75222

Star Film Co.
79 Boblink Lane
Levitown, NY 11756

State University College
at Buffalo
Buffalo, NY 14200

STERLED
Sterling Educational Films
241 E. 34th Street
New York, NY 10016

Stoney Associates
The Brook Studio
South Country Road
Brookhaven
Long Island, New York 11719

Straightface Films
149 Mercer Street
New York, NY 10012

Stray Cat Productions
50 E. 10th Street
New York, NY 10003

Sunburst Communications
39 Washington Avenue
Pleasantville, NY 10570

Swank Motion Pictures, Inc.
201 S. Jefferson Street
St. Louis, MO 63166

Syracuse University
Center for Instructional
Communications
Syracuse, NY 13210

Temple University
Department of Radio-TV Films
Philadelphia, PA 19122

Tennessee State Museum
Extension Services
War Memorial Building
Nashville, TN 37219

Tennessee Valley Authority
Film Services, Box 1050
500 Union Avenue
Knoxville, TN 37902

Terra Productions, Inc.
140 West End Avenue
Apt. 14-G
New York, NY 10023

Texas Department of Human
Resources
John H. Regan Building
Austin, TX 78701

Texture Films, Inc.
1600 Broadway
New York, NY 10019

Thorne Films
1229 University Avenue
Boulder, CO 80302

Thunderbird Films
3500 Verdugo Road
Box 65157
Los Angeles, CA 90065

Thurber Productions, Inc.
P.O. Box 315
Franklin Lakes, NJ 07417

Time-Life Films, Inc.
43 West 16th Street
New York,NY 10011

Time-Life Multimedia
100 Eisenhower Drive
Paramus, NJ 07652

Time-Life Video
100 Eisenhower Drive
Paramus, NJ 07652

Tom Davenport Films
Route 1, Box 124
Delaplane, VA 22025

Tony Silver Films
325 West End Avenue, 3B
New York, NY 10023

Tricontinental Film Center
333 Sixth Avenue
New York, NY 10014

Twentieth Century Fox
10201 W. Pico Boulevard
Los Angeles, CA 90064

United Artists
729 Seventh Avenue
New York, NY 10019

Universal Education & Visual
Arts
6930-1/2 Tujunga Avenue
North Hollywood, CA 91605

Universal 16
425 N. Michigan Avenue
Chicago, IL 60611

Universal Studios
100 Universal Plaza
Universal City, CA 91608

University Community Video
425 Ontario, SE
Minneapolis, MN 55414

University of California at LA
405 Hilgard Avenue
Los Angeles, CA 90024

University of California, EMC
2223 Fulton Street
Berkeley, CA 94720

University of Iowa - AV Center
C-5 East Hall
Iowa City, IA 52242

University of Minnesota
A-V Library Services
Minneapolis, MN 55414

University of New Hampshire
WENH-TV
Durham, NH 03824

University of North Carolina
Office of Folklife Programs
North Carolina Department
of Cultural Resources
Raleigh, NC 27611

University of Southern California
Broadcast Production and Media Center
Davidson Conference Center
University Park
Los Angeles, CA 90007

University of Washington Press
Box 5569
Seattle, WA 98105

USIA
U.S. Information Agency
400 C Street, S.W.
Washington, DC 20547

Vedo Films
85 Longview Road
Port Washington, NY 11050

Veriation Films
518 Hamilton Avenue
Palo Alto, CA 94301

Vermont Center for Cultural
Studies
RFD 2
Stowe, VT 05672

Vermont Public Radio
Box 895
Windsor, VT 05089

Verve Films, Inc.
733 Green Bay Road
Wilmette, IL 60091

Vestron Video
911 Hope Street
Largo Park
Stamford, CT 06907

Vineyard Video Productions
Elias Lane
West Tisbury, MA 02575

Vision Associates, Inc.
665 Fifth Avenue
New York, NY 10022

Vision Quest, Inc.
7715 North Sheridan Road
Chicago, IL 60626

Visual Publications, Ltd.
197 Kensington High Street
London W8
England

Visual Resources, Inc.
1 Lincoln Plaza
New York, NY 10023

WDEMCO
Walt Disney Educational Media
500 S. Buena Vista Street
Burbank, CA 91521

Walter Thomas
2131 College Avenue, #7
Berkeley, CA 94704

Warner Brothers Non-Theatrical
Division
4000 Warner Boulevard
Burbank, CA 91522

Warner Home Video
3 East 54th Street
New York, NY 10022

WAVE-TV
P.O. Box 32970
Louisville, KY 40232

WCAU-TV
City Line & Monument Ave.
Philadelphia, PA 19131

WDVM-TV
Brandywine Street, NW
Washington, DC 20008

Westinghouse Learning Corp.
2400 Ardmore Boulevard
Pittsburgh, PA 15221

Weston Walch
321 Valley Street
Portland, ME 04104

Weston Woods Studios
Weston, CT 06880

WGBH, Boston, Distribution
Office
125 Western Avenue
Boston, MA 02134

Whitney Museum
945 Madison Avenue
New York, NY 10021

WMHT-TV
Box 17
Schenectady, NY 12301

Wilderness Women Productions
c/o Annick Smith
Star Route
Bonner, MT 59823

William Darnell Productions
340 E. 80 Street, #11-F
New York, NY 10021

Winterthur Museum
Greenville, DE 19807

WKYC-TV
Montage
1403 E. 6th Street
Cleveland, OH 44114

WNET Media Service
356 West 58th Street
New York, NY 10019

Wombat Productions
Little Lake, Glendale Road
P.O. Box 40
Huntsville, TX 77340

World Vision Enterprises
600 West Fifth Street
New York, NY 10036

WQED Pittsburgh
4802 Fifth Avenue
Pittsburgh, PA 15213

Xerox Films
245 Long Hill Road
Middletown, CT 06457

Yale University Media Design
Studio
305 Crown Street
New Haven, CT 06520

Zipporah Films
1 Richdale Avenue, Unit 14
Cambridge, MA 02140

Alphabetical List of Titles

Numbers below refer to entry, not page, numbers. Consult the Subject Category Outline in the front following the How To Use This Catalog section for further help. A second annotation for a title means that it is listed in more than one section of the catalog. For example, Act Of Congress, An is listed in History (H-E-1) and Political Science (PolS-I-1).

A

Aaron Siskind	Art-C-1
Aaron Siskind	Art-C-2
Aaron Siskind	Art-C-3
Abe Lincoln In Illinois	H-J-1
Abnormal Behavior: A Mental Hospital	Sy-H-1
Abstract Expressionism, New York School	Art-C-4
Abstract Paintings: The Gestural Tradition	Art-C-5
Act Of Congress, An	H-E-1
	PolS-I-1
Adams Chronicles, The (Eight Parts)	H-I-1
Admiral Byrd	ST-F-1
Admiral Richard E. Byrd	ST-F-2
Adolescent Responsibilities: Craig And Mark	Sy-Cb-2
AEF In Siberia	IR-A-35
African-American Relations	IR-B-1
Afro-American Tradition In The Decorative Arts, The	F-E-1
Afro-American Worksongs In A Texas Prison	F-B-1
After Jackson Pollock	Art-B-1
After The Ball: A Treasury Of Turn-Of-The-Century Popular Songs	PopC-A-1
Age Of Ballyhoo, The	H-K-1
Age Of Exploration, The	H-F-1
Age Of Revolutions, An	H-I-2
Age Of Revolutions	IR-A-1
Agee, James, Evans, Walker: Let Us Now Praise Famous Men	Li-A-1
Agricultural America: United States Geography	G-Art-1
Agriculture And The New Deal	EH-E-59
Agricultural Midwest, The	EH-E-58
Aghveghnimi – At The Time Of Whaling	An-B-1
Ahora No. 94 These Festivals Of Summer	PA-C-1
Ain't Nobody's Business	An-H-1
Alaska: The 49th State	G-F-1
Albert Einstein	ST-F-3

Art In America: Sculptures (Part 8)   Art-D-2
Art Of Huckleberry Finn, The   Li-A-3
Art Of Huckleberry Finn II, The   Li-A-42
Art Of The Real: U.S.A. 1948-1968   Art-C-13
Arthur Crudup: Born In The Blues   F-B-3
Artists In The Schools: Bob Aiken   Art-E-8
Arts America II   PA-A-2
Arts Of The United States   Art-A-1
As Long As The River Runs   PolS-P-3
Assassination Of President William McKinley   H-J-4
At Issue: Crime And Punishment   PolS-H-2
Atlantic Slave Trade   EH-B-19
Atomic Cafe, The   H-K-7
                                                           IR-C-1
Attica   Sy-H-3
Audubon   ST-F-6
Audubon's Florida Wildlife   ST-F-7
Aunt Arie   Sy-I-2
Authority And Rebellion   Li-A-4
Autobiography Of Miss Jane Pittman, The   PolS-M-1
Automobiles And Roads   EH-E-34
Autumn: Frost Country   Li-B-1

                              B

Background To The Constitutional Convention   EH-B-10
Ballad Of The Iron Horse   EH-D-14
                                                           ST-D-2
Balance Of Power   IR-F-1
Baltimore   Sy-A-3
Banjo Man   F-B-4
Bank Holiday Crisis Of 1933, The   EH-E-11
Banners   Art-E-9
Barrio Murals Of Santa Fe   Art-B-7
Basketmaking In Colonial Virginia   ST-C-5
Battle Of Newburgh, The   PolS-O-3
Bearden Plays Bearden   Art-F-2
Beau James   PolS-D-1
Beauty Knows No Pain   Sy-D-2
Before The Industrial Revolution   ST-C-6
Beginning At Plymouth Colony, The   EH-B-15
Beginnings   PA-A-3
Beginnings And Growth Of Industrial America   EH-C-1
Being A Joines; A Life In The Brushy Mountains   F-C-1
Benjamin Banneker, The Man Who Loved The Stars   ST-F-8
Benjamin Franklin: Scientist, Statesman, Scholar And Sage ST-F-9
Benjamin Franklin: Symbol Of The American Revolution   H-I-10
Ben's Mill   ST-C-7
Berlin Airlift,The: Turning Point   IR-A-6
Bert Morris   Art-D-16
Between Rock And A Hard Place   Sy-F-2
                                                           EH-E-43
Big Lever, The: Party Politics In Leslie County Kentucky   PolS-S-2
Billboard Environment, The   Art-B-8
Billie Jean: A Study In Motion   PopC-F-3

C

California Custom Care	Art-B-9
California Design '76	Art-E-10
California's Challenge	Sy-A-5
Call It Bluegrass	PopC-A-8
Campaign	PolS-C-2
Campaign: American Style	PopC-E-3
	PolS-C-3
Candidate, The	PolS-C-4
Careers And Babies	Sy-Ca-4
Carl Sandburg	Li-B-4
	Li-B-5
Carl Sandburg Discusses His Works	Li-B-6
Carl Sandburg Discusses Lincoln	Li-B-7
Carolina And Red, White, And Blue Grass	PopC-A-30
Carolinas Peyton: Black Farmer	Sy-I-5
Case Against Sacco And Vanzetti, The	PolS-H-6
Castle On The Plain	H-C-2
Cattle: Birth Of An Industry	EH-D-19
Cattle Drive	F-D-2
Cause I've Already Been To Hell	IR-B-6
Celebrating A Century: The 1876 Philadelphia Centennial Exhibition	H-J-5
Celebration Of Black Women In Literature, A: Alice Walker	Li-G-1
Central America: Sphere Of Interest Or Influence?	IR-B-7
Century Next Door, The	EH-D-8
Ceramic Sculpture: Six Artists	Art-D-3
Challenge Of Change	EH-E-45
Changing Course: A Second Chance	Sy-Ca-5
Chaplin: A Character Is Born	PopC-B-5
Charge And Countercharge: A Film Of The Era Of Joseph McCarthy	PolS-P-5
Charles Burchfield	Art-C-17
Charles M. Russell	Art-C-18
Charles Proteus Steinmetz	ST-F-10
Charles Sanders Peirce	ST-F-11
Checkmate On The Hudson	H-I-11
Chester Grimes	F-C-2
Chicago	Arc-B-2
Chicago Blues	F-B-6
Chicago Conspiracy Trial, The	PolS-H-7
Chicago Murals	Art-B-10
Children Of Pride, The	Sy-Ca-6
Children Of Violence	PolS-P-6
	Sy-Cb-3
Chillysmith Farm	Sy-Cc-2
China Scene, The	IR-B-8
China's Chair	IR-A-7
Chinese American, The	An-E-1
Chinese American, The: The Early Immigrants	EH-C-41
Chisholm: Pursuing The Dream	PolS-C-5
Choctaw: Choctaw Indian Fair	F-I-2
Choreography By Balanchine, Part One	PA-A-4
Choreography By Balanchine, Part Two	PA-A-5
Christmas Ornaments	Art-E-11
Chuck Davis Dance Company, The	PA-A-6
Chulas Fronteras	F-B-7
C.I.A., The	IR-E-3

D

E

Eagle Has Landed,The: The Flight Of Apollo 11	ST-H-5
Eagle On The Street	EH-E-20
An Eames Celebration: Several Worlds Of Charles And Ray Eames	Art-E-13
Early Balloons	Sy-D-3
Early Morning	Sy-I-3
East 103rd Street	Sy-H-4
Easy Rider	PolS-P-9
Economic History	EH-B-5
Edgar Allan Poe: Background For His Works	Li-A-8
Edison, Persistent Genius	ST-F-12
Edison The Man	ST-F-13
Edward R. Murrow	Lj-A-4
Edward Steichen, Photographer	Art-C-23
E.E.Cummings	Li-B-8
Effective Communication: Better Choice Of Words	La-A-2
Egypt	IR-A-17
Eight And The Ashcan School,The	Art-C-24
1876; Labor And Violence	EH-D-25
Eighteenth Century Life In Williamsburg, Virginia	EH-B-18
Einstein: The Story Of The Man Told By His Friends	ST-F-14
Eisenhower Years, The	PolS-K-2
El Barrio - The Puerto Rican	An-D-1
El Salvador: Another Vietnam	H-K-11
Elderhostels	Sy-Cc-1
Elections, The--How Votes Are Packaged	PolS-C-7
Election Of 1932	PolS-C-8
Election Process, The	PolS-C-9
Electric Flag, The	PopC-C-6
Electric Rainbow,The	PopC-C-7
Electroworks	Art-C-25
Eli Whitney	EH-C-24
Eli Whitney Invents The Cotton Gin	ST-F-15
	EH-C-35
Eliza	H-B-3
Emerging Giant,The: The U.S.In 1900	H-K-10
Emerging Woman, The	PolS-P-10
Emily Dickinson And Marianne Moore	Li-B-9
Empire Of The Sun	Sy-I-4
Energy---The American Experience	EH-A-12
English Language,The: It's Spelling Patterns	La-A-3
Enrico Fermi	ST-G-4
Equality	Sy-G-2
Era Of Good Feeling	EH-C-3
Era Of The Common Man	EH-C-2
Era Of Water Commerce, 1750-1850	EH-C-6
E-R-I-E (The Erie Canal),The	EH-C-8
Erie Canal	EH-C-7
Erie War,The	EH-D-6
Ernest Hemingway	Li-A-9
Essay On Watergate	PolS-K-3
Eugene O'Neill	Li-A-10
Europe And The Age Of Discovery	H-F-3
Europe's New Look	IR-A-18

F

For You, Mr. Bell	ST-F-16
Forever Young	Sy-Cc-3
Forgotten West, The	F-D-4
Forms From The Earth	Art-E-14
Forms In Metal	Art-D-6
Four Day Week, The	PopC-F-7
Four Days Of Gemini, The	ST-H-6
Four Generations Of Women Poets	Li-F-1
Foxfire	PopC-E-5
Frank And Ollie: Four Decades Of Disney Animation	PopC-D-7
Frank LLoyd Wright - Organic Architect	Arc-C-3
Franklin D. Roosevelt, Part 1; The New Deal	EH-E-21
Franz Boas	An-A-1
	ST-46
Franz Kline Remembered	Art-C-31
Frederick Douglass	PolS-M-4
Frederick Remington	Art-C-29
Free Press Vs. Fair Trial By Jury	PolS-H-10
Free Show Tonite	F-C-4
Freedom And Security: The Uncertain Balance	PolS-H-11
From These Beginnings	ST-D-4
From This Land	EH-E-62
Frontier America: The Far West	H-C-5
Full Of Life A-Dancin'	PA-A-12
Fun And Fantasy: Contempory American Crafts	Art-E-15
Fun Factory	PopC-B-9
Fur Trade, The---Big Business	EH-C-30
Furniture	Art-E-16

G

Gang Ain't Nothing But Friends, A	Sy-Cb-1
Gary Snyder	Li-B-12
Gasoliine Age: History Of Transportation In The United States, Part 1	EH-E-36
Gatecliff---American Indian Rock-Shelter	Art-F-6
	ST-B-2
Gemini G.E.L.	Art-C-32
Gene Deitch, Animating Picture Books	PopC-D-8
Geography, Climate,And Natural Resources In The Northcentral Region	G-D-5
Geography, Climate, And Natural Resources In The Northeast	G-D-6
Geography, Climate, And Natural Resources In The South	G-D-7
Geography Of Alaska And Hawaii	G-F-2
Geography Of The Five Pacific States	G-D-8
Geography Of The United States	G-A-4
George Segal	Art-D-7
George Washington And The Whiskey Rebellion	H-I-16
George Washington And The Whiskey Rebellion: Testing The Constitution	EH-B-11
Getting Straight	Sy-H-6
Ghosts Of Cape Horn	H-J-11
Giant Sequoia	G-E-4
Gibbons Vs. Ogden	EH-C-9
Gimme Shelter	PopC-A-18

H

I

In The Best Interests Of The Children	Sy-Cb-6
In The Rapture	F-G-2
In The Year Of The Pig	PolS-Q-3
In White Collar America	Sy-I-11
Independence	H-I-17
Indian Artists Of The Southwest	Art-F-7
The Indian Experience	Sy-Ba-5
Indian Potter Of San Ildefonso	H-A-3
Indian Pottery Of San Ildefonso	Art-F-8
Indian Reorganization Act, The	H-A-2
Indomitable Blacksmith, The: Thomas Davenport	ST-F-18
Industrial America	G-A-5
Industrial Revolution: Beginnings In The United States	ST-E-5
Industrial Revolution, The Beginnings In The United States	EH-C-25
Industrial Revolution, The (Three Parts)	EH-C-5
Industry, Agriculture, And Commerce In The North Central Region	G-D-12
Industry, Agriculture, And Commerce In The Northeast	G-D-13
Inheritance	Art-E-18
Inheritance, The	EH-E-50
Inherit The Wind	PolS-H-17
Inland Waterways In The Development Of American Transportation	EH-A-22
Innovation---American Enterprise	EH-A-16
Inside/Out	PolS-H-18
Interior West, The: The Land Nobody Wanted	G-D-14
Interviews With Mylai Veterans	PolS-Q-2
Inventions In America's Growth, 1750-1850	ST-F-19
Inventions In America's Growth, 1850-1910	ST-F-20
Investigative Reporting	Lj-B-2
Iowa's Ancient Hunters	H-A-4
Iran	IR-A-21
Irish, The	H-B-9
Is Everybody Listening?	PopC-C-10
Israel	IR-B-13
Island Called Ellis, The	An-C-3
It Ain't City Music	PopC-A-21
Italian American	H-B-10

J

Jack Johnson	PopC-F-9
Jack Kerouac	Li-A-18
Jackie Robinson	PopC-F-10
Jackson Years, The: The New Americans	H-J-16
Jackson Years, The: Toward Civil War	H-J-17
Jacksonian Democracy	H-J-15
Jade Snow Wong	An-E-2
James Michener	Li-A-19
James Rosenquist	Art-C-33
James Thurber's The Night The Ghost Got In	Li-A-20
Jamestown	EH-B-14
	H-H-2

K

M

O

P

U

V

W

Willmar 8, The	Sy-D-14
Winslow Homer	Art-C-56
Winterthur, The Benchmark Of Excellence	Art-E-27
Witches Of Salem, The	H-H-8
With These Hands	Art-E-28
Wizard Of Waukesha: A Film About Les Paul	PA-C-29
Wizard Who Spat On The Floor: Thomas Alva Edison	ST-F-25
	EH-D-13
Woman's Place	Sy-D-12
Women Artists: Clay	Art-D-18
Women Artists: Clay, Fiber, Metal	Art-E-29
Women Artists: Metal	Art-E-30
Women In Advertising	Lj-B-8
Women In Communications	PopC-B-28
Women In Prison	Sy-h-14
Women In Sports	PopC-F-20
Women In The Civil War	H-B-30
Women Of Cane River	H-B-29
Women Writers: Voice Of Dissent	Li-F-4
Women's Fiction	Li-F-5
Woodenworks	Art-E-31
Woodrow Wilson: A Portrait Of Power	H-K-45
Woodstock	PopC-A-40
	PopC-A-41
Woody Allen: An American Comedy	PopC-B-29
Word Is Out	Sy-I-33
Working For The Lord	H-G-2
Working Places	ST-E-9
Works Of Edward Ruscha, The	Art-C-57
World Of Andrew Wyeth, The	Art-C-58
World Of Franklin And Jefferson, The	H-I-26
World Of Differences: B.F.Skinner And The Good Life	ST-A-6
World Human Rights: Policy And Practice	IR-B-21
World Resources And Responsibilities	IR-D-8
World Terrorism: What Can Be Done?	IR-F-10
World Turned Upside Down, The	H-I-27
Writer And The City (Great Minds)	Li-D-17
Writer In America: Janet Flanner	Li-D-18
Writing: An Interview With Irving Stone	Li-A-46
Wynn Bullock	Art-C-59

Y

Yankee Craftsman	ST-89
Yankee Go Home: Declining U.S.Power?	IR-B-22
Yankee Painter: The Work Of Winslow Homer	Art-C-60
Year Of The Communes	Sy-I-34
Years Between, The	H-E-4
Yellow Cab	Sy-I-35
Yellow Trail From Texas	EH-E-69
Yes Ma'am	F-A-8
	Sy-I-36
Yesterday's Farm	EH-A-4
Yesterday's Witness: A Tribute To The American Newsreel	Lj-A-12
Yo Soy Chicano	An-D-4

Z

About the General Editor

Howard B. Hitchens is a Communications Consultant in Frankford, Delaware. He was editor of *Audiovisual Instruction/Instructional Innovator* magazine for twelve years when he was with the Association for Educational Communications and Technology. He has contributed articles to the *International Encyclopedia of Education*, *The Encylopedia Americana*, *Public Relations for Libraries* (Greenwood Press, 1973), and *Educational Media International*.